GILMAN
Voices

1897–1997

EDITED BY
PATRICK SMITHWICK '69

GILMAN SCHOOL

Baltimore, Maryland

The aerial shot of Gilman School on the preceding pages, taken between
1956 and 1961, shows how leafy the suburbs surrounding the school still
were, and how undeveloped the campus still was. Within the next four
decades, campus buildings proliferated, using up some of the campus open
space shown here.

Going clockwise, starting on the left side of the photo: faculty housing was
built in the woods, by the baseball diamond, next to what was then Belvedere
Avenue. A parking lot was constructed out of the woods, near The Cage, at
the southeast corner of the campus. A swimming pool was built, linking The
Cage with the gymnasium. In the woody area south of what is now Carey
Hall, beside The Alumni Auditorium, The Middle School was built. The Lower
School, at the corner of Belvedere and Roland, has been added onto several
times, and plans in 1997 called for a total rebuilding.

Note that the entrance to the school was then off Belvedere, near The Lower
School. There was no concrete wall running along between Belvedere (now
Northern Parkway) and the playing fields. Instead, there was a steep slope, with
thick grass, up which coaches would demand their charges to run, sometimes
backwards and on all-fours. The dreaded command often barked out was,
"Up to Belvedere!"

Gilman Voices, 1897–1997
is dedicated
to the Gilman boy,
to the Gilman boy in the Gilman man,
and to Walter Lord '35,
a Gilman boy forever.

❧

Table of Contents

1950s

1960s

1970s

Preface

Gilman—I have come to realize over five years of working on this book—is a confederacy of contradictions, a panoply of paradoxes, an incongruous fête of sacred traditions jitterbugging with the latest fads. It is also, as I have always known, an inexorable force, headed, slowly but surely, in the right direction.

The first time I came up against these complex, intriguing, and powerful undercurrents in connection with *Gilman Voices* was during my first meeting with the Gilman Centennial Book Committee—when I was being interviewed for the job of writing a history of Gilman School. Nervously standing before the committee of ten, I was quickly aware that half of the committee assumed that the book to be written would be a scholarly, historical overview of the school's history. The other half wanted something more anecdotal, they weren't sure what, such as, "Conversations with Alumni." This half thought that the main problem with the recently printed histories of colleges and schools which they had examined was that they were unread by today's rushed populace—a serious problem indeed. They wanted something more user-friendly for the fast-paced 1990s and the new millenium. And they wanted something that would lure all types of alumni into reading at least certain sections of the book.

"What do *you* think, Pat?" came the question from Alex Armstrong '33. Hmm, what to do? Here I was caught in a classic Gilman imbroglio—much like ones I'd been in as a student. I had the task of pleasing both these groups in order to get the job, and here, in a few seconds, I could be determining the very nature of the job, the book, my future five years as a writer/editor/researcher. There were some imposing figures before me: Brad Jacobs '38, Sunpapers editor/writer for years and author of *Gilman Walls Will Echo*; Walter Lord '35, historian and author of dozens of renowned books; Alex Armstrong '33, my past English teacher; Nick Schloeder, my past history teacher; Cary Woodward '53, English teacher; David Drake, director of development; Bill Paternotte '63, managing director at Alex. Brown & Sons and head of the committee; Bill Passano '48, president of Waverly Press; Tommie Caplan '64, published novelist; Liz Dausch, archivist and Gilman parent. These committee members had been meeting, and I knew all agreed on one basic point that had been made by Walter Lord: this history of Gilman should be not only about what happened inside the walls and on the fields of Gilman School, but should show how life at Gilman reflected the bigger picture of what was going on in the country, in the world, at the time, and how Gilman proactively, in many cases, and reactively in others, responded to these times.

We agreed upon a general outline which now forms the backbone of the book: Ten chapters, one for each era, or, loosely, each decade. Each chapter would begin with a historical essay, written by an alumnus or member of the Gilman family, which would show how Gilman both reflected the times and reacted to the times. And it would be followed by five to seven more personal essays—memoirs. I would direct the writers of the memoirs to write about specific incidents, to focus on the educators who made a real difference in their lives, and to recreate the experiences on the page—to show them from a close-up, having-been-there, personal point of view, and thus to develop a narrative like that of a short story. In this way, through the combination of historical essays and personal essays, we could come up with the best of all possible worlds. A book could be constructed that would give a solid representation of Gilman over the past 100 years—from a historical, sociological, psychological, literary, and even demographic viewpoint.

First was the task of picking out writers for the historical essays. I wrote hundreds of letters to alumni and Gilman teachers asking for names and ideas, and finally settled on what is a classy stable of writers: Brad Jacobs '38, Arthur Machen '38, Walter Lord '35, D. Randall Beirne '43, Peter Wood '60, Nick Schloeder, Michael Sarbanes '82, and J. B. Howard '81. Each was picked to write about a specific period, and each went out of his way to research the period. Most were also picked because they could rely on personal memory of the time. Each read drafts of essays by the others. Walter Lord was the first to turn his in, followed by Brad Jacobs and Arthur Machen. The writers of these historical essays provide the foundation for the book, the underpinning. Read these eight overviews in sequence, along with those by A. J. Downs, Redmond C. S. Finney '47, and Archibald Montgomery '71 and you will have a solid understanding of how Gilman responded to the winds of change that swept across America in the late 1900s and throughout the 20th century—post–Civil War boom, WW I, Roaring 20s, Depression, WW II, Fifties' security, Sixties war and division, Seventies change, Eighties boom, Nineties sobriety.

As first drafts of memoirs and historical essays ended up in my mailbox, I began to develop a puzzle-portrait of 100 years of Gilman history. When I wrote a new potential contributor, I would head him or her in the direction of the missing piece. The 1950s section-puzzle was filling in very quickly. Yet—how about Henry Callard? I had some good general stuff on him, but I wanted to see him in action. I

Notes from a
Thankful Editor

Above all, I would like to express my thanks and gratitude to Alex Armstrong, Class of 1933, for his help and patience and inspiration throughout the five years of work on this book, and especially during the last year when I mailed him every "finalized" essay—completely edited, fact-checked, revised—and he promptly returned each with grammatical corrections, spelling corrections, subtly worded questions about awkward phrasing, and the most interesting marginalia, wittily written in exquisitely formed *New Yorker*-ish phrases that at times had me chuckling out loud, and at others touched my heart.

I could hear Alex's voice, clear and calm and projecting, just as I had heard it 30 years earlier in Tenth Grade English class, as I read over his intriguing comments on past students and teachers. He drew from an incredible treasure chest of a memory filled with eight decades of Gilman lore, much of which found its way into the book. Alex was the manuscript's first reader. He was my test run. He was my critic. He also was the first to turn in his memoir—clear, smoothly flowing prose; handwritten, double-spaced, on legal sheets—which I can remember reading in bed with a wool quilt pulled over my legs on a drizzly November Saturday upon returning from my son's soccer match. It made my day, my weekend. That son was 12 then; he is 17 now.

Walter Lord '35 was the first to turn in a historical essay. Unable to walk, confined to a wheelchair, and barely able to stir sugar into his coffee, he wrote it the same way he wrote *A Night to Remember*, by hand, with a pencil. "Piece of cake," he'd say. Over the five years I met and worked and drove and dined with Walter, and as the Parkinson's stripped away more and more of his physical strength, I never once heard him complain. I learned and witnessed what it is to be brave, to be courageous—the subject of most of Walter's work. And it was a wonderful experience to witness this man's love for Gilman and its boys.

It was through Harry Turner '70 that I originally came to know Walter. I hadn't seen Harry since I used to chase him, unsuccessfully, across the playing fields at Eighth Grade recess. One afternoon, Harry called me and asked if I'd be interested in writing the history of Gilman School for its Centennial. Shortly after that, he sent me a copy of a letter recommending me to Walter Lord for this job. Soon, urged on by Walter, I was meeting with Headmaster Reddy Finney and Director of Development David Drake, and finally, with the Gilman Centennial Book Committee.

Walter contacted me often in the first couple of years of work. In fact, anyone who knows Walter (a New York City bachelor) knows that he calls at odd hours—say, 10:00 Sunday night. He'd ask me how it was going. He had the uncanny ability of a great editor/mentor to call just when I needed a prod, a push, an idea. I might be stymied on an issue, and with the experience of a shelf of award-winning books behind him, he'd cut right through the morass, and point out a path I had not seen. He always asked how I was, and my family.

Every Easter, for the life of the work on this book, I'd drive over to Anne Deford's in the Long Green Valley to have breakfast with Walter, his mind nimble, curious, and showing an amazing memory for detail. The conversation would begin at a fast pace and remain at that pace. The first year, Walter and I spent hours going over potential contributors and subjects and themes to be covered. Walter was at times outrageous or hilarious, and at others incredibly insightful in helping to narrow down the list. In a five-minute period we'd go from discussing Reddy Finney to *The Titanic* to Pearl Harbor to the latest Civil War book to the sport of playing marbles at Gilman. Soon we'd move to a sitting room, the light pouring in through the expansive windows. We'd have lunch, and before I knew it, it would be time for Anne and Walter to up and hop in the car and head over to the timber races—the Manor or the Grand National—where Walter hoped to see Reddy win a race, and there I'd be, watching the two of them drive out, feeling like a race horse left in the starting gate.

Cary Woodward '53, book committee member and Gilman English teacher since 1966, was a special help in coming up with ideas for potential contributors and discussing different themes to be covered. Over the summers of 1992 and 1993, while he attempted to vacation in Deer Isle, Maine, we exchanged letters on who would be good on this subject, who on that. During the same summer, I read the transcripts of over 25 oral interviews with important and interesting members of the Gilman family, conducted by Mary Ellen Thomsen a few years earlier. These interviews, now stored in typescript as well as high-quality cassette tape in the Gilman archives, provided a wealth of background material.

And then, there was Roy Barker. I sent Roy, English teacher at Gilman 1946–82 and department chair for most of that time, a long outline of people I had assembled as possible contributors. He wrote back, in turn, complimentary, acerbic, caustic, glowing, loving, cryptic, devilish descriptions, recommendations and denunci- ations of everyone on the list, reminiscing on papers turned in 40 years ago, and eccentric grammatical and syntactical problems certain students had and never did conquer and which he still had to witness these "students" producing—without the release of applying red ink!—in books and newspapers and magazines every day. Fourteen pages, handwritten, front and back, black ink on white, unlined paper.

After sending that long letter, Roy communicated with me through short Gilman-like notes. When he had an idea, or after he received a letter from me (typed, proofread five times, 30-year-old Gilman-issued *Warriner's* consulted once or twice), he would fire off a stamped, addressed, index card—the tiny type we were supposed to use for notes for speeches at Gilman—with what was to me very im- portant material scrawled down the card and then running up along the sides. Then Roy died at a hospital in Hyannis, Massachusetts, on September 12, 1993, of pneu- monia, and I regret not having found the time to visit him at his home at Cape Cod once we had begun our lively correspondence.

Brad Jacobs '38—retired newspaper writer/editor and author of *Gilman Walls Will Echo, The Story of The Gilman Country School, 1897–1947*—was one of the strongest supporters of insisting that *Gilman Voices* tell the full story of Gilman's history. Brad would occasionally call me at work, volunteer his help, and with an erudite phrase and a clear-eyed focus, wipe away problematic concerns that had weighed on me for months. His flowing, seamless essay on the early, Homewood years of the school, "The Lady Vanquishes," was one of the foundation historical essays for the book; it is a textbook example of form and style fitting subject matter.

And it was Brad who opened the doors to finding an excellent designer for the book. I was telling him over the telephone one afternoon how I was having a diffi- cult time locating a good book designer and printer. "Call Jack Goellner at Hopkins Press," he said. "Tell him I sent you."

Moments later the renowned and retired director of Johns Hopkins University Press picked up his telephone at home. "You say the name 'Brad Jacobs,'" he as- serted, "it opens doors. What can I do for you?" Within four days, he introduced me to Gerry Valerio, an experienced free-lance book designer in Annapolis.

And then there was the time that I was having mixed feelings on what to do about a particular essay. A few test-readers had told me they thought it should be "toned down." I confided this to Brad.

"Tone it down?" I heard over the telephone wires. "Tone it down? If anything, I think you should rev it up!" I left every single conversation I had with Brad over a five-year period with a sense of renewal, feistiness, and exuberance. Finally, it was through a generous gift to Gilman from Brad that the research, writing, editing, design and printing of *Gilman Voices* was made possible.

And then there was Liz Dausch, Gilman's archivist. The entire time I worked on the book, I mailed, faxed, and called in questions to Liz, many of them pertaining to seemingly obscure details. And she would find the information. She also dug up out of her empire of archives correct spellings, dates of events, years a teacher spent at Gilman, and was an essential factor in getting the facts straight, for me as well as for many of the contributors of the book. I am also indebted to Liz for gathering the material that went into making up the lists in the appendix and for helping pick out the photographs.

David Drake was director of development while I worked on the book. His in-the-bone-marrow knowledge of and respect for Gilman, and his sense of humor about Gilman and its eccentricities, were all a constant source of replenishment.

Nick. Nick Schloeder. His unquenchable youthful spirit, his caring about the school, his focus when one-on-one, the way his blue eyes burn into your own. If Ed Russell is one of the most influential teacher/coaches of the first half of the book, then Nick Schloeder had the greatest impact, as a teacher/coach, in the second half. And here Schloeder would be—this historic figure about whom I would be reading again and again—in my office, a glow of limitless energy around him, telling a story, so in love with history and football and Gilman and his students and his athletes. Nick's passion for the school, his love of Callard and Finney, his individualistic, iconoclastic outlook, his sense of humor, would lift me. Many a late afternoon found me hiking up the narrow, wooden, turn-of-the-century stairway to Nick's 1950s office—election bumper stickers plastered across a wall, Reddy Finney's old manual Royal typewriter in the brick fireplace, and in front of his desk an old beaten leather chair into which I would slump and listen to parables and stories that were so good I'd feel guilty for not having a tape recorder along.

And Reddy: his glow, his inspirational quality, his contagious exuberance. From my Gilman book journal: "9/1/94 Just got a call from Reddy—he's apologetic about taking so long on his essay. Says how patient I am. He'll drop the piece off Tuesday. I hang up. He matters, I think. I want to please him. It is true what so many of the book contributors have said about Reddy—he is a moral conscience. He has a power. I haven't felt this way about anything or anyone all day—until I see the note to give him a ring. *His voice is so soft.*"

One autumn day in 1995, in his farm clothes and work boots, Redmond C. S. Finney barrels through the labyrinth of desks and chairs, steps and doorways, that make up the Gilman development office, to my desk. He sits across from me, and we begin to go over his essay. I stand, preparing to come to his side of the desk, so he can sit and I can stand. "No, no, Patrick," he says, moving quickly, forcefully, around the desk to my side, standing on my right. Leaning forward, he goes over the handwritten changes in his essay, explaining them, underlining them, circling them, his big reddened outdoorsman hands looking so out of place with a pencil between the fingers. He reads the last sentence, makes one final stab where the last period goes. "That's it."

He is up and outside and speed-walk-rambling along, stopping to talk to music teacher John Merrill, hearing that Ludlow Baldwin is in an infirmary, and then he is in his too-small-for-him faded-maroon car, the door open, answering my question by telling me that, yes, he'll go visit Ludlow right at that moment, "There's no time like the present!" as the car starts to roll down the slight incline outside the Alumni Auditorium and I say, "Reddy, Reddy—the car is moving!"

He whips around, pulls up the emergency brake. "Look at that," he says, looking first at the shiny new van now just inches ahead of his front bumper and then at me. "I could have hit that nice car." Shaking his head and laughing at himself and cranking the engine, "I'm just such a klutz," he says, and sputters away, off the campus, to visit his predecessor as headmaster at Roland Park Place.

Ludlow Baldwin—another inspiration. I had the best time corresponding with and getting to know Ludlow. When I first wrote Ludlow a three-page letter trying to lure him into writing a piece for *Gilman Voices*, I received a neatly handwritten letter back, dated October 27, 1992. In answer to my request for a written memoir, Ludlow first explained he'd caught a virus which had sapped his strength, and then continued,

"In part because of this ailment, but mostly because of another reaction that confronts me, I am going to decline your flattering invitation for an 'essay' . . . This other 'reaction' is simply that whenever I write about myself, I forge into self-flattering and boasting. Being educated in the Classics, I classify this as Hubris, which the Greeks considered the most dangerous of all sins, evils, and/or character weakness—for after it then inevitably follows a 'Fall,' before which, 'Pride Goeth.' At age 87 (next month), I do not wish to start boasting, viz.—" He then went on to give the bare facts of his Gilman career, beginning with coming to Gilman at the age of 15—having graduated from City College and been accepted at Johns Hopkins—for a year of maturing, and becoming a one-year Gilman graduate in 1922, before attending Hopkins.

I had a grand lunch with Ludlow, at his favorite spot, the Hopkins Club. The next morning, on arriving at work at St. Paul's School at 8:30 a.m., I found an envelope addressed to me at the receptionist's desk. The receptionist, Jean Bendis—what a help she was through the first years of contributors stopping by and calling me!—informed me that an older gentleman, perhaps my grandfather, had left it off earlier. It was a thank-you note from Ludlow—who had treated me to lunch. Later, I learned from Ludlow's godson Harry McDonough that this was a Ludlow trademark. After a meeting or even a phone conversation, I would always get a neat, handwritten note—often with "hand delivered" written on the envelope—clarifying what we had discussed or when we would next meet.

I had many magical moments corresponding through the mail and talking over the telephone with my writers and sources. I thank them all. I wrote Roy Barker the following on October 29, 1992: "Dear Roy, The very second I was sealing a manila envelope to you, containing the originals of letters past students have sent you, the phone rang here at work. . . . I picked up the receiver and there was Tom Fenton speaking to me from London, as clearly as can be: 'I like the idea of writing something about Roy Barker, along the lines of what you'd written in your letter. He changed the direction of our lives. I'd probably be in some god-awful business right now if it hadn't been for that night with Roy.'"

Knowing Roy was ill, I sent Fenton's essay to him as soon as I received it. My letter triggered all sorts of memories, and Roy wrote me back a delightful letter about Tom Fenton's junior year, Roy's first at Gilman, (The *Cynosure* was dedicated to Roy that year), concluding with a post-Gilman anecdote about the adult Fenton which ended with this sentence: "And now you know that I am probably the only ex-faculty member from Gilman to have Scotland Yard put out an APB on him."

Here's a note in my files from Frank Deford '57. It is typed, seemingly on a manual typewriter, onto a 3-by-5 index card, and signed by hand. And it was discovered when throwing some old magazines into the recycling pile. It had inadvertently found its way between the pages of an unread catalogue. "Thank you for your very nice note. . . . I'd be honored to do a piece for the Centennial . . . You can count me in." Another time, I was listening to Deford's morning sports commentary on the way to work. I got out of the car, walked to my office. The phone rang. Picked it up—took a step back: it was that same exact voice to which I had just been listening. "Hello. This is Frank . . ."

And here comes Cooper Walker '33—we discuss meeting Marlene Dietrich in the Ritz during the War in one breath and a deep-felt, life-long thankfulness to wrestling coach Ed Russell in the next. We work on fine-tuning his essay, which mainly means taking out any hint of "hubris."

And Headmaster Arch Montgomery '71—the magic of seeming to bump into him at exactly the right moment. One day I was driving my old pick-up by Gilman on Roland Avenue. I thought, I haven't been on the campus in a pick-up in 25 years. I pulled in, rumbled through, pulled up in front of Carey Hall, gave the cupola and front door a nostalgic look. As if it had been rehearsed, Arch stepped out the main door. I waved him over, he climbed in the truck, and I gave him a ride over to his campus house. We sat in the cab and talked about educating our sons. With Arch sitting there in the hay-strewn cab of the truck, I was transported back 30 years: taking Arch out on Daffodil, a chestnut pony, teaching him to ride (he could have been a contender), and then, after dinner in the summer, stepping out onto the lawn and into the fireflies, pulling on old frayed leather boxing gloves, laughingly helping each other tie the laces, and going at it for a few rounds.

For five years I worked on *Gilman Voices* while having a full-time job, three of the years working as director of publications and public relations at St. Paul's School, and two in the same capacity at Gilman. Thank you, St. Paul's Headmaster Bob Hallett and then-Director of Development Geordie Mitchell, for encouraging me to edit the history of Gilman School while working at St. Paul's. Having a full-time job meant working on the book on the weekends in my garret in the old Monkton Hotel, and it meant writing and editing at 5:30 a.m. during the week. Who helped me carve out this time? Who put up with me talking about Gilman, listening to stories about Gilman, being asked about Gilman, receiving calls from Gilman alumni, around the clock, for five years? My wife Ansley—and to her I owe the most gratitude of all—her patience, her encouragement, her handling of our three children while I was working.

For five years, I received drafts of essays in the mail when I got home from work. It was like receiving Christmas presents year-round. I wouldn't open them at that moment with the phone ringing and the children dancing around; I'd save the opening for a special, quiet time.

It has gotten so that I cannot imagine *not* working on this book. I cannot imagine *not* finding one more piece of information to splice into the 100-year puzzle, one more essay on one more dedicated teacher/coach. I cannot imagine *not* receiving my missives in the U. S. Mail from contributors all across the country.

In reality, this book will never be finished as long as Gilman continues to turn out students who give and care and create and serve. Thank you contributors, thank you Book Committee members, thank you Gilman alumni and teachers and headmasters and parents, thank you classmates—especially Rob Deford and Tom Whedbee—for your help, support, and inspiration in producing *Gilman Voices, 1897–1997*.

PATRICK SMITHWICK

23rd December 1995
Monkton Hotel, Maryland

"In thy face I see the map of Honour, Truth, & Loyalty."

Dr. Daniel Coit Gilman, 1897
First President of Johns Hopkins University

On the following pages, the entire student body, and a youthful lot at that, gathered for
the first school photograph in the spring of 1898 of The Country School for Boys of Baltimore City.
The boys are sitting on the steps of Homewood, their school building from 1897–1910,
and now a museum on the campus of Johns Hopkins University.
Front row (left to right): George Hinman Abel, Joseph Edwin Mabbett, Henry Greenway Albert,
Henry Patterson Harris, Albert Graham Ober, Jr., Wilson Bowen Robinson, France Lawrence Goodwin,
Lennox Birckhead Clemens, Williams Fitzhugh Turner, Clapham Murray, Jr.,
Gerald DeCourcy May, Harpur Allen Gosnell.
Second row: Henry Coleman May, Samuel Stansbury Brady, Jr., Irwin Manning Brown,
Benjamin Franklin Bennett, Lewis Kinney Robinson, Hugh Lennox Bond III, Henry Findlay French,
Arunah Shepardson Abell Brady, Christopher Hughes Manly, John William Stansbury Brady, Jr.,
Robert Bell Deford.
Third row: John Gilman D'Arcy Paul, Francis James Carey, Francis Wanton Robinson,
George Alexander Pope, Jr., Solomon Hillen McSherry, Donald Newcomer Gilpin, John Sterett Gittings,
George Buchanan Redwood.
Fourth row: William Van Wyck, Mr. John H. Chase, Raymond Pleasants Stabler,
Walter Booth Brooks, Jr., Mr. Frederick Winsor, headmaster, Lyman Colt Josephs, Jr., Richard McSherry,
Mr. Henry H. Ballard, Brooke Gwathmey Bird.

1896
1910

1896

Anne Galbraith Carey wonders what to do about school for her eight-year-old son Frank. She decides that he would benefit most by living at home while attending a school in a country setting with rigorous classes in the morning, a hot meal for lunch, study hall, and sports in the afternoon. Then, home to dinner with the family and homework before bed.

1897

In response to the inspiration and hard work of Mrs. Carey, a committee consisting of William A. Fisher, Daniel Coit Gilman, Charles J. Bonaparte, Herbert B. Adams, William Cabell Bruce, William H. Buckler, and Francis K. Carey sends out a circular letter inviting a number of other Baltimoreans to become members of the Board of Trustees for management of a new school.

January 21

The first trustee meeting is held. William A. Fisher is elected president.

June 25

The Country School for Boys of Baltimore City is incorporated. Anne Carey begins a hectic summer of almost single-handedly redecorating and preparing Homewood.

September 30

The Country School for Boys opens for classes in Homewood House, now part of The Johns Hopkins University campus. Thirty-two students enroll. Frederick Winsor is the first headmaster.

Headmaster S. Wardwell Kinney (1903–09) and faculty member William Myers attend a baseball game. Kinney was a major proponent for moving the new school out of Homewood. In 1907, he told the trustees that the school's "usefulness and efficiency are greatly hampered by its outworn and out-grown buildings." It wasn't until the fall of 1909 that the trustees contracted to buy 68 acres in Roland Park.

Anne Galbraith Carey, at the age of 32, conceived of and established The Country School for Boys. Mrs. Carey continued to be active in civic affairs throughout her life.

Gilman's first headmaster, Frederick Winsor, was a Harvard-educated Bostonian who had been teaching English and history at Exeter.

1900
Roland J. Mulford becomes headmaster.

The Blue and The Gray, the School's literary and news magazine, is first published. It publishes continuously under this name until 1970, when it becomes *Vantage*. In the 1980s, it becomes *Paragon*.

1903
The first class graduates with four members: Henry Findlay French, France Lawrence Goodwin, Clapham Murray, Jr., and Lewis Kinney Robinson. Samuel W. Kinney becomes headmaster.

The William A. Fisher Medallion is awarded for the first time at graduation.

Louis Robinson runs the 100-yard dash in 10 1/5 seconds, clipping 3/5 of a second off the schoolboy record.

1904
The Country School baseball team records its first undefeated season.

1905
The Country School football team records its first undefeated season.

1906
The Alumni Association is organized.

1909
Edwin B. King becomes headmaster. Construction of the main building on the new Roland Park campus is begun in September.

1910, October 4
The Country School for Boys moves from Homewood House into the main building on Roland Avenue. The school opens its doors to 175 day and boarding students while 200 bricklayers, carpenters, electricians, steam fitters, plumbers, and mechanics continue to work.

1910, December 20
The Country School for Boys officially becomes The Gilman Country School for Boys, in honor of Daniel Coit Gilman, one of the brightest luminaries in American education, and first president of Johns Hopkins University.

Dr. Daniel Coit Gilman was first president of the Johns Hopkins University when he lent his valuable support to the formation of The Country School for Boys in 1897. Gilman died in 1908. On December 20, 1910, with the agreement of Gilman's two daughters, the school's name became The Gilman Country School for Boys. It was not until 1951 that the "Country" was dropped, and the school's name became Gilman School.

The Country School baseball team of 1899.

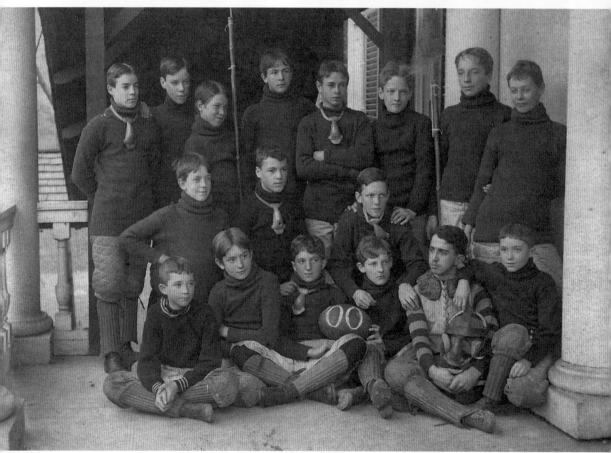

Above far left, Princeton graduate S. Wardwell Kinney was headmaster of The Country School from 1903 until his premature death in 1909.

Above left, The Country School for Boys housed in Homewood—a jewel of Federal, neo-classic architecture on North Charles Street—opens for classes on September 30, 1897.

Left, the 1900 football team is dressed in full uniform and ready for a game. Note the "nose-guards" hanging from the necks of several players.

In what would become a time-honored tradition, Country School students work diligently in late afternoon study hall as the light angles in through the large windows. Note that to maintain discipline the instructor has opted to sit behind the students instead of at the more traditional position in the front of the room.

Far left, sailor suits, wide collars, bow ties, ankle-high lace-up boots, four-button jackets, and hair parted in the middle mark these Lower School students in both photos taken on the porch of Homewood as the forerunners of the dapper Gilman Lower Schoolers of today.

Left, the first play of the Country School Dramatic Association, in 1902, was "Ici On Parle Français." Sitting: Findlay French, List Warner, Pat Harris, Julian Ridgely, and Arunah Brady. Standing: Lawrence Goodwin, Clapham Murray, Iredell Iglehart, and William Cooper Walker.

Below, a Country School running back sprints through snow and tacklers for a touchdown.

9

The graduating class of 1905: Top row, Harry Hardcastle and Albert Ober. Bottom row, Hambleton Ober, Julian Ridgeley, and Douglas Ober. Below, the track team of 1904 is ready to run.

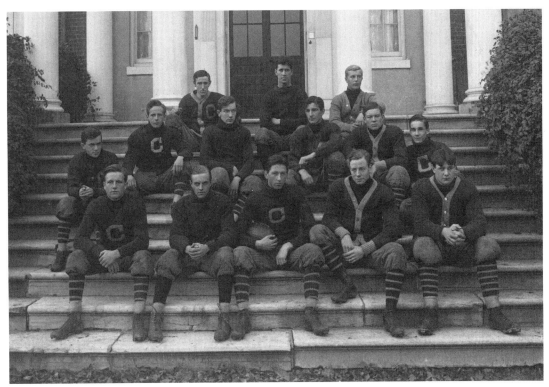

By the fall of 1910, The Country School had bigger and older players, and varsity football teams started to give other schools a bruising. Below, the 1910 Baseball Champions.

11

Above, football team captain Renouf Russell '11 relaxes before leading The Country School to a 17–11 victory over Dunham School in 1909.

Right, Iredell Iglehart '04 prepares to hit a homer.

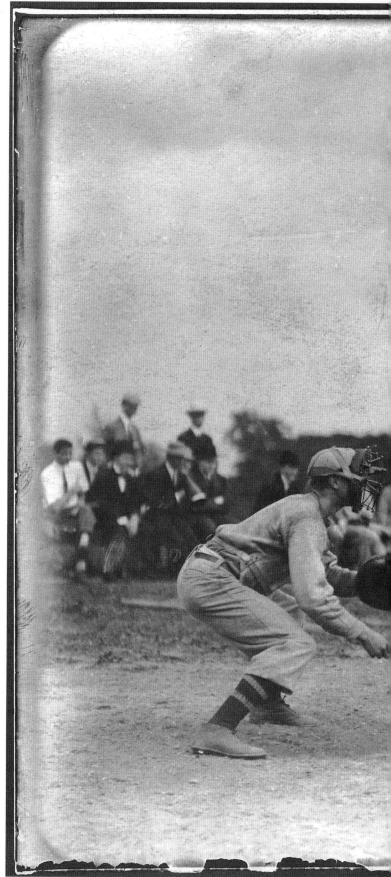

Above, E. Boyd Morrow began teaching at The Country School in 1906. He followed the school through its move to Roland Park, and was twice passed over for the headmastership. Finally, in 1926, he was chosen by the trustees to serve as headmaster.

Left, the faculty and staff of The Country School enjoy tea, biscuits, and light reading on the steps of Homewood. The stocky terrier will be replaced with a swift and svelte greyhound in future years as the school mascot.

The Lady Vanquishes

How the Country Day School for Boys of Baltimore City is born and spends 13 years—shaky, unsettled but determined—at the beautiful mansion called Homewood.

BRADFORD JACOBS '38

Late in 1896 Anne Carey was on her way south on Charles Street, by carriage, from lunch at the Elkridge Kennels when she began to wonder: What to do about school for her eight-year-old son Frank?

The question presented a formidable puzzle, but Anne Carey was the formidable young woman to deal with it. The answer she was to produce would imprint on secondary education—over the long range, across the nation—an entirely new pattern. The starting point, she quickly found, was trouble at short range and close up.

Part of the trouble lay with the dismal state of Baltimore schools. At best, the public system offered patchy teaching. Most young Baltimoreans quit classes at 16—or, gloomily, at 12—to work in clothing sweatshops and canning factories. At worst, school buildings huddled in hard-bitten neighborhoods. Teachers struggled along under low pay with classrooms stuffed 70-strong or worse. Subject matter seldom rose above elementary. In some cases it was politically tilted, to assuage Baltimore's demanding German-language wards. Recreation in the city was a bad joke. For sport, boys chased cats up alleys cobbled with garbage left to fester for weeks.

Charles W. Chancellor, a member of the Maryland Board of Health, paid a startled visit to one Baltimore public school of the period and reported:

> *The heat and stifling air and nauseating effluvia in some of the rooms is indeed such as a human being has hardly been compelled to live in since the time of Jonah.*

As late as 1911, H.L. Mencken—who loved the city—would ask: "Why is Baltimore such a pesthole . . . ?"

Local private schools, while better, presented private hangups. Friends and Calvert Hall carried their own religious flavors. Marston's and Dunham's, both run for profit, had seen better days. McDonogh was founded and shaped to fit boys low on money and, besides, was military. St. Paul's was for choir boys; it stopped short of college preparation. Tome was lost somewhere in darkest Cecil County.

What, Anne Carey asked herself, was she to do with young Frank? How about that famous New England composite school, tested and proven for years as a shaper and teacher of outstanding young men? Yes, how about St. Grottlesex?

Anne Carey gave St. Grottlesex serious thought and, as she sadly wrote, rejected it because: ". . . to send a nine-year-old boy away to boarding school and then to college, and perhaps to the Harvard Law School, meant that when he came back to Baltimore to make his living, he *was never exactly of us.*"

Consider that wistful observation: "he *was never exactly of us.*" In its perceptively motherly way, here lies the very genesis of the country day school idea. St. Grottlesex and its stiffly righteous kin were monumental schools, to be sure; their flaw was that they robbed the cradle, stole away the son at a too-tender age. The melancholy result was that afterward "he *was never exactly of us;*" he was of somebody else, somebody alien and maybe—who knows?—somebody hostile. Something better had to come about. Something closer to the warm embrace of home.

Add to all this sober reflection the fear of fleshpots, specifically, fleshpots lying in ambush in New York City for Baltimore boys in transit to St. Grottlesex. At least until the 1940s, it was necessary for northbound passengers to change trains at Pennsylvania Station. This need consume no more than a half-hour; a boy bound on adventure, however, could arrange for a four-hour delay in New York, where at the Stork Club its enterprising manager slyly provided for the club's future expansion by furnishing free drinks to teenagers. Carey-type mothers suspected this ploy and laid their own defenses. So much for St. Grottlesex.

So what to do with young Frank Carey?

Most mothers would have been terminally daunted, would have surrendered one way or the other. Not Anne Carey. What soon dawned on her was this simple but enormously challenging fact: she would have to (a) invent a whole new school and (b) bully her friends and acquaintances into backing her, then (c) personally make the school happen. She did all three, nearly alone.

Anne Carey had no professional qualifications. Appropriate to her generation, her own formal education had been limited to arts and graces. At 32 years old she was a mother, that's all, unqualified a century later for a teacher's job at the lowest, least demanding level. What's remarkable is that, also a century later, the educational concept she was to bring to life would mature into a wholly new turn in the philosophy of schooling—a day school of the first rank for boys, a school located in the country. She was that rare hybrid, a practical visionary.

She was also, two grandsons would recall many years later, personally intimidating. They called her "Granny" but when he did something Granny disapproved of, one grandson recalled, still shivering at age 64, she "would just look at me."

"My God," said the second grandson, "My God—'The Look.'" He was 65.

Anne Carey, however chilling she could be, was not operating in a vacuum. Going for her in the 1890s, along with her own perceptions and personal momentum, was the freshening state of Baltimore as a city. Pre-Civil War Baltimoreans were an amiable if parochial lot. War woke them up to the city's "Jonah"-like accommodations, noted above. War stirred imaginations, opened opportunities. It made them, if grudgingly, more northern. By a geopolitical fluke, slovenly old Mobtown found itself snapping erect on the winning or Yankee side of the line. This new Baltimore blinked in astonishment. Must the city pull up its still-Southern socks? Take on the brisk, slick postures of the New Yorkers, Philadelphians and Chicagoans who, money in hand, were busily snapping up the old Baltimore-owned businesses?

The 20 years after Appomattox found Baltimore in a ferment. Immigrants were dumped ashore by boats from Germany, Ireland, Russia—still more, black and white, crept North from the benumbed American South. New industries smothered the downtown in smoke, fed hungrily on cheap Baltimore labor. New banks formed and fattened; insurance companies parlayed the newcomers' insecurities into sturdy institutions. Railroads, brought to ripe vigor by wartime tensions, spread profitably west and south; Baltimore enthusiastically joined the nation. Shipping lines reached out to Europe and Asia; Baltimore began joining the world. Comfy old ways had to change. Life in Baltimore turned not-so-comfortably earnest.

It took nearly two decades to digest the city's post-war prosperity. All that money! To be sure, new Yankee owners siphoned off the juiciest profits elsewhere. But Baltimoreans who cashed in their old holdings were feeling an unfamiliar flush. What to do with the delightful new dollars?

Fresh, invigorating notions of culture seeped through Baltimore's emerging elite, happy in its *nouvelle richesse.* The now-defunct Cavalier South, while exploiting black slavery, had also produced in Charleston and Savannah a plantation gentility—art, music, European entertainments—scarcely known in earlier Baltimore. To the North, Boston and New York had long led the nation in graceful living; must Baltimoreans look on forever from outside, perpetual country cousins?

William and Henry Walters thought not. Railroad tycoons, they collected art around the world, then established it in a small, splendid museum. Johns Hopkins, Baltimore's foremost merchant prince, thought not too. He established a university and a hospital, each with enough *éclat* to define Baltimore for the next century. Enoch Pratt, with his free library, hoped to make Baltimore the city that reads. Like Hopkins and Pratt, John Goucher and John McDonogh recognized improved education as Baltimore's most urgent need, then handsomely underwrote their convictions. Garretts and Fishers, Bruces and Bonapartes joined in. A band of greasy-thumbed political bosses hustled to cover; a reformist city charter arose triumphant. The folkways of a once-hairy old city were becoming outright refined.

It was against the city's dawning enlightenment that Anne Carey perceived the shadow of hopelessly inadequate schools. But when she suggested creating a new school to Francis King Carey, a rising young corporation lawyer and her husband, he just didn't—as women a century after would say—get it. "I received the subject rather coldly," Mr. Carey would confess later. "The suggestion, when she first made it to me, seemed to me impracticable."

Frank Carey was not alone. It seemed impracticable too to Dr. Griffin, dean of the Johns Hopkins faculty. Also to Dr. Basil Gildersleeve, one of Hopkins' brightest luminaries, and to Dr. Ira Remsen, later to be Hopkins' president. Impracticable also to most of the professional educators she wrote to for guidance. Their replies, she wrote, were "brutally discouraging."

Ordinary, nonprofessional fathers—like her own husband—gently pooh-poohed Anne Carey's idea:

> . . . those fathers who had gone to school in Baltimore had affectionate recollections of the old-fashioned, cultivated gentlemen with whom they had prepared for college . . .
> In their day there had been open lots to play on and a few large private gardens. Perhaps after we had listened patiently to their reminiscences for half an hour they would let us tell them that by 1896 the cultivated gentlemen had died or grown old—the grace of the old day was dead. Moreover, there were no vacant lots . . . times had changed . . .
> The mothers knew all this, but the fathers had to be reminded.

It was Daniel Coit Gilman who, at this bleak hour, reached out a helpful—and immensely distinguished—hand. He showed a broader understanding than his fellow educators and a deeper sympathy than Frank Carey and other "coldly" doubtful fathers. Besides, he was enormously admired in the educational world and beyond. He lent Anne Carey his prestige, his contacts, and his guidance. She quite worshipped him, and she brushed the troublesome shadows away.

Later in 1896, allies began to rally round, notably Louise Bruce, another young mother and Anne Carey's loyal friend. Together this pair encircled Judge William A. Fisher, Louise Bruce's father, and for many years a member of the Supreme Bench of Baltimore city. Now they were cutting some ice: together, Dr. Gilman and Judge Fisher provided a magnetic, even commanding community presence for Anne Carey's hitherto lonesome enterprise. They needed money; however, when recruiting founders they looked not for the richest men in town but for the best. One was William H. Buckler, a young lawyer of distinguished education, who would become a nationally known diplomat. Another was Charles J. Bonaparte, fresh from a bold—and successful—undertaking to reform Maryland politics; he would become Secretary of the Navy and Attorney General under Theodore Roosevelt. Next was Herbert B. Adams, a prominent scholar who had organized the history department at Johns Hopkins. Then came William Cabell Bruce, law partner and son-in-law of Judge Fisher; he would become a United States Senator from Maryland.

These four joined Frank Carey, Judge Fisher, and Dr. Gilman in the first con-crete steps to make the country day school dream a reality. They met throughout the late windy months of 1896, most often at Judge Fisher's handsome old city residence at 8 West Mount Vernon Place, sometimes at one or the other's downtown law office. For putting their conclusions into a formal prospectus, they turned to their highest educational authority. In writing, Dr. Gilman explained to future trustees the framework of this unprecedented school:

> *It is proposed to establish a country boarding and day school for boys, designed for the education of the sons of parents who wish their boys to be trained from the beginning of their school years under the best methods approved by modern education and with surroundings which will protect their health and character.*

Was there a faint fudging visible here in the word "boarding"? Was it stuck in as a prudent hedge in case Anne Carey's original idea—a Baltimore "day" school, not a faraway St. Grottlesex—didn't quite catch on? Perhaps, but the little knot of boarders would broaden the base of the school which followed and, besides, lasted for many decades without apparently blurring the clarity of the day-school principle.

Early in 1897, out to potential trustees went Dr. Gilman's prospectus, along with a circular letter setting forth the new school's promising details. Baltimore's freshly blooming suburbs were to offer a location: "a gentleman's country place." The putative headmaster would be "superior." Classes would be non-sectarian, despite a "distinctly religious influence"—a neat trick, how done neatly unspecified. In practice, the Country School's early years would be heavily WASP years, a pattern destined to continue until broader tolerance took over in the 1960s. Day boys would stay all day, eat a hot meal at mid-day, fill out the afternoon with sports and a study hour—then go home to their parents. Anne Carey's enterprise was taking on a working shape.

Which raised a working question: what about money to get going? As noted, the original seven founders were not chosen for wealth. Of that lot, Judge Fisher alone seems to have been not only professional and public-spirited but also more than comfortably well off. In his case, Fisher family money had been happily swollen by a substantial influx which came along with the Judge's bride from Cincinnati, the heiress Louise K. Este. It was their daughter, Louise Fisher Bruce, who was Anne Carey's best friend and co-mother in this essentially maternal exploit. Others would help financially, but the essential nugget at the beginning was a Fisher nugget. Fisher money would underwrite a handsome dining hall, a revered medallion, a trophy tragically inspired by the premature death of Mrs. Bruce's young son. Others would catch the generous spirit. None would dominate the scene in the way Hopkins and McDonogh and Pratt dominated their own establishments.

A $10,000 foundation fund was deemed vital. At $200 apiece, 50 people with sons, grandsons or other visible prods to generosity were solicited. An "endowed school," they were told, was the objective, not an entrepreneurial school.

The first trustees meeting was held January 21, 1897, including five of the seven originals. To them were now added Dr. Harry Fielding Reid, a Hopkins geology professor; Allan McLane, a rising young lawyer of a prominent Baltimore family; and Dr. William S. Thayer, chief assistant to the brilliant Hopkins doctor, Sir William Osler. Judge Fisher was elected the first president. Money only dribbled in.

Two brighter developments in May were the lease of Homewood, an exquisite jewel of Federal, neo-Classic architecture on North Charles Street, and the hiring as headmaster of a 28-year-old Bostonian then teaching English and history at Exeter: Frederick Winsor. Homewood had been built a century earlier near the intersection Merryman's Lane, later University Parkway, made with Charles Street, not yet "extended," not yet even paved. There was a tollgate. The building, three connected wings of pink Baltimore brick, had been built for Charles Carroll, Jr., a dispirited alcoholic, who had abandoned his fortune, house, and wife. Homewood, with 12 wooded acres, had fallen to the Wyman family, who rented it out to the Country Schoolers for $1,000 a year. At its low pinnacle, the house had a tiny eyeball window from which the masts of ships in Baltimore's inner harbor could be seen miles to the south.

Frederick Winsor's tenure there was short but busy. Quickly he hired two other young masters—John H. Chase, a Harvard man like Winsor, who would teach mathematics and classics; and Henry H. Ballard, a Johns Hopkins Ph.D., who would deal with science and mathematics. Classified advertisements appeared in the *Baltimore American* inviting "a limited . . . number of applications." On June 25, the school was formally incorporated as "The Country School for Boys of Baltimore City." Whereupon the *American* of the following day carried a story under this headline:

NEW SCHOOL FOR BOYS
———

Incorporation of a Country
Institute of Learning
———

Prominent Baltimoreans
At Its Head
———

To be Conducted On Similar Lines
As Those of Johns Hopkins
University—But of A
Lower Standard
———

No Capital Stock—First Academic Year Begins
Next September, Frederick Winsor of Harvard
Headmaster

Applications began to turn up by July on Headmaster Winsor's desk. To get ready, Judge Fisher and Cabell Bruce all but drained the school's $11,500 foundation fund. They slipped in a quadrangle behind the north side of Homewood; a gymnasium, a dining room, a handball court, and servants' quarters blocked it off. Plumbing, draining, heating were dutifully extended. To greet boys coming to school by the new electric cars from downtown, they slung a long boardwalk winding from St. Paul Street, where the car stopped near its present intersection with 33rd Street, west across the line where Charles Street would soon be paved, then up the hill to Homewood. Authorized to spend $3,500, they spent $8,000—this on a place only rented. If parsimoniously, Anne Carey spent the rest. Soapy water flew, followed by paint—some soft green, some a rich colonial yellow—to repair the woodwork and walls she found in "a shabby condition and of such a hideous color." What was left of the Carroll/Wyman furniture, she found in "shockingly bad taste": she combed Baltimore's second-hand shops to replace it. Sturdy oak tables appeared, some round and some rectangled refectory. Windsor chairs with gently curved backs ringed the tables, many to continue in service through the years in the existing school common room. Anne Carey pinched each penny, scrupulously writing down every item including a bucket and foot tub ($2.50) and a four-cent pepper pot.

What emerged by September was a building not only homelike and attractive but an architectural masterpiece. Built some 95 years earlier, Homewood's interior now presented a delicacy almost too dainty for the slam-bang boy life about to burst in upon it. Windows and doors were large, some handsomely leaded in floral patterns. Carved walnut framed walls and fireplaces; Mrs. Carey had these patterns picked out in precise white. Hardwood floors were covered in the blocked, colored cloth fashionable in the late Eighteenth Century. This newly rehabilitated Homewood was in every sense radiant of domestic civility.

Would its dozens of new young occupants appreciate it? Or, instead, rip up its elegance under heedlessly thundering heels?

Probably neither actually occurred. None knows—or at least none has recorded—any undue reverence among students for Homewood's graces. As to damage inflicted as many feared it would be, Johns Hopkins itself brushes aside the threat. A later university publication cheerily reported: ". . . a menace which, by some happy chance, never materialized. It is too much to say that the pupils who swarmed through the building were aware of its architectural significance; certain it is, however, that they felt something choice had been put under their protection. At any rate, there was not a single mark or an intentional defacement to show for the boys' occupancy . . ."

Shortly before 9 a.m. September 30, 1897, the Country School for Boys of Baltimore City warmed to life. Thirty-two youngsters, uneasily eyeing their hastily jumped-up little school, walked through the great doorway framed in by Homewood's southern flank. They were just on the verge of their teens, 11 to 13. Almost uniformly, each head of hair was parted in the middle, each jacket a blue serge box with four buttons up the front. Pants were short and tight. Stockings were long and black, shoes high-laced, caps small and visored. A couple of sailor suits, be-dickied, set their wearers apart. So did a handful of gold watch chains, airily draped across waistcoats. None of this lot had shaved—ever.

Most had ridden 15 minutes by electric car, the Waverly, from downtown. Home addresses included 24 East 25th Street, 28 East Mt. Vernon Place, 12 West Madison Street, 2225 North Charles Street, 13 East Lafayette Avenue, 926 St. Paul Street, 2219 Maryland Avenue. These were the addresses of fashionable, well-off Baltimore, all for the most part clustered matily in the neighborhood of the Washington Monument, generally within an easy carriage ride of one another. Zippy electric cars, cousins of the Waverly, would shortly erode such social cohesion but had not yet. Only a handful of boys hailed from distant Brooklandville, Lutherville, Catonsville, Hampton. These clop-clopped in behind horses.

Homewood and its 12 comfortably rolling acres presented a reassuring pastoral scene, Anne Carey's dream come to pass. To the east lay the little village of Waverly; the west was rugged with Wyman's woods. A few blocks south the city began, home to most boys. At the north there spread a few smiling grassy estates and, beyond them, the largely un-plumbed mysteries of Baltimore County, fenceless, bosky, peopled by a scattering of the resolutely bold. Homewood, already a century old, lay serene among hollies and southern red oak of settled seniority. Plenty of room for a ballgame, plenty for a quick exchange of knuckles.

Inside the old Carroll house the new arrivals met a sterner reality. English—literature and compositions—mathematics, and, for older boys, Latin lay in wait. Oddly, as a presumed ally of Latin, manual training was offered. You build a sound box, the reasoning went, you construe a sound Latin sentence. 50 was passing, 40 wasn't. Or maybe you misbehaved—spit, swore, gambled, got caught smoking. "Rounds" were sternly imposed—endlessly-walked circuits of the pebbled driveway, classmates jeering all the way. Then a hot dinner, an hour's study, a game outdoors, home by the Waverly electric, and more study for tomorrow. With its special home dimension, a Country Day School day was completed.

Life was not all Spartan. Games at first were highly informal. Incredibly, to later generations, these boys didn't yet know how to play most games. Besides, at eight to thirteen, they were too little to take on Baltimore's older, better muscled schools. What they did take on with gathering success was a mixed bag called the "Lanvales," the "Stonewalls," and the "John Street Athletic Club." They also acquired some morale-boosting school colors—blue and gray, apparently meant to be a reflection of George Washington's blue and buff, the buff somehow distorted by a shirt-maker to gray.

Soon the Country School boys grew heavier, stronger and faster. By 1901 they faced up to Deichmann's, the Warfield School, Walbrook, the Washington School, Poly, St. John's prep, and Marston's. In 1903, Louis Robinson, a sensational Country School runner, blew Dunham's off the track with a sizzling 100-yard dash run in 10 1/2 seconds, clipping 3/5 of a second off the schoolboy record.

Dances began in 1902. Should the U.S. sell the Philippines to Japan? debaters asked. The first school play was a frolic called "Ici On Parle Français." To record all this, the year 1900 brought forth a boy-run magazine, *The Blue and The Gray*, destined to be a vibrant depository of Country School doings. Here was history as it was lived. *Blue and Gray* editors took their responsibilities seriously: F. Brayton Wood, an aspiring tackle, was lectured—"Never turn around and push with your back." Fighting and gambling were discouraged with such delighted vehemence as to suggest emotions secretly mixed. Literarily, Gilman Paul emblazoned the magazine's pages in 1903 with this rousing fictional sally: "The Princess Rosalind rushed in betwixt the enraged combatants and exposed her lily neck to the savage rapier thrust with a scream. . . ." There was lots of that.

Prudently, *The Blue and The Gray* accepted paying advertisements including the offer of tidy boxes from Williams & Wilkens, Engravers, of 8 S. Calvert Street; "Natural Milk vs. Machine Manipulated Milk" from Pikesville Dairy; and horse blankets from Vordemberge, saddler, at 816 Madison Avenue. L. Slesinger & Son, of 106 Charles Street North, offered high-button shoes at $5 the pair. No such shoes appeared, however, in a school picture taken on Homewood's front steps.

In 1902, after a school trip to Washington, William C. Walker wrote solemnly of visits to the Library of Congress and the Corcoran, but with more enthusiasm of "a glimpse" the boys got "of President Roosevelt . . . as he left the White House grounds for a ride on a fine black horse."

Nor was the faculty spared a little teasing: "Mr. Post was heard to say a few days ago that he was going to install a whipping post in the school." Or was it teasing?

By 1908, the magazine swaggered forth with an official seal composed by two faculty members: an arrangement of Stars and Bars in blue and gray; a learned-looking volume, open; a couple of decorative stars. The legend: "In tuo lumine lumen." Three years later, a fancier shield showed a gold cross and star, plus three bees.

A truly distinctive feature of the Homewood campus—distinctive, at least, by more modern standards—was the privy located 100 yards just north of the main building and framed, then as later, by a pair of venerable southern red oaks. This privy was—still is, having been studiously preserved by Johns Hopkins operatives—a seven-holer, four holes on one side, three on another. Artwork on the interior walls was inspired by—specifically, grew out of—natural creases and knotholes in the wood. Anatomy on display, both male and female, seems more exaggerated than probable but, either way, highly enthusiastic. "I love . . . do you?" is instantly answered below: "Yes I do!" Initials—some carved in the wood, some scribbled in ink—abound: "J.S.," "James E.," "J.B., W.S." So do names: "John Silk," "L. Hickman," "Will Clinkhofer," "Pierpont," "Webb 09." Something unspecified, something pleasurable, it is hinted, could occur at either "1615 Burton St." or at "308 Madison Ave." Privy walls offer a heady mix, not always a clear one.

Considering all the joys it bought, Country School tuition in 1897 was not high—$150 for each of the first three years, $200 the second three, $250 the third. Dinner cost $1.50 per week. Not surprisingly, the school's treasury was only marginally in balance throughout the Homewood period. Net profit for the years 1908 and 1909 ran between $1,500 and $2,000. Homewood rent, at $1,000, was a bargain. Salaries for teachers were the big expense, but trustees were content. The Country

School, they told themselves, was "the best in the Southern states." Indeed, the school catalogue boasted that "no one of its graduates has ever failed an examination to enter any college."

June of 1907 saw 28 boys graduate. They split 10 each to Johns Hopkins and Princeton, three to Harvard, two to Yale, one each to Swarthmore and Earlham. One forswore college. That same spring, a denominational count of the 90 boys enrolled produced this religious breakdown: 49 Episcopalians, 16 Presbyterians, 13 Roman Catholics, two Friends, two Lutherans, two Methodists, two Baptists and two Christian Scientists. Two were unaffiliated. No non-Christians appeared.

After its first decade the Country School was surviving, if in some aspects narrowly. One spot was so sore as to be an outright embarrassment. This was the startling turnover in headmasters. Between 1897 and 1912, four highly touted educators bounced into the front office, shortly to bounce out. For the most part, they went unwillingly—possibly reflecting a flaw in Anne Carey's original family-style concept of a country day school. As she would later report, Dr. Remsen at Johns Hopkins—"pessimistic" about the concept from the start—had warned her about how important a headmaster would be:

"It is the man," he said. "Nothing else matters."

"We thought," Anne Carey said, to the contrary, "the boys were the school."

Perhaps here lurked a built-in conflict. Perhaps "the man" so insecurely rooted at the top was the victim of an aura, aggressively familial, exuded by the school's motherly founders and its too-vigilant trustees. Was the faculty hugged to death? Or, anyway, to resignation?

By January, 1900, Frederick Winsor found three years in the Country School quite enough. He resigned, ostensibly to found a school of his own elsewhere. Years later, a daughter or granddaughter wrote that Mr. Winsor "did not see eye to eye on school problems." She did not say with whom.

In 1901, to the headmastership came Roland J. Mulford, of Harvard, a veteran instructor at St. Mark's and at Pomfret. Presumptuously—or so the trustees termed it—Mr. Mulford took on a new master without consulting the board. He was shoved out in 1903; this time, the boys—and some parents—were outraged. *The Blue and The Gray* openly mourned his leaving. The following fall, for the first and only time, the number of students enrolled fell: from 80 to 72. The missing eight, some of whom followed him elsewhere, were called "the Mulford exodus."

S. Wardwell Kinney, of Princeton and Harvard, was a tragic case. Briskly British by attitude, not by birth, Kinney in 1904 stiffened Country School collars. He thereby supplied an Anglican "tone" the trustees found quite stimulating. Unfortunately, early in 1909 Kinney sickened and died, leaving the headmaster's office empty yet again.

Next, in the Spring of 1909, came Edwin B. King, who would also stumble across the Country School trustees. King was fired at the end of the school year, 1912, for reasons never completely clear. A contemporary observer commented on a "disturbance to much of the school body." A letter from the Sixth Form and a petition from the school expressing regret at King's departure were presented to the Board.

The uncomfortable conclusion is that its first decade and a half left the Country School on perilously thin ice. A going concern, yes, but its status was murky. Its faculty was jumpy and uncertain. The whole enterprise seemed shaky. If jocose, a passage written in the 1972 Alumni *Bulletin* by Francis Beirne '08, unwittingly made part of the perilous situation clear:

> *In the fall of 1903 the football team of the Country School for Boys was approaching the last and crucial game of the season. It was in excellent shape except for one weakness, and that was a serious one. It had no substitutes . . .*
>
> *In the crisis somebody thought of a Sixth Former of decent proportions who despised athletics but up to that point had miraculously escaped them. Notwithstanding, he was slapped into uniform and made to run out with the team. His indignation alone gave him a ferocious look that struck terror into the hearts of the opposing eleven. Fortunately none of the regulars were hurt during the game, and the unwilling substitute got no farther than the bench.*

Still, who won the game? Frank Beirne, perhaps delicately, does not say. One authoritative onlooker put the whole matter pretty bluntly:

> *For ten years, following the Baltimore beginning in 1897, the experiment created not the slightest ripple of educational interest anywhere else. The old mansion was architecturally famous, and architects often stopped off to see it. But no one appears to have perceived the enormous significance of the educational experiment going on there, and no one ever came by to study it as a possibility for study elsewhere. The trustees themselves seemed not to feel sure of the plan, added a protective anchor in the form of a boarding department and, in 1899, sent a representative to ten Southern cities to arouse interest in it.*

Worse was ahead. A charming testing ground, Homewood wasn't to endure. As early as 1898, calls were heard to move to some place larger and more permanent. In 1902, Homewood was handed over to Johns Hopkins University: as *The Blue and The Gray* saw it—"MR. WYMAN GIVES US AWAY." By 1909, Hopkins made plain it was planning to move in: Would the Country School kindly move out? A panicky land search ensued, and half a dozen doubtful possibilities turned up. One was the old A. S. Abell mansion, "Guilford." Another—the John S. Gittings property, "Ashburton"—was so appealing that a tentative building plan was drawn up and labeled "Ashburton School." Potentially the most imposing opportunity lay on a peaked hill just north of the railroad track newly put down by the Northern Central through the heart of the Green Spring Valley. It had been the Avalon Inn; later, after the Country School passed it up, the property was acquired by General Douglas MacArthur. He built a grand chateau and called it "Rainbow Hill" after his famous World War I division.

Ultimately a lucky strike settled upon Roland Park, just then an early and daring experiment with suburban planning. But the Country School itself was an experiment, wasn't it? And surburbia—plenty of trees, connected by carline to downtown Baltimore—was thought just the ticket. The trustees, then an enthusiastic if faintly unworldly lot, borrowed $75,000 to take 68 acres at the corner of Roland and Belvedere Avenues. This set the stage for a future editor of *The Blue and The Gray* to use as his pen-name "Roland Belvedere."

It set other, scarier stages which D. K. Este Fisher, a trustee and an architect, was there to observe and to report in vivid detail:

> *There was on the land no building capable of use, and to build was an indispensable necessity if the school was to continue in existence. How was it to be paid for? This was a stunning question, when the land was already mortgaged to the hilt and there were but a few months before Homewood must be vacated. The trustees were not to be halted in their determination . . . it was decided to ask for subscriptions from the trustees, their families and the friends of the school to certificates of indebtedness, with interest . . .*

After the greatest effort, $248,500 was raised. The new school was built, landscaping completed, school reopened in 1910. If the re-establishment of the school in Roland Park was an exercise in perilous finance, the actual design of the new building—named Carey Hall in 1990—was a model of careful, sensitive architecture. The architect was David Hamilton Thomas, Jr., born in what is arguably the finest house in the city—Hackerman House, later part of the Walters Art Gallery at No. 1 Mt. Vernon Place. David Thomas, a graduate of Johns Hopkins and M.I.T., may well have been Baltimore's foremost designer. Listed to his name are the Alex. Brown building, the Belvedere Hotel, the Bank of Baltimore, the renovated St. Paul's rectory. (His original Gilman drawings, on linen, were uncovered in the 1980s in a tower under the school's cupola.)

Let's turn here to commentary by W. Boulton Kelly, Jr. '46, who performed the first architectural analysis of the building since it was opened in 1910. Bo Kelly is himself a leading Baltimore architect, a prime mover in Preservation Maryland and selected by Vieilles Maisons Françaises as its representative here.

A portion of the Kelly analysis:

> *The trustees seemed to feel that establishing the school temporarily in "Homewood"—a distinguished Federal House (1806, neo-Classic) built by Charles Carroll, the signer, for his son Charles, Jr.—matched to a large degree the aspirations of the school. The warmth of the red brick, the residential scale of the five-part house, the historic aura, all combined to reinforce Mrs. Carey's concept of a country school.*

> *Carey Hall is a very impressive building with strong echoes of Homewood . . . The really distinguishing design features of the Thomas building are three—the white wooden octagonal tower directly in line with the entrance, springing from the gambrel roof in two stages to an octagonal open belfry, capped by an octagonal dome and grasshopper weathervane, then two symmetrical end pavilions, three bays wide, which project forward of the main block toward Roland Avenue . . . These two pavilions have higher ceil-*

ings than the main block because they were originally designed for special uses—dining in the north pavilion, assembly in the south, with elaborate paneling, decorative shields and the like. These plus the original library, at the east, have decorative barrel vault plaster ceilings.

Many changes have occurred since 1910, but one space which has never changed is the Common Room, directly accessible from the front entrance. This space with Mrs. Carey's windsor chairs and refectory tables has collected students at all times of day, acting as a sort of mixing and holding room between events, an important focal point of enormous social significance to the school.

Just this side of the Common Room is the Carey Reception Room. This is Mrs. Carey's own addition, a relic of Homewood, a relic of old Southern custom: in an earlier day, a visitor was steered to the reception room to await the lady of the house, who was notified by the butler. Only then would the lady herself appear or, in dubious circumstances, not appear. This room has been kept up by William P. Carey, Mrs. Carey's grandson, whose handsome donation later invited the new name of the building.

For all its crisp new building, its sweeping new acreage and ever larger student body, a blur hung about the school. Its name, The Country School for Boys, had brought complaints as early as 1907 from alumni embarrassed at college. Had they learned there to milk cows? jeering classmates asked. Hoe the cabbage patch? Alumni strongly advised a new name.

Daniel Coit Gilman may well have been over-rewarded for his useful but modest part in getting the school started. He was not a founder, not a trustee. He never went to a meeting. What he did was encourage Anne Carey and Louise Bruce in this often lonesome struggle and steer them for advice to professional educators. Perhaps his name was spread upon the new school letterhead mostly as a marketing device; it was a name which commanded broad community respect at a time when The Country School did not. Perhaps, in retrospect, the name Carey would have been a symbol more fairly earned. But that is only in retrospect and, besides, Carey Hall today puts the symbolism where it belongs. The Country School needed a boost, a sharper image, and in December of 1910 it got it. Henceforth, the school would be known as Gilman Country School for Boys, and later, Gilman School.

Beneath the 1938 *Cynosure* photograph of Bradford Jacobs—a shot of him looking dreamy and debonair in a bow tie—editors wrote, "Sophistication is the key to Brad's personality. But it is a quiet, unobtrusive sophistication, which knows by instinct the proper approaches for the different environments in which he finds himself." That was Jacobs in 1938, and that was Jacobs 1992–97 when he contributed the above chapter to this book and served on the Centennial Book Committee.

Jacobs attended Gilman 1929–38, with his favorite subject being English and his favorite teacher Archie Hart (English). By his senior year, he was Secretary of the Dramatic Association and singing in the Glee Club. Jacobs was a member of the Sixth Form Dance Committee and the Areopagus Debating Club, a four-year member of the Literary Club, Associate Editor of the *Cynosure*, and Co-Editor-in-Chief of *The Blue and The Gray*. (His writing style has a close resemblance to that of "Roland Belvedere," a frequent contributor to *The Blue and The Gray* during Jacobs' editorship.)

Jacobs moved on to Princeton, where he furthered his studies in English. Out of college in '42, he spent four years on active duty in the U. S. Army, rising to Captain in Military Intelligence. He assisted in the invasion and occupation of Germany, and was awarded the Bronze Star, the Croix de Guerre (France), and three battle stars.

Returning home in '46, Jacobs began a 40-year career at the Baltimore *Sun*. He also began researching the history of Gilman School. In 1947, Gilman published *Gilman Walls Will Echo*, The Story of the Gilman Country School, 1897–1947, an elegant and sophisticated history of the school written by the youthful Bradford McE. Jacobs. Jacobs continued working at *The Sun*, as a reporter, editorial writer, foreign correspondent, and Washington correspondent. In 1968, he was appointed editorial page editor of *The Evening Sun*, a position he held until 1980. He retired from The Sunpapers in 1985 after publishing *Thimbleriggers: The Law versus Governor Marvin Mandel*, which delved into the background of corruption charges against the Maryland governor. In the 1990s, he was co-editor of H. L. Mencken's *Thirty-five Years of Newspaper Work*, and chairman of the Baltimore Council of Foreign Affairs. All along, his specialties were politics and foreign affairs, and the writing of exquisitely turned-out paragraphs.

Jacobs and his wife, Molly Bruce Jacobs, can be found at Gilman on grandparents' day, trooping along to class with their grandsons, Bradford Shea '02 and Garrity Shea '07.

1910
1929

1911

In response to fears of contagious diseases prevalent at the time, Gilman starts the Open Air School. Pavilions open to the elements in all weather conditions are erected to the south of the main building, where the youngsters huddle under hoods to learn their lessons. Heated soapstones that sometimes burn their way into the desktops provide the only warmth. Nine students are enrolled in the first year of the Open Air School, followed by 28 the next. By 1919–20 the total Open Air student body has swelled to 102.

Thirteen boys graduate; their diplomas are the first to bear the name, The Gilman Country School for Boys.

1912

Frank W. Pine is appointed the school's fifth headmaster. He stiffens the school regulations and scholarly expectations. He stands up to the Board of Trustees.

1914

The first issue of The Gilman *News* comes out on January 13. Articles include a column on the proposed gymnasium: "The trustees have announced that sometime in the near future they expect to erect a splendid gymnasium, which will be one of the finest in the country." To be built "near the spot upon which the tackling dummy stood last fall," it will contain a 100-foot long, heated swimming pool "with the purest of water."

A *News* sports writer gleefully records that the varsity soccer team whipped the faculty seven to one. "Mr. H. Froelicher shot the Faculty's goal while Mr. Morrow played well at center halfback." This is E. Boyd Morrow, who 12 years later will become headmaster.

The pastoral beauty, the symmetry and balance, of Gilman's new campus is manifested in this early photograph of the east side of the main building.

A long story in The Gilman *News* details the plot of the dramatic association's annual play, "The Ladies' Battle" ("Un duel en Amour") to be performed at Lehmann Hall.

1916
May Holmes begins a 60-plus year career at Gilman.

1917
The entrance of the United States into World War I creates financial havoc for the school. Loans are called due, and the school's future is in doubt until friends of the school relinquish the certificates of indebtedness that had financed construction of the main building.

1918
Headmaster Frank W. Pine dies in the Great Influenza Epidemic.

The first *Cynosure* is published. Nineteen graduate.

The Areopagus and Pnyx debating clubs are founded.

1919
Captain L. Wardlaw Miles becomes headmaster. Miles had been awarded the Distinguished Service Cross and the Congressional Medal of Honor for his heroics during World War I. The French had awarded him the Croix de Guerre and made him a member of the Legion of Honor. The Italian government had presented him with the Italian War Cross.

1920
May Holmes leaves Gilman to head McDonogh School's business office.

1920–21
A young man named Henry H. Callard teaches manual arts in the Open Air School while he attends graduate school.

1921
The first Gilman Circus is held. The tradition of Sixth Form speeches is introduced.

1922
Henry H. Callard begins teaching full-time at Gilman. He teaches 1922–24, 1925–27, and is headmaster 1943–63.

The football team is undefeated. Classes are first held in the new Lower School building. The Open Air School experiment is ended with no dissenting votes.

1923
Capt. Miles persuades May Holmes to return from McDonogh School.

1924
The varsity wrestling team, coached by Ed Russell, wins the league championship, beginning a streak that continues until 1932.

1926
E. Boyd Morrow, who has taught at Gilman since its Homewood days, becomes headmaster.

1928
The Gymnasium and Cage are constructed.

Far left, in 1910, mules still provided most of the power for plowing, heavy landscaping, and hauling materials to the building site from the railroad siding of the old Ma and Pa line that ran along the eastern edge of the campus.

Left and below, construction of the main building on the new Roland Park campus of The Country School for Boys was begun in September of 1909. Trustees sought a building that would be as fireproof as possible. Floors and walls were made of thick concrete. The frame was steel.

Mrs. Francis T. Redwood offered to give Gilman Country School the handsome set of front gates shown in this artist's rendition, but the school turned down the proposal. Gilman has never seemed to be the type of institution that needs a grandiose set of gates. For years, there was not even a sign out in front of the school. And for years, alumni and guests have simply driven up to the front of

Carey Hall and walked in, or jogged over to the track and athletic fields of the campus from the sidewalk on Roland Avenue, or hiked up to the headmaster's office from expeditions along Stony Run, or walked over from Bryn Mawr School or Roland Park Country School to classes in Carey Hall.

E. Boyd Morrow, future headmaster, at bat in 1910. Behind the catcher's mask is Douglas Ober '05.

Note the ornate "G's" on the uniforms of the 1912 track team.

Below, members of the baseball team of 1910 assemble in their Country School uniforms. The next season, the "C's" would be replaced with "G's."

Edwin B. King, was headmaster of The Country School for Boys 1909–12.

Below, Gilman Lower School students perform their calisthenics outside one of the open air classrooms of the early 1900s. At this time, open air classrooms were considered a stimulating and healthy environment, especially by the Johns Hopkins physician-trustees sitting in warm offices who mandated them.

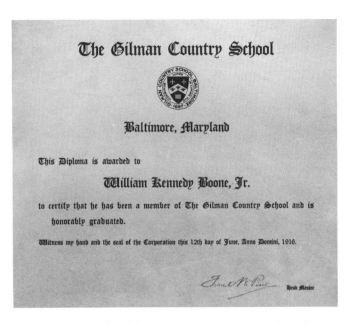

Above left, Frank W. Pine was headmaster 1912–19. The 1916 diploma—awarded to William Kennedy Boone, Jr.—displays the signature of "Head Master" Pine. Frank Pine's son, Jim Pine '21, taught history at Gilman 1929–70, and his grandson Frank Pine '59 taught at Gilman 1966–67.

Above, on May 7, 1910, the Dramatic Association performed "I've Written to Browne" for a Gilman audience. Boys played both male and female parts.

41

L. Wardlaw Miles taught at The Country School 1902–05. At the conclusion of WWI, Captain Miles returned to Gilman as headmaster. A highly decorated war hero, Captain Miles had been struck down in both legs by a volley of German fire, and had two bullets in his arm, when he had himself mounted on a stretcher and continued to lead his men. Miles had a B.A. and a doctorate in English; he was also a graduate of the medical school at the University of Maryland.

Below, the new state-of-the-art kitchen of Gilman Country School.

Upper right: the main building of Gilman in the late teens.

Lower right: Open Air School classrooms, on the southern side of the main building, with all windows open on a snowy February morning.

Gilman Lower School students studying in the open air classrooms were given heavy, hooded cloak and heated soapstones for their hands and feet. It was thought at the time that the ample supply of

esh air would prevent the spread of contagious diseases. Begun in 1911, the Open Air School oper-
ed until 1922 when the new Lower School building opened.

Football has always been a popular sport at Gilman, starting with the 1905 Championship Team and extending into the present. In the upper two photos, cleats, padded pants, and a leather helmet appear to be the only protective equipment used. For the younger boys, in the bottom photograph, helmets seem to be optional.

Above, the 1923–24 wrestling team. Seated: William Graham '25, Stuart S. Janney, Jr. '25, Redmond C. Stewart, Jr. '24, Harvey R. Clapp '24, Charles B. Alexander, Jr. '26. Standing: John Whitridge, Jr. '26, R. Arden Lowndes '27, Holmes M. Alexander '24, Colin MacRae '25.

Left, one individualist of the early teens dares to sport short pants and a sleeveless shirt while his tennis teammates are clothed in the more conventional long pants.

47

The Developing Years

ARTHUR W. MACHEN, JR. '38

On October 4, 1910, The Country School for Boys opened its doors in its brand new building on Roland Avenue exactly one year, one month, and eleven days after ground was broken for the reckless financial undertaking. Although the bedrooms, dining room, kitchen and classrooms were finished, much of the rest was still under construction. In his Founders Day address the following spring, the headmaster, Edwin B. King, described the chaos:

> *Until after Thanksgiving we had almost 200 workmen in this building every day. Some of you are householders. Did any of you ever try to keep house when 200 bricklayers, carpenters, electricians, steam fitters, plumbers and all kinds of mechanics had possession of the house, and if you did, did you have at the same time to serve dinner every day to 175 hungry boys and masters?*

Despite the inconvenience, the school persevered, and 13 boys received diplomas at the end of the first academic year in the new surroundings. Theirs were also the first diplomas to bear the name, The Gilman Country School for Boys. Daniel Coit Gilman, after whom the school was named, had been neither a founder nor a trustee, but, as president of Johns Hopkins University, had lent valuable support to Anne Carey and Louise Bruce in their efforts to get the school started on the Homewood campus. With the consent of Dr. Gilman's two daughters, the new name was adopted by the trustees on December 20, 1910.

A turning point in the life of the new school with the new name occurred on January 18, 1912, in the middle of the ensuing academic year when the trustees—with the appointment of a particular new headmaster firmly in mind—abruptly dismissed the current headmaster, Edwin B. King. King had been reelected to the office the previous June 11, and the minutes of the board provide no clue as to the reasons for his sudden termination. The trustees turned aside without comment petitions and letters in his support as well as his own plaintive request for a statement of cause. Instead, at the same meeting at which the dismissal was approved, a nominating committee was appointed to explore the matter of offering the headmastership to Frank W. Pine of The Hill School in Pottstown, Pennsylvania. The committee was given power to act, from which one may infer that discussions with Pine must have previously taken place.

At the next meeting of the trustees the committee exercised its authority by announcing the appointment of Frank Woodworth Pine as headmaster. Edwin King left during the spring vacation, and Pine assumed his new duties the following fall, snapping the Gilman administration into line. Hired at $2,500, Frank Pine was a genuine professional.

Three months after he took over, the new headmaster asked the trustees if he could hire a baseball coach for two months at $35 a month. He was told that would require formal board action. Pine was not pleased.

Four months later, who resigns? Not Headmaster Pine. It's Dr. Joseph Ames, president of the Board of Trustees, who steps back. In a formal note of apology, he compliments Pine and says he himself, as president, has been accused of "interfering." He will not do so again.

The principle was established. Gilman's soft old Southern way was put aside, whereupon Pine installed a first-class education machine, with a crisp northern smack. He was the first headmaster to assert himself as the chief executive officer of the corporation, and with his arrival the Board of Trustees withdrew from its meddlesome interference in day-to-day administration and retreated to its proper role as a policy-making and fund-raising body. By now the Gilman model was being followed in new country day schools in New York, Philadelphia, Boston, Richmond, Buffalo, and Kansas City.

Fund-raising proved to be a major preoccupation over the next five years. The school was debt-ridden, and the trustees refused to raise tuition to a level that would cover operating costs. Instead, tentative arrangements were made with the Roland Park Company to sell school land for development. "For Sale" signs lined the Roland Avenue border for months; land was priced at $40 a front foot. That uneasiness soon faded, but the school was still running at a loss. Debts mounted. War with Germany was declared in 1917, and in the subsequent war hysteria, the credit of the school vanished, and the banks pressed for payment.

Unless something could be done to restore its credit and increase income to prevent deficits, the doom of the school was sealed. Crisis hung in the air until the day before one bank loan had to be paid. One trustee, Jere H. Wheelwright, rose to the occasion with a personal gift of $27,000 on the spot. It was enough to keep the bank at bay, then to send the other trustees out to gather up the $248,000 in certificates (representing nearly $2,000,000 in 1992 dollars when adjusted for inflation) still outstanding.

Every certificate was rounded up. Once investments, they were made outright gifts to the school. A bronze tablet on the north wall of the Common Room commemorates the lifting, at last, of a huge debt which had hung over the school since the move to Roland Park.

Among other events of significance during the early days of the Pine administration was the experiment in open air education for boys in the lowest grades. A cadre of physician-trustees from the Johns Hopkins medical institutions, convinced that open air in all weather conditions was therapeutic for consumptives, concluded that the regimen might also be salutary for normal people. This notion spawned the Gilman Open Air School. Pavilions, open to the elements in all weather conditions, were erected to the south of the main building where the youngsters huddled under hoods to learn their lessons. Heated soapstones that sometimes burned their way into the desktops provided the only warmth. The school's catalogue (the *Register*, as it was then called) extolled the success of the Open Air School in these words:

> *The experiment has proved a complete success, the results having exceeded the expectations of the promoters of the School. The first Winter of the existence of the School (1911–1912) provided as severe a test in weather conditions as it will in all probability ever meet. No boy experienced discomfort on any day during the extreme cold of December, January and February.*

One wonders whether the students would have echoed this warm tribute to the Open Air School. Nine students were enrolled in its first year, followed by 28 the next. By 1919–20 the total had swelled to 102. It is unlikely that the names of the members of the faculty of the Open Air School would strike a responsive chord with most of the readers of this book—except one. That was the instructor in manual training in 1920–21, a young man named Henry Hadden Callard.

When the new Lower School was opened in 1922 on land to the north of the main building, the Open Air School was folded into it, but to a limited extent the concept lingered on as the corridors in the new building were left open to outside air and only the classrooms were provided with windows. Eventually, the corridors were also closed in, and thereafter the Lower School was disparagingly referred to by the older boys as the "Hot Air."

The entry of the United States into war with Germany in 1917 had a significant impact on the life of the school for the next two years. In addition to the financial crisis already mentioned, the school faced the prospect of dwindling enrollment as a result of the draft. By 1918, when the draft age was lowered to 18, Gilman had 10 boys who were exposed to the call and 21 who would shortly reach the age of 17. There was also mounting pressure from parents and others to show the flag with some form of military training. After some delay and vacillation on the question, Pine announced to the board on September 11, 1918, that drilling would be instituted immediately under proper supervision and that parents would be notified accordingly.

The Armistice on November 11, 1918, brought an end to Gilman's venture into the military world. On December 2, 1918, the trustees voted unanimously to disband the Students Army Corps and to absorb a bill of $435 from a New York clothing store for undelivered uniforms.

More permanent innovations during the Pine years included the introduction of a school newspaper, the Gilman *News*, in 1914; the first senior yearbook, the *Cynosure*, in 1918; and in the same year the formation of two debating clubs, the Areopagus and the Pnyx. It was, however, Frank Pine's strong executive leadership and his insistence on the highest standards of scholarship and personal honor that left the most lasting marks on the institution. His untimely death from a streptococcus infection on February 3, 1919, left the school in a state of shock.

Waiting in the wings to succeed him was E. Boyd Morrow, who had joined the faculty as a teacher of mathematics in the Homewood days and since 1916 had been listed in the catalogue as assistant headmaster. Before that he had been designated on the faculty roster as senior master, the second in rank below the head, and must have had aspirations to succeed Edwin King in 1912. Even now, however, seven years later, his ascendancy to the top spot was not assured as the trustees named him Acting Headmaster and appointed a search committee to look for Pine's permanent replacement.

The minutes of the Board of Trustees of April 15, May 1, June 3, and July 2 all report progress in the search process, but no names are mentioned on the record. Finally, at a special meeting on July 19, 1919, attended by only four trustees and with both the president and vice-president being absent, Captain L. Wardlaw Miles was named Gilman's sixth headmaster.

Miles was no stranger to the faculty, having taught German at Homewood 1903–05. He was a war hero, having been awarded the Congressional Medal of Honor for outstanding bravery in hand-to-hand combat on the Western Front resulting in the amputation of one of his legs. He had an impressive academic record with an A.B. and Ph.D. from Johns Hopkins and an M.D. from the University of Maryland. Before the war, he had taught English literature at Princeton. He delivered the commencement address at Gilman's Founders Day exercises in 1919 and so impressed the trustees that they offered him the headmastership.

Once more passed over for promotion, E. Boyd Morrow stayed on as assistant headmaster and for the next seven years discharged many of the business functions of a chief executive, Captain Miles having made no secret of his distaste for business details. The trustees approved a resolution of thanks and a $1,000 bonus to Morrow in recognition of his dedicated service as head of the school since the death of Pine. (In 1912 he had been similarly awarded a $200 bonus for his extra work in the spring of that year following the departure of Edwin B. King).

In addition to the new Lower School, opened in 1922 as previously noted, the '20s witnessed the construction of two brick double houses for faculty use, a home for the headmaster, and a frame building known as "the cottage" for administrative offices. There would have been no room for these and many other improvements to the physical plant over the years, had it not been for the abandonment of plans for developing a major portion of the 68 acres of land acquired in 1909. The date when this decision was made is not recorded in minutes of the trustees, their last mention of the subject being on March 22, 1910. Yet, it is certain that the school could not have grown and prospered as it has if its substantial acreage had been sold for short term profit instead of being preserved for future expansion.

Over the years the only significant conveyance of land by the trustees to a third party was one to the Baltimore City School Board in 1922 as a site for the Roland Park Public School. At first, the trustees refused the advances made by the school board, but, when faced with a condemnation threat, the trustees relented and put a price of $37,500 on the tract. The bad news was that this acreage, although relatively small, could have been put to good use in later expansion; the good news was that the acceptance of Gilman's price by the city provided the lion's share of the $56,477 cost of the new Lower School.

The school's athletic program made remarkable strides during the Miles years, particularly in the sports of wrestling and football.

Wrestling was first recognized as an organized sport in the academic year 1919–20 under the aegis of Edward T. Russell. The next year he formed the Interscholastic Wrestling Association of Maryland with four participating schools, Gilman, Friends, Severn, and City College, and in that first year of competition Gilman produced four champions: Stuart S. Janney, Jr., Redmond Stewart, Arthur Foster, and Charles Williams. By 1929, Gilman had achieved complete domination of the sport on the local scene, winning all seven dual meets while giving up only eleven and a half points in the season. All members of the Gilman team made it to the finals of the Interscholastics, four of them walking off with gold medals: G. Douglas Wise, William A. Fisher, Jr., R. Houghton Hooker, and Stockton Lowndes, the latter having been captain of the team and a champion four years in a row. The next year, 1930, the team again made a clean sweep of the dual meets and produced five champions in the Interscholastics: G. Douglas Wise, William A. Fisher, Jr., C. R. Houghton Hooker, Captain John C. Legg III, and Charles H. Classen.

Coached by the legendary Ed Russell, Gilman teams continued to enjoy their unquestioned supremacy over the sport in Maryland until 1933 when McDonogh won the tournament with 28 points to Gilman's 27.* A dynasty was broken, but a tradition had been established that continues to this day as Gilman challenges the current dynasty of Mount St. Joseph.

Yet, it must be mentioned that it was not only for his skill as a wrestling coach that Ed Russell is so well remembered, but even more for his care and devotion to Gilman students. Ludlow Baldwin '22, the future headmaster, vividly recalls his early days as a Gilman student:

> *I was only 115 pounds when I came to Gilman as a senior. I had just graduated from*
> *City College at 15 and had been accepted to Hopkins but my parents—under the advice*

---

*For more on this tournament, see Cooper Walker's "Of Ed Russell and Wrestling Reminiscences," page 81.

of Fred Gibbs, a Gilman graduate—thought I was too young to go to college, and I ought to take a year at Gilman. I was far more immature than 15. I had never had a date. I'd never been away from home. When I got to Gilman I was a shrimp. I arrived there, from the public schools, into this higher atmosphere of the Blue Book and Social Register, and I felt very much out of it. Ed Russell came up to me, as almost a total stranger, and said, 'Ludlow, I've got a place for you. We need somebody in the 115-pound class on the wrestling team.' So he made me feel quite at home. He was a very kindly soul. A lot of people wonder about his teaching ability, but he was a very kindly soul. He was my savior. He gave me status, so to speak. I had never wrestled before and he made me the 115-pounder on the wrestling team. And I was a reasonable success. I lost the inter-scholastics, but I was runner-up. I owe a great deal to Ed Russell. He did it out of the kindness of his heart—taking me on as a protégé—and if you ask me who I remember above all others at Gilman or on the Gilman faculty, it would be Ed Russell.

As for football, the team of teams, coached by Bernard A. ("Bud") Hoban, was produced in 1921, one that recorded the following victories: Mount St. Joseph (40–0); McDonogh (45–0); Army-Navy Prep (55–0); City College (62–7); Peddie (31–7); Friends (49–14); Episcopal High School (14–6); and Tome (66–0). The star performer was the incomparable Jacob W. ("Jake") Slagle who graduated in 1923 with 14 varsity letters and went on to Princeton, where he was a candidate for All-American recognition on the football team.

The Pine-Miles years also brought together a cadre of gifted teachers who were dedicated to the highest standards of academic excellence. Among those on the roster were the following:

ARTHUR L. LAMB, the eldest master, who had graduated from Johns Hopkins in 1888 and taught geography and chemistry. Short in stature and soft in speech, he was much revered, but his gifts did not include prophecy. He is said to have told a class, "Boys, you can forget about aviation. Man was never intended to fly."

JOSIAH "JOSH" BARTLETT, a graduate of Brown in 1888, who taught mathematics. A stern disciplinarian and not as popular as some of the masters, he was respected as a teacher who knew his subject as well as anyone.

HERBERT E. PICKETT, who had graduated from Yale in 1913 and taught history. He also coached dramatics and ran the Hyde Bay Camp in Cooperstown, New York, attended by many Gilman students. He was a tall, imposing figure with a gift for articulating the spoken word.

THOMAS LEE LIPSCOMB, who had graduated from Randolph-Macon in 1914 and taught English. A Virginia gentleman, he would often dismiss his class with the quip, "Young men, you have now added one cubit to yo' stature o' knowledge."

MEREDITH MINOR JANVIER, who had received his B. S. degree from the University of Virginia and taught science. A shy, diminutive man, he was well liked by all who knew him.

EDWARD T. RUSSELL, a graduate of Princeton in 1915, who taught Latin and coached varsity wrestling as well as the J.V. football team. No one on the faculty was more beloved than Ed Russell.

GEORGE CLARK BELDEN, a graduate of Harvard in 1921 and known to the boys as "Juicy." He was an excellent teacher of French, but students sitting in the front row were advised to wear raincoats.

D. MILES MARRIAN, Johns Hopkins '25, one of the best teachers of mathematics on the faculty. A Minor League baseball player, he was also a gifted chalk-thrower who could curve a piece of chalk around one boy's head in order to strike another on the noggin.

RICHARD O'BRIEN, a 1920 graduate of Teachers' College of New York State, who would become one of Gilman's most distinguished French teachers in decades to come.

In short, Gilman School was riding the crest of a wave in the early to mid-1920s. It had a charismatic headmaster, a visibly successful academic and athletic program, and a physical plant that sparkled as a gem in the northern suburbs of Baltimore City. In 1920, the trustees had finally increased tuitions to levels that would match operating expenses. The once struggling, debt-ridden institution was now virtually debt-free and poised to make the most of the second half of the roaring '20s.

In the middle of this decade at a meeting of the board of trustees on April 5, 1925, Captain Miles dropped a bombshell. E. Boyd Morrow had been offered the headmastership of another school and was at the very moment looking over the opportunity. As if in a state of panic, the trustees directed Miles to reach Morrow by long distance telephone—no easy task in 1925—and urge him to take no action without consultation with the Gilman trustees. Dr. John M. T. Finney, the president of the Board, was authorized to make with Morrow whatever arrangements he deemed necessary. The trustees wanted no stone unturned to assure Morrow's continued availability for the top job.

At the next meeting of the board on May 8, 1925, Captain Miles announced his intention to resign as headmaster at the end of the academic year 1925–26. At the same meeting Dr. Finney reported with pleasure that Morrow would remain at Gilman. His salary was increased by $1,500. The crisis had passed, and the Crown Prince (or the "Clown Quince" as the boys called him) was in line to be installed as "The King." There was no search committee, no attempt to find other candidates. As if confirming a *fait accompli*, the trustees on February 1, 1926, unanimously approved Finney's motion that E. Boyd Morrow be appointed the school's seventh headmaster to take office at the end of the current school year. It had been a recognition long awaited, twice denied, and much deserved.

Morrow lacked the personality, the warmth and ease of communication of some of his predecessors and successors.* Nevertheless, Morrow had the ability, the

---

*Ludlow Baldwin '22, 73 years after the occurrence, recalls the following wrangle in 1921 with E. Boyd Morrow, then assistant headmaster, which exemplifies Morrow's style of relating to the students:

In the Sixth Form I was a boarder at Gilman and very small. So was Hubert Royster, the year behind me. He was so small they called him 'Peanuts,' 'Peanuts' Royster. And so Hubert and I were wrestling

temperament, the experience, the sound business judgment and, most of all, the resolve to lead the school through the difficult times of the Great Depression and the pre-war years of the 1930s.

The only major changes in the physical plant during his administration were the new gymnasium and cage, both opened in 1928 at a total cost of $315,523, the bulk of which was covered by pledges already paid into the gymnasium fund. These improvements, world-class at the time, were sufficient for the school's needs until the post-war boom in enrollment required new construction for faculty housing, the auditorium, the Middle School, the science building and other structures.

The Developing Years 1910–1929 were filled with crisis, challenge and achievement. They were critical and exciting ones in the life of Gilman School.

Entering Gilman in 1929, Arthur Machen had a reputation as a public speaker by the time of his 1938 graduation. ". . . here it is (public speaking) that his ability shines forth in its greatest brilliance," notes the *Cynosure*, and, "A good conversationalist, he is at his best in an argument, invariably slaughtering his opponents through his eloquence and adeptness of speech." It seems that even at a young age, Arthur Machen was headed for law school.

At graduation, Machen was co-winner of the John M. T. Finney Debating Medal, awarded to the two boys judged to have delivered the best speeches in the Final Debate. He also won The Vocational Prize, awarded to the senior who submits the best written report upon a profession he is investigating as a career. Topic: the legal profession.

In his last year at Gilman, Machen managed the football and wrestling teams, was vice-president of the Glee Club, vice-president of the Pnyx Debating Club, president of the Literary Club, associate editor of the *Cynosure*, alumni editor of the *News*, and secretary of *The Blue and Gray*. His favorite teacher was Tom Lipscomb (English and Latin).

Machen concentrated on the study of classics at Princeton, graduating Magna Cum Laude and Phi Beta Kappa. He served in the South Pacific during World War II as a reserve Naval officer on the battleship USS *Massachusetts*.

After graduating from Harvard Law School, he joined Venable, Baetjer and Howard in 1951 as an associate and worked there as a partner 1957–93. From 1959 to 1960, Machen served as president of the Gilman Alumni Association, and 1958–61 as an Alumni Trustee. He served with Cooper Walker '33 and Edmund N. Gorman '32 as Special Committee of the Alumni Association which started the Gilman Fund, predecessor of the Annual Fund, in 1956. Two sons, John P. '69 and Henry L. '77, attended Gilman.

---

in his room on the lower south corridor where Sixth Formers were berthed, and one of us threw the other one down with a BANG *and we kept wrestling hard. Five minutes later we looked up from the floor to see the assistant headmaster in the doorway—*E. BOYD MORROW. *He was rough. A cold fish. And he just stood there. So we got up. I was a Sixth Former, a senior. He took me by my ear, and Royster also, led us to the stairway, down the stairway, and took us into "A" study hall—me a senior—by the ear. He sat me down, said I'd stay there a week or two. I'll tell you, Morrow was rough.*

Half a century after he won The Vocational Prize on Founders Day for his authorship of a paper on the legal profession, Machen again picked up the pen on behalf of his chosen vocation, producing the book, *A Venerable Assembly, The History of Venable, Baetjer & Howard, 1900–1991*, published in 1991. Machen continues to work as a Senior of Counsel at Venable; yet, a major ambition is "to learn how to retire gracefully and productively."

1930s

1930

Tuitions are raised from $25 to $200, and a large new running track is built between the gymnasium and the football field.

1930

After an unprecedented three overtimes, Gilman's Jack Legg beats Severn's Chung Hoon in the 155-pound semifinals of the Maryland Interscholastic Wrestling Tournament.

1932

Varsity lacrosse is started by coach and faculty member Edward W. Brown.

As the repercussions of the Depression hit Gilman, Headmaster E. Boyd Morrow makes an across-the-board 10 percent cut in all faculty and staff salaries, followed soon thereafter by another 10 percent cut.

1933

Sixty-three student tuitions are either unpaid or only partially paid, making a total of $25,601 owed the school.

Football teammates Clark Barrett, Dickie Janney, Chris Lowndes, and Ham Welbourn whip Gilman's arch-rival and heavily-favored-to-win Tome School with the risky, notorious, and surreptitious "Conversation Play."

1934

Faculty member Edward W. Brown starts the ice hockey team.

1935

The 118-pound football team, coached by Miles Marrian, and known as "Marrian's Mighty Mites," scores 301 points to its opponents' zero. Howard Baetjer scores over 100 points.

Effects from the Depression continue. Enrollment drops. The Upper School student body falls from 238 in 1930 to 178 in 1935, meaning a $39,600 drop in tuition income. The boarding department falls from 85 in 1930 to 22 in 1935.

Walter Lord delivers his senior speech on the sinking of *The Titanic*. The preparation and research for the speech served Lord well. Twenty years later, the publication of *A Night to Remember*

To the left, Herbert Pickett draws a map on the blackboard as students seated at study tables listen attentively. Pickett was a history teacher at Gilman for 25 years: 1913–17; 1919–40. Director of the annual school play, adviser to the Gilman *News*, director of Areopagus and Pnyx debating clubs, Pickett also served as dean under Headmaster E. Boyd Morrow. Note how the walls of the high-ceilinged classrooms were designed so that prints could be hung.

launched Lord's career as a historian, making his earlier senior speech one of Gilman's most renowned.

The "Cod Liver Oil Committee," headed by Doctors J. M. T. Finney, George Finney, and J. Hall Pleasants, concludes that the administration of cod liver oil is the responsibility of the parents, not the school.

1936

Enrollment is up to 293 and Headmaster Morrow reports to the Board that he is able to restore part of the reduction in masters' salaries.

1937

Gilman celebrates its 40th anniversary and its successful emergence from the Depression.

1938

Students begin to wear well-tailored blazers, similar to those worn in New England boarding schools, with one pocket covered in gold-and-silver bullion fashioned into the Gilman seal.

Editors of *The News* send reporters off campus "to bring back a story." Robert M. Thomas pursues actresses to Pennsylvania Station. Thomas G. Hardie II interviews a German boy on beer, co-eds, and swing music. Soon, T. Courtenay Jenkins starts a sports' column, "Batter Up." *The News* becomes less a semi-official mouthpiece of the school and more a voice of the boys themselves.

1939

Charles D. Plitt, George C. Westerlind, and M. Tyler Campbell lead Gilman into its third ice hockey championship, and retire the Harvard Cup, offered to stimulate school-boy interest in ice hockey.

60

Opposite at top, The Songbirds show off their musical talent. That's William C. Whitridge, Upshur Lowndes, E. Rowe Zimmerman, Jr., and Wilmon W. Hartman, all Class of 1932.

Opposite below, Samuel B. Symington '32 and friends joke around in an old jalopy juxtaposed with a big modern sedan of the 1930s.

Opposite bottom, Sixth Formers relax at the Lowndes' house, directly across Roland Avenue from Gilman. Left to right, Robert R. Peard, Zenas Sears, Barton Harrison, E. Rowe Zimmerman, Jr., Wilmon W. Hartman, and William C. Whitridge.

At left, Pepper Constable '32, with ball, was captain of the 1931 team, played quarterback, and was named All-State in 1930 and 1931.

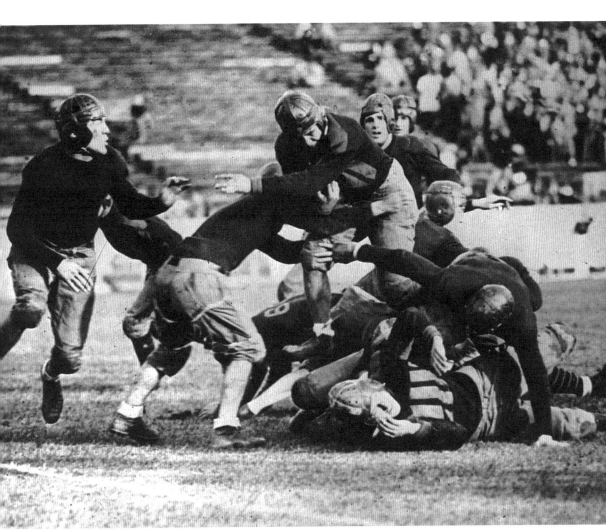

Running back Edward Simmons '32 busts through a line of defenders as Pepper Constable, one of Gilman's all-time great backs, watches.

E. Boyd Morrow, known by students and alumni as "The King," provided stern and disciplined leadership as headmaster through the trying times of the Depression and the early WWII years. Morrow was headmaster 1926–43.

Right, "A" Study Hall in the 1930s, with Mr. Thomas L. Lipscomb presiding. In the 1980s, "A" Study Hall became the Art Center. With its high ceilings and the flooding of natural light, it was a favorite for artists. Yet, the room took a beating. In 1996, the Art Center was moved to the third floor of Carey Hall, and "A" Study Hall was restored to its former grandeur and renamed Centennial Hall.

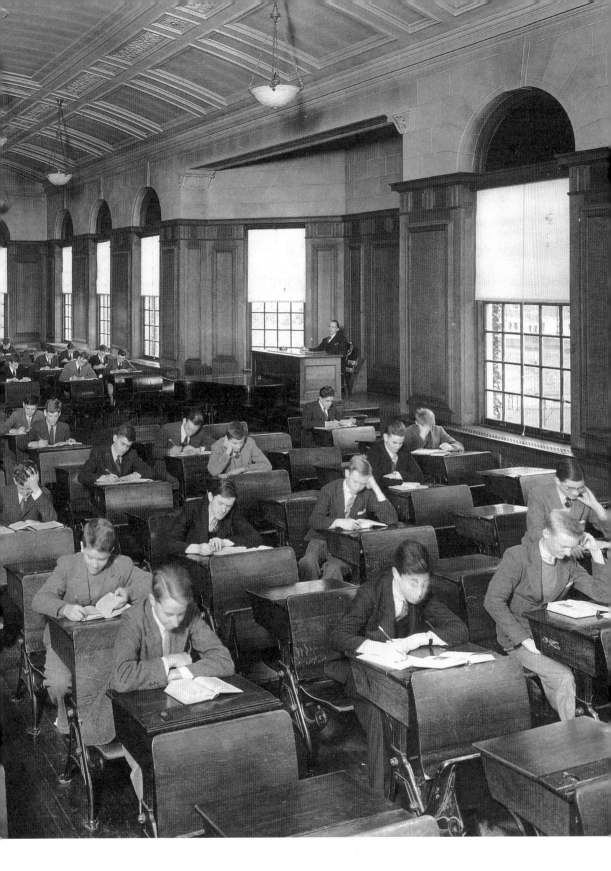

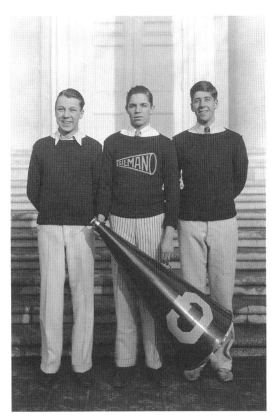

Cheerleaders of 1933 are ready for the game.

Alex Armstrong '33, gesticulating, stars as Cyrus Martin in the comedy "It Pays to Advertise," produced in 1933 and performed at the Maryland Casualty Auditorium. That's Edgar Smith '33 on the right with the girl, playing the part of Armstrong's son. The two continued to pursue their Thespian interests in college, both belonging to the Triangle Club at Princeton, and acting in many plays together, including one where Smith played Armstrong's mother. Left to right, the cast is Bill Schmeisser '34, Bob Linthicum '33, Armstrong, Richmond Holden '36, Bob Janney '33, Smith, and Jim Finney '33.

It is early spring 1937 and May Holmes, on the far right, prepares to head off the campus with three Lower School teachers: Lillian M. Elliott, Helen Stevens, and Bernie Cronquist.

Founders' Day, 1933, was held in the gymnasium.

Edward W. Brown, above, was a beloved Gilman faculty member from 1923 to 1940, when he left to become the headmaster of Calvert School. Brown coached the Gilman varsity football team 1929–39, and was the founder of the ice hockey and lacrosse teams.

Right, Coach Charles Mitchell, Jr. '16 gives his varsity ice hockey team of 1936–37 a talk as players eagerly await practice.

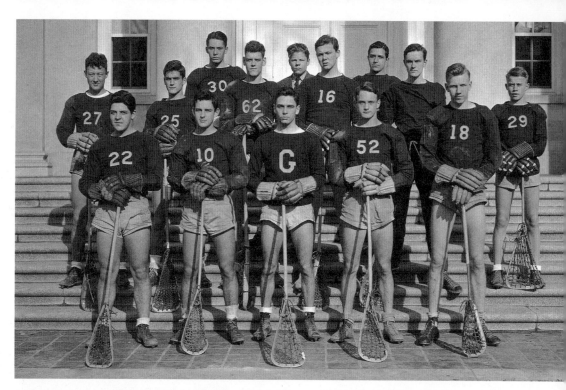

Upper left, the 1938 varsity lacrosse team.

Lower left, Varsity Wrestling Coach Ed Russell directs his wrestling disciples in the art of the take-down. To be on Mr. Russell's wrestling team was synonymous with being one of the most carefully scrutinized and well-cared-for athletes in Gilman's history, as Cooper Walker '33 highlights in his essay "Of Ed Russell and Wrestling Reminiscenses."

Top, the varsity football team of 1938 lines up for a group shot in front of the gymnasium, now called "The Old Gym."

Left, though overshadowed by wrestling, basketball in the 1930s was growing in popularity. Seated varsity players of the 1937–38 team are Harry Nance, Raymond Brown, and Gordon Allen. Standing are Charles Brooks, Samuel Cook, and George Stewart.

71

Gilman in the 30s:
A No-nonsense,
No-frills Education

WALTER LORD '35

For one Gilman boy, the Great Depression spelled modest prosperity. As prices crashed, my allowance—two dollars a week—stayed the same, and its purchasing power soared. Movie tickets—normally 75 cents for a loge at Loew's Century—fell to 35 cents. Hershey bars formerly cost a nickel; suddenly they were three for a dime. Phonograph records—always 75 cents at Kranz or Hammonds Music Shops—were now only 35 cents. Taxicabs—a form of transportation previously beyond the wildest dreams of a Second Former—soon could be had for 25 cents for the first three and a half miles, five cents for each additional half-mile. Even Mr. Marrian's slowest math students knew that this was a better bargain than the trolley at a dime a head.

There were other benefits too. Seats at the movies were easier to find. Parking downtown was a cinch. An excellent faculty at Gilman was more or less frozen in place. Few teachers wanted to take the chance of looking around in times like these.

For Gilman itself the situation was very different. With virtually no endowment, the school depended almost entirely on tuitions to find the cash to keep going. This practice worked as long as there was a steady supply of full-tuition boys, but that was no longer the case. As the Depression deepened, families spent their savings, used up their credit, cashed in their stocks, hocked the car, and there still wasn't enough to keep going. Some took their sons out of Gilman and shifted them to less expensive private schools or to the public high schools, City and Poly.

Enrollment in the Upper School fell from 238 in 1930 to 178 in 1935, meaning a drop in tuition income of $39,600. Even more alarming, perhaps, was the case of boys who remained enrolled but whose parents were trying to cut a deal with the school delaying payments. In 1932, some 46 accounts were delinquent, totalling $15,741. In 1933, the figure rose to 63 accounts in arrears totalling $25,601. Where to find the money needed to run the school?

The problem fell squarely into the lap of E. Boyd Morrow, the headmaster who had replaced the charismatic Captain Miles in 1925. Morrow was a cool, austere realist. His relations with the student body were remote—the boys hardly knew him—and because of his aloofness he was invariably referred to as The King.* Yet he was probably the right man for the job at this particular time. The school's plight called for hard decisions, and Boyd Morrow could make them without flinching.

A good place to start was the mid-day meal. The school's philosophy had always been that a Gilman education not only prepared boys for academic and athletic excellence, but also for the life of a gentleman. With this end in mind, students assembled every day in the paneled elegance of the Fisher Memorial Dining Hall for a formal hot luncheon, served on real linen tablecloths, with real linen napkins, and by real waiters in starched white jackets. The result was reasonably successful, except for the occasional gifted lad who knew how to use his knife to flip a pat of butter up to the ceiling and make it stick.

Now the era of civilized dining was coming to an end. It didn't all happen at once, but gradually the napkins, the tablecloths, and the obliging waiters all vanished from the scene.

Other economies brought a distinct touch of second-hand goods to the world of textbooks. For years the custom had been for every boy to buy a completely new set of books at the start of every term. Suddenly someone discovered that the books rarely changed; so why shouldn't an incoming Second Former take over the books used by his predecessor, who had now moved on to the Third Form?

Second-hand became the byword in athletics too. In the fall, nearly everybody took football, and each year brought brand new uniforms, complete with helmet and shoulder pads, for a period that amounted to a couple of months. The irony was that the boys who liked football the least bought the most. They invariably abandoned new equipment at the end of the season, while the boys who truly enjoyed the game tended to hang on to lucky helmets, socks, sweatshirts, and the like. Now, the drift to the second-hand meant that everybody looked like a seasoned player, even if he never did more than warm the bench.

Parents chipped in with their own economies. The custom-tailored suit from DePinna gave way to ready-made slacks and a jacket from Hutzler's. Vests disappeared completely. So did knickers; boys now went straight from short pants to long trousers, no stop in between.

None of these measures were enough. Enrollment continued to slide, and the school's countermeasures continued to fall short: Fees were eliminated for commencement speakers . . . Fire insurance was reduced on the main building from $200,000 to $175,000 . . . Receipts from the circus, traditionally earmarked for a

---

*Not many knew that this austere headmaster was an accomplished violinist.

swimming pool fund, were diverted to general maintenance. Funds designated for two major scholarships were (with the approval of donors) spread out so as to cover additional needy students. On one occasion, trustees, arriving for a meeting, were each dunned $50 on the spot.

In the fall of 1932, Morrow took an especially drastic step. With the approval of the Board of Trustees he made an across-the-board 10 percent cut in all faculty and staff salaries, followed by a second 10 percent cut a little later. Prep school masters didn't get much to begin with—the rationale was that the tweedy atmosphere and long vacations made up for lack of money. Now a master making $2,000 was expected to live up to the same standards on $1,620.

Gilman's ordeal continued. On April 18, 1933, the school's treasurer, W. Bladen Lowndes, confronted the board with the dismal news that a special drive to clean up back bills had netted only $3,000 of the $23,000 owed. He recommended still more cost-cutting measures: eliminate sandwiches at morning recess . . . cut out away-games with distant rivals . . . close down the school magazine, *The Blue and The Gray* . . . do away with the *Cynosure*, the seniors' yearbook.

Mr. Morrow was more inclined to go to the heart of the matter: find more boys. He argued for (and finally got) an expanded Lower School, which enabled the school to carry students all the way from kindergarten to the gates of college. (There's no record of what Calvert, Gilman's principal feeder, thought of this.)

The headmaster also worked hard to build up the boarding department. After all, a boarder paid roughly twice as much tuition as a day boy. He urged the trustees to go out and find likely prospects. He issued a new catalogue designed to appeal especially to prospective boarders. He sent three of his faculty stars—Herbert Pickett, Ed Russell, and Eddie Brown—on headhunting trips to the provinces.

Unfortunately, they were up against the city's demographics. Baltimore was rapidly expanding to the north. This trend found Gilman becoming less a country school and more a school of the suburbs. The parents of potential boarders were usually looking for a Currier & Ives setting in New England, or the Old Plantation South for atmosphere. Gilman's location offered a rather bland alternative. The school's boarding department gradually slid from 85 boys in 1930 to 22 in 1935.

Curiously, the boys seemed almost oblivious to the situation. Generally speaking, they were aware of the Depression, but saw little connection between it and the school. To them the empty freight yards, smokeless factory chimneys, and the neatly dressed men selling apples on the sidewalk, had little to do with their own lives. It was almost as though the school and the parents had conspired to shield them from an unattractive mess.

Not that the boys needed any shielding. They had all the right instincts, and would have been happy to help those less fortunate. But it was hard to find them. In the confined world of upper-class Baltimore at this time, the average Gilman boy had little contact with the rest of the city. The nearest poor people seemed to be in a mountain school in Hindman, Kentucky. Every year bundles of frayed shirts and unraveling sweaters were dumped into bins in the common room and packed off to

Kentucky. During the winter a special "Hindman School Dance" was held, with the proceeds also going to Kentucky. Nothing went to any worthy cause in Baltimore. The concept of Gilman and community service still waited to be born.

It must be remembered that there were no visible ethnic problems at Gilman during the 1930s. Most of the boys were Protestants (today they would be called WASPs) plus a sprinkling of Catholics. Park Heights Avenue was a distant, unexplored land somewhere west of Carlin's Amusement Park.

The closest thing to an ethnic problem was posed by the boys who lived in the Green Spring and Worthington Valleys. It was said that you could always tell a Valley boy by his tweeds and the leather patches on his sleeves. Valley kids also seemed to know a lot about horses. The suburban boys looked upon them with a faint mixture of envy and suspicion. This was a factor that never entered the world of sports and athletics, but vaguely emerged in social life and conversation. The school did its best to homogenize the student body by dividing it into two groups called "Blues" and "Grays." The boys were smart enough to regard this as an artificial division and never paid much attention to it.

Regardless of cliques, daily life followed the same routine for everybody—a standard mixture of classes and study hall, punctuated by lunch. At 3:15 the whole school trouped over to the gym to dress for athletics. By 5:30 they were finished and heading home, which really meant an evening of homework. Every day was the same.

Except Wednesdays. This was the day designated for haircuts and doctors' appointments. At 3:15 nearly half the boys raced for the orthodontist's office. These worthies operated on a first-come first-served basis, and laggards were doomed to spend most of the afternoon in the waiting room reading and rereading old copies of NATIONAL GEOGRAPHIC.

The only other way to a free Wednesday afternoon lay in making the "Over 70 List." This was the reward given to every boy who had averaged over 70 in his academic work during the previous two-week period. It proved a worthy goal. Freed immediately after lunch, these chosen few were on the trolley by 2:15, rocketing down Roland Avenue toward the intoxicating world of the big movie theaters on Lexington Street. Sitting in the dark luxury of Loew's Century, listening to the giant Woerlitzer organ, it was hard to believe that in just a few hours the same old grind would begin.

Every year was the same, yet every year was different too. Each was studded with events and incidents that somehow gave it an individuality all its own . . . moments that would strike special chords of memory in the years to come.

In 1930, such an event occurred in the Maryland Interscholastics Wrestling Tournament when Gilman's Jack Legg took on Severn's Chung Hoon in the 155-lb. semifinals. No one who saw it would ever forget. "It was an epic," Cooper Walker later wrote in the 1955 Alumni Bulletin. "Chung Hoon was a cat, lithe and quick; Jack Legg a bear, strong and cunning." After an unprecedented and unbelievable three overtimes, the "bear" finally won.

Only once a decade does a truly great football player emerge at Gilman, and in the '30s it was Pepper Constable, playing at the peak of his game in 1931. Big, fast, and immensely powerful, he completely dominated both sides in the City game, played in the old Municipal Stadium. One scene lingers: it was late in the fourth quarter, and the players were barely visible in the gathering dusk. But there was Pepper, with half the City team clinging to him, barreling 40 yards through the line for one more score in the fading twilight.

The decade's greatest performance, however, did not involve the heroics of Pepper Constable, but the guile of the whole varsity football team two years later in 1933. Gilman's arch-rival Tome had earned a 0-to-0 tie with mighty McDonogh, which then trounced Gilman 33 to 0. Sensing an easy victory, Tome arranged for several top New York sportswriters to cover the game. All began as predicted, with Tome pushing Gilman around easily. But they never quite scored, and midway in the second quarter Gilman through some fluke found itself on Tome's three-yard line. Two plays got nowhere. Now it was third down, and Gilman lined up again. Suddenly halfback Clark Barrett asked for the signal to be repeated. Quarterback Dickie Janney barked, "Barrett, can't you get anything right?" The Tome linemen stood up to watch this interesting exchange and Gilman's center Chris Lowndes snapped the ball to halfback Ham Welbourn, who strolled through the Tome line into the end zone for a touchdown.

The conversation play, as it was called ever after, not only won the game, 6–0, but possibly put the whole Tome School out of business. Tome was already in dire shape due to the Depression, and it was hoped that the stories to be carried in the New York papers would give it a much-needed shot in the arm. Now there was no story, except for the epic of Gilman's triumph over a befuddled rival. Several years later Tome closed its doors.

But the most impressive football performance of the decade came not at the varsity level, but in the season enjoyed by Miles Marrian's 118-lb. team in 1935. This remarkable "band of brothers" ran up a total of 301 points while holding their opponents scoreless. In fact, only once did any opposing back penetrate as deep as Gilman's 20-yard line, and this rash fellow broke his leg on the play. There has never been another team like it, either before or after, and its success has never been satisfactorily explained, except by a story that Coach Marrian had a mysterious access to the playbook of Colgate University, also undefeated in that unique season.

Two new sports kindled their own special memories. Lacrosse, long a favorite Maryland pastime, was introduced in 1932 through the efforts of coach and faculty member Edward W. Brown and became an immediate hit. In 1934, Mark Kelly became the first of three consecutive Gilman goalies to win All-Maryland status.

More surprising was the introduction of ice hockey—again a push made by Ed Brown—in 1935. Thanks to the development of artificial ice, the sport was no longer the monopoly of fancy New England boarding schools. Gilman could do it too, as was quickly demonstrated in 1936 by Bobby Bordley, a remarkable skater who glittered like quicksilver as he flashed around the ice. There was one feature of ice hockey which made it either more attractive, or less so, depending on the point of view. Gilman had no rink, and its teams had to use the Sports Center, a commercial facility in a part of town sprinkled with soda fountains and movie theaters. Nobody has ever been sure how many of the skaters really liked hockey, and how many were drawn by the side attractions of North Avenue. Little matter. Nothing was more exciting than a close Friday night game, with the Gilman crowd roaring their encouragement as the scoreboard clock wound down toward zero.

It was about this time that McDonogh replaced Tome as Gilman's chief rival. It was not difficult to make the switch. Tome was obviously fading, and McDonogh—considered a band of farmers—was coming on fast. When in 1932 the Cadet football team beat Gilman for the first time in history, it was a black day on Roland Avenue. Nor did it help when McDonogh's headmaster condescendingly invited the Gilman football squad to train at his camp in the future. The Gilman trustees politely declined, regretting that the idea "was not practicable."

These memorable moments of the '30s covered far more than sports. In 1932 there was, for instance, the sudden appearance of the yo-yo in the halls of Gilman. How it came about, who was responsible, where it came from, are questions that have never been answered, but of the fact that it happened there is no doubt. Within a single week, every boy in the Upper and Lower Schools seemed thoroughly versed in the art of making the yo-yo "sleep," twirling it "around the clock," and a dozen other demonstrations of skill. The fad died out as quickly as it had come. Similarly, "knock-knock" jokes came and went with breathtaking suddenness. They were sometimes highly topical:

> Knock-knock.
> Who's there?
> Worcestershire.
> Worcestershire who?
> Business is the Worcestershire it's ever been.

Even more memorable was the sudden advent of miniature golf in the spring of 1932. It was the very bottom of the Depression, and in times like these the pastime seemed an especially inappropriate bit of frivolity. Nevertheless, a course was laid out in the grove just west of the gym. In no time at all putters were sprouting everywhere, and eager foursomes of boys and masters were pitting their skills against each other. The minutes of the Board of Trustees offer no clue as to who gave this elaborate gift to Gilman. They simply say "one of the parents" made it possible. It was a bad investment. Within weeks the course lost its novelty and by mid-summer it lay abandoned in rusty ruin.

All boats rise together on a rising tide, runs the saying, and Gilman was no exception to the rule. Whether it was due to the New Deal, or to the new defense industries which were booming as the threat of Hitler grew—whatever the reason, there was a distinct business surge in the fall of 1936. At Gilman, this took the form of an increase in enrollment, more prompt tuition payments, fewer parents seeking financial relief, and a decision by the trustees to restore five percent of the 20 per-cent cut in faculty salaries.

The lift in business was accompanied by a new style in popular music, which was so much a part of growing up. The saccharine strains of Guy Lombardo and Hal Kemp gave way to the blaring syncopated beat of Benny Goodman, Tommy Dorsey, and Artie Shaw. They were the high priests of this new style, which came to be known as "swing." It was embraced by the teenagers of the late '30s as enthusias-tically as their own children would seize upon rock. Even today the clarinet solo of Shaw's "Begin the Beguine" evokes vivid recollections of rumble seats, saddle shoes, bobby socks, Vitalis, cokes at the Campus Inn, a radio console in the living room, and corsages for the one-and-only at the Fifth Form Dance.

By 1939, both the Depression and the decade were all but gone. To what degree were the Gilman boys of this period changed by these ten years? They were a little more serious. The senior poll no longer carried headlines like "most popular with the flappers" and "biggest shiek." They were beginning to be worried by the signs of war just over the horizon. On the other hand, they weren't consumed by this threat. The same senior poll voted that their favorite topics of conversation were: the Euro-pean situation, 1; the weather, 1; girls, 24.

Academic excellence remained the touchstone of the Gilman experience. The school took marks seriously. The term "preparatory school" was taken literally, with the emphasis on getting into college rather than on the challenges to be faced after admission. Every June found the school giving Fourth and Fifth Formers a week of cram courses in preparation for the coming College Boards. During this week spe-cial help was pounded into the students. For instance, one of the most enterprising English teachers, Archie Hart, had his students memorize a few lines of off-beat poets, not because of their merits, but because he thought a little name-dropping might impress the College Board markers. Conversely, courses in art and music were neglected; the student didn't need them for College Boards. Gilman's music teacher was paid only $500 a year. Art appreciation cost even less, thanks to a Carnegie grant.

Worldly and sophisticated the average Gilman graduate was not; but he had something much more basic. His no-frills, no-nonsense education (plus a lot of exercise and homework) gave him a discipline and quickness of mind that would serve him well in the hard years of war that lay ahead. Beyond that, he would have a set of values that would make him a better citizen. Above all, the friendships he forged in this intimate, if somewhat insular world of Gilman in the '30s, would give him pleasures and satisfaction for the rest of his life.

Crediting Upper School history teacher Herbert Pickett with sparking his interest in American history, Walter Lord has fond memories of his student years at Gilman, as well as of his Gilman-infused summers as a camper and later tutor at Hyde Bay Camp in Cooperstown, NY, a sort of Gilman summer outpost from 1927 to 1970, where Lord eventually became known as "The Commodore."

In his senior year at Gilman, Walter Lord was a member of the track team, President of the Areopagus Debating Team, President of the Literary Club, Editor-in-Chief of *The Blue and The Gray*, Copy Editor of the *News*, and Associate Editor of the *Cynosure*. "Gilman was another home to me. I practically lived there, especially on Saturdays and Sundays when up against an editorial deadline."

On his graduation in 1935, Lord was awarded The William Brodnax Cameron Debating Medallion for excellence in debating as well as The Princeton-Gilman Alumni Cup for the best Sixth Form Speech of the year—a speech on the sinking of the *Titanic*, later the topic which launched his career as a historian.

Lord attended Princeton, graduating in 1939. He entered Yale University's Law School, but his studies were interrupted by the advent of war. Joining the Office of Strategic Services (OSS), he was working in Secret Intelligence in London by the end of the war.

Lord finished his law degree at Yale, and went to work as an editor, writer, and copywriter. Following up on a life-long interest in the Civil War, he worked evenings on an annotated version of *The Fremantle Diary*, based on the diary of a British officer who had toured the South in 1863. (Years later, it was the major inspiration for the novel, *Killer Angels*, and the movie, *Gettysburg*.)

By the time *The Fremantle Diary* was published in 1954, Lord was researching the sinking of the *Titanic*. The success of *A Night to Remember* (it has been through over 50 printings, with millions of copies sold) resulted in Lord's embarkation on the life of a full-time writer. He has authored 13 books, and for all of his career has been drawn to the close examination of human courage.

Lord served as a Trustee of Gilman School 1962–80 and on the Gilman Centennial Book Committee 1992–97. On May 13, 1995, The Walter Lord Library was dedicated and opened in John M. T. Finney Hall, the new Middle School building. In late 1996, Lord bequeathed to Gilman his residuary estate worth over $1 million. Lord directed that the funds go toward faculty education and faculty sabbaticals.

Of Ed Russell and Wrestling Reminiscences

COOPER WALKER '33

Early in 1945—it was during the Battle of the Bulge—we were flying transport planes into Paris, bringing wounded boys back to the States. The mail, naturally, was terrible during the war, and people at home would often ask us, "Would you please take this letter to my mother in Paris?" and we'd usually do it. Well, one day back in the States, a friend, Captain Lawrence, asked a favor. His wife was a friend of Marlene Dietrich, and was trying to get a letter to her. "Would you deliver this letter to Marlene Dietrich at the Ritz in Paris?"

"Hell yeah."

Soon, there I was, having cocktails with Marlene in the Ritz Bar, and in walked fellow wrestler C. B. Alexander '26 and H. R. Fenwick '42—they were in the American Field Service and had just driven down from the front. They'd been up with the tough stuff and were the dirtiest, grimiest, scruffiest-looking guys you'd ever seen. With snide pleasure I stood up, "I want you boys to meet Marlene Dietrich." We all had a drink together, Marlene left, and the immediate impression of Marlene gave way to reminiscences with C. B. of wrestling days at Gilman with Ed Russell.* I know of no way to point up more quaintly the effect this individual sport, and its equally individual coach, had on boys fortunate enough to participate in wrestling at Gilman. The coach and the sport were virtually synonymous.

---

*"After a drink, or two, we walked outside," explains Cooper Walker. "Bobbie (H. R. Fenwick) found a horse-drawn cab, had a talk with the driver and commandeered the vehicle by jumping up on the back of the horse and giving him a kick in the belly. What a wonderful, wonderful night we had—with Bobbie up there astride the horse in wartime, and C. B. and I in the back. We went all over Paris, up to Montmartre, to the Moulin Rouge. How Bobbie ever got us back I don't know. They drove me out to Orly Field. Luckily, the flight was delayed and I took a shower, shook my head and got off all right. They drove right back to the front. The lines were very close. C. B. was killed that day."

Ease your way with me, if we can, past lotus shores of nostalgia—the feel of the triceps and the inevitable query about weight; the tiers of the old gym, and the tears upon occasion; the whine of the old hand-crank phonograph before meets: "Don't know why, there's no sun up in the sky, stormy weather . . ."; the dreams of drinking water when losing weight—ease with me back to some historic fact.

Wrestling started at Gilman in 1920, according to Florence Russell, because Ed Russell had been placed as a coach of soccer and spent his waking hours figuring out a way to get indoors. In the beginning, the grappling sport in Maryland was without form. Ed saw his way to staying indoors in the winter and fashioned the Interscholastic Wrestling Association of Maryland, composed of Severn, Friends, Baltimore City College, and Gilman. The weights ran from 85 to 155 pounds.

Great Gilman names immediately emerged from the agonies of the early mat: Stuart Janney, Winny Graham, Arthur Foster, Redmond Stewart, and Brice Goldsborough. The sport became second to football in popularity. In 1921, the interscholastics were won handily.

Tom Lowndes was named an alternate in the 1928 Olympics. In 1928, Gilman won every weight in the interscholastics except one and took second in that. In 1929, the team scored 195 1/4 points to its opponents' 11 1/2.

At Princeton, Ed had been keen about wrestling, and though incapacitated for varsity competition by a severe knee cartilage operation, had served as assistant coach for two years. Princeton freshmen soon appeared on the schedule, the matches being wrestled at night early in January. The meet was a social event, with many spectators appearing in tuxedos. Absolute silence was *de rigeur*. Applause was restricted to the clapping of hands. In 1931, Gilman defeated the Princeton freshmen 27–0.

Ed was short, really rather roly-poly. His most distinguishing feature was a lock of hair which he carefully stretched across an otherwise bald pate. Sometimes this lock would bend loose from the side of his head, giving the appearance of a handle on a pot.

Ed used to delight in wrestling with the lighter boys on the squad, not full strength. (His garb was a white sweatshirt and white sweatpants with a drawstring at the waist.) He would designate the degree of effort to be used, "40 percent," "50 percent," and thus we learned sliding sit-throughs, double wristlocks, armrolls, figure-four scissors, cradles, cross-body rides. . . .

In 1933, I had the great good fortune of being captain of the wrestling team. Without a doubt I can say that the years of struggle under mentor Ed Russell, leading up to that honor, totally influenced my life. School became a joy, not just a place for assiduous study. Had the die not been cast, my whole life might have been different.

"I never proselytize. Never. But you must come out for wrestling next year."

Those, perhaps, were the first words Ed Russell ever spoke to me. I did not know what proselytize meant, but I sure found out. The remark was made early in the Upper School, where I first played "guard" on an undersquad basketball team with the talented Taylor twins and Walter Woodward. Ed made the above remark after I had somehow beaten Francis Swann in the finals of the annual intramural wrestling meet, the weight-class, I think, just over 100 pounds.

Then began an influence on me through wrestling and Latin which shaped my years at Gilman and took me as an UL (unskilled laborer) to Hyde Bay Camp with the great Pickett clan.

Ed's power to inspire by merely taking your left triceps between his thumb and forefinger and asking, "How's your weight today?" was akin to the laying on of hands.

Never a pep-talk, only the creaky wind-up gramophone in the dressing room before a meet—"You, you're driving me crazy"—and you'd go out on the mat with a zeal unknown since the crusades.

Ed's preoccupation before a meet was well-known and lovingly played upon. One Friday in the winter of my Sixth Form year—I was seated in Fisher Memorial Dining Room at Ed's left—he chanced out of a reverie to say, "Cooper, why are the boys on the wrestling team blond?"

I replied, "That's right, Morris Emory's blond."

"Yes," said Ed, "and Dickey Janney."

"And, I'm blond," I said.

"Yes."

"And Steve Mann." (The shades grew darker.)

Then looking at Mac Patterson, the black-shocked captain of the soccer team, I averred, "And Mac Patterson's blond . . ."

"Yes, Mac's blond."

Then with a sudden realization, mock indignation, bulging of the cheeks, "No, he's not blond!"

Gilman had won nine interscholastics in a row when the tournament of 1933 came around. We'd won all our dual meets, beating McDonogh 16 1/2–6 1/2, I believe. (Jake Classen broke his ankle in that meet at McDonogh but with encouragement carried on. Of course, Ed did not know the ankle was broken.)

Before the interscholastics, Ed juggled weights so as to be sure, or relatively sure, of winning four of the eight weight classes. Woody Gosnell, a steady winner at Gilman, had gone on to Severn, and we figured Gilman would win four firsts, McDonogh three and Severn one.

The banner up for the *News* was printed,

"GILMAN WINS TEN IN A ROW"

Incredibly, Woody Gosnell lost to McDonogh.

At 7:30 p.m. on Saturday in the consolations, flashbulbs exploded on the mat around referee Tubby Miller as Herbert Smelser sought to salvage a possible victory. In the end, Gilman lost to McDonogh 27 1/2–26 1/2. Ed took the loss more philosophically than the team—or at least I think he did.

I soon ended up teaching English at Hyde Bay Camp during summers while at Yale, suddenly on a faculty with Ed Russell, Jim Pine, Al Townsend, Miles Marrian, Jim Dresser, Herbert Pickett—the old maestros. It was both fun and awesome.

The tutoring school was an adjunct of the camp, which had opened in 1927, the brainchild of Herbert and Emily Pickett. The many-acred facility lay at the northeast end of Lake Otsego, the area made famous by James Fenimore Cooper's *Leatherstocking Tales*. At the southern end, where the Susquehanna flows out of Lake Otsego and courses south to form the Chesapeake Bay, were Doubleday Field and the Baseball Hall of Fame at Cooperstown. Miles Marrian, Gilman's baseball coach, taught math at Hyde Bay. On Sundays he'd slip away and play semi-pro ball at Doubleday Field.

The campers slept in World War I surplus army tents, six to each. My first year, I was counselor of a tent as well as tutor of English. What a rowdy tent I had: Billy Robertson, Frank Lynn, Walter Koppelman, Fred Levering, Herbert Smelser, all virtually my peers.

Except for those in tutoring school, Hyde Bay campers were free to do as they chose: swim, play tennis, ride horses, sail, or just lollygag around. (Ed Russell had a wrestling facility near the shore of the lake.) But reveille, taps, and meal hours were obeyed by all.

The "Unskilled Laborers," boys who got their summer free in exchange for work, had built the entrance gate to the camp somewhat askew—a UL could not afford to be perfect with plumb and level, else he would belie his name—and one day found me riding through that slightly crooked gate in the Russell car bound for Cooperstown.

Florence Russell was at the wheel; the road was dirt. About a mile on the Cooperstown side of Pathfinder, Ed came out of a reverie and asked, "Florence, where's your sewing basket?"

(Now remember, Ed for years had been carefully cultivating several increasingly thin strands of hair, running from left to right, over his otherwise bald pate.).

Florence replied, "Ed, why on earth do you want to know?"

"Well, I want those scissors to cut off this damned lock. I've been wanting to do it for years."

So, on the dusty road to Cooperstown, occurred the rape of Ed's lock.

Back at Camp he put it in the Russell Bible, and I think it is still there to this day.

In later years, I came to know Ed as the perennial secretary of the Alumni Association. As self-dubbed "Mister Minutes," he was annually called upon at the banquet to give his report. In this role he outshone Robert Benchley; the report would contain *nothing* of the minutes of the association meetings, but would have the gathering in convulsions.

In one report he told this story on himself:

A project of mine has been a drive for a neat campus. I've told the students that at Gilman there are three classes of people: the third class throws litter on the ground and lets it lie there; the second class picks up only the litter they themselves have dropped; but the first class picks up litter whenever they see it. Well, the other day on the grass between my house and the school I picked up a sheet of paper and on it was written, 'Greetings from a third class person to a first class person.'

Ed Russell influenced my life in a subtle way, never articulated by me before—but urged on me to express, despite my misgivings, by the editor of this book. In the First Form of the Upper School I was a bookworm.* After I began my wrestling efforts I experienced an irresistible epiphany, a conscious desire to forego strict academe and to have some fun. A real sense of camaraderie with fellow classmates resulted. One of our schemes which caught on was starting an ice hockey team, coached by Eddie Brown, at Carlins Park. Later it switched to the Sports Center on North Avenue. While getting in time on the ice, I was successful in wrestling in my Fifth and Sixth Form years—and upon graduation I had dropped back to 12th in my class academically.**

Maybe, just maybe, if I had not been busted out of my academic cocoon by Ed Russell, I might not have taken up flying, thereby missing out on having cocktails in the Ritz Bar in Paris with C. B. Alexander, H. R. Fenwick and Marlene Dietrich in 1945.

---

*Walker had led Gilman in scholarship with an average of 81.96. Harrison Garrett, a Sixth Former, was second.

**Walker won the Maryland Interscholastics in both his Fifth and Sixth Form years.

Attending Gilman 1924–33, Cooper Walker found his overriding scholastic interest in the Classics and English, as is easy to tell from the scintillating allusions to A. E. Housman and the crisp quotations from Shakespeare which he can toss off during a conversation. During his senior year, he was a member of the Literary Club, associate editor of the *News*, the *Cynosure*, and *The Blue and The Gray*, and vice-president of the Pnyx Debating Club. His favorite teacher/coach was Ed Russell.

While winning awards for scholarship in the Lower and Upper Schools, Walker found time to be a *four-sport* athlete. He was a three-year member of the varsity wrestling team, captain his senior year; two-year member of the varsity lacrosse team; two-year member of the hockey team; and spent one year playing varsity football. Yet it was in wrestling, under the coaching of Ed Russell, that Walker flourished, winning the M.S.A. championship his junior and senior years.

At Yale, Walker continued his studies in English. He was on the lacrosse (captain his senior year) and wrestling teams for all four years and played intramural ice hockey. After graduating in 1937, he taught English at Hotchkiss School for two years and worked as a Baltimore *Sun* reporter for a year before joining the Army Air Force as a pilot in Air Transport Command. He flew in all theaters 1942–46, and worked for the Department of State 1947–48.

Walker developed real estate 1948–60, and then started the Walker–Wilson Travel Agency. All along he has worked as a freelance writer and fine-tuned his travel skills.

Walker was president of the Alumni Association 1955–56, a member of the Board of Trustees 1956–69, and instrumental in starting the Gilman Fund, predecessor of the Annual Fund, in 1956.

The Lighter Moments

ALEXANDER ARMSTRONG '33

A little nonsense now and then
Is relished by the wisest men.

Anon.

It was back in the days of the Fisher Memorial Dining Hall, when Gilman was much smaller and when at lunchtime each master presided over a table of 12 students. There were tablecloths, and we actually had napkins that could be used, if you were quick enough, to catapult a pat of butter to the ceiling.*

It was fish day, and Josh Bartlett, formidable head of the Math Department, prepared to serve the students at his table. One student promptly made his feelings known.

"Sir, I don't want any of that dead fish."

Just as promptly, he found himself on report for insolence. When the weekly demerit list was posted, however, his name was not included. Mr. Bartlett, miffed, went to see the dean.

The dean was historian Herbert E. Pickett, another large and formidable presence, who, moreover, had the well deserved reputation of never having been bested in a verbal exchange. Josh demanded to know why the student had not received a demerit.

"The only issue here," replied the dean thoughtfully, after a pause, "is whether the fish was actually dead. Was it dead?"

"Of course it was dead, you damn fool," said Josh, with heat.

---

*For an alternative butter delivery see "A Small and Silent Symbol of Audacity," by Tim Baker '60. Alex Armstrong notes, "The napkin method is the only one I knew, and it worked well, a sort of snap sling-shot from between the knees."

"Ah!" said the dean.

According to legend, the student escaped unscathed.

In the course of my years as a student and as a faculty member, I heard this story many times. On formal occasions such as the annual alumni banquet and commencement, one hears of the school's virtues, its high goals, its achievements academic and athletic, and that is as it should be. But when alumni gather informally, issues have a way of dissolving into reminiscence of moments that by accident or design relieved the tedium of the daily grind.

Relief for the student is not always relief for the teacher. In spring and fall the large, screenless windows of "A" study hall give easy access to birds, which then negotiate the high ceiling in long sweeping flight back and forth, evoking apprehension below. Or a student may be galvanized into sudden and desperate evasive action by an errant yellow jacket, to the delight of fellow students.

In class, likewise, there are moments of diversion or interruption, depending on whether you are a student or a teacher. One winter day when as a teacher I was laboring to make a point, an alumnus, presumably overcome by nostalgia, landed his helicopter on the football field. That ended the point. I was gratified to see lower formers in recess pelt him with snowballs.

For those teaching in the old music room, later the VI Form room at ground level in the rear of Carey Hall, there was the dread moment when the coal delivery truck lumbered into the back court, turned, backed to the coal intake below the classroom window, elevated its load, and lowered its chute. For several minutes thereafter communication was impossible until the last coal had thundered into the cellar.

But it was the Baltimore Orioles who furnished the supreme interruption. Arriving in town in the spring of 1954, they came to practice on the Gilman field. The gentle breeze carried into our open windows the crack of the bat and the shouts of coaches and players. How other teachers fared I can't say, but I was teaching *Idylls of the King*, and found at once that "Elaine the fair, Elaine the lovable, Elaine the lily maid of Astolat" was no match for Bullet Bob Turley and his cohorts. The class and I suffered together until the bell brought merciful relief.

Whole collections have been published of bloopers written by students. I offer my two Gilman favorites. A Third Former, writing on an Ivanhoe test, asserted ". . . the fair Rowena had a line of golden churls down her back." And a Fifth Former, reproducing a memory passage for teacher A. J. Downs, was not satisfied that Claudius should reveal his guilt to Hamlet by a mere "blanch," and wrote, "If he but belch, I know my course."

I cannot vouch for the accuracy of every detail of every story I heard in my years as a student and teacher, but this is not a court of law; moreover, such stories often involve memorable personalities in Gilman history, the more reason not to stumble over trivia.

In this category is a story involving the amiable math teacher James L. Dresser. Some may dispute the adjective, but to my frequent pleas for help in my worst subject he always responded patiently and cheerfully. In this corner it's "amiable." He was teaching a class in one of the first-floor rooms when students in the rear of the class were startled to see an antlered deer looking into the open window, apparently contemplating a leap inside. Consternation—until a sideways swaying motion revealed that the head was bodiless, that it depended on overhead support. When laughter erupted, the head vanished upwards. Via stairway, so did Mr. Dresser, but he found neither deer nor students.

A diversion of a more subtle and elaborate nature occurred in a history class conducted by Mr. James C. Pine in a ground-level rear classroom. Whenever he turned to the map or the board to make a point, a voice would remark, "Sir, that's old stuff. You gave it to us last week," or perhaps "Gee, Mr. Pine, do we have to learn this stuff?" No one appeared to have spoken, and no one admitted to having done so. Finally the light dawned. Mr. Pine strode to the back of the room, picked up a wastebasket, and extracted a speaker. It was connected to wires that went out the window, across the court, and into a window on the opposite side, from which the funster with a microphone could monitor Mr. Pine's every move.

The justly indignant Mr. Pine threw the whole contraption out the window.

Huck Finn says, "You don't know about me without you have read a book by the name of *The Adventures of Tom Sawyer*." Likewise, you don't know about Gilman unless you knew, or at least know about, Thomas Lee Lipscomb. English teacher and strict grammarian—I can still see the diagram of one sentence that covered the entire blackboard—coach of the champion 105-lb. football team ("Give 'em the cold steel, boys."), he was above all the perfect Virginia gentleman. Courteous, slightly formal in manner, he was on occasion eloquent in faculty meetings. He would follow the argument carefully, in later years with his hand cupped to his ear to aid his failing hearing, and then deliver his opinion in beautifully balanced prose. He could quote Shakespeare to good effect, as when he once began his answer to a charge with "Ne'er shake thy gory locks at me."

It was the end of the school year. In the English office we had corrected final exams and written failure reports and were embarking on the delicate and difficult task of writing advisee reports. To praise is pleasant and easy, but to discuss shortcomings in a helpful and tactful manner is challenging. It was wretchedly hot, and we were tired.

Mr. Lipscomb's bachelor quarters were just across the hall. The door opened and he appeared, neatly attired in the brown suit he always wore, including jacket and tie, and showing no signs of heat or fatigue.

"Gentlemen," he said, "if I may have your attention for a moment, I believe I have discovered the all-purpose advisee report."

We gratefully put down our pens and sat back to listen. "Madam," he continued, "if your son would get off his ass and work, there would be no problem."

As we roared our approval, he permitted himself a slight smile, turned, and went back to his room.

It wasn't until the end of my first year as a teacher that Mr. Lipscomb said to me, "Alex, call me Tom." During the first week, however, I felt Ed Russell's soon-to-be-familiar grip on my upper arm as he said, "Alex, call me Ed."

So "Ed" it was and is. A Latin teacher known to some as "Cupie" for his cherubic appearance and to scores as "Uncle Ed," he is enshrined in Gilman history as the coach of nine consecutive state-champion wrestling teams. I spoke of Ed to Cooper Walker '33, a "Russelling team" champion in those glory years.

"Cooper, is it true that Ed was so excited during a meet that he stepped into a water bucket?"

"No, but during a meet he did throw his hat down directly into the water bucket."

"How about the story that he set himself on fire in class by putting his pipe into his coat pocket?"

"That's true, but it happened more than once, both in class and in summer camp. The first warning was usually a little wisp of smoke."

Unfortunately, on the only occasion when a glowing pipe in his pocket would have served Ed well, it wasn't there. He had his pocket picked in Rome.

Once more into the golden haze of legend—and this time I was there: The Sixth Form speech in those days was delivered from the desk platform in "A" study hall, before the assembled Upper School. My classmate Sam George even then had an interest in ornithology which led just three years later to fame for co-discovery (with Tom Gilliard) of the remains of the extinct great auk on Funk Island, Newfoundland. On this occasion he planned to speak on the owl. For illustration he brought in a caged owl and before the students assembled placed it in readiness behind the desk.

The bell rang, silence prevailed, and after scripture and prayer the Sixth Form speaker was announced. Sam mounted the platform and faced the student body.

"Mr. Morrow, members of the faculty, and fellow students." Then with a gesture toward the desk, "I have beside me a great horned owl."

But he didn't. He had forgotten to place the owl on the desk before he began. Students saw only the round, solemn, slightly forbidding face of Headmaster Boyd Morrow.

It was nearly a minute before order could be restored.

Embarrassed, Sam reached down and brought the cage up to the desk. The unexpected apparition of a real owl beside Mr. Morrow created another tumult.

I do not remember the speech.

One would not surmise, looking at the superb and highly regarded watercolors of R. Jack Garver, former head of Gilman's Art Department, that he could also be a merciless cartoonist. If you were in a faculty meeting, however, after a long day of teaching, coaching, and conferences, and were feeling just a little bit droopy, you might become aware of his calm eye upon you while his pencil moved as if taking notes. Somehow the result would enter surreptitious circulation, and there you were, instantly recognizable, with no sagging muscle or drooping eyelid overlooked, exposed in all your inattentive weakness. Yet he himself never seemed sleepy, and never missed a single detail under discussion. Maddening but salutary. He kept us alert.

A distinguished Hopkins professor once observed: "Out of chaos comes order. Out of order comes nothing." One who might have agreed was Roy C. Barker, Chairman of the English Department. Since he was also chairman of the Fifth Form Committee, a member of various other committees, coach of varsity tennis, an occasional consultant to the headmaster, and like all other English teachers a constant corrector of papers, the top of his desk can only be described in terms of mass, a sort of indiscriminate pile. Small wonder that his oversize coffee cup was stained brown, and that under constant pressure he sometimes displayed a short fuse, resulting in the nickname "Old Blowtop."

Someone was bound to think of it. In the round, bold handwriting of Headmaster Henry Callard, this note was forged:

Roy—Please see me as soon as possible. HHC

It was backdated a week and carefully inserted at the bottom of the pile. We waited. Several days passed, then . . . "Oh, my God!"

There was a split in the atmosphere as Roy left the office. Several minutes passed. We heard him ascending the stair.

"All right. Who did it?"

To which after all these years I still say, "Gee, boss, I dunno."

But it took a student, Dave Robinson '63, to devise a torment of truly Byzantine ingenuity. Noting that my desk in the front room of the English office commanded a view of Mr. Barker's desk in the second room, he said, "I can fix it to give you control of the lamp on his desk."

And working with professional neatness when Mr. Barker was in class, he did just that. If Roy's lamp was on, all I had to do was press my knee against a switch under my desk and it would go off until I chose to turn it on.

"Now don't overdo it," said Dave. "Pick your moments, and we can keep this going for days."

It was term-paper time. I picked my moments, and when Roy and a student had their heads together over a paper, his lamp would mysteriously go out. After he had turned the switch several times and given it a shake or two, it would come on again. Enough for the time being.

It should be noted that Mr. Barker's encyclopedic knowledge of grammar and literature was in inverse ratio to his knowledge of matters electronic. Dave was right; with restraint we kept it going for days. Finally, as Roy and a student were once again plunged into twilight, Old Blowtop erupted. He shook the lamp, angrily put it down, and came and stood over my desk.

"Armstrong, I don't know how you're doing it, but STOP!"

I had a glimpse of Dave outside the office door, helpless with laughter.

The scene changes. In an A-V classroom on the second floor of the auditorium, A. J. "Jerry" Downs waited . . . and waited . . . and waited. Surely this was the period and place he met with his Sixth Form Honors English section, yet the bell had rung and not a student had appeared. Except for himself, the room was empty. Were they meeting with a college dean? No, as college counselor he would have known about that. He waited another minute or so, then rose to leave.

The door to the room's large storage closet opened, and a member of the class stepped out and announced: "Second floor. A. J. Downs Honors English."

Whereupon the entire class solemnly emerged from the closet and took their seats.

Mr. Downs joined in the laugh, and being a man of considerable ingenuity himself, bided his time.

It came soon enough. The History Department scheduled a trip to Washington, and most of his Honors English class was included. It happened that he had scheduled a test on *Oedipus Rex* the day following the trip. Accordingly, he wrote the following essay topic:

In an essay of about 250 words, discuss the significance of Mt. Cithaeron in the play.

A fair topic? Not if you consider that Mt. Cithaeron is mentioned only once in the play, and that but a bare reference. The students not included in the trip were informed and briefed on how to react.

Next day the class met and the test topics were handed out. The few in the know read the topic, nodded with feigned satisfaction, and went vigorously to work. The others—and they included some of the form's top scholars—were stunned. They looked around in confusion, noted the students who were already writing, saw Mr. Downs solemnly reading a book. There were muttered protests. Some made attempts to get started, then crumpled their papers, threw them aside, and started over.

Their misery lasted only a minute or two. Mr. Downs burst out laughing, took up the horrors, and gave out the real test.

All even.

A few vignettes on headmasters can serve to end this lighthearted ramble.

Back to "A" study hall. Early in my career I was in charge one day when I noted two figures coming from the Common Room. One was Gross, indispensable man of all work and sole operator of the "Gross machine," a large floor waxer.* The other was Henry Callard, who was wearing a baggy sweatshirt. They were carrying a 12-foot ladder. Mr. Callard smiled and waved to me. They propped the ladder over the door. Gross held it steady while the headmaster mounted nimbly and fixed whatever was wrong with the clock. He descended, smiled and waved again, and the two of them departed with the ladder.

It was my introduction to another side of the man, so idolized by the students,

*James Barry Gross was a member of the maintenance staff.

who could patiently listen to all views in a faculty meeting and guide us to a proper conclusion. So I was not surprised when he came one day to help fix a roaring john in the English office, or when near 7:00 one evening, in darkness, I hailed a kneeling figure in front of the auditorium with "Hey, fellow. Working kind of late, aren't you?" and Henry Callard replied, almost apologetically, "Yes, Alex, but I haven't been able to get to planting these bulbs all day."

It was a sultry September day early in the career of future headmaster Redmond Finney. He was teaching a history class. For some reason the large, wide windows, so familiar to every Gilman student, were shut, and the heat was oppressive. As he talked, Mr. Finney extended an arm to the window near him and pressed upwards. Nothing happened. He went on with the point he was making, then reached and pressed again. Again nothing happened. Convinced that the window was stuck, Mr. Finney took a stand in front of it and pressed up hard with both hands.

No wood-and-screw assembly that dated back to 1910 could withstand such a surge from muscles that had achieved All-American honors in two sports. The ancient lock burst its moorings and the window flew up, to the delight and awe of the class.

Another future headmaster, Ludlow Baldwin, served many years as dean before succeeding Henry Callard. When on duty one weekend, he smelled smoke. As the minutes passed, the air became hazy and the smell increased, but no flames were visible and no source could be found. The smoke thickened. The former Naval officer, veteran of 12 major engagements in the Pacific in World War II, decided it was time for action. He called the Fire Department, described the situation, and asked that a man be sent to investigate. Then he waited.

Almost at once sirens wailed in the distance, then rapidly drew nearer. Fire engines roared and clanged up Roland Avenue and into the Gilman driveway. To Mr. Baldwin's dismay, firemen in helmets and full regalia, armed with axes, entered the Common Room.

The cause of the "fire" was soon located: a smoldering blackboard eraser in an overhead light. A triumph of student accuracy.

"I went into hiding," says Mr. Baldwin.

One final foray into the distant past. It was in the late thirties, during the headmastership of E. Boyd Morrow. The annual alumni banquet was held that year in the ballroom of the Elkridge Club.

During the main course Mr. Morrow rose and announced that the speaker of the evening, the Greek ambassador, was detained on official business but was expected to arrive in time to deliver his address.

Just as the dessert was being served, there was a slight commotion at the entrance, and there stood the ambassador. I can still see him, a dark-haired, very handsome man, broad-shouldered, of medium height. Angled across the front of his tuxedo shirt was a wide red ribbon, in the center of which gleamed a silver decoration.

We stood and applauded, and he smiled and nodded in gracious acknowledgment. Mr. Morrow advanced and conducted him to the head table.

The usual Alumni Association business concluded, Mr. Morrow rose to introduce the speaker. He outlined his distinguished career, including his recent assignment to Washington, and mentioned that his son was entered at Gilman. (Applause).

The ambassador rose. To our astonishment, he spoke not in polished English with perhaps a slight accent, but with comically garbled syntax and vocabulary reminiscent for older alumni of Lew Lehr's fractured German. As he spluttered on, we found the urge to laugh almost irresistible, but that would have been insulting.

I looked at Mr. Morrow's impassive face and resolved that if he could show such control so could I, though it strained every rivet in my body. Others were suffering also, and I didn't dare catch a friend's eye.

At last the ordeal ended, the ambassador sat down, and we found relief in lavish applause. Whereupon he rose again and delivered a superb address in flawless English.

We had been duped, and we knew it and loved it and admired him for it. This time the applause was sincere and prolonged. The evening was a great success.

It was not until a day or so later that word began to spread that the "ambassador" was a hired entertainer. It was rumored but never confirmed that the daring scheme was the brainchild of C. B. Alexander '26. Most appealing, however, is the glimpse afforded behind the iron façade of the "King," Headmaster Morrow, for he must have been included from the start.

So even the King, under whose stern gaze a First Former is said to have vanished in a puff of smoke, even he had his lighter moments. In her second century, may Gilman never be without them.

 Alex Armstrong attended Gilman 1926–33 with his main intellectual interests being literary and musical, and his most influential teachers being Dick O'Brien (French) and Tom Lipscomb (English). He served as editor-in-chief of the *Cynosure* and *The Blue and The Gray*, and president of the Pnyx Debating Club. Armstrong especially enjoyed singing in the Glee Club and being a cast member of the school play. On spring afternoons, he could be found on the tennis court with varsity teammates. Along with Coach Don Hoffman and many classmates, he raised tropical fish. Upon graduation, he was awarded the school's two debating prizes.

Attending Princeton 1933–37, Armstrong majored in English and was in the casts of three Princeton Triangle shows. (As a freshman, he was on the swimming squad. "Raw cod liver oil, a full cup, after every practice.")

He attended law school for one and a half years before transferring to Johns Hopkins to study English. His studies were interrupted by Pearl Harbor in 1941. As a commissioned Ensign USNR, Armstrong was assigned to the heavy cruiser U.S.S. *Chicago*. He served as Battery Officer, Radar Control Officer, and Senior Radar Control Officer. *Chicago* was involved in the Battle of Coral Sea; an attack by Japanese midget subs in Sydney Harbor; the

Occupation of Guadalcanal; the Battle of Savo Island; and the Battle of Rennell Island, during which it was sunk by aerial torpedoes on January 30, 1943. Armstrong ended the war stationed at Guam and retired as a Lt. Commander in 1945.

Returning to Hopkins, Armstrong finished his Masters and became executive director of the United Nations Association of Maryland before joining the Gilman faculty in 1951. He taught English 1951–79 and edited the Gilman *Bulletin* 1955–74, infusing it with his wit, humor, and gracefully flowing prose. Among his fondest Gilman memories are the many Gilman/Bryn Mawr plays he directed.

A voice student for most of his life, Armstrong sang in the Baltimore Handel Choir and the Church of the Good Shepherd (Ruxton) Choir with his wife, Louise. The Armstrongs have four daughters, and one son, Alexander, Jr., who graduated from Gilman in 1973.

Archie Hart,
That Dear Man

BILL MUELLER '35

Archie Hart was one of my best teachers at Gilman and became one of my most cherished friends. What sparked the friendship which brought us together and kept us together until his death?

On one particular Friday, Archie asked our class to read about some well-known figure and be prepared the next Friday to write in class a short biography of our chosen subject. At the time I was madly in love with a cute, snub-nosed blonde and was in no way about to replace dreams of her with the gathering of far less exciting biographical material. Come the next Friday, the day assigned for the writing, and I had nothing to say—until my imaginative disposition plucked the Maryland name Chace Ridgely out of thin air and wrote of him as second only to the Bard of Avon, though known to few outside his home town of Frederick.

For several days after I turned in my fakery, Archie viewed me with increasing puzzlement. By the fourth day he had caught on, asked me to stop by after class, and blasted me with words I remember verbatim: "Damn you, Mueller, you've tricked me. I spent hours at the Pratt and the Hopkins libraries checking every poetry reference book in existence. There never was, is not, and never will be a Chace Ridgely. And I had to spend hours finding that out."

Archie, of course, enjoyed the joke, and we were blood brothers from then on.

Attending Gilman 1928–35, Bill Mueller won the Fisher Medallion upon graduation, as did his son, William Henry Mueller II, 35 years later in 1970.

Mueller was a member of the Areopagus Debating Society and the Glee Club. His main athletic interest was in track; he was on the varsity team in 1933, '34, and '35.

At Princeton, Mueller concentrated his studies on philosophy and literature. In 1939, he graduated from Princeton and enrolled in Harvard Graduate School with his major being English literature. He has taught literature and religion at Williams

College, Santa Barbara College, University of North Carolina at Greensboro, and Goucher College, and has been a visiting professor at Princeton and the University of Pennsylvania.

Mueller served on the Gilman Board of Trustees 1966–72. He continues to write and lecture, and is the author of the memoir, *Apology for the Life of William Mueller, The Growth of an Existentialist,* as well as a series of scholarly books, including *The Prophetic Voice in Modern Fiction; The Testament of Samuel Beckett,* coauthored with Josephine Jacobsen; and *Celebration of Life: Studies in Modern Fiction.*

Memoirs of a Faculty Child
or
Life at Gilman from Within

LAWRENCE K. PICKETT, M.D. '37

The invitation to reminisce on Gilman through the eyes of one faculty "child" 70 years from when I arrived at Gilman, is flattering and a great challenge. The faculty member is Herbert E. Pickett, my father, hereafter referred to as HEP. As he was first of all my father, then teacher, coach, extracurricular advisor, and lastly my good friend, you will note that the relationship was very special.

HEP taught at the school 1913–1940 with two years out during World War I when he was asked to leave by Mr. Pine, then headmaster, because there was no appropriate place for a pregnant woman in the school building. Mother and Father lived on the ground floor of the main building, and my older brother was becoming increasingly obvious. After one year at the Episcopal Academy in Philadelphia and one year at the Pingree School in Elizabeth, New Jersey, HEP returned in 1919 at the request of Mr. Pine.

The war had decimated the ranks of the faculty. Mr. Pine promised that appropriate quarters would be found for the addition to the Pickett family. This was accomplished in rented apartments. Though born in 1919, I didn't appear on the Gilman scene until 1923 when the school built a faculty dwelling, a duplex, near what is now the old gym. We moved into the east side while Stuart Link, mathematics teacher, and his wife Helen and three children, Helen, John, and Christine, moved into the west side. At that time there were only four other faculty children on campus, Frank, Sarah, Sam, and Jenny Miles, all somewhat older than we were. Wardlaw Miles succeeded Mr. Pine as headmaster and lived in the headmaster's house.

There was much open space between our house and the Ma & Pa Railroad. Since the gymnasium wasn't built for several years, we had a rural environment right in the middle of Roland Park. The Links had a pony which we helped take care of. We had chickens and rabbits. The woods over towards the Ma & Pa Railroad were tempting for exploration but were forbidden territory as many vagrants camped there.

The structures around the school changed considerably at this time. When the main building was built in 1910, the gymnasium was in the basement underneath "A" Study Hall, and the locker rooms were along the basement corridor. As the student body expanded, the gymnasium was taken out of the basement and was replaced by "K" study hall and a mathematics classroom. The school built a barn-like gymnasium, to the south of the football field, as a temporary structure which lasted for about seven years. It contained a wrestling room, basketball courts, locker rooms, and a maintenance garage, but little else. The principal custodian of that building was John Starr, known as "Chief," a great friend of all the students and certainly of the faculty children. When the gymnasium was replaced in 1928 by the so-called "new gymnasium," the Chief had a much larger domain to oversee. This gymnasium was built to the right of our house, about 50 yards to the east. For three years we were surrounded by construction since the City of Baltimore soon built a public school immediately behind our house. It was the bane of my mother's existence—two little boys and lots of Maryland mud!

Somewhere around 1930 or '31 the Link family moved to Sewickley, Pennsylvania, where Mr. Link became Headmaster of the Sewickley Academy. Meredith Janvier and his mother lived in Link's side of the house for several years. Edward T. Russell and his wife, Florence, very important people in our life, moved in next door. Ed and my father were long-term friends, teaching together both at Gilman and at Hyde Bay camp.

In the early days before I went off to the Lower School in 1929, I joined the group of other faculty children to be befriended or tolerated by the maintenance men for the school grounds and building. I followed them around doing their tasks when they were on our part of the campus. They became part of my life. There was Mr. Finley, the superintendent; Charlie, the carpenter and plumber, who also drove the rickety bus to take the five-day boarders to and from the train; and Richard, the groundsman. John did the heavy work, and Parker drove a horse and wagon for trash collection. Parker was very gruff and chased me away so that I wouldn't be hurt or spook the horse. As I recall, the old mare was well past the age when she might be spooked.

Captain Miles resigned as the headmaster in 1925. When E. Boyd Morrow, long a teacher and assistant headmaster, took over, the Miles moved out to a home in Roland Park. The headmaster's house was renovated for a number of families to live in as Boyd and Eleanor Morrow lived in an apartment on the ground floor of the school building.

On the top floor of the renovated house lived George B. Moulton, principal of the Lower School, with his wife Mona and son Warner. On the second floor were Palm and Eleanor Oscarson and their two sons David and Donald. Later Al Townsend moved in from his bachelor quarters in the new gym after he married Virginia Stuart, the dietitian for the school as well as house mother for the younger boarding boys. On the bottom floor was Adolay Hausmann with his wife, Joy, and later a daughter, Cynthia. Along with the Links, the group made up a small play school watched over by the mothers.

From age five to nine I attended Mrs. Freye's school in Roland Park. Many of the eight boys in my class went on to Gilman with me and entered the Fourth Grade. Teachers in the Fourth, Fifth, and Sixth Grades were Mrs. Mary Richardson, Miss Lillian Elliot, Miss Anne Van Vlack and, in my first experience with male teachers, Mr. Pryor and Mr. George Murdock. I can remember Mr. Murdock in the important Sixth Grade as being a loud and strict disciplinarian, who used, for the first time in my academic career, the threat which I was to hear often in subsequent years, "Behave yourself or I will tell your father."

Leaving the Lower School in 1931 and entering the Upper School in '32 was a bit of a shock. Teaching was carried out by subject matter and not by class. All the teachers were male and long-time friends of my father and mother. Before entering the First Form we had always referred to the close friends as Uncle Ed, Uncle Tom, Uncle Al, etc. Upon entering school, it was immediately Mr. Russell, Mr. Lipscomb, Mr. Townsend, all of whom were most frequently addressed as "Sir." The school uniform was suit and tie at all times, occasionally with a sweater under the suit. School began at 8:30 a.m. with chapel in "A" study hall; it included reading of the Bible, singing of hymns and announcements. Classes ended before lunch. There was a formal lunch hour in the dining room with students seated at a table of eight or 10 and supervised by one of the masters. After lunch a 15-minute recess was followed by study hall in "A," or extra-curricular activities, until 3:15, at which time we went to athletics.

From the First Form to the Sixth Form, life took on a different dimension. There was an ever closer awareness of the many roles HEP had in the Upper School. He taught several grades of both ancient and American history. He supervised study halls. He coached the J.V. football team with Ed Russell. He supervised and directed the two debating clubs. He directed the annual school play put on by the Dramatic Association. He was advisor to the Gilman *News*. Most importantly, he functioned as the dean, there being no assistant headmaster under Boyd Morrow's regime.

The demerit system, I am sure, is remembered more by some than others, as an unpleasant series of episodes. The infractions, whether major or minor, were reported to the dean on a piece of paper known as a slip. HEP investigated the episode, spoke to the master, confronted the perpetrator, and the matter was closed with a sentence. This generally meant staying after school or coming in on Saturdays, depending on the seriousness of the crime. Time was served more by doing such useless things as copying dictionary entries for perfecting penmanship rather than by doing homework.

The urge to see how much one could get away with was rather short-lived in my case. I thought the sentence imposed for one infraction represented undue punishment for a most insignificant episode; nevertheless, the time was served. At home the night following the report Father told me, "These men are friends of mine trying to do a job of teaching and you are making life miserable for them." There were some choicer words for major infractions, but it served to make me an infrequent miscreant and to mend my ways.

Both my brothers and I were made to understand by HEP during early Upper School life that he would always act, whether it was in the classroom, in extracurricular activities, or on the athletic field, so that no one could accuse him of showing favoritism to his sons. I used to consider this the 10 percent rule: 10 percent lower grades, 10 percent more demerits for reported infractions.

One particular episode which I recall was giving my Sixth Form speech. For reasons unclear to me now I chose the topic "Horace Mann the Great Educator." It could be that I was stupid enough to feel that it might impress the judge and jury embodied in the person of Herbert Pickett. The speech was given and that night at home there was considerable silence at the supper table. I was told to go to the office and wait. I shall shorten this by paraphrasing a most articulate diatribe. I was threatened with being disowned if I ever again stood up before an audience and gave a talk on a subject in which I had no interest and about which I knew very little, or if I ever again spoke in a low monotone without addressing the audience, or if I ever again read from notes while shifting my feet and talking so fast that no one could understand me. What I gained from this experience has stood me in good stead the rest of my life. HEP was an excellent public speaker.

Lest the reader conclude that my school life was plagued by events such as these, it was not. Our family was a very close one. There were words of approval and praise for a job well done, friendly criticism when it was not so good. HEP was a man of great principle who had concern for all of us.

My football career was not a distinguished one. Outstanding in my memory is the 105-pound team coached by Tom Lipscomb. The year was capped by a disastrous defeat by the rival, McDonogh. Tom Lipscomb would often reminisce, stating that the only thing missing in that game was any vestige of tackling, blocking, or running with the ball on the part of the Gilman team.

On the junior varsity team with Ed Russell and HEP as coaches, I spent an equal amount of time on the bench and the playing field. The post-game discussions at home made me aware of how I could do better. Improvement was hard to discern.

On the varsity I did a little better with Eddie Brown as coach, assisted by Jim Dresser for the ends, and Jake Slagle for the backs. Friday nights there was a general critique of the teams and individual performances. Football was not one of my strong points.

The wrestling team was different. It was an individual sport where we had a lot of extracurricular coaching as well as "post mortem" sessions on all our meets and tournaments with Ed Russell over coffee at our house. It is no wonder the three Pickett boys living next door to Ed Russell and 50 yards from the gymnasium ultimately performed well in wrestling at the scholastic, college, and NCAA level. Brother Bob went further than Herb and I when he became coach of the Harvard wrestling team for 20 years following his finishing college at Syracuse in 1950.

We had access to the Gilman gymnasium seven days a week. Graduates who had been on the wrestling team and had gone on to wrestle in college often stopped by during vacations to see Ed Russell. He would arrange for a workout in the gymnasium with one of the three of us as we spanned the spectrum of weight classes.

In the spring, coached by Don Hoffman, I worked at the shotput and the discus on the track team. There were no dual meets, but we took part in regional meets and scored modestly well. A Dartmouth graduate, Mr. Hoffman was on a federal pension because of impairment from injuries in the first World War and had a unique position on the faculty as track coach and supervisor of study halls. It was assumed that he had been gassed during the war and had a pulmonary disability. Much to our amusement, he rolled his own cigarettes. We saw a great deal of him as he lived at one of the faculty apartments at the front of the gymnasium, and he introduced us to raising tropical fish. That hobby grew in our house under his coaching for many years.

The Depression left its mark on the school as it did on many other businesses. Decreasing enrollment was soon followed by decreasing faculty salaries. First cut was 10 percent, followed not too many months later by a second cut of 10 percent. This pattern had an expected effect on the Pickett household, changing our lifestyle somewhat. My mother and father pointed out how lucky we were, #1—to have a job, #2—to have a house to live in, and #3—to have enough to eat. Some boys left school because of the hard times. We did not. HEP took us downtown and showed us the long soup lines. He told of numerous individuals who had had good jobs with excellent incomes but who had to resort to this public dole to survive. It was a very impressive visit and made us realize our good fortune.

As the economy began to pick up and some of the school salaries were restored, I can remember HEP's amusement at the way restoration of salaries occurred. He pointed out that if a salary was decreased 20 percent and then was restored at 20 percent of the new base, the resultant salary fell far short of the original. Somewhat in jest he pointed out the discrepancy to Mr. Peter Blanchard, the business manager at the school. Mr. B did not appreciate this form of humor.

A synopsis of the Pickett wrestling history:

HERBERT E. PICKETT, JR.   Gilman '35, Yale '39, Union Seminary

 1933 3rd place Maryland Scholastic Association Meet
 1934 3rd place MSA
 1935 Heavyweight champion MSA

 YALE UNIVERSITY
 1936 Freshman numerals
 1937 3rd heavyweight Eastern Intercollegiate Tournament
 1938 2nd heavyweight Eastern Intercollegiate Tournament

 1940–42 Member of the New York Athletic Club wrestling team, champion of AAU
          wrestling tournament
 1944 Member Baltimore YMCA wrestling team

LAWRENCE PICKETT   Gilman '37, Yale '41, Yale Medical School

 1936 165-pound champion MSA
 1937 Unlimited champion MSA

 YALE UNIVERSITY
 1938 Freshman numerals Undefeated Dual Meets
 1939 3rd Eastern Intercollegiate Tournament
 1940   2nd heavyweight EIT
 1941 Champion heavyweight EIT
 1941 2nd heavyweight NCAA Tournament

ROBERT A. PICKETT   Gilman '38 to '40, Governor Dummer Academy '41 to '42

 1938 155-pound champion MSA
 1939 175-pound champion MSA
 1940 Heavyweight champion MSA
 1941 Heavyweight champion New England Scholastic Tournament
 1942 Heavyweight champion New England Scholastic Tournament
 1943 Yale wrestling team
 1944 U.S. Navy
 1945 Far Western AAU Champion 191 pounds, Outstanding Wrestler Award
 1946 U.S. Navy
 1947 Syracuse University, Eastern Intercollegiate Champion 175 pounds
 1948–50 Freshman wrestling coach, Syracuse
 1950–68 Head wrestling coach Harvard University
 1961–62 President NCAA Wrestling Association
 1968–78 Wrestling Official Eastern Intercollegiate Wrestling Association

A number of faculty members were involved with or ran summer camps. This included Stuart Link in the earlier days, and Jake Slagle, who was affiliated with Camp Wallula, and Ferris Thomsen.

Herbert Pickett and Ed Russell formed a partnership and started Hyde Bay Camp, near Cooperstown, New York, in 1927. Ed dropped out of the partnership after the first year but remained with the tutoring school. From 1928 on, the camp, located on Otsego Lake, was run by HEP and family.

In the early years, most of the counselors, as well as the teachers, came from Gilman, thereby continuing the Gilman association for some boys throughout the entire year. Boys could attend the tutoring school to make up courses in which they had performed poorly or failed. Some took courses to lighten the load for the following year.

I graduated from Gilman in 1937 and went on to Yale. My life on the school grounds came to an abrupt end except for very brief vacations. Even at the time of my graduation I could sense a growing feeling of unrest on the part of HEP, by this time dean of faculty. He spent one week in June each year grading the College Board examinations in New York, carrying on a long-time friendship with a number of teachers from other schools. Through this association and reading and talking to others in the profession, he felt that Gilman should update the curriculum and take on a more progressive role in education. This was directly in conflict with E. Boyd Morrow's conservatism. Motivated by this rift and an assumption that Boyd Morrow would remain headmaster for years to come, as well as by a long suppressed desire to run his own school, HEP resigned from Gilman in 1940. My younger brother, Bob, went off to prep school at Governor Dummer Academy in South Byefield, Massachusetts. Mother and Father packed up and went to Cooperstown, where, after many negotiations, the Cooperstown Academy was resurrected from years of inactivity. Two Gilman teachers, George Chandlee and Al Kerr, joined the new effort: a small school of Fourth through Eighth Graders.* With these two teachers and the continuation of the Hyde Bay Camp for several years, we kept our contacts with Gilman.

In retrospect, I realize what a fortunate life I have had. I attended an excellent preparatory school for nine years, enjoyed superb athletic facilities, associated with a number of excellent teachers and friends, and lived in a very nice home with all maintenance taken care of by the school. Although the salary income from Gilman was most moderate, the fringes of our home and tuition more than made up for it. The experience of being a student at Gilman offered a unique opportunity to have

---

*After four years of teaching and coaching in Gilman's Lower School, George Chandlee went with Pickett to Cooperstown Academy, where he taught for two years before enlisting in the Army. Upon the completion of his military tour in 1946, Chandlee rejoined the Gilman faculty as an Upper School teacher of mathematics and lacrosse coach. His first team won the 1947 Maryland Scholastic Association championship, ending the fabled St. Paul's winning streak at 74 games. Over 23 years, Chandlee's teams compiled an amazing .800 winning percentage.

close contact with my father. He was a remarkable person. He had great humanity and wisdom mixed with humor. After the period covered by this memoir, Cooperstown Academy—a noble experiment from which many boys profited—closed in 1950, and HEP continued to live a full life, running a home for the retired and becoming District Governor of the Rotary. Life with him was a joy until his death in 1962.

Gilman has grown in many ways in the past half century. I still keep in touch with many classmates and surviving faculty.*

---

*In preparation for the writing of this memoir, Larry Pickett had several conversations with both of his brothers, Bob and Herb. He would like to note that the details and insights they provided were invaluable to him.

Lawrence K. Pickett, M.D. attended Gilman 1928–37 with his main intellectual interests being math and science, and his favorite coach, Ed Russell. In his senior year he was co-editor-in-chief of the *News*, Associate editor of the *Cynosure*, a member of the Literary Club and the Pnyx Debating Society. And he wrestled: MSA Champion of 1936 and 1937. He also was a member of the varsity football and track teams.

As a pre-med student at Yale, Pickett majored in biology. He wrestled all four years, was captain of the 1941 team, Eastern Collegiate Heavyweight Champion, and finished second as a NCAA heavyweight. He continued at Yale Medical School, specializing in pediatric surgery.

Pickett was in private practice as a pediatric surgeon 1950–64, professor of surgery and pediatrics at Yale Medical School 1964–84, chief of staff of Yale New Haven Hospital 1972–84, and associate dean of Yale Medical School 1972–82. He became Emeritus Professor in 1983 and has since worked as a medical consultant, supervising new products and marketing as well as an employee health and wellness program for a medical instrument company.

Anyone
for Marbles?

"Knucks up knee high, no knee bend"

COOPER WALKER '33

When and why the game of marbles disappeared from the Gilman landscape is as mysterious as the passing of dinosaurs. When I was in the Lower School and the early years of the Upper, shooting marbles was the preferred entertainment divorced from school regimen. In the lower forms "little ring" was played; in the Upper School, "big ring."

In "little ring" a line was drawn some 12 feet back and the players tossed their shooters toward the encircled marbles. Then the shooting would begin. I suppose the original marbles were fashioned from the stone of the same name. Our marbles were mostly of glass of different hues: bloodies, milkies, cats-eyes . . . But agate was preferred for shooting.

During recess, or at any other free time, boys would be seen, in what was then dirt and what is now the paved area between the Lower School and the Cottage, on one knee aiming a small spherical projectile held between thumb and forefinger at marbles in a ring. The ring was drawn rudely on any flat earthen surface devoid of grass.

If an opponent hollered "Knucks up knee high, no knee bend," the marble shooter had to stand with a locked knee and shoot from the unbent kneecap.

The boy's marbles were carried by the owner in a drawstring bag, probably sewn by his grandmother. I know mine were. In the morning the lad might have 20 or so marbles in his bag. At night the number varied, depending upon the number of other boys' marbles he knocked out of the ring compared to those of his. Each boy ponied up marbles for the ring. If you knocked a marble out of the circle, you kept it.

Often marble players would be frowned upon at home because their knelt-upon knee-pants would wear completely away, leaving their knee-cap smiling joyfully through.

Each boy had his own preferred projectile, his "shooter"; the sine qua non was a sphere of agate about three-quarters inch in diameter. A glass shooter might shatter on contact; agate never, though upon each hard contact, a small "moon" would appear in the polished surface. Hence they were known as moon-agate marbles, or just "moonies." My favorite "shooter" was a coal black agate with three pure white concentric circles around the middle, rather like Saturn. Unlike Jupiter, it had a million "moons"!

In the Lower School I beat Bobby Deford in the marble tournament. Come to think of it, the game of marbles must have gained some sort of school recognition. I gave the prize, various moon agates, to Bobby Pickett.

There were two methods of propelling the "shooter." One was called "cunnythumb" and was looked on with disdain as used only by hackers. A cunnythumb shooter held his marble in the curl of his forefinger and propelled it with his thumb behind. The other method had no name, but it was quite sophisticated: the thumb was cocked behind the curl of the middle finger and the "shooter" held between the knuckle of the thumb and the tip of the forefinger. This position gave the maneuverability of a cueball in billiards. The shooter could be made to stop dead upon impact; underspin could make it draw backward, and topspin make it travel with the struck marble. Angles would position the shooter for the next strike, quite like billiards.

In the Upper School only "big ring" was played. The area on which the four-foot diameter ring was etched was under a tree outside room 18. This classroom was an extension of "K" study hall, creating the short leg of an "L" at the south portion of the school. Stuart Link taught arithmetic in that classroom.

Marble players and onlookers would congregate under the tree. Participants' marbles would be grouped tightly in the ring's center, not neatly racked as at the start of a pool game, but bunched as tightly as bare hands could do.

The first boy to shoot from the ring's edge, if he were first-rate, had an advantage. A firm shot striking a single one of the huddled marbles would surely drive one on the far side out of the ring, a requisite for him to continue to shoot.

Sometimes, as first shooter, I could "clear the ring," giving me the soubriquet of "ringworm." If the center group of marbles was unsuccessfully fractured, the next shooter could enter the ring by picking off strays near the edge and work his way in from there.

All good fun, joking, kidding and laughing. But then came an older player named Sloan into our midst with a shooter made of steel. Much debate took place about the legality of a "steelie" as a shooter. The debate waxed. My memory wanes. I don't remember much about marbles after Sloan and his "steelie" came into the game.

A profile of Cooper Walker appears on page 85, following his essay "Of Ed Russell and Wrestling Reminiscences."

Gilman and My Mentor,
Miles Marrian

DAWSON FARBER '35

I came to Gilman in 1927. My great uncle, Robert B. Ennis, who was the head of the Democratic party in Maryland, had many associates who had sons at Gilman. He had no children, and he arranged for me and my brother Bob '36 to attend. My father was a doctor with Bethlehem Steel at Sparrows Point, and so we became five-day boarders.

Gilman at the time certainly was a school for the well-to-do. Baetjers (Venable Baetjer), Blacks (A. S. Abell), Garretts (Robert Garrett & Sons), Griswolds (Alex. Brown), Willards (B & O), Leggs (Legg & Co., which is now Legg Mason), Lanahans (W.W. Lanahan) and on and on. John M. T. Finney, M.D. was president of the Board of Trustees and held the same position at McDonogh. As a student from "across the tracks," I remember the chauffeur-driven cars dropping off day students—in particular the Baetjers' Pierce Arrow.

Across the street from Gilman, on the other side of Roland Avenue, was the home of the Lowndes family. In their basement were two bowling alleys, two rifle ranges, and a pool table. Sixth Formers and particularly Sixth Form boarders, had privileges to use these facilities at certain times.

Headmaster E. Boyd Morrow—"The King"—and Mrs. Morrow lived in an apartment on the ground floor, the space now occupied by the Development Office. The top two floors of Carey Hall were for boarders, with the south end of the top floor divided into cubicles. On the top floor was an infirmary with an apartment for a full-time nurse, Miss Kerr, and an apartment for a "House Mother," Mrs. John M. Clemmitt, who supervised the cubicles, which were little more than partitions with curtains across the entrances.*

---

*Miss Mary Ethel Kerr was the resident nurse at Gilman for 25 years.

Boarders all remember Thomas Lee Lipscomb ("T. L."), who had an apartment at the top of the main stairs on the second floor. Here was the true "Virginia Gentleman." Head of the English Department at the time, he was a superb teacher. As a disciplinarian he was tough but fair, and students had great respect for him.

Dinner for boarders was in the north wing of Carey Hall. Blue serge suits with stiff white collars were expected to be worn by the younger boys. We took for granted the linen on the table with individual napkin rings and the African-American waiters.

Then came 1929 and the crash and times were difficult. Enrolled in my class were as many as 63 members over the years. In 1935, 26 graduated: 14 Princeton, two Yale, one Harvard, one MIT, one Hopkins and three to other universities and colleges. Three or four did not attend college.

During the Depression, most of my classmastes who left Gilman before graduation did so for financial reasons, but if your parents could afford it, college entrance was no real problem. For those students who wished to enter the medical profession from Gilman, acceptance into Princeton and eventually Hopkins Medical School was almost automatic.

While I boarded from 1927 to 1935, we were conscious of changes brought about by the Depression. There was a large turnover of boys, tablecloths were eliminated at meals, and students began to help with service. However, our beds were still made and rooms cleaned by the maid.

Relationships with faculty members were very personal. Several in particular had a great influence on my life. Miles Marrian, math teacher, sensed early that I was having an adjustment problem and became a close friend and counseled me on a regular basis. Ed Russell had a great influence on all the boys and constantly urged us to seek higher levels of achievement. Ed Brown was a role model: an excellent teacher, superb coach, and a wonderful human being. The upset victory over Tome School (6–0, 1933) with the famous "Conversation Play" portrays what he was capable of obtaining from his players.*

Boarding at Gilman gave you an opportunity to have closer relationships with the faculty. After dinner there was a one and a half hour supervised study period. There also was extra time in the morning and before dinner to interact with the faculty. I remember long punting duels with Ed Brown and Herb Pickett after football practice and before dinner.

As we grew older, we moved from the cubicles on the upper south corridor to upper north and then to lower north. Finally, as Fifth & Sixth Formers, we moved to lower south.

Single masters had small apartments scattered on the two upper floors. Married faculty had houses located on the southern fringe of the Gilman property between Roland Avenue and the gym; at this time Gilman property stretched to Deepdene Road.

*See page 77 of Walter Lord's "Gilman in the 1930s," for the full story on the Conversation Play.

A master was seated at the head of each table for all meals. The headmaster had an oval table of eight to ten seats in an alcove on a raised platform. Grace was said at all meals. Besides morning chapel, there was an evening chapel before study hall.

In the mornings between 6:00 and 7:00 the MA & PA (Maryland & Pennsylvania) would come through the school property. The track was set on a steep grade and the train wheels would spin and squeal as the engine huffed and puffed. (We boarders sometimes covered the rails with skunk cabbage as far as the supply permitted, thereby increasing the spinning and squeaking.) That, along with the blowing of a whistle for the Belvedere crossing, gave warning to us that wake-up time was near.

One of the aspects I most thoroughly appreciated about boarding was getting to know boys from all over the country: sons of diplomats in Washington, sons of officials in the State Department and in the military. This diversity was a plus.

In 1934, I was rooming with Gary Black. We decided one night to sneak out and go to the circus. Everything went well, we thought. Yet, upon our return, we had a welcoming committee led by Mr. Healy, the night watchman and custodian. For this escapade we each received 40 demerits. At the time, a student was allowed 14 demerits for an accumulation of infractions. Over 14, each demerit would need to be worked off at half an hour a crack by running on the track, policing the grounds, or coming back on Saturday.

It was Miles Marrian who became my ongoing mentor. I met Miles Marrian when I was 10 years old and in the Lower School, which only had three forms then: Fourth, Fifth, and Sixth.

When I first came to Gilman from Sparrows Point Elementary School, Miles Marrian sensed my anxieties. A coach of football, basketball, and baseball at different levels, he noticed that I had a great interest in athletics but little ability.

One afternoon he pulled me aside after practice and told me that if I worked hard he would go out of his way to teach me the fundamentals of baseball. When he learned that I was left handed, he began calling me "Lefty," a nickname that followed me through Gilman and Princeton. Baseball was his first love, as he had been a pitcher at Johns Hopkins. We would work on pitching fundamentals for hours. (I remember his raising the pitching mound to its highest legal limit, which made my style more effective.) He recommended that I play summer baseball, and he and Ed Russell made the arrangements. Pitchers were not supposed to hit, it was said. He did not agree, and with hours of practice I became an above-average hitter. I pitched my first game in Clifton Park with Ed Russell, Miles Marrian, and Al Townsend among the spectators.

More important than the athletics was Miles Marrian's insisting that any goal in life was obtainable if you were willing to make the sacrifices. This philosophy also came through loud and clear from Ed Russell and Ed Brown. All three were my football coaches at different levels, and when I went out for football at Princeton, the skills of blocking and tackling put me ahead of boys from other schools.

Miles Marrian was more than a coach; he was a superb math teacher and a tough disciplinarian who allowed no nonsense in the classroom. Classes were small, and we did a lot of our work at the blackboards. Beware if you did anything out of order—a piece of chalk would whiz by your head and be reduced to powder on the board.

While at Princeton I made the freshman football team and later spent four springs on the Princeton diamond. Marrian was delighted, and I felt that in some degree I had justified all the work he had done with and for me over the years. I was grateful. I still am.

Dawson Farber Jr. '35—"Lefty"—attended Gilman 1927–35, with his main intellectual interest being history and his favorite teacher/coach Miles Marrian, who taught math and coached Farber in football, basketball and baseball.

Farber played three years each of varsity football, baseball, and basketball. He was captain of the baseball and basketball teams his senior year. Upon graduation, he was awarded the Alumni Baseball Cup.

Attending Princeton 1935–39, Farber played two years of football and four years of baseball. He was on the Princeton Baseball Team of 1939, which played Columbia in New York in the first sporting event ever televised.

Farber spent 1940–45 in the army, retiring as a captain after earning a Silver Star and a Bronze Star. He then worked as vice president of marketing for National Brewing 1945–75, chairman of the board for Carling/National Brewing 1975–79, and president of Carling/National Brewing Company 1979–82.

Farber and his wife Patricia, "Patty," have five sons who attended Gilman: Dawson III '65, Peter '66, Michael '70, Mark '73, Jonathan '75. Peter won the Fisher Medallion. Mike was captain of the varsity lacrosse and football teams.

Dawson Farber, vice president of the Board of Trustees 1975–80, and then a Trustee Emeritus, has accumulated over 30 years of service to Gilman as a Board member. He served on the Home and Grounds Committee 1964–70, Athletic Committee 1973–74, and Priorities Committee 1973–75, and was secretary to the Board 1973–75. He continues to work hard for Gilman. As a sampling, in 1995, he was on the Committee on Trustees, Committee on Human Relations, Committee on Financial Aid, and Committee on Financial Development. Above all, Dawson Farber has directly and generously assisted Gilman students in a variety of ways that affect them the rest of their lives.

"What has impressed me most over these years," notes Farber, "is that every one of the Gilman family has striven to improve the quality of the school. I have enjoyed it all, especially working with Reddy Finney. Reddy was a wonderful blend of Henry Callard's 'Heart' and Ludlow Baldwin's directional approach. My personal relationship with Reddy was and is one of the most rewarding of my life."

1940s

1942

Illness forces E. Boyd Morrow to discontinue his duties as headmaster. Edward T. Russell and Meredith Janvier are appointed acting headmasters.

Dr. John M. T. Finney dies, having led the Board of Trustees from 1912 to 1942, longer than any other president before or since.

1943

Henry H. Callard becomes headmaster.

Anne Galbraith Carey, originator of the idea for the Country School, dies.

1947

Gilman School celebrates its 50th anniversary; 43 students graduate. *Gilman Walls Will Echo*, a stylishly-written history of Gilman's first 50 years by Bradford Jacobs '38, is published.

An effort to raise funds for War Memorial Scholarships begins.

First-year lacrosse coach George Chandlee directs an experienced lacrosse team to its first MSA championship, ending St. Paul's famed 72-game winning streak and seven consecutive MSA titles. Captain Richard B. C. Tucker '47, and seniors Robert R. Boyce, Redmond C. S. Finney, William J. Carroll, and Theodore Gould III lead the team and begin a 32-game winning streak. In the championship game against Boys' Latin School, Gilman trails 6–2 with five remaining minutes. Center middie Reddy Finney wins five straight face-offs, and Gilman fires in five unanswered goals, winning the game.

Commando training during World War II. At top of the barricade: Owen Daly II '43. On the ground, Martin L. Millspaugh, Jr. '43 and D. C. Finney '43.

113

Above, Graeme Menzies '47 returned to Gilman to teach in the Lower and Middle School 1956–92, and to coach lacrosse. Here he displays 1940s haberdashery in his senior photo.

Above right, Ludlow Baldwin '22 in his Navy Days. By war's end the future Gilman headmaster had accumulated five Campaign Ribbons and 12 Battle Stars, and retired with the rank of Commander, USNR. He also accumulated a passionate store of knowledge on ancient history from reading *Plutarch's Lives* in the ship's library.

Left, read Gibson Carey's "Adventures and Escapades as a Boarder" and you may come up with a different picture of boarding life from the plush, well-mannered, and studious lifestyle shown in this 1937 photo of a seven-day boarder's room.

Lower right, James C. Pine '21 taught history 1929–70 and was chairman of the history department 1940–70. His father was Frank Pine, headmaster 1912–19.

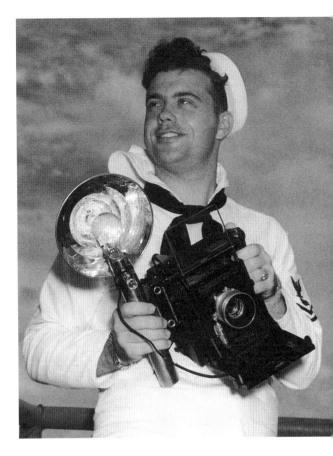

Opposite left, the heavy cruiser U.S.S. *Chicago* was in the Battle of Rennell Island on January 30, 1943. The cruiser suffered partial flooding from torpedo hits the night before and was sunk by Japanese planes the next afternoon. Aboard was Alex Armstrong '33.

Opposite bottom, anti-aircraft fire punctuates the sky near the Pacific island of Tulagi on August 8, 1942. The photograph was taken from the *U.S.S. Chicago*. (The three ship photos are official U.S. Navy photos.)

Above left, Alex Armstrong '33 shows his "Gilman forbearance" in this send-it-home-to-Mom snapshot of the young Navy man with an Hawaiian model taken in 1944 in Honolulu.

Left, torpedo damage to the bow of the *Chicago* is shown in this U. S. Navy photo taken after the Battle of Savo Island, August 9, 1942. An American task force was taken by surprise 2:00 Sunday morning, sinking four cruisers and damaging the *Chicago*.

Above right, Percy Meredith Reese as a U. S. Navy photographer in Puerto Rico, 1941–42. Reese taught and coached at Gilman 1950–79, and was especially known for his Eighth Grade course in ancient history.

Opposite, the Sixth Form Dance Committee of 1943: seated are Owen Daly II, Chairman D. C. Finney, William Gracie. Standing are Randal Beirne, Ralph Thomas, Matthew S. Atkinson III. See Daly's "You Never Quit" and Beirne's "A Time of War."

Roy Barker, top, is one of the most renowned and controversial of Gilman teachers. He taught English at Gilman 1946–82, chaired the English department, expanded and improved the drama department, coached tennis, and was a confidant to three headmasters. Check essays by Tom Fenton '48, Clapham Murray '49, and Mitch Miller '63 for Barker's influence on students' lives.

Left, Waldo Newcomer '48 soliloquizes in "But Not Goodbye."

Thomas L. Lipscomb, known by many as "The Southern Gentleman," taught English at Gilman 1921–63.

Below, Gilman tennis players prepare for practice. Hugh Rienhoff '46, William Blalock '48, George Thomsen '48, Robert Rich '48, William Passano '48, Clapham Murray '49, and William Tytus '48. Be sure to read Murray's mercurial memoir, "In Pursuit of Matters Cultural."

Lawrence Shoemaker '43 looks for extra yardage in a 1942 game.

Jim Gorter '47 connects for a base hit. A member of the football, wrestling, baseball, and track teams, Gorter was a four-sport varsity athlete. In his essay, "A Classmate of Reddy's," Gorter states, "He [Reddy] played center on the football team when I was the tailback. Nick Carter would say, 'Finney, you open the hole and Gorter, you follow him.' It worked."

121

A Time of War

D. RANDALL BEIRNE '43

The decade 1940–1950 was full of change for Gilman and sent the school in new directions. The school had struggled through the years of the Depression under the leadership of E. Boyd Morrow. It was slowly recovering in 1940 when it received the impact of World War II. Gilman, like the country, had to adjust to war austerity from 1940 to 1946.

During this period the school also suffered from the illness of both Mr. Morrow, the headmaster, and of Dr. John M. T. Finney, who had been president of the Board of Trustees for 30 years. Charles S. Garland took over the position of Dr. Finney as president.

Through a series of penny-pinching devices, Mr. Morrow had saved the school financially during the lean 1930s, but worse was to come. By 1941 the war and the unsettled financial situation of parents caused a heavy drop in enrollment. Too many tuitions went unpaid. Most of the administrative personnel and other help left to work in war industries. Mr. Morrow handled this crisis by setting up a student work program assigning the boys to domestic activities such as waiting on tables.

E. Boyd Morrow, "The King," was an intimidating presence. He exerted his strongest and most direct influence on students in the teaching of math, and was a believer in the value of discipline and rote learning. Few First Formers of the early '40s will ever forget their first lessons in discipline in Miles Marrian's math classes. When Mr. Marrian became Major Marrian during the war and taught plebes at West Point, he was considered one of the best teachers the Academy ever had. (Let the chalk fly where it may!) Also associated with this method of teaching was Jim Dresser, who later switched to the new math and introduced the teaching of computers.

One of the key methods of keeping the school solvent during the early '40s was to retain boys whose tuition was paid but not to pass them until they had positively learned what was required. Thus, the school had a number of boys who never seemed to graduate. Too often classes were a mix of bright young boys who hadn't reached puberty, and older, physically mature boys who were almost men. This was fine until the war, when many of the older boys were drafted. Later, some of these boys returned after several years in the service, and Gilman had to find a way to test them and grant diplomas.

A new informality crept into what boys wore. Gilman had always had a serious dress code requiring coats and ties. In 1938, smart blazers were introduced with one pocket covered in gold-and-silver bullion fashioned into the Gilman seal. By 1940, this natty outfit was challenged by some students who wore white, Princeton-type "beer jackets" and jeans, and who justified these as suits. In both cases, the necktie was still a strict requirement.

In 1939 and '40, the sports program was studded with stars. Names like Franke in football, Plitt in ice hockey, Pickett in wrestling and Campbell in lacrosse are still remembered. The 1940 and '41 football teams were some of Gilman's greatest, with two consecutive Maryland A Conference crowns.

George Franke became one of Gilman's all-time greats as he made the All State Team in 1940 and 1941. The combination of his size and speed allowed him to blast through and devastate most opposing teams. His ice hockey mate, Charlie Plitt, became the outstanding hockey player in the city. Together with George Westerlind, Tyler Campbell and others, they dominated Baltimore hockey, becoming so good that they were able to beat some college freshmen teams, including Princeton.

One of the most popular teachers at Gilman, whose career carried over from the Depression into the war years, was Ferris Thomsen. He was athletic director, mathematics teacher, and supervisor of many study halls. Some of the older athletes even had the nerve to call him by his first name. Mr. Thomsen was notorious for collecting notes from his mailbox and stuffing them into his pockets, where they became lost for weeks at a time.

The year 1940 saw the departure of Herbert Pickett, who had started teaching at Gilman in 1913. He had risen to be Mr. Morrow's assistant, but left to start his own school in Cooperstown, N.Y. Many Gilman students knew Mr. Pickett through Hyde Bay Camp, where they worked in the summers as his ULs (unskilled laborers). Few will forget their happy summers there, where regimentation was kept to a minimum. Many spent their morning hours at Hyde Bay being tutored in math by Mr. Marrian and Mr. Dresser, and their afternoon hours engrossed in such enterprises as hunting buried treasure concocted by Walter Lord.*

Gilman was just emerging from the Depression when World War II began in 1939. Although the United States didn't enter the conflict for two more years, Gilman graduates and students willingly volunteered to serve. Most graduates eventually entered military services, and many students summered in factories and

---

*For more on Hyde Bay and Herbert Pickett, read Larry Pickett's "Memoirs of a Faculty Child," Cooper Walker's "Of Ed Russell and Wrestling Reminiscences," and Jamie Spragins' "Theater and Gilman Culture."

on farms to bolster the country's manpower needs. After the United States entered the war in 1941, more military manpower was needed, and by 1942 the government was drafting 18-year-olds out of Gilman's halls and playing fields.

Over 900 Gilman alumni and faculty members saw service. Of those alumni who served, approximately 4.5 percent died. Most of the members of Gilman's classes from 1940 through 1945 served. The statistics by class are as follows:

CLASS	1940	1941	1942	1943	1944	1945
PERCENT SERVED	76	89	91	85	92	55
NUMBER KILLED	4	1	2	4	1	0

One of the first to sacrifice his life was Sam Miles '32, M.D., son of the earlier headmaster, Capt. L. Wardlaw Miles, who was killed in action in Guadalcanal in 1942. A Navy doctor, he was administering to a wounded Japanese prisoner when the prisoner pulled out a grenade and killed them both.

Many older graduates had completed college before entering the service. Some, such as Gilman's class of 1939, were in college when the war began. Tyler Campbell (Marion T.), Jack Thomas (John G., Jr.), and Ned Baetjer (Edwin G.), who were roommates at Princeton, later lost their lives. A total of 38 Gilman alumni and one teacher, John H. Ballantine, Jr., were killed during the war.* Most of those at Gilman or in their first year of college went directly into the services or into a service-controlled college program upon reaching 18. Some became pilots and died on missions or in training. Others served in the Navy and went down with or escaped from their sinking ships. Some won outstanding distinction in combat.

A number from the classes of the early '40s saw much combat, especially those rushed into battle as infantry replacements. Dick Baughman, Tim Lanahan, and Ralph Thomas, all from the class of 1943, and Tyler Campbell '39 and many others died in ground combat between 1943 and 1945. Dick Baughman landed with the first wave on Omaha Beach in Normandy on June 6, 1944 and was killed there. His name is carved on the 1st Division monument that overlooks Omaha Beach.

Others, such as D. C. Finney, Bill Gracie, and John Bissell from the class of 1943, had harrowing combat experiences in Europe. Bill was captured in December 1944 during the Battle of the Bulge. As a P.O.W. he escaped from a prison near Berlin but was re-captured and placed in solitary confinement. Later, while on a work detail, he escaped again and finally reached American lines. John Bissell, who discovered at a Gilman reunion that he had been in the same infantry division as D. C., suffered the loss of part of his hand.

In 1939, faculty members began to leave for service. By 1943, 16 faculty members had left, and students began taking over administrative jobs. Older faculty took on more students and extra duties in the athletic department and administration.

---

*A list of the 38 alumni and faculty members who lost their lives in war is given in the appendix.

Football lost Nick Carter and Red Massey. Miles Marrian went to teach at West Point, while George Chandlee, who had left Gilman to go to Cooperstown with Herbert Pickett, became an Army hospital technician.

Faculty member Tom "Hank" Greenough was a large man who had starred in football in college. He addressed each student at Gilman as "meatball." As coach of the 100-pound football team, he loved to lift each player by the belt and physically place him into a position. In 1939, he received word that he had been accepted by the American Field Service to serve in France. Motivated by his selection, he went out and celebrated on a school night. The next morning Mr. Morrow saw no reason for the celebration: he ended Hank's teaching career at Gilman. A year later an article appeared in The Baltimore *Sun* relating a breathtaking story of Hank's capture by the Germans, his breakout of a prison train by overpowering the guards, and his escape to England.*

Alex Armstrong '33 joined the Navy in August of 1940. Within a month after Pearl Harbor he was on a transport going out to join the U. S. S. *Chicago*, a heavy cruiser. The *Chicago* fought in the Coral Sea Battle, was attacked by Japanese midget subs in Sydney harbor, and was part of the occupying task force at Guadalcanal on August 7, 1942. Two days later, it had its bow blown off in the night Battle of Savo Island. With a new bow, it returned to action and was sunk in the Battle of Rennell Island on January 31, 1943. By that time Armstrong had become Senior Radar Control Officer.**

Ludlow Baldwin '22 was also in some of the thickest fighting in the Pacific. He had been working at Terminal Warehouse 1933–42, eventually becoming president, a position he liked because it provided him with a springboard into activities in the City. He enlisted in the Navy at the age of 36 on January 7, 1941. "I enlisted because I was sure that if I'd allowed myself to become an officer, they would have made me something in the Port of Baltimore, in charge of warehousing or something, and that wasn't my idea of going into the Navy or into the war."

When Baldwin went down to the old Post Office to enlist, he was interviewed by an acquaintance who had worked for him on the Willkie campaign. Baldwin had been chairman of the "Democrats for Willkie," and his interviewer had been one of Baldwin's division officers.

Baldwin relates the story as follows: "My interlocutor said to me, 'You, Ludlow, don't want to be just a Seaman Third Class. Isn't there something I can make of you?'

"'I don't know anything you can make me,' I said.

"'Have you ever shot a gun?'

"'Sure,' I said.

"'Well then, we'll make you Aviation Ordinanceman Third Class,' he said. This was the greatest thing in the world because after Boot Camp at Norfolk they imme-

---

*Thomas O. Greenough taught English, history, and geography at Gilman 1937–39.

**Though grateful for survival, Armstrong, who taught English at Gilman 1951–79, bemoans the loss of a new Hohner accordion that had cost 54 pounds in Sydney.

diately shipped me out to a carrier, the USS *Wasp*, up in Maine's Portland Harbor."

One day the Squadron Commander of the *Wasp's* dive bombers asked Baldwin why he didn't put in for aviation training. Baldwin replied that at 36 he was a little over age for rank.

"How about your education?" the commander asked.

"What do you want to know?" replied Baldwin.

"You went through high school?"

"Yes, I did."

"Did you go on to college?"

"Yes, Johns Hopkins."

"Did you go any further?"

"Yes, Harvard Law School."

"All right," he said, "I'm putting you up for officership."

Though unwilling to discuss his battle experiences, Baldwin expounds on the direct relationship between being in the Navy and deciding to go into teaching.* "I had, ever since law school, lodged in the back of my mind that I wanted to be a Baltimorean and help out in things in the City. Indeed, in my summers off from law school I had a very good job at a bank in New York, and they wanted me back after graduation. I took my job in the Baltimore Trust Company at about half the pay I would have gotten in New York because I wanted to be a Baltimorean.

"I had developed a taste for service and usefulness, and my experiences being on charity boards gave me the feeling that I really wasn't accomplishing much, and that it would be better to get into a line of activity, or profession, where my livelihood was identified with an undertaking of direct use to the community.

"While I was floating around in the Pacific for three and a half years, I thought more and more about teaching, and I was reading a great deal of stuff, particularly having to do, oddly, with ancient history. Our library on the carrier was rather extensive, including *Plutarch's Lives,* and histories of Greece and Rome and the Middle East."

After the war, Baldwin enrolled in graduate school at Hopkins to study archaeology, ancient history and Greek. First, he went to Henry Callard, by now Gilman's headmaster, to ask how to get a job in the public schools. Callard sent him down to City College, where the principal said he had no course in ancient history and besides, he couldn't hire Baldwin because he had no teaching credits. At the time Baldwin was a graduate of City College, Gilman (a year of post-graduate work), Johns Hopkins, Harvard Law School, and was halfway through a master's.

Baldwin returned to Callard, who told him, "While you're working on your master's next year, come and teach ancient history at Gilman. Take one section, and we'll pay you $500." Baldwin finished his degree, married Anne Gordon Boyce, and the following year was hired full-time to teach three sections of ancient history, and

---

*Ludlow Baldwin's battle experiences and awards are listed on page 209 of Ambler Moss's "Ludlow Baldwin: Master of the Socratic Method and the Personal Touch."

Bible. Thus began the career in education of one of Gilman's future headmasters.

As the war progressed Gilman seniors took over more and more faculty administrative jobs. Fortunately, those who had served at Hyde Bay Camp as counselors had had experience working with small boys. Members of the Sixth Form Committee took turns for five-day duty in the cubicles on the boarding corridor. Those who had never worked with young boys before learned to be fathers in a hurry.

Local military activities, as well as returning graduates and faculty in the service, kept the students mindful of the battles being fought. Tanks rolled down Roland Avenue. Enlisted faculty members dropped by to visit the school. John Ballantine, a former teacher of mathematics, visited students and was later killed in action. When a student with a brother in the service was suddenly called home from school, other students suspected that his parents were having to break bad news to him.

Gilman organized programs to get students physically and mentally prepared for war. An obstacle course was built and all boys were required to master the course. Don Hoffman, a faculty member who had been badly gassed in World War I, organized rifle training and selected students who were taught how to shoot.

The curriculum had to be adjusted to accommodate the needs of the armed services. Emphasis was placed on teaching advanced math and navigation. With over 50 boys anticipating the draft upon reaching the age of 18 in 1943, the school accelerated programs so that a boy could receive his diploma upon his 18th birthday.

Gas rationing reduced the use of private automobiles. Gilman, as an educational institution, had priority in the issuance of gas coupons. Boys from Baltimore County took the Northern Central train into Mount Washington where a school station wagon met them at the station and took them up to the school. Other students walked, rode bikes, or depended on public transportation.

In 1944, the Army-Navy game in Philadelphia was canceled because of wartime restrictions on rail traffic. Instead, the West Point cadets were allowed to have a "training mission;" they traveled by boat to Baltimore to meet Navy. Gilman furnished quarters for the great Army team that made famous the names of Glen Davis and "Doc" Blanchard. German prisoners, incarcerated at Fort Meade, were called in to help prepare cubicles at Gilman for the team. While the midshipmen arrived in Baltimore by bus, the entire cadet corps arrived by boat.

Headlines blazed from the Gilman *News*:

ARMY TEAM HERE
BEFORE BIG GAME
VICTORIOUS TEAM SLEEPS OVERNIGHT;
MR. LIPSCOMB SUPERVISES
SLEEPING ARRANGEMENTS

The reporter points out that Mr. Callard and Mr. Russell each took a few players into their own houses, there not being enough room on the boarding corridors for the full squad of 55 players, and continues: "While the team was at Gilman, they requested that the place be as quiet as possible; consequently, Mr. Callard asked the student body not to disturb the guests in any way. Saturday all conditional classes were canceled, as was demerit work, and everyone was requested to keep away from the school. The boarders remaining at school waited on the tables when the squad had meals."

After whipping Navy, the Army team marched from the city stadium, now called Memorial Stadium, back to Canton, reboarded, and steamed down the Bay into the ocean and through the U-boat infested waters to West Point.

By 1942, Headmaster Morrow was too ill to take an active part in running the school. Ed Russell was so well liked by students, faculty, and parents that the Board felt he was the ideal man to deal with these three groups. Meredith Janvier, on the other hand, had handled much administration for Mr. Morrow, and the Board felt he could handle this part of the Headmaster's job most effectively. Mr. Russell and Mr. Janvier became acting headmasters.

Mr. Russell ("Uncle Ed") is remembered as one of the most popular teachers Gilman ever had. Generations of Gilman alumni tell stories about Ed, his wife Florence, and his highly successful wrestling program. One story concerns his pipe, burning sparks, and a student remarking, "Mr. Russell, sir, you are on fire." And so he was! Another concerns Ferris Thomsen, who was trying to keep the attention of his class, when suddenly a finger protruded through a hole over a doorknob and waggled at the class. Ferris, finally losing patience, swatted at the finger with a ruler and pulled open the classroom door. Whom should he see but Ed Russell holding his damaged finger!

Mr. Russell and Mr. Janvier weren't the only faculty members who took over many extra duties to keep the school running. Dick O'Brien, a knowledgeable and inspiring French teacher, managed the Lower School for four years in addition to his regular schedule of classes. Others who took over key jobs and continued on at the school under Mr. Callard were Adolay Hausmann, Jim Dresser, Jimmy Pine, Tom Lipscomb, Alfred Townsend, Ferris Thomsen, Don Hoffman, and Dr. P. J. P. Oscarson.

Dr. Oscarson, known to the boys as "Doc," is remembered for his lengthy stay at the school and for his mastery of many languages. The boys always heard he was writing a book that linked all these languages. A large, easy-going person, he was often the target of student pranks. One afternoon a mischievous student tied a carrot to the end of a string and lowered it from the second floor so that it dangled outside the window of Dr. Oscarson's classroom. Also attached was a note that said, "What's up, Doc?"—the infamous greeting used by Bugs Bunny.

The arrival of Henry Callard in 1943 was a major turning point in the school. Having suffered through the Depression, the impact of the war, and the illness of Mr. Morrow, the school needed new leadership and direction. In Henry Callard the school received not only a gentle, kind, understanding man, but also perhaps the best mind on the faculty.

Mr. Callard believed that students should be taught citizenship and responsibility. They should be aware of current events and issues. To carry this out he stressed broader training and more reading.

He also felt that school responsibility was in the hands of too few students. The old Sixth Form Committee was not representative of the student body. He organized a Student Council that drew from the four upper forms.

A strong advocate of community service, Mr. Callard believed the school had become isolated. He felt the school should foster student involvement in the community. To diversify the student body he recommended giving more scholarships to well-qualified boys.

The inauguration of the scholarship program had to wait until the war ended. Begun in 1947, the scholarship program served to honor the 39 alumni and faculty lost during the war. Each scholarship was named for one of the deceased. By 1948, nine boys had been awarded War Memorial Scholarships, totaling $3,500.

Mr. Callard thought boys should learn to work with their hands. He encouraged work projects as part of community service. In addition, he introduced an industrial arts program. Shop became a respected course, and boys looked forward to exercising originality in their creations. (Few remember that 1922–24, while Mr. Callard was an undergraduate at Johns Hopkins, he taught crafts and assisted in athletics part-time in the Lower School.)

As an administrator, Mr. Callard was fortunate to have Miss May Holmes as his secretary. Having an incredible memory, he kept almost no records. He never wrote things down and yet could remember every word he had had with a parent a year earlier. His desk was a mess, but he could reach into a pile of papers and bring out whatever he needed.

Mr. Callard always had the interest of Gilman first in his decisions. He led by example. He was often seen performing some physical activity to improve the looks of the school. On one occasion he came into "A" study hall with a bucket and several empty cans and went around the room bleeding all the radiators. Fascinated students stopped studying to watch.

Throughout the Depression and war years Gilman struggled to survive and had made few changes in the curriculum. Mr. Callard, from the start, implemented changes. Art and music were introduced in the Middle and Upper Schools. Although art had been taught in the Lower School, neither art nor music had been part of the course of study in the Upper School. In addition, religion was added.

When the war ended, most of the pre-war faculty who had been in the service trickled back. Nick Carter and Red Massey returned and quickly took up coaching again. Carter resumed the leadership of the football team, which since 1943 had been coached by Ferris Thomsen, Ed Russell and Jim Dresser. Lt. Col. Miles Marrian returned and found that teaching at Gilman was not the same as teaching at West Point. To forestall too many meetings with parents, Mr. Marrian scheduled meetings for 7 a.m. in his office. Other memorable impressions of Mr. Marrian persist. Alumni still remember his most common comment on their math paper, "CTCWP," (Coming to class without pencil).

When the student body increased rapidly at the end of the war, Mr. Callard set out to recruit new teachers, some of whom were to leave their imprint on the school for the next 30 years. Roy Barker was a gifted English teacher who stressed writing skills and creative art. Charlie Gamper arrived in 1946 and initially taught geography, French, and math. Later he became baseball coach. Gamper succeeded Adolay Hausmann in 1958 as Gilman's athletic director. He held the post for 10 years, retiring in 1968. Gamper was also president of the Maryland Scholastic Association for 12 years, 1973–84.

"Becoming president of the MSA was one of the nicest honors that I ever experienced," notes Gamper. "The MSA was the only such organization in the country that did what we did—private, public, or parochial. It was one of the greatest things this town had, to see the coming together of all of these schools and their ability to understand each other, the ability to get along. We had our arguments. We had the riot down at Dunbar, which has been smoothed over by now—it took a long while. I feel that without the MSA, the City of Baltimore would have had much more in the way of racial problems than it did have."

Gamper was nicknamed The Duck by his students—in study hall when he yelled, "Quiet!" it sounded very close to "quack."

Another master who came out of the service at this time was John Robinson. An inspiring teacher, Robinson taught in the Lower School for 15 years and was the basketball coach of many successful varsity teams.

Page Smith, who later received national recognition, including being selected to the Book of the Month Club and winning the Kenneth Roberts Memorial Award for his biography of John Adams, arrived in 1946 to teach English. Smith, from the class of 1936, had been badly wounded in Italy. After teaching a year at Gilman, he left to work on his Ph.D. at Harvard under Admiral Samuel Eliot Morrison.

Major changes took place in the science curriculum. Gilman graduates had usually done well in the arts, but in college many had difficulty with science. Only in biology had they been able to compete with other schools. A few Gilman students who wanted to pursue engineering had felt it necessary to transfer to Poly. All this changed in 1947 when Bill Porter joined the faculty and proceeded to strengthen the physics and chemistry courses. In 1962, a new science building was completed, and Porter himself was recognized by the American Association of Physics Teachers for his "exceptional competence in subject matter."

After the war Gilman quickly gained eminence in lacrosse. During the early '40s the sport had been dominated by St. Paul's School. When Ferris Thomsen left Gilman to coach lacrosse at the university level, George Chandlee stepped in and built four championship Maryland Scholastic Association teams in a row. These teams were led by some of Gilman's greatest players: Bo Willis, Cy Horine, Alan Hoblitzell, and Charles Stout.

The 1940s represent one of Gilman's most turbulent periods as well as a period of growth. By 1950, under Mr. Callard's leadership, the problems of operating a boys' school in wartime had receded, the school was solvent for the first time in 20 years, and a new, broader philosophy of commitment and community service was in place.

Coming to Gilman in the fall of 1937, D. Randall Beirne soon became a very busy Gilman student and athlete, with his favorite teacher/coaches being Miles Marrian (math), Ed Russell (wrestling), Ed Brown (geography), Dick O'Brien (French), and Ferris Thomsen (lacrosse). By his senior year he had served as associate editor of the *Cynosure*, the *News*, and *The Blue and The Gray*. Beirne was a three-year man on the varsity lacrosse, wrestling, and football teams.

Upon graduation, Beirne went to the United States Military Academy (West Point), where he majored in engineering and continued a strong interest in geography. From 1948 to 1962, Beirne worked his way up to Major, while being stationed in Korea, Germany and finally, Gettysburg College. From 1963 to 1965, he taught physics at Loyola High School, while earning a Masters at Johns Hopkins. In 1965, he began teaching at the University of Baltimore, while also earning a doctorate in geography from the University of Maryland. Between 1965 and 1994, Beirne taught geography, anthropology, sociology and science at the University of Baltimore.

Beirne's father, Francis F. Beirne, graduated from the Homewood campus of what was then called The Country School for Boys in 1908, and was a member of the Board of Trustees of Gilman 1935–50, and a Trustee Emeritus until his death in 1972. Beirne's son, Daniel, is a 1977 graduate of Gilman.

You Never Quit

OWEN DALY II '43

I t didn't always happen then, and it certainly is not necessarily true today, but it is not altogether rare that the best octave in a young man's life is between the ages of 11 and 18. To have it happen to a large extent at Gilman School was a great opportunity and experience, cherished by many for a lifetime.

It may be difficult to think of Gilman's First Form Upper School as a pseudo-melting pot way back in 1937, but my classmates and I came from some varied economic circumstances in the struggling Thirties. Many of us moved up from the Lower School; just as many came from Calvert, but a significant smattering also emerged from Roland Park Public, Miss Fry's, the Normal School (Towson Elementary), Timonium Elementary, and as far away as Annapolis. And with what were then anxious and inquiring minds, some 40-plus students were unceremoniously squeezed into "A" Study Hall for morning chapel. You shared a desk with an upper former from September to June, and it wasn't long before you knew everyone in the Upper School. (You always knew the guys ahead of you!) Soon we adjusted to our home base of "K" Study Hall and proceeded to find our way to the various classrooms we would frequent for the next six years.

The teaching styles of our masters were as varied as our primary school origins. Miles Marrian's mathematics class in Room 18 was, and is, a living saga of "undivided attention or else" that remains with Gilman alumni to their dying day. If your pencil rolled off the inclined bench desk, you picked it off the floor and placed it on his desk. It was his pencil from then on. Mr. Pine's geography class was a classic. Who can forget him rubbing his hands across his face at some inattentive student's inane question, all the while peeking through his fingers at the class reaction? Tom Lipscomb was the consummate gentleman from Virginia, who persuaded many that proper English grammar and composition could be fun. He was also a whiz at handling a tough passage of Second Form Latin, but you had to catch him upstairs in his apartment, which would be filled with the sweet scent of pipe smoke, five minutes before morning chapel.

We had our athletic teams too. Hank Greenough's 100-pound football team wasn't too much to talk about. Mr. Lipscomb at the 110-pound bracket would drill us in the fundamentals, and before it was scrimmage time, he would invoke the World War I cry, "We'll have some of the cold steel now, boys." Mr. Marrian had coached football, basketball, and baseball in the Lower School, but the graduate course came on the 120s, where he still offered Andy Kerr's (Colgate's coach) double wing formation with a balanced line. This symmetrical formation of the day was perfectly in keeping with the dedicated and orderly mind of this bionic man, whom many still regard as a paragon—in the classroom or on the field.

On the not-so-much fun side of the game, a few of us took our blows early in the season, and we still can remember Walter Dandy, among others, with a cast on a knee or an ankle by the first week in October—three years in a row.

By the Third Form we had some additional "leavening" with the arrival of Rene Crouch and Tim Stobbart from England. They were sent here by their parents to avoid the Nazi bombs. At about the same time, in Mr. Markriter's English class, we became conversant with the works of their late countryman, William Shakespeare.

It was also about this time that some openings and opportunities appeared for us in the other activities within the school, such as the *News*, *The Blue and The Gray*, Literary Club, Christian Association, Dramatic Club, and others. We did some nudging into some varsity teams, too. It wasn't hard to realize why math teacher and basketball coach, Bill Formalt, deserved the 14 letters he earned in college—if you ever challenged him for a rebound under the basket.

Many of my friends were wrestlers. After weighing in the morning of a meet, they were invited to Ed and Florence Russell's for tea (lots of sugar), orange juice, eggs, bacon, and toast with strawberry jam. Good wrestling teams continued, and in the next two years under Nick Carter, we were MSA football co-champions. Besides our modest claims to success on the field, and to show we were somehow very tough, we substituted some new lyrics to the "Battle Hymn of the Republic."

> "We block on trees by day
> and we slide on roads by night
> And we work in the factories
> Till our muscles are just right."*

Then came Pearl Harbor and change. Teachers in a mounting wave began to leave for various branches of the service. By the fall of 1942, at least ten had gone, and Messrs. Russell and Janvier replaced a very ill Boyd Morrow as acting co-head-

---

*Owen Daly and classmate Carroll Jackson worked at Booz Brothers Shipyard, directly across from Domino Sugar in the Inner Harbor, for 40 cents an hour over the summers. Other teammates worked at Western Maryland Freightyard at Port Covington and at Crown, Cork & Seal. Over Christmas of 1942, Daly and classmates delivered mail. "The best job of all was to deliver the mail in one of the big army trucks."

masters. Transportation changed drastically, and we even rode the street car to Homewood Field to play McDonogh. We came out of a warm gym to a frigid 40-knot wind to start the second half. I held the ball for D. C. Finney—president of our class for four years straight—at kickoff and automatically became the safety man. A good McDonogh back carried it 95 yards for a touchdown. To this day a few of us don't know where we were on that play. I was shivering and miserable; I must have "relaxed" for a moment. We lost 14–12. I finally learned—you never quit, not even for a second, never!

Our social life consisted of a movie at the Century or Keiths Theater downtown and maybe a chocolate shake at the Nibble and Klink, catty-corner from the current Senator Theater. (You'd drive in, park, and they'd slap a tray to the side of your car.) School dances also became part of the growing pains, and negotiating with the local orchestra leaders was often a lesson in futility.

The boarding corridors were full at this time, partially because of the gas rationing; yet, the school was short of masters to monitor the boarders. During the week, two of us on the six-member Sixth Form Committee would spend the night at Gilman from Sunday through Thursday. The five-day boarders would go home on Friday, and over the weekend one of us would stay on the corridors. Bill Gracie, from Cumberland, was a very popular boarder, and the most exciting night for a boarder consisted of watching Bill Gracie's movies.

We had a great class. We all worked well with the acting headmasters. In April, 1943, the Sixth Form Committee was taken to the home of Mr. Garland, the new president of the Board of Trustees, to "participate" in the selection of Henry Callard as our new headmaster. What a way to wind up a Gilman experience!

As I look back some 50-odd years later, I don't believe any member of the faculty could have had a selfish bone in his body. How could there be when sometimes he was on call 24 hours a day for all of $1,600 a year? These were masters in a very real sense. The likes of Russell and Marrian, Lipscomb and Pine, Townsend and Hausmann, Dresser and O'Brien, Brown and Carter, don't come along every day, and fortunately their work is not yet completed. For in a teacher or a coach, it is not easy to measure his ultimate success in his profession; you never know when his influence will end. You only know that it lasts for generations. And—that's the way it was at Gilman.

Owen Daly II attended Gilman 1936–43, in 1937 winning the Gold Medal for Scholarship in the Lower School. In the Upper School, his favorite teacher was Miles Marrian. As associate editor of the *News*, *Cynosure*, and *The Blue and The Gray*, Daly showed an early interest in writing, editing, and journalism. He also sang, was a member of the Areopagus Debating Team, and was vice president of his class his junior and senior years.

Daly played on the varsity football, basketball, and baseball teams, and one year on the varsity lacrosse squad. He was co-captain of the varsity basketball team during the 1941–42 season and captain during the 1942–43 season. In the spring, Daly jogged back and forth from the diamond to the tennis court, winning the Senior Tennis Cup in 1941, '42, '43, and the Junior Tennis Cup in 1939, '40. At graduation he won the William Cabell Bruce Athletic Cup.

Three weeks after graduation, Daly entered the V-12 program, through which he attended college for 14 months before being sent to midshipmen school at Northwestern University. He then spent a year and a half in the Pacific as Assistant Gunnery Officer on the destroyer USS *Compton*. Out of the Navy in the summer of 1946, he entered Princeton in September and graduated—in an accelerated program with a heavy course load—in June of 1948.

The youthful veteran began working at the Mercantile-Safe Deposit and Trust in 1948. In the fall of 1950, he was called up by the Navy for the Korean War. He returned to Mercantile in 1952, where he remained until moving to Equitable Trust Co. in 1965. From 1967 to 1982, he was president and then chairman of the Equitable Trust and Equitable Bank Corporation. Daly is married to Marian Riggs Bailliere Daly. They have four boys, two of whom, Owen III '70 and Clinton '74, attended Gilman.

Son of O. Gordon Daly '12, Owen Daly has been a trustee of Gilman since 1952. He was president of the Board 1969–75, during which time Gilman launched and concluded its first major capital campaign, for $6 million, headed up by Daly's classmate Richard Thomas.

A Letter from London

TOM FENTON '48

I don't know whether he planned it that way. Perhaps I give him too much credit, but the evening Roy Barker spent with me in Paris in 1961 was a major turning point. He nudged my life in a direction that has taken me from Baltimore to Samarkand, and a thousand points in between.

Some of the details are dim now. It was 32 years ago, but I believe we finished off an entire bottle of cognac. Very good stuff, too.

There were questions, the kind you would expect from an English teacher to a former student, 13 years out of Gilman and nine years a naval officer. I thought I was one of his better students, but Roy never said that. Instead, he asked what had I been writing since then?

"Mostly fitness reports, Roy. That's what you do in the Navy."

Well, it didn't take long for that to sink in. Simone says I spent a number of sleepless nights after that, endlessly discussing with her what I should do. The answer was preordained. I chucked my plans to go to business school, just as I had earlier dumped law school to marry Simone.

Did Roy know what that decision cost? I gave up a life of what could have been respectability. The road from the European Business School was supposed to lead from Fontainebleau to the upper echelons of the big multinationals. The road that I took led to dingy police stations in the urban blight of 1960s Baltimore.

The first job was hard to find. It was the Baltimore *Sun* that finally hired a former naval officer with no experience in anything except destroyer tactics and the delights of foreign travel. It did not take long to find out why no experience was needed.

The police beat was where you began. You rarely *wrote* anything, of course. You dictated details to a rewrite man in the City Room. Still, I will never forget my first story. It is gathering dust in a trunk somewhere, a three-line filler proudly pasted on the first page of my first scrapbook. It was a $1.69 purse snatch.

Did Roy read the item? Or my next find, a story about a dead mule somewhere in South Baltimore?

The only qualities required for what I was doing in those early days were the ability to wheedle a few details out of a desk sergeant and a knack for reading a police blotter upside down. Come to think of it, that's about all you need to be a journalist.

Surely Roy must have read my first front-page story. I was in the City Room when the hurricane hit the Eastern Shore. Old Caulfield scanned the half-empty room from the city editor's chair, and focused on me—now inside and doing obits.

"Fenton, you got a car?"

"YES, SIR!"

That's about all I owned in those days on a salary that was too small to permit such luxuries as the payment of rent. We were living rent-free in my uncle's stables.

By the time I got back from Rehoboth Beach, my heart-rending description of the devastation of the beach resort of my childhood was bannered on the front page, with a BYLINE. That's what The *Sun* usually gave you in lieu of a raise. I bought a dozen copies of the paper from the first newspaper stand I saw. I haven't reread the story since then. Probably just as well.

In retrospect, I realize these were wonderful days for me and lousy days for Simone. She was raising a family on wages that would qualify us these days for food stamps.

We hit the gravy train when The *Sun* sent me overseas after five years in Baltimore. The paper in those days was a family affair, remarkably stingy in paying its local staff, but lavish with expenses when it came to its foreign correspondents. There were no fewer than six of them, for a paper with a circulation of only 200,000.

Going abroad was like going from night to day. As a local reporter, I had to present the managing editor's secretary with the stub of a pencil to get a new one. All that changed the day her boss, Buck Dorsey, called me into his office and said I was the new Rome Correspondent. First class air travel. An apartment full of 18th century antiques in Rome. And, oh yes, a full-time maid who couldn't believe I owned only one pair of shoes.

There was no turning back. Buck Dorsey let you more or less write your own ticket. I went where I wanted, wrote what I wanted, and The *Sun* printed it all: a medieval banquet at the court of Haile Selassie, a revolt in the Horn of Africa, a trip into the wild interior of Royalist Yemen, the Six Day War, arrest and internment in Egypt. It's all a blur now, half-remembered moments of a life on the road with new wonders at every turning. By this time, I was beginning to thank Roy for saving me from respectability. This was much more fun.

The *Sun* sent me to Paris, where I eventually jumped ship and signed on with CBS News. CBS sent me back to Rome, then to Tel Aviv (for another Arab-Israeli war), on to Paris, and finally to London as the Chief European Correspondent.

That wasn't the end of my writing, Roy. Now I speak what I write, and use (. . .)

instead of punctuation. But even after 22 years in front of the camera, I still watch my grammar. You may be listening.

My life with CBS is spent on the treadmill of history . . . wars, revolutions, coups, the end of communism, the end of the Soviet Union, the end of Yugoslavia, and no end of excitement. To quote another Baltimore *Sun* alumnus, it beats working.

What if you hadn't dropped by to see me in Paris? I sometimes think about that. Fenton the big shot Washington lawyer? Fenton the corporate raider? Or even Tom and Simone running a little hotel somewhere in Provence (with perhaps a mention in the *Michelin*). But all that is the road not taken.

No regrets, Roy. I wouldn't have it any other way.

 His favorite Gilman teacher being Roy Barker, Tom Fenton was president of the dramatic association, feature editor of the *News*, editor-in-chief of the *Cynosure*, and a member of the Literary Club and the Areopagus Debating Club in his senior year at Gilman. Fenton was a two-year member of the varsity track team, and when not writing, editing, or debating, could be found at the easel, painting. At graduation he won the Sixth Form prize for scholarship and was a co-winner of the Latin prize. The prophecy in the yearbook came close to hitting the target: "Winner of Gold Oscar for movie script. . . ."

Fenton majored in English and American literature at Dartmouth. Upon graduation in 1952, he joined the Navy, where he served until 1959. From 1959 to 1966, Fenton worked as a local reporter at The Baltimore *Sun*; 1966–68 as The *Sun's* Rome correspondent; 1968–70 as the Paris correspondent. In 1970 Fenton went to work for *CBS News*, as the Rome correspondent 1970–73, Tel Aviv Correspondent 1973–77, and Paris correspondent 1977–79.

Since 1979, Fenton has been the Senior European Correspondent of *CBS News*, stationed in London 1979–94, and in Moscow in 1994. In a quarter century as a foreign correspondent, Fenton has covered most of the major stories in Europe and the Middle East. For the future, he hopes "to keep on flying to hot spots." He and his wife, Simone France Fenton, have two children, Ariane and Thomas.

The Heart of the Matter

WALDO NEWCOMER '48

For me, the essence of Gilman was no single teacher, no single experience, not even several. Rather, Gilman was scores of experiences, events, and relationships—academic, athletic, and personal—within a fine ethical framework of sportsmanship and integrity. We were richly challenged in mind, body, and spirit. We thus learned much about ourselves, and forged and tested key traits of character, at least a few of which have endured over the ensuing five decades. Work hard, persevere, be considerate of others, be sportsmanlike—gracious in either victory or defeat—do your share and more, help others, strive to do your best; the list is long but its focal points are tolerance and integrity. Within these two can be subsumed almost all the traits of importance.

The teachers did it. Who else? All were at least very good (if not, they did not return). Many were great—Roy Barker, Jim Pine, Charlie Gamper, Tom Lipscomb, Ed Russell, Doc Oscarson, Al Townsend, Ad Hausmann, Jim Dresser, Ferris Thomsen. Beyond being our classroom teachers, they were our coaches for both intramural and varsity sports, and our referees and umpires at the intramural and JV levels. They were also our counselors and advisers for extra-curricular activities. And some had administrative duties, for in fact it was the teachers who ran the school. Good thing, too, for the school and for us.

What resulted was a surprisingly integrated personal environment—with Henry Callard a larger-than-life figure over it all—in which we studied about, saw in others, and had personal experience with issues fundamental to our future lives. In history and the great literature of the world, we read about and came to understand on one level fundamental issues about the humanity—and sometimes inhumanity—of mankind. Few of us were interested in the Greeks and Romans, medieval history, and the Renaissance; I certainly was not. But as we went on to study Shakespeare, Lamb, Emerson, Hardy, and others, we saw these same themes played out in novels, poetry, drama, and essays. The seemingly daily essays we had to write made us think through these issues for ourselves. And in all the aspects of our daily lives at the school—classes, athletics, study hall and homework, work details, and extra-curricular activities—our teachers/coaches/advisers reinforced these principles in our behavior. For Gilman's Honor Code, and its stress on sportsmanship on and off the field, was founded on these same principles.

This did not make us philosophers, or even scholars; it did give us practical, strong principles upon which to build our lives and our relationships with others. We learned by doing how to think through for ourselves many of the kinds of issues that would confront us in life. Of course, not all was learned at Gilman. Family, friends, other schools and institutions all had their impact before, during and after our Gilman years. Most, it is fair to say, has been learned—sometimes relearned—in the University of Life. Gilman focused, as no other institution has, on the issues embodied in *tolerance* and *integrity*. Gilman built the foundation.

Tolerance. Now I must confess to two favorite teachers: Jim Pine and Roy Barker. They are my favorites because they made interesting, challenging, and worth doing two subject areas in which I had no interest, no inclination, no ability—history and English. Roy and Jim therefore get the main credit—along with Henry Callard—for whatever I learned at Gilman about tolerance for other viewpoints, ideas, philosophies. For both history and literature reflect a wide range of concepts and philosophies; both are also replete with examples of actions taken in intolerance, and the sometimes cruel consequences thereof.

Tolerance, we discovered, goes far beyond accepting as peers people who differ from us. It goes beyond reaching out to understand them, their experiences, and their viewpoints. Tolerance also means listening to and debating thoughts and ideas which may even be abhorrent to us. For we also discover, in doing so, that we clarify and thus strengthen our own thinking as we seek to rebut, not always successfully, positions contrary to ours. And sometimes—just sometimes—we can even find in the most extremist views the germ of an idea that can be developed into something useful. One of the greatest strengths of this nation is its diversity—of races, religions, and ethnic origins—and therefore of beliefs, objectives, and priorities. We have tolerated and ought to tolerate even the extremists in our midst. Without them to spur our thinking and rouse our passions, we might sit comfortably secure in the rightness of our views while the world, in constant flux, changes around us. To us students, however, that all seemed pretty heady stuff to be inculcated with; 50 years later it still does, perhaps because it has worked.

Integrity. Gilman was not subtle about integrity. The Honor Code was omnipresent. It stared us in the face each morning as we walked in; sat on our shoulders throughout the day, whether in class, study hall, or work detail, or on the athletic field; and went home with us at night. Here were high standards, clearly stated, and strictly adhered to, and the responsibility was solely our own, individually. No excuses. An explanation might be useful to learn from, but no excuses.

Holding to one's integrity is rather easy when those around you do the same. Gilman may have provided a level playing field, but the world at large does not. "Ready, protect yourself, wrestle," has been a useful metaphor. Life outside of

Gilman and since continually tests the depth and strength of what Gilman taught us. No one of us is perfect, and we do have legitimate rights as individuals; so the classic struggle of good versus evil repeats itself in each of us. We do things we are proud of, things we are ashamed of. But no triumph is sweet if not fairly won; and in times of despair our own integrity is the foundation upon which we stand and rebuild. More particularly, many decisions we face in life—and surely the most difficult and agonizing ones—require choosing among competing moral imperatives. It is our integrity at the core of our character that gives us the courage to do so and the equanimity to accept the results.

And that is the heart of the matter.

Waldo "Bo" Newcomer's main intellectual interests at Gilman were in mathematics and physics, with his favorite teacher/coaches being Roy Barker, English; Jim Pine, history; and Charlie Gamper, baseball. A member of the varsity football and baseball teams, Newcomer, in his senior year, was vice-president of the Dramatic Association, vice-president of the Areopagus Debating Club, a member of the Literary Club, managing editor of the *News*, secretary of the Sixth Form, and a student council member. At graduation he was awarded the William A. Fisher Medallion, the Gold Medal for the Head of the Upper School, the Sixth Form Speaking Prize, and the Mathematics Prize.

Newcomer attended the Massachusetts Institute of Technology, where he majored in engineering and business and played on both the football and lacrosse teams. Upon graduation he signed on with the Navy, remaining on active duty as a carrier pilot 1952–57, and serving in the reserves 1957–63. From 1957 to 1974, Newcomer was on the Senior Staff and from 1974 to 1981, the Consultant Staff, of Arthur D. Little, Inc. From 1981 to 1988, he was a partner at Canny, Bowen Inc. Newcomer and his wife, Linda, live in Florida and are the parents of Laura and John.

In Pursuit of
Matters Cultural

CLAPHAM MURRAY '49

Fifty years ago, my father, Clapham Murray, was reminiscing about his Gilman days for Brad Jacobs, who was putting together a book about Gilman's first 50 years, and now, 50 years later, I am doing the same thing. Oddly enough, as my father was reliving his Homewood days, I was experiencing Gilman on Roland Avenue. I remember thinking, Fifty years, such a long time ago; how could my father have been part of such ancient history? He was the oldest living graduate, a distinction he held, I think, from the moment he received his diploma, and a distinction of which he and I were very proud. He returned to the school once when I was a student, and delivered his famous "Let the Bells Ring Forth" speech, modeled upon his Ciceronian orations against "Lucius Goodwinicus," Lawrence Goodwin, his 1903 classmate. I feigned embarrassment, but for a lifetime, whether on stage or before a body of students, I have tried to emulate that ancient, oratorical style, whenever appropriate.

What do I recall from so long, long ago: 1943–1949? Many of the great moments in Gilman sports, of course. Who could forget John "The Count" Kunkowski snapping out of his corner like the end of a bullwhip, slamming his opponent to the mat, and retiring in triumph, all in a matter of seconds. He was a forerunner to "Rambo," terrifying but exciting.

Although never recorded in the Gilman chronicles, my own athletic prowess was quite memorable. My father, an omniscient man, taught me never to get in the way of a moving object or falling projectile. If something is coming at you, he said, step aside, my son, let it go by. If something is falling toward you, step back, my son, let it hit the ground first. During my athletic career at Gilman, my injuries were minimal. I did, however, experience one traumatic blow. One year I foolishly went out for Big League Football. Dickie Marshall tried to make a defensive tackle out of me. During a scrimmage, Doug Green, ball under his arm, and knees coming up and out of him like pistons, bowled me over before I could put my father's wisdom into action. I was placed on "injured reserve" and, fortuitously, the next morning, came down with a terrible cold. My mother sent me to school with a note requesting that I be excused from all athletic activities. Sensing that she was tiring of writing the same note daily, I generously suggested to my mother that she tag on the phrase, until further notice. My best friend and classmate, Frank Adams, who also had a cold, had his mother write a similar note.

"Until further notice" came on the first, warm day of spring, when Frank, not possessing my perspicacity, went to the lacrosse pitch, and I to the tennis courts. During the time of our long illnesses, Frank and I pursued matters cultural, attending the mid-week matinees at the Gayety Theatre, the old burlesque house on Baltimore Street. For 25 cents we went in a side door and up a long, steep, wooden staircase to the "peanut gallery." If Georgia Southern was in town, we'd go back for a Friday or Saturday evening performance. Years later, when I was writing my master's thesis, I devoted a whole chapter to the "Gayety."

Some of my fondest memories of Gilman are associated with her teachers. I came to Gilman from a rural, elementary school in southern Maryland, where there was some confusion over the verbs "sit" and "set." "Y'all children, set down now, ya heah."

"Hens set and people sit," Tom Lipscomb would say to me in that slow, wonderful drawl of his. Whenever I draw upon a southern accent, I prep myself by conjuring up an image of Tom Lipscomb and repetitiously recite "fo" and "fo'teen." He was my First Form English teacher. I'd turn in my weekly theme, and he'd bleed on it. One error, your grade dropped to 75; two, to 50; three or more, and you simply didn't score. I think it was just before Christmas when I got my first 50. I had a seat in his class, next to the window, and in the Spring of '44 or '45, or both, the minor league Orioles were using the Gilman baseball diamond for spring training. Travel was restricted during the war years. Mr. Lipscomb kept turning my head back to the matter at hand, a diagrammed sentence on the blackboard. Every time I tried to sneak a look, he'd snap me back. He had eyes in the back of his head or a magic mirror on the board. Didn't he know what was going on out there? Couldn't he hear the crack of the bats, the whack of the leather? It was spring training, for God sakes! Spring Training!

Years later I learned from Roy Barker that Tom was an avid Yankee fan. Roy told me Tom used to smoke three cigarettes a year, one on his birthday, one at Christmas, and one when the Yankees won the World Series. The man, obviously, had to have been a nicotine addict. What a wonderful teacher he was. He introduced me to my first Thomas Hardy, *The Return of the Native*, and then Maugham's *Of Human Bondage* and Dickens and Walpole. He was a gem, a sweet man.

From Tom Lipscomb I went to Clarence Lovelace. He read the first story I ever wrote, and his response sent me soaring through the clouds. He had a special Saturday session, which you could attend or not. I attended. It was he who introduced me to T.S. Eliot. Imagine, T.S. Eliot, Fourth Form. I'm sure I didn't understand it. I'm not sure I do now, but he made it sound so wonderful. "Prufrock" is still one of my favorites. Lovelace made me aware that words, like music, can rise above meaning.

And then there was Roy Barker—the classroom, the literary club, the tennis courts; it couldn't get any better. By a quirk of fate, an accident really, I became a teacher, and Roy, without either of us knowing it, became my mentor. He insinuated his way into my conscience; he was the measure for excellence. He was there when I wanted him, and he was there when I didn't want him. I think I realized he wasn't going to leave me, or I wasn't going to leave him, when I encountered his picture in a fraternity composite at college. He was on the stairwell wall, leading to the second floor. I had to pass it every night on the way to my quarters. Talk about, "He knows when you've been bad or good." We meet now at that fraternity for reunions, and neither one of us is on that stairwell wall.*

Roy's specter, and I've told him this, has appeared to me on several occasions, but the most ominous time was during my first year teaching, when I deliberately and with forethought cut a class. Surely, in the teaching profession that is a mortal sin. I was in my apartment, which I shared with a colleague, and we were watching the World Series on a rented TV. The time for my class was approaching, came and passed, as Don Larson completed the ninth inning of his "perfect" game. Roy appeared in my dreams for weeks after that. Had I only known that he was a baseball buff and a Yankee fan to boot. How would the specter have haunted me, had I walked away from that historic moment? In recent years Roy and I have kept up a correspondence, which I have found extremely rewarding. Although no longer an apparition, Roy continues to be a tremendous inspiration. Of Gilman's teachers, he is truly one of the Olympians.

During my early forms at Gilman, I was something of a Latin scholar; I was an outstanding "conjugater." I didn't know what the word meant, but give me the verb and I was off and running. Without Latin, my academic average during those formative years would have been more abysmal than it was.

What a shock when I suddenly came up against Ad Hausmann. I didn't know "diddly squat," and here we were translating "Julius Caesar." I was always prepared to divide Gaul into three parts; it was the only section I knew. I played it like a lottery ticket, but why I thought he would call upon me, one student out of 15, to read that section, I'll never know. It always went to the likes of Phil Fenton, Bill McCarthy, or John Welch, who not only partitioned Gaul, but went on to wage the full campaign while I was left struggling to get poor Julius across the English Channel or headed back toward the Rubicon. My explanation for the sudden plummet in my Latin grades was simple. Mr. Hausmann didn't like me. "Sounds logical to me," responded my father, in a way that told me he wasn't buying any of it. As a teacher,

---

*This essay was written two years before Roy Barker died at a hospital in Hyannis, Massachusetts, on September 12, 1993, of pneumonia.

I was to learn that when you felt an antipathy toward a student, you bent over backwards to be fair.

Anyway, I finally came to the reality that I was going to have to knuckle down if I was to overcome Hausmann's negative attitude. It took a while, but, like that first 50 from Tom Lipscomb, I began to attain respectability. Years later, this man, who didn't like me, summered in Conway, New Hampshire, and was a season ticket holder to the Barnstormers Theatre in Tamworth. He'd come backstage, maybe twice a summer, usually when I was playing a significant role, and in time, in his own way, he gave me to believe he was a fan, this man who didn't like me.

I can't leave Gilman's wonderful teachers without mentioning J. C. Pine. He was one of my favorites. If my children could have taken his geography course, they'd know where the hell they are today. And his U.S. history course was the "crème de la crème." I had some very good history professors in college, but no one to equal J. C. Pine.

And of course the head Olympian, Henry Callard. Anyone there during his years knows that he was the figure who made it all happen.

Fifty years from now, when I'm the oldest living graduate, remind me to tell about the outrageously undisciplined Gilman actor, who, albeit in character, in a scene with Nicholas Probst, now Pryor, stepped out of the script, walked over to the telephone, picked it up and said, "Turner on this end; what's on yours?"

Drama, theater—acting and directing—have been the passions of Clapham Murray's life. Murray began at Gilman in 1943 and was soon a member of the Pnyx Debating Club and Dramatic Association. With his favorite sport being tennis—a three-year varsity man—and his favorite subject being literature, it is a sure bet that Roy Barker, varsity tennis coach and English department head, was his most influential teacher/coach.

Murray majored in theater at Wesleyan University, Connecticut, and studied theater one more year at Emerson College. He then taught at Westbrook Jr. College in Maine; Roanoke College in Virginia; and the New England College in New Hampshire and in Arundel, Sussex, England, where he is currently Emeritus Professor of Theater. Murray is also working as Artistic Director and Actor with the Barnstormers Theatre in Tamworth, N.H., and, between acts, is writing a novel.

Adventures and Escapades
of a Boarder

G. GIBSON CAREY IV '51

My years at Gilman (1941–51) coincided with the heyday of the school's boarding program. I was a boarder for nine years, from the Lower School through graduation. As I look back on these years, this was a wonderfully colorful and shaping experience for me, filled with adventures, relationships, and memories that are the very fabric of my fond feelings for the school.

There were "seven-day boarders," who lived at the school full-time, and "five-day boarders," who went home over the weekends. Boys boarded at the school for a variety of reasons. Some came from a great distance simply to attend Gilman: There were contingents from Washington, Philadelphia, and York, Pennsylvania, among others. Some boarded for academic reasons, the idea being that enforced nightly study hours would prove beneficial to their grades. In the early 1940s the school's enrollment was perilously low, so Messrs. Russell and Janvier went on a swing through the South to find new students, who would also be boarders. They returned with a number of colorful new boys in tow: notably, the Nolands and Pardees from New Orleans, the Palacios brothers from Curaçao, and the Byingtons from Rio.

The boarding program grew dramatically during World War II and peaked at about 60 boys. Some boys lived too far out in the country to make the daily commute during gasoline rationing. A number of boys' mothers followed their husbands on military assignments for as long as possible before they went overseas, consigning their sons to the school's care for the interim. My father was assigned to the Pentagon for much of the war, and later took a position in Washington with the fledgling CIA; so, I boarded five days a week, and the family reassembled on our farm in the Greenspring Valley over weekends.

I doubt that anyone boarded longer at the school than Jim Griffin from Princeton and I. We both started in the Fourth Grade when we were about nine years old. Jim was a seven-day boarder, however, giving him some kind of claim to "Super-Boarder" status.

Lower School boarders lived in "the Cubes": cubicles located on the third floor over the South Corridor. (Single female teachers—Miss Stevens, Miss Bard, Miss Bell, and others—had third-floor rooms over the North Corridor, and the rear wing was the infirmary). The cubes had no doors, and the walls were only about six feet high. If you jumped on your bed with sufficient zeal, you could just clear the top and have a view into the adjoining cube. We spent a lot of time boring holes in the tongue and groove walls with our penknives so we could whisper to our neighbors at night, and a vigilant staff spent a lot of time refilling them with plastic wood.

There was a housemother who supervised the nightly ablutions of the younger boys and dressed us in blue suits for supper: Fifth and Sixth Graders were spared these indignities, except in the most extreme circumstances of inadequate hygiene. We sat at a separate table for supper, went to Prayers with the Upper Schoolers, and then were marched off to our evening study hall in Mr. O'Brien's Room 5. A number of young bachelor teachers had rooms at the school, and a particularly likable newcomer named Bill Gerardi, an Upper School math teacher, lived in rooms adjoining the cubes. He was nominally charged with keeping after-hours discipline, a thankless task, indeed. Life was never dull.

Upper Schoolers had proper rooms on the second floor. Boys from the First through Third Forms were on the North Corridor, and from the Fourth through Sixth on the South. The rooms were sparsely furnished with two metal beds, and somewhere around 1945 there was an influx of surplus Navy gray metal desks and bureaus.

The move to the North Corridor, coincident with the move into the Upper School, was a profound rite-of-passage. No more housemother. No more special table in the dining room or special study hall. We had roommates. The hormones were kicking into high gear at this juncture, as well. Most boys were now shaving at least weekly, whether they needed to or not. And there were non-stop speculative discussions about the gently nurtured, long into the night, night after night: it was the only topic. We tried desperately to unravel the great myths and half-truths of the fair sex, which have been passed from one generation of mystified but obsessively curious boys to the next since Biblical times.

The subsequent move to the South Corridor was simply another step up on the stairway to manhood . . . but a wonderfully significant one. There was just a touch more independence now, and not quite as much supervision. If you were on the Honor Roll, you could study in your room during evening study hall. Speculative debate about the fair sex continued, of course, but now the older boys were actually dating, and there were first-hand experiences to be reconciled with the myth and rumor of earlier years. Many boys were smokers, too: there was a nightly gathering, presided over by Jumbo Gibbs, on the roof of "A" Study Hall.

And we ate. Lord, how we ate! After athletics, we trekked down to Doc Davidov's for a milk shake, or to Delvale's, if there was sufficient time and funds. We got back to school just in time for supper. The school food was no better than it should have been, but we were driven by powerful appetites and learned to eat everything in sight, a valuable skill in years to come. After study hall, some of the more enterprising students who kept hot plates under their beds (a strictly forbidden practice) would cook up cans of spaghetti, meatballs, or whatever had been liberated from pantries at home. In the wintertime, we kept stashes of ice cream and other perishables outside our windows, squirreled away in the ivy.

After dinner, there was the nightly prayer service in "A" Study Hall for all boys, Upper and Lower School. These were led by Sixth Formers who read a brief passage of scripture pre-selected by Mr. Callard, a prayer or two, and a hymn of their choosing, accompanied by Mr. Kerr at the piano.

The Lower School boys were then dismissed to their juvenile studies, while the Upper Schoolers settled in for two long hours in "A" Study Hall, most often supervised by Track Coach Don Hoffman who doodled drawings of trout flies, and dispensed what assistance he could to boys struggling with their nightly homework assignments.

The minute evening study hall was over, we made a great show of dashing to the few telephone booths for critically important calls to the ladies of our hearts. Boys on the Honor Roll had a distinct advantage in this regard: they always got to the telephones before those condemned to "A" Study Hall, and kept them pretty much tied up for the rest of the evening. The school switchboard was operated, at night, by a boarder. This was a position of great power—in putting some boys' calls through, while selectively disconnecting others. I recall this clearly. I had this influential job for a year.

We were supervised, in the North and South corridors, by officers of the Student Council who generally lived at the school as boarders, even if their homes were in Roland Park. I don't recall their being particularly effective in this role, especially with their peers on the South Corridor. Over and above these student proctors, various members of the faculty took turns keeping an eye on things and enforcing the parietals. This task most often seemed to fall to the handful of bachelor teachers who lived in rooms scattered about the second floor. Al Kerr, Charlie Gamper, George Chandlee, Messrs. Bannon, Turner, Reese, and, in later years, Finney all took their turn. Wise old foxes like Tom Lipscomb, or married faculty like Doc Oscarson, Al Townsend, Roy Barker, Ad Hausmann, or Ed Russell—all of whom lived at the school—somehow seemed to avoid these tiresome duties.

In any case, the supervision was none too effective, and there were plenty of opportunities for adventures and escapades; especially for five-day boarders, many of whom had automobiles parked in the lot behind the kitchen, where it was understood they were to stay for the week. This never deterred Sandy Cassatt, who would sneak over to Pimlico at dawn to time the workouts of the race horses, which had happy consequences on his betting at the track in the afternoon, under the cover of a doctor's appointment. There were excursions to The Block, where there was generally a matinee at the Gayety, or the Globe and Clover across the street, with bored women and baggy-pants comedians performing halfheartedly for almost empty houses; but we thought it was pretty spicy stuff! Nocturnal visits to the two local girls' boarding schools—Garrison Forest and St. Timothy's (then in Catonsville) became a regular event until a few boys were caught and heavy punishment was meted out.

A number of five-day boarders, including me, convinced our parents that we had to be at school in time for study hall on Sunday nights; there was not a speck of truth to this, but it gave us a wonderful opportunity for weekly nocturnal excursions free of all supervision and curfews, and we would creep into the school and our beds on the South Corridor long after lights were out, aided and abetted by a conspiratorial night watchman we called Chiefie.

Weekends could be dreary affairs for the seven-day boarders. Many spent the weekends at the homes of their classmates. The school was all but empty. There wasn't much to do. Television hadn't happened. Sunday mornings were devoted to a walk to a Catholic service, or to the Church of the Redeemer. Mr. Callard fretted about the hard lot of the seven-day boarders, and he and Mrs. Callard graciously gave an annual dance for the boarders in their home, with a small band from Rivers Chambers, usually led by the ubiquitous Tee. Like so many things Mr. Callard did for the boys, it was enormously appreciated. (There is a legend that, in the depths of the war, with help impossible to find, Mr. Callard personally got up in the middle of the night to tend the huge coal-fired boilers in the school. This was no myth: the boarders saw him do it on many an occasion.)

Looking back on those years, I feel a special bond and nostalgia for the school which I suspect other boarders probably share. Gilman was our home-away-from-home, and the faculty were our surrogate parents during adolescent years when, psychologists tell us, our lifetime values are established.

In particular, I remember the faculty. Most students knew them only as teachers, or perhaps coaches. The boarders lived with them, and knew them when they were "off-duty." They were a very special breed: Lipscomb, Russell, Barker, Pine, Gamper, O'Brien . . . the list goes on and on. Gentlemen, all. I developed a special respect for Al Kerr, growing from a shared love for classical music. He took me to the monthly Philadelphia Orchestra concerts at The Lyric whenever our family tickets were not otherwise spoken for; and he nurtured my interest with his own fine collection of records and the Glee Club which he so capably directed. Presiding over it all was Henry Callard, respected and loved by every boy in the school. He set standards, and by his own example established expectations which have been a lifelong challenge for us all.

These were very good men, and those were very good years.

G. Gibson Carey IV's main interests at Gilman, which he attended as a five-day boarder 1941–51, were classical music, writing, and hunting and fishing. Roy Barker was his inspiration in English and writing, while Al Kerr lured him into the mysteries of music. In the Upper School, Carey was chairman of both the Fifth and Sixth Form Dance Committees, and in his senior year, president of the Dramatic Association, and managing editor of the *Cynosure* and *The Blue and The Gray*. He was a four-year member of the Glee Club and of the Literary Club, and worked on the *News* for three years.

At Princeton, Carey majored in English, while continuing his interest in music, and scheduling time to hunt and fish on the weekends. Upon graduation from Princeton, he put in a two-year stint with the U. S. Army, and then, in 1957, went to work for the Procter and Gamble Company in advertising, where he has remained since. Working out of the home office in Cincinnati, Carey specializes in advertising human resources and marketing services and is vice president of Procter and Gamble Worldwide. He has served as a chairman for the Cincinnati Country Day School, the Cincinnati Opera, and the Cincinnati Free Store/ Food Bank.

Married to Anna Kirwan Steck Carey, Ph.D. (Bryn Mawr School '53), Carey is the father of four children. When he retires, he plans to live peacefully "with lots of good fishing, good opera, and maybe a little writing."

A Classmate of Reddy's

JAMES P. GORTER '47

I n September, 1939, at the age of nine, I entered a man's world: Gilman. My first four school years had been spent at the Roland Park Country School—an establishment for young ladies that grudgingly admitted a small group of boys far too young to appreciate the unique opportunity afforded them. At any rate, at nine my parents deemed me ready for Gilman's rough and tumble life. I was there for eight wonderful years, from 1939 to 1947.

Many experiences are indelibly etched in my memory—learning Latin from Mr. Townsend and math from George Chandlee, chemistry from Mr. Janvier and trying to learn French from Mr. O'Brien. Headmasters Morrow, Russell, and Callard; working on the Gilman *News* and the *Cynosure*; study halls; the Gilman Fair in the Cage; athletics with Ferris Thomsen and Nick Carter; my term as a boarder in a third floor cubicle, and last but not least, the Bryn Mawr girls next door.

The friendships made at Gilman were important ones lasting intensely through college, but in my case, tapering off when I moved to Chicago shortly after graduation from Gilman. It was a particular privilege to have been a classmate of Reddy Finney. He really hasn't changed much over the years—thoughtful of all; dedicated to excellence and what is right, demanding both of himself and others, but fair in all his dealings. These qualities were evident when he was a student at Gilman and even more so at Princeton and in his later career as Headmaster. He led by example, both in the classroom and on the athletic field.

At Gilman, Reddy was (and still is) so much stronger than anyone else. He was a true farm boy, much more used to manual labor than any of his city-slicker friends. He played center on the football team when I was the tailback. Nick Carter would say, "Finney, you open the hole and Gorter, you follow him." It worked. We had a good team in 1946 with a record including a 20 to 6 victory over McDonough and even one over a much larger and more sophisticated Lawrenceville: 19–6.

In football we were teammates, but in the school wrestling championship we were opponents, and in those days wrestling was the major winter sport at Gilman.

The school championships were attended by the student body, faculty, and parents—a major event. The first round heavyweight match was Finney vs. Gorter. It was also the shortest wrestling match in Gilman history, and you know who won. But I always felt it wasn't too bad to lose to an All-American athlete.

Gilman made a lasting impression on me, and had I stayed in Baltimore I would have wanted my sons and grandsons to be Gilman boys. What more can one say!

 James P. Gorter attended Gilman 1939–47. His favorite classes were in math, Latin and history. A class officer, he also worked on the Gilman *News* and the *Cynosure*. He was a four-sport varsity athlete, a member of the football, wrestling, baseball, and track teams. Among the varsity letters he earned were two in football and three in track.

In his senior year, Gorter was awarded the Gold Medal for the Head of the Upper School, the Cameron Debating Medallion, the Walter Lord Prize for General Proficiency in History, the Alumni Baseball Cup, the Culver Football Cup, and the William Cabell Bruce, Jr. Athletic Prize.

Gorter attended Princeton where he majored in economics, studied the classics, played varsity football and ran varsity track. Graduating Summa Cum Laude, he then studied at the London School of Economics before joining Goldman Sachs & Co., Chicago, in 1956 and becoming a partner in 1965. He is married and the father of three children.

Reflections upon Gilman Headmastering, 1968–1992

REDMOND C. S. FINNEY '47

April, 1968, seems like a long, long time ago. The decision that the Gilman Board made at their spring Board meeting to select a young, inexperienced teacher-coach with minimal administrative background to succeed Ludlow Baldwin as headmaster was a courageous action. But times were simpler then; boards of trustees were more laid back, and those involved in determining independent school leadership placed more emphasis upon the head being "head teacher" than upon knowledge of organization or expertise in management skills.

Henry Callard virtually "did it all" himself. During his 20 years of brilliant and compassionate leadership, he was everything to the school, including moral example, role model, head teacher, chief counselor, chaplain, business manager, and grounds keeper. I have omitted "development officer"; Gilman and a lot of other independent schools of the 1950s and '60s had yet to establish such offices. Also, Mr. Callard hated anything to do with soliciting or fund raising, or with what is now termed "public relations." He would much rather have given someone a dollar than ask for one, and he was suspicious of anything that suggested façade or contrived image. He was a self-effacing, modest man, and he only felt comfortable striving to be himself and, at the same time, having Gilman work to be its honest-to-goodness, authentic self.

I consider it my greatest good fortune to have followed Henry Callard and Ludlow Baldwin and to have had the privilege to have worked closely with these two fine school men and gentlemen. They were similar in a lot of ways, especially in their steadfast striving to fulfill the highest ideals of Gilman. Both men were strong personalities who led by example, but Mr. Callard was more the old-time traditional headmaster; whereas, Ludlow Baldwin launched Gilman into a more modern phase of administrative organization.

Although Mr. Baldwin's five-year tenure as Gilman's headmaster might be considered relatively short, he made major contributions. In achieving a more sophisticated level of administrative organization, he selected an administrative team, and he delegated specific leadership responsibilities. He also inaugurated the practice of meeting regularly with his Executive Council. His previous experience as a lawyer, businessman, and naval officer influenced and shaped his leadership style. Although he did not like fund raising any more than Mr. Callard did, he viewed it as a necessity for the future well-being of the school. Accordingly, he established a permanent Development Office with Charles "Chuck" Emmons '23, as director, and he increased emphasis upon the annual giving program which had been inaugurated in 1956 by the alumni association as The Gilman Fund under the dynamic leadership of Cooper Walker '33.

I was also fortunate to have worked under and learned from some remarkably fine Board presidents, including Dr. Ridgeway Trimble '18, Owen Daly '43, William McCarthy '49, J. Richard Thomas '43, George E. Thomsen '48, and George Hess '55. Each of these gentlemen was the finest example of absolute devotion to Gilman. I was further blessed to be associated with many outstanding individuals who served on the Board.

Dawson Farber '35 served as a trustee throughout my 24 years as headmaster. The level of his contribution and the quality of his service remain unmatched. He has been a faithful adviser to four headmasters now over a span of more than 30 years. He has been on every long-range planning committee since the 1960s, and his service on key trustee committees such as Faculty and Staff has been extraordinary. I will never forget the advice and counsel he gave to me. His comprehensive business background and his knowledge of management skills were an invaluable resource.

The same can be said of Owen Daly, whose Board presidency occurred during those crucial early years when my learning curve as a new headmaster needed a special boost. Like Dawson, Owen went far beyond the level of normal trustee assistance and guidance.

Another remarkable trustee of long service is Dr. Theodore "Ted" Woodward. What a wise and compassionate man! And how magnanimous. It is fitting that Gilman's new and beautiful health center is named in honor of Dr. Woodward. If it were not for Dr. Woodward and for another like-minded trustee and physician, Dr. Earl Galleher '44, Gilman would not have the high quality of health services and facilities which the school offers.

It is gratifying to note the increasing number of women who have joined the Board over the past 25 years. Mrs. Betsey Spragins not only founded the Gilman Parents Association, she also chaired the Long Range Planning Committee which developed the blueprint for Gilman's development in the 1980s. The legacy of what

Betsey Spragins accomplished in the founding of the Parents Association takes on special significance when one considers the tremendous contribution this association makes to the school today. Betsey was always a most thoughtful, perceptive, and deeply caring voice.

One of the earliest Korean-American families to become part of Gilman was the family of Dr. and Mrs. Jai S. Lee. Mrs. "Julie" Lee and her husband Dr. Jai Lee enrolled their eldest son Gregory in the Lower School in 1974. "Julie" became the ultimate Gilman parent volunteer. She worked in the library, helped lead the Parents Hospitality Committee, served on the Parents Association Executive Council, and mobilized a large contingent of the Baltimore Korean-American Community toward becoming supportive of Gilman. In 1987, she was elected to the Board of Trustees. The Lees' sons, Greg '86, and Jerry '93, achieved outstanding records at Gilman.

The best piece of advice I ever received as a fledgling headmaster was from Mr. Callard, who wrote me a letter in the summer of 1968, a letter which I have kept to this day. The essence of Mr. Callard's message was (1) to resist the temptation to make changes too fast, and (2) to place primary emphasis upon giving one's presence and personal attention to the school community. Henry Callard himself lived this advice to the fullest. The memory of his special warmth and the individual attention he gave repeatedly to every member of the school community has always remained with me. Everyone knew that Mr. Callard cared deeply. There was no mistaking that his caring and, if you will, his love were directed toward others unconditionally because he always wanted what was best for them. Because faculty and students came to realize this, they learned to care too, and they thought twice before doing something that might displease their headmaster.

Special people have the most to do with shaping our lives and comprise the primary influence of "the Gilman experience." This influence manifests itself in terms of the particular role that specific individuals play, i.e., what they teach or coach, but even more in terms of their unique personalities and how they relate to others. How can any of us who were so fortunate as to know Edward T. Russell ever forget his unqualified love for every Gilman boy, his beguiling sense of humor, and his complete devotion to the school? And when we think of the epitome of what it means to be a "gentleman," who can come up with a better example than T. Lee Lipscomb? As further examples of unparalleled dedication to Gilman School, countless numbers of Gilman alumni and faculty will place May Holmes or Helen Stevens or Charlie Gamper or Reg Tickner at the top of the list.

As I look back on the 24 years I served as headmaster, I think about the people, especially faculty, staff, and students. These memories are stimulated by recollections of special issues and important changes which took place in the school. Frequently, particular individuals and important happenings are inextricably interrelated. Indeed, I express everlasting gratitude to certain people who were the catalysts and leaders in undertaking certain initiatives. I will never forget the role Bill

Campbell '52 played in the increasing diversification of Gilman. At the outset of his time as a Gilman teacher/administrator/coach, he was committed to the goal of opening Gilman to a greater variety of kids from different races, religions, and backgrounds. In pursuit of that goal, he never hesitated to tell people where he stood and to express the importance of Gilman moving in this direction. Together we coined the phrase "Baltimore Community School," implying that Gilman should be a school whose student body reflected the composition of peoples living in the greater metropolitan area.

Thanks to Ludlow Baldwin's support, Bill and I had the opportunity in the summer of 1967 to found Gilman Upward Bound, a federally funded program for center-city kids from poverty backgrounds. This program, which is still in existence today under the outstanding leadership of William Greene, has had a major and most positive impact upon the hundreds of Baltimore city public school students who have been involved, as well as upon those from the Gilman faculty and student body who have served in teaching and support roles. The entire Gilman family should be proud of Gilman Upward Bound, for most of our Upward Bound graduates would never have finished high school, much less have gone on to college and to other postsecondary school educational experiences, without the influence of this program. The Upward Bound formula of consistent personal attention, steady encouragement, readily available counseling, and an unwavering insistence upon staying in school and mastering the basic fundamentals of learning has produced many success stories. A large debt of gratitude is owed to Bill Greene and his Upward Bound staff, which has always included significant contingents of Gilman faculty and Gilman Upper School students, in addition to a solid cadre of Baltimore City public school teachers. It is gratifying to know how many Gilman Upward Bound graduates are productive citizens today and how appreciative they are of their Gilman experience.

Bill Campbell and I first met William "Bill" Greene in the spring of 1967 when we were interviewing both prospective teachers and students for the first Gilman Upward Bound summer program. At the time, Bill Greene was teaching mathematics at Gwynns Falls School in southwest Baltimore, and we persuaded him to accept a position on our summer faculty. Following the 1968–69 school year, my first as headmaster, Bill Campbell and I persuaded Bill Greene to join the Gilman faculty on a full-time basis. Accepting this position was a major and, indeed, a courageous decision on Bill Greene's part, for not only was he leaving the employment of the Baltimore City public schools, but also he was the first African-American to become a Gilman teacher. Initially, he taught Upper School math; subsequently, in 1970 he succeeded Bill Campbell as director of Gilman Upward Bound, a position he has filled with great distinction into the 1990s. In the early 1980s, he was named assistant headmaster and appointed director of Middle and Upper School admissions.

Bill Greene has been one of the principal ambassadors for Gilman School. Gilman's positive and healthy relationship with Baltimore City, and in particular with the Baltimore City public schools, is the direct result of the work of Bill Greene. In addition, Mr. Greene has been a surrogate father, confidant, and ongoing support to countless numbers of students and teachers, especially Gilman's increased minority population. Many African-American students, parents, and faculty would not have felt as welcome or secure at Gilman, or might not even have joined the Gilman family, were it not for Bill Greene's support and friendship.

I do not believe that those of us who represent the historically traditional Gilman fully appreciate how difficult it can be to be in the minority in a competitive and socially aware environment like Gilman's. As I think back on those early years when the first African-American students enrolled in Gilman, I recall how composed and disciplined and discreet they were. In a real sense, the likes of Greg Emery '68, David Robinson '68, Stuart Simms '68, and Willard Wiggins '68 were pioneers. My respect and admiration and love for these gentlemen, and for many who followed them, remain undiminished to this day.

Becoming a more diverse community has had a major impact upon Gilman. Although I am considered by some to have been the principal leader of this happening, so many others deserve equal or more credit, starting with Henry Callard and then Ludlow Baldwin, and subsequently including many like-minded faculty and trustees. I doubt if any of us really fathomed at the time the real depth of the change that was taking place and the benefits that were to come to the school through becoming a more diverse community. One need only survey the pages of successive *Cynosures* and Gilman *News* to understand the outstanding contributions that have been made by "students of color." And one would be amazed at the extent of the positive feelings that both the students, now alumni, and the parents of this "new generation" of Gilman have toward the school and their "Gilman experience." Above all, the increased sensitivity to others and the significant growth of understanding and appreciation of differences throughout the school family are among the greatest benefits.

As I reflect further upon individuals who have had a special impact upon the school, I am compelled to mention one of the greatest teachers during my Gilman tenure who, unfortunately for me and Gilman, retired too soon. A brilliant English teacher and an empathetic leader, A. J. "Jerry" Downs has never stopped growing. His enthusiasm and his love for kids were and continue to be unquenchable. He never stopped thinking about more creative ways to teach, and he never ceased exploring how to inspire his students and how to build their self-esteem. It was also Jerry Downs who was the principal leader of the faculty during the formative days of coordination with Bryn Mawr and Roland Park Country. Jerry had a vision of what coordination could become, and this vision combined with his remarkable ability to inspire others, had much to do with bringing about the rich three-school coordinate program we know today.

Jerry Downs was a devotee of the creative arts. For years he was a mainstay of the Gilman drama program, and he was the principal founder of the Gilman Summer Theater, now popularly known as The Young Victorian Theater. Thanks to teachers like Jerry Downs, Alex Armstrong, and Roy Barker, drama is alive and well at Gilman. When I joined the faculty in 1954, the number of plays had been increased significantly since I graduated in the 1940s, especially after the construction of the Alumni Auditorium in 1956. And thankfully so. Much of the credit must go to Roy Barker, English department chair. There had been but one play a year when he began at Gilman in 1946. He introduced a play at each of three levels, Seventh–Eighth Grade; Ninth–Tenth; Eleventh–Twelfth.

I must admit that I never appreciated the great value of the drama experience—the poise, confidence, and sensitivity, as well as the discipline it can nurture and build—until I had been on the faculty for several years and had the opportunity to watch people like Jerry Downs and his drama pupils in action.

One cannot refer to the growth of dramatics at Gilman without mentioning the entire creative arts experience. One can go back to the Fifties and the time of Harold Wrenn, who brought his outstanding art history course to Gilman utilizing his rich professional experience and his remarkable selection of illustrative slides to expand the knowledge and sensitivity of his students to the legacy of the world of art. And Gilman can never forget Hunt Hilliard, who developed Gilman's industrial arts and woodworking program into a unique and outstanding offering. It was the fulfillment of Henry Callard's vision that led to the construction of the original shop in the summer of 1948 and then brought Hunt Hilliard to Gilman in the early 1950s. What a blessing was Hunt Hilliard, whose leadership and devotion led to the woodworking and architectural design program being incorporated into all three school divisions.

And what a perpetual joy and fulfillment music has been to the school community, especially under the magnificent leadership of John Merrill, a brilliant teacher and superlative human being! During John Merrill's 30 years of teaching at Gilman, the music program has expanded and flourished. Comprehensive programs of both choral and instrumental music have been established at all three school division levels, and under the directorship of John's associate, Ronald Bange, the Gilman Band has achieved remarkable results, bringing Lower, Middle, and Upper Schoolers as well as students from our two coordinate neighbors into one integrated ensemble. It has been said that music is a universal language, an adage John Merrill brings into reality with every performance of his outstanding Glee Club. Many is the time I have had tears come to my eyes while listening to the beautiful blend of voices John Merrill has coached. And he achieves this quality year in and year out!

I cannot fail to mention my close friend and long-time associate Nicholas Schloeder. Although profane at times and iconoclastic, Nick Schloeder could be at once Gilman's sharpest critic and most loyal supporter. Early on, Nick was among those who were ahead of the times as he envisioned the Gilman of the future. He also has exemplified throughout his long Gilman professional career the epitome of what is best in the teacher/coach philosophy. He continues to be unusually gifted in both the classroom and on the athletic field. Many of his students have been awakened to excitement about history and to political action and a greater sense of their responsibilities to the larger community through Nick's American Government and U.S. History courses. And countless numbers of student athletes have benefited from his coaching. Rarely will one find an athletic coach who is able to combine such a high level of teaching the fundamentals of sport with such a sophisticated and ingenious strategical approach.

Although it has been difficult to maintain the teacher/coach tradition, principally owing to the forces of rapidly expanding knowledge and the increased specialization required in attendant teaching, Gilman has done a remarkable job. Most Gilman faculty still coach at least two seasons while carrying a full four-period classroom load. This is good and healthy for teachers as well as for students. How else can a student or a teacher have the opportunity to see and to get to know one another in two such completely different settings? Among a number of benefits is the higher level of mutual appreciation and respect that I am convinced results.

I could name many others as outstanding examples of the Gilman teacher/coach, including Sherman Bristow, Joe Duncan, Tim Holley, Peter Julius, Marty Meloy, Jack Thompson, Jerry Thornberry, John Tucker, and Alex Sotir. Serving as athletic director for ten years, Alex Sotir taught only one class, but by his energy and the example of his own self-disciplined life and his belief that his Gilman teams could measure up to any competition, he taught many Gilman student-athletes that they could achieve at higher levels than they ever thought possible. Sherman Bristow, currently both athletic director and dean of Upper School students, joined the Gilman faculty in 1971 following his graduation from Princeton, and he has been a prime example of excellence as a teacher/coach ever since. The faculty leader of the Ninth Grade English course for two decades, Sherman loves literature (he wrote his thesis on Jane Austen), and he loves to teach. He is an outstanding leader of young men, and he excels as a coach. Year in and year out Sherman Bristow's athletic teams achieve considerably above their potentials. Why? I am convinced that it has to do with an inspirational quality and ability to relate to young people that is special and unique. Some teachers have it, some don't. Both groups might be good teachers, but there are those special people, those "stars" if you will, that you want to make sure you have on your faculty.

Each year as we planned for the following academic year and had the opportunity to interview teacher prospects, I tried my best to envision who might be those special "stars," those candidates who had that extra "plus" and that special inspirational, relating quality. I confess that on several occasions I urged our division heads to hire certain people even if we did not have a specific opening. We could "manufacture" one, and the needs to fill always seemed to arise. In addition, one simply cannot have too many teachers on the faculty who are inspirational leaders and genuine role models for our students.

It would be unfair and indeed grossly incomplete to give the impression that the people of primary importance on a school staff are classroom teachers, teacher/coaches, and leaders of special programs. There is no doubt that these categories make up the vast majority of the employees of Gilman. However, there are others who are of vital and inestimable value to the school. They range from the devoted people who provide much-needed secretarial and office services to the wonderful staff who care for Gilman's beautiful buildings and grounds.

How can many generations of Gilman alumni ever forget Miss May Holmes? No person was more devoted to Gilman and the Gilman ideals. The Gilman archives which we treasure today are largely the result of what she maintained over many years and brought together with such loving hands. And I cannot fail to name the current headmaster's secretary, Barbara Hawks, without whom the headmaster's office would not have survived during my tenure. Her organizational talents, her tact, and her ability at human relations are irreplaceable. Without her attention to detail and to human needs, many people would go away much less happy, and countless numbers of students, parents, and visitors might feel unfulfilled.

Let me conclude by mentioning one other person who has made a major contribution to Gilman and whose leadership was there at a most crucial time in the school's history. I am referring to JoAnn Davison, our head librarian, whose vision over the past 25 years has enabled Gilman to achieve one of the most advanced library and media systems of any secondary school in the country. JoAnn Davison first came to Gilman in the last years of Mr. Callard's headmastership but left to raise a family. Most fortunately, the school was able to persuade Mrs. Davison to return just as Gilman embarked on a major study of our total library needs, when we knew that it had become necessary to expand significantly our over-all library facilities and capabilities. Mrs. Davison headed a committee, including library consultants from the state and national levels, which addressed both the physical and technical needs and planned the move of the Upper School library from the old library, now known as the Gilman Room, into what is now known as the Fenimore Library, made up of the old Fisher Memorial Dining Hall and new adjoining Cochran Room. This historic move was finally accomplished in the spring of 1971. At the same time, when the then-new Middle School was built, a brand new library media center was planned and constructed in the John M. T. Finney Building, and a library team of three professionals plus support staff was appointed to elevate all three school divisions to the cutting edge in library-media service and technology.

JoAnn Davison has continued to lead and to plan. All three Gilman libraries have availed themselves of modern computer technology and readily access library resources in other libraries across the city and state. In addition, the variety of print and non-print material available for teaching and learning purposes has grown significantly. And now Gilman's new Middle School, the completely redesigned and rebuilt John M. T. Finney Building, houses one of the most sophisticated library-media centers and information retrieval systems one can imagine. JoAnn Davison and her team of librarians, along with the respective school division heads, especially Middle School Head Ron Culbertson, have made it possible for Gilman to be an integral part of the information highway which is going to be such a central and necessary part of education in the Twenty-First Century.

Redmond Conyngham Stewart Finney was an 11-year student at Gilman, starting in 1936; for many of those years he had not just the nickname, "Reddy," but also one other, "Ducks." ("I used to raise them," he says.) In his Upper School years, it was Roy Barker who awakened Finney to the beauty of literature and books. Fred Williams drew him into the study of biology, especially botany. Headmaster Henry Callard taught him religion, which became a life-long interest. Ed Russell and Mr. Callard were his most lasting role models.

Finney was secretary of the Sixth Form, secretary of the Student Council, co-business manager of the *Cynosure*, feature editor of the *News*, and a member of the Pnyx Debating Team. At graduation, he was awarded the Fisher Medallion.

Because of a back injury, Finney was out of team sports during the fall and winter of his junior year. However, this gave him more time for riding horses and other parts of country life which he loved and which were nurtured in him by his grandmother, Katharine Small (Mrs. Redmond C.) Stewart.

Finney played varsity football in 1946 and wrestled varsity for three years. In 1945, Finney won the MSA 136-pound wrestling championship, and in 1947, the MSA 175-pound championship. He played four years of varsity lacrosse.

Upon graduation, Finney went to Princeton, where he majored in religion with a focus on the Old Testament; he was especially interested in the prophets and wisdom literature. He stuck with his formula of football, wrestling, lacrosse (which he liked in that order), becoming the only athlete—with the exception of the great professional running back Jim Brown—to ever become an All-American in two sports in one academic year, football and lacrosse. During that senior year he was also captain of the wrestling team.

Finney contemplated applying to divinity school, but his grandmother, Katharine Stewart, urged him to go into education, asking whether he would rather spend his life working with older people, as would be the likely outcome of divinity school, or young people. (He had also considered enrolling in agriculture school and becoming a full-time farmer.)

After serving in Korea in the Amphibious Corps of the Navy 1951–53, Finney came to Gilman in 1954. He coached, and taught history, mathematics, and religion 1954–68. Over the summers of 1956–58, he earned a Masters of Education from the Harvard Graduate School. In the Sixties, he served as Upper School director of morale and discipline under Headmaster Ludlow Baldwin. From 1968 to 1992, Redmond Finney served as headmaster of Gilman School. In 1966, Finney was named Maryland Scholastic Football Coach of the Year, and in 1970, he was inducted into the Maryland Athletic Hall of Fame.

Following retirement from Gilman, Finney has continued with his passions of coaching and teaching, though in a different form: he has gone into breeding and raising thoroughbred race horses on his farm, Landslide, in Upperco, Maryland. Ivory Poacher, a horse owned by Redmond Finney and his brother, Jervis, won the 1993 Maryland Hunt Cup. Gilman's past headmaster hopes to win another Hunt Cup, win the Virginia Gold cup, win a Maryland Million race, and fox hunt until he is 85!

Finney and his wife Jean have two sons, Stewart '77, and Ned '79, and two daughters, Jean and Beth, a son-in-law, David Emala '74, a daughter-in-law, Cheryl, and six grandchildren. Finney's father, George, was a member of the class of 1917, and his grandfather, John M. T. Finney, was president of the Board of Trustees 1912–42.

1950s

1950
Decade-long effort to expand offerings in music, art, dramatics, and community service begins.

1951
The "Country" is dropped from The Gilman Country School for Boys, and the school's name becomes Gilman School.

1952
Gilman is granted a Cum Laude honor society charter.

1952–53

Headmaster Henry Callard, on a Fulbright Exchange, teaches at Kings School, Somerset, England.

Ludlow H. Baldwin '22 is acting headmaster.

1955
Under the leadership of Cooper Walker '33, president of the Alumni Association, an annual giving program is launched. Walker nominates a committee called the Hughes Committee (Thomas R. Hughes '24, chairman). Hughes, as well as Edmund N. Gorman '32, leading another committee, recommends that Gilman adopt an annual giving program and that the school use the "light touch, the soft sell, not the baksheesh cry of the street beggar." The fund would be cumulative—all interest to be reinvested in the fund.

May Holmes visits the Goucher College development office, modeling the original organization of the annual giving program after Goucher's program, which had been partially modeled after Princeton's.

1956
Under the inspiration and supervision of self-taught architect and Superintendent of Maintenance John Krizek, the Alumni Auditorium is completed. Science teacher Bill Porter is a major catalyst in the planning and design of the building.

1957
$13,959 collected for the Annual Fund.

1958
Coached by English teacher Roy Barker, the varsity tennis team wins its first "A" conference championship.

Black tie and formal dresses were *de rigueur* at Gilman proms in the 1950s.

Final debate between the Pnyx and the Areopagus, 1951. That's Jack Cooper speaking while George Cassels-Smith keeps the time.

Below, the Traveling Men, 1951: Henderson Dorsey, Bill Merrick, Alexander Cassett, G. Gibson Carey, David Mohr, Wylie Faw, Tom Parr, John Gettier, Noel Volz, Thomas Offut, George Cassels-Smith. That's Robert H. Swindell at the piano.

Top, George Chandlee '32 served as captain and midfielder on Gilman's first varsity lacrosse team. As coach 1947–70, he led the team to six MSA championships. He was inducted into the Hall of Fame in 1977. Robert Turnbull '50 is on the left and Charles Brown '50 on the right.

Lower left, a varsity golfer shows off his driving form.

Below, Bob Russell '51 follows his blockers for a first down. Russell was the president of his class and the only graduate in Gilman's history to win both the Fisher Medallion and the Bruce Athletic Cup. As a senior, he won varsity letters in four sports: football, basketball, lacrosse, and track.

Ludlow Baldwin '22 taught religion and ancient history at Gilman 1946–68. He was headmaster 1963–68 and acting headmaster 1952–53.

Right, Paris in Room 5, Richard O'Brien in action. For more on one of Gilman's greatest French teachers, read John Dorsey's "On Learning about Learning."

169

Opposite above, Headmaster Henry Callard and his wife, Clarissa, in front of Carey Hall, 1963. Callard taught at Gilman 1922–24, 1925–27, and was headmaster 1943–63.

Opposite, Sixth Form Dance Committee members of 1957, John Kyle, Frank Deford, Tom Garrett, and Warren Hills, appear earnest about their obligations for the upcoming dance.

Left, English teacher extraordinaire Roy Barker—sometimes called "Old Blow-Top"—meets with the Literary Club.

Below, the Class of 1953, in the second grade, stands at attention. Shorts and collarless jackets—with the shirt collar worn outside the jacket—were still preferred by some parents but by few students.

172

Members of the Class of 1960 clown around in both of these shots for a yearbook photographer. Far left, in the telephone booth shot, is Paddy Neilson, drinking from the milk carton. (Neilson, the second-string quarterback on the varsity football team, was voted "Class hasn't-got-ten-up-in-the-morning-yet man" on the class ballot. Hiking the ball to Neilson was J. Griswold, who was voted "Class shouldn't-a-gotten-up-in-the-morning man" on the class ballot. Teammates were glad practices were held in the late afternoon.)

173

Right, Gibson Carey '51 and Tom Parr '51 hold a mock duel. Both were avid hunters and crack shots with a pistol. To impress dates, the duo took their charges to a junk yard where Parr would shoot a bottle, at a good distance, out of Carey's hand. The two still duck hunt together in the 1990s. For the life of a boarder at Gilman, read Carey's "Adventures and Escapades of a Boarder."

Below, a member of the Class of 1951 shows off his sports coupe.

174

Above, crank up the boogie-woogie, it's jitterbug time.

Opposite, George Wagner '51 has Bill Merrick '51 all cooped up. Middle, Jimmy Griffin '51 keeps warm in a raccoon coat.

On this page, Merrick overwhelms his dance partner at the prom with his Fred Astaire charm and grace. Merrick has taught in the Lower School since 1958. See Josh Civin's "A Wonderful Present" for snapshots of Merrick in action as a teacher.

Gilman in the 1950s:
An Open and
Challenging Environment

PETER H. WOOD '60

The past is a foreign country, and for most Americans, young and old, the past before the 1960s is a very foreign country indeed. During the 1950s—the decade after Roosevelt and before Kennedy—some of us inhabited a small portion of that country known until 1951 as The Gilman Country School for Boys.

Viewed from a satellite, it would have been tiny, a dot in the middle of Roland Park, near the edge of Baltimore, beside Maryland's Chesapeake Bay, on North America's eastern coast, in the earth's northern hemisphere. But Sputnik belonged to the Russians, and Americans had not yet seen themselves from outer space. Gilman, therefore, seemed extremely large. It became our country and our culture, with its own shifting styles of dress and manners of speech, its own teams and celebrities, its own food and newspaper, its own calendar and rituals. It even had its own coat of arms, like Peter Sellers' Duchy of Grand Fenwick in the *The Mouse That Roared*.

Ours was a nation of commuters. A handful of boarders lived on the third floor under the supervision of Mr. Lipscomb, Mr. Reese, and others. A small contingent walked to school or rode the Roland Avenue bus, carrying their books in assorted satchels and bags. (Backpacks in those days were only for true mountaineers like Edmund Hillary and Tenzing Norgay, who scaled Mount Everest in 1953.) Others in the vicinity rode bicycles, and a few would-be Marlon Brandos even gained permission to ride motorcycles. (The school installed driveway bumps in the '50s.) Denizens of the Green Spring and Worthington Valleys occasionally

177

arrived in a pick-up truck—farmer chic. But for most of us, cars played a big part in every school day.

Eventually we might have our own "wheels" or borrow Dad's, but for most of our Gilman years we were passengers in a family car. Foreign-made autos remained a rarity, so most of these machines were cumbersome station wagons and chrome-covered sedans from Detroit. Their tailfins varied from year to year, rather like our haircuts, but they were our Staten Island Ferries, methodically hauling us to and from our school.

I am surprised how vividly I can still recall daily sights and repeated motions; my body recollects the numerous twists and turns of the old Falls Road like a skier remembering a familiar slope. And always there was the radio, spouting new hit songs and distant news. I was staring at the radio dial of my father's Chevy when Dallas Townsend on the CBS Morning News informed us of the death of Joseph Stalin.

The nation of Gilman differed markedly from the troubling world that our parents inhabited, and yet themes that were occupying America's adult citizenry at the time also found their way into our lives. The longest shadow of all was cast by the ominous mushroom-shaped cloud of the Cold War. Many of us were too young to remember the anti-Axis propaganda of the early '40s. By the time we were old enough to read the Baltimore *Sun*, the Marshall Plan had been declared, and West Germany was a fledging "front-line state" in the new struggle against our former Russian allies. Berlin was no longer a target for U.S. bombers, but the destination for a massive airlift. We knew about the Korean War, if only because athletes like Ted Williams changed uniforms, and we certainly knew about Senator Joseph McCarthy.

What we learned about the world during those Cold War years usually came from linking something tangible and close to something remote and obscure. My mother, an inveterate teacher, especially with her own five children, had a special gift for making complex issues concrete. She would point out specific houses as we motored around the outskirts of pre-Beltway Baltimore. If memory serves, a tidy house near Towson was the home of Owen Lattimore, the scholarly liberal and sometime State Department advisor whom McCarthy denounced publicly and implausibly as "the top Russian espionage agent" in the United States. An enormous hilltop mansion in the Green Spring Valley was the property of Douglas MacArthur, the famous general who had been ordered home from Korea by his civilian commander-in-chief and who reminded an emotional session of Congress that "old soldiers never die."

But at school we learned to be circumspect about discussing current politics in the classroom. After all, even the distant New Deal remained a topic of heated division among our teachers. (I recall how Mr. Baldwin boldly began our American History class with a unit on the 1930s, explaining that in past years the school year had ended before he could get to this controversial era. "Darn it, boys, I think you should know about this stuff.") Once or twice, however, the issues of the Cold War became real. After Russian tanks crushed the Hungarian Revolution in the fall of

1956, for example, the school took part in collecting food and clothing for refugees, and a few months later a Hungarian teenager, Aurel Hollan, newly arrived in Baltimore with his family, became a member of our class. Aurel and his family were given one hour to get out of the home which his family had occupied for 600 years. They left as though they were taking a Sunday walk.*

Such dramatic and intimate connections were exceptional, however. Usually our knowledge was of the multiple choice variety, demonstrated once a year on the "*Time Magazine* Current Events Test for Young Readers." With luck, we could locate the Yalu River, the Suez Canal, and the island of Formosa; we could identify Jonas Salk, Roy Cohn, and John Foster Dulles. These annual quizzes transmitted one more premonition of how the adult establishment would be working when we reached it. *Time* epitomized a genre of surface glibness that was gaining headway in American life, and for young readers the message seemed clear: learn a little bit about a lot of things and don't bother with underlying connections or causes. Instead, match up important names and faces so that you will never feel awkward or ignorant in the right circles. Current affairs, it seemed, were like the rules of Latin grammar or English punctuation, the moves of dancing or playing tennis, the principles of religion or lacrosse—something you needed to have a feel for if you were to meet the ideal of a well-rounded Gilman boy.

What better to counter this notion of slickness introduced from outside than evidence of serious thought and writing produced locally and shared within. If any one thing worked to offset, or at least humanize, the *Time* view of global conflict, it was the ritual of the Sixth Form Speech. Since every senior went to the lectern, we each heard roughly 200 of these presentations as we made our way through the Upper School. In the early 1950s, Chapel was held in "A" Study Hall every morning, and it challenged the skill of any speaker to hold the attention of fidgeting schoolmates packed two to a seat behind the fixed wooden desks, half of which faced away from the podium. In the mid-50s there was the added distraction, for months at a time, of a large new brick building going up less than a good eraser toss from the study hall windows. Finally in April of 1956 the new auditorium was complete, and speakers stood high above their peers, behind a pale green podium, to experience their agonizing 15 minutes in the limelight.

Some speeches, despite Mr. Barker's best efforts, no doubt remained poor. A few, where speaker and topic meshed perfectly, achieved soaring success. But most of these talks proved surprisingly competent. (The Sixth Form speech began as the Fifth Form term paper. The topic had to be approved as significant and worthy of research. Then, the paper was carefully corrected and graded. In the Sixth Form

---

*At first, when Aurel Hollan had something to say in class, he would rise and stand stiffly at attention. Because of his accent, teachers had trouble understanding him. His themes were a challenge to correct. He would meet with his English teachers and go over every line. Yet, he was known to rarely make the same mistake twice. Aurel graduated from Gilman with honors, went to Harvard. He's now a Ph.D.

year, it was revised for the speech and then rehearsed.) The nervous orator not only survived the ordeal but usually managed, perhaps far more than he realized, to alert fellow students to certain names and places, ideas and controversies, that they had never heard of or taken seriously before. Since many dealt with recent issues in foreign affairs, they often served as a forum for testing out our own hopes and fears about the shadows of the Cold War. My brief talk, "Experiment in Democracy," dealt with Nehru's India. I explained how important it was that the new old country limit its population and expand its economy, and I ended rhetorically with the hope that western development techniques, not communist alternatives, would lift India "out of the darkness of poverty into the light of opportunity and freedom."

Not all the idealism and piety of Sixth Form Speeches was directed toward foreign affairs. Mixed in among the presentations were talks on science, history, and culture, along with numerous discourses on domestic issues, some of which seemed as pervasive and shadowy as the Cold War itself. And one domestic theme stood out among all others in these years—race relations. As W. E. B. Du Bois predicted in 1903, "The problem of the 20th century will be the problem of the color line—the relation of the darker to the lighter races of men." He might have gone on to say that in America each decade would approach the matter differently; each community and class, each family and school, would write its own individual history. In suburban Maryland in the 1950s, the color barrier seemed as unsettling to adults as Winston Churchill's "iron curtain," as transparent and impenetrable to adolescents as the "invisible shield" in toothpaste commercials.

I still recall the Monday in May 1954 when I grabbed the sports section of the newspaper after school, anxious to read about how an American shotputter, Parry O'Brien, had just broken the 60-foot barrier. "You might want to read the front page also," my mother said gently. "I think this is an event everyone will remember." I glanced at the headline she was handing me: "SUPREME COURT RULES IN FAVOR OF SCHOOL INTEGRATION." The "separate but equal" era of American education, sanctioned by the ruling of an earlier Supreme Court decision in the case of Plessy v. Ferguson in 1896—one year before the founding of Gilman— would now come to an end. But only with "deliberate" speed, and only in the public schools.

Our independent state of Gilman was insulated from the swings of the American legal system in ways that we did not fully understand. For most of us the United States Supreme Court seemed remote indeed. As clever Gilmanites, we somehow believed ourselves more likely to sit on the high court than to be constrained or guided by its decisions. After all, my own redheaded classmate (and later college roommate), Roger Brooke Hopkins, was descended from Chief Justice Roger B. Taney, the Marylander who had ruled in the Dred Scott decision of 1857 that the nation's founders regarded Negroes as "a subordinate and inferior class of being" who therefore had no rights as citizens. Now all of a sudden Baltimore, the southern city that Mr. Lincoln had slipped through at night in order to reach his inauguration in 1861, faced a reworking of its fundamental social arrangements, and we were looking on from our station wagons and our tree-covered campus in Roland Park. Like contestants on the "$64,000 Question," we were shut into an isolation booth, peering out through the glass.

The isolation was virtually complete, for schools represent the culture that created them, and with regard to race relations Gilman had many of the attributes of a Maryland plantation or a post-bellum country estate. In the old kitchen, amid the clatter of metal pans and the rumble of the mysterious "dumbwaiter," black women were among those who cooked the food, ladled it into serving bowls, and washed our dirty dishes. In the dark basement hallway, James Barry Gross, of the maintenance staff, parceled out chocolate milk and cheese crackers between morning classes. Outside, black men mowed the athletic fields and picked up the trash, a never-ending harvest of milk cartons and "Big Town" wrappers. In the gym, Harry Wilson,* known to us only as Harry, washed our football uniforms, mopped our basketball court, handed out towels to wrestlers, and swept out the mud that baseball and lacrosse players tracked endlessly into his Augean stable.

Like most young Americans, we contemplated race primarily through the prism of sport. Hiking to Westminster to watch August practice sessions or filing into the noisy confines of Memorial Stadium, we watched Weeb Ewbank's integrated Baltimore Colts. We cheered for Lenny Moore, newly arrived from Penn State, and for Gene "Big Daddy" Lipscomb, whose alma mater was listed in the program as "Miller High School, Detroit," but we cheered more loudly for the white stars such as Unitas, Berry, Ameche, and Marchetti. When the Browns migrated from St. Louis to become the Baltimore Orioles, we glimpsed Larry Doby of the Indians and other early black American Leaguers. But race relations throughout the Maryland Scholastic Association changed with great slowness, especially in Roland Park. On rare occasions we took part in athletic events against integrated schools, and by the end of the decade all-black teams sometimes visited Gilman. I remember one of our first baseball games against Dunbar—but mostly because I ended a hitting drought that had lasted half a season.

We Gilman students who recognized Chiang Kai-shek and Gamal Abdel Nasser from the cover of *Time* could not identify Frederick Douglass or Paul Lawrence Dunbar. But we did notice, through the windows of our isolation booth, the strange careers of people our own age as they were suddenly thrust onto the national stage. In 1955, a 14-year-old black youth named Emmett Till was murdered in Mississippi for supposedly whistling at a white woman. In 1959, when Ike sent National Guard troops into Little Rock, white teenagers jeered at black youths attempting to attend Central High School. Whatever their race or gender, whatever their particular roles in the unfolding drama, we could not miss the fact that they were our own generation. As Pogo, a leading commentator of the decade, had observed in another context: "We have met the enemy, and it is us."

How was Henry Callard to deal with his small portion of this smoldering na-

*Harry Wilson was custodian of the gym from 1946 to 1973.

tional brushfire? The dedicated headmaster, who had come to Gilman in 1943, was at the height of his career. His brick home on Roland Avenue overlooked the campus; his sons were active participants in the student body; and he was the surrogate father for a generation of Gilmanites. Hair prematurely white, head cocked to one side, he read scripture to us in the morning, patrolled the front walk for stray paper in the afternoon, said grace when the boarders sat down to supper at night. The gentle elder in the rumpled suit seemed less an administrator than a walking conscience. He patrolled the cavernous entrance hall and the spacious front steps the way a pastor attends the doorway of his church, ministering individually and informally to his varied parishioners. His caring manner and open humility could be an easy target for teenage sarcasm, but like it or not he was a formative moral force in our world, cajoling and encouraging us with his quiet voice and furrowed brow.

Nothing furrowed his brow more deeply than "the American Dilemma" of sordid race relations in an otherwise idealistic nation. Inheriting a Protestant temperament that seemed more Quakerish than Anglican, Mr. Callard appeared more troubled than many Baltimoreans by school segregation. But he knew that it was based upon long-standing racism within the culture and that it would not be challenged without considerable disruption and upheaval. Open controversy was not something he relished, either for himself or his school.

Eager for change but wary of criticism and open dissent, the headmaster began working in the '50s to include persons on the Board of Trustees who could move Gilman away from its segregationist tradition. But these moves were too cautious, veiled, and tentative to yield any immediate fruit. Mr. Callard sensed, whether rightly or wrongly, that if he pressed the matter to a decision he would not receive sufficient support to win a policy change. He might, given the atmosphere of the moment, polarize the Board, divide the faculty, disrupt the student body, and jeopardize his own job. These were not risks that he was willing to take.

Instead, Mr. Callard labored to improve the atmosphere in the school in ways that might prepare the road for subsequent change. Whenever possible, he encouraged visits by provocative adults whose strong credentials prevented criticism. I recall, for example, a classroom appearance by C. Vann Woodward, the revered historian of southern segregation and a wise critic of Jim Crow. He was a professor at Johns Hopkins and the father of a Gilman student. More importantly, Callard poured his energy into vitalizing and diversifying the faculty that was to be the school's greatest asset in those years.

To enhance the recruitment of a new generation of teachers and to increase their influence on students, he pushed for the creation of more on-campus faculty housing. Beside homes where the Russells, the Dressers, and the Gampers already lived, a new residence complex appeared, completed in 1956, and soon to be dubbed "Faculty Row." Located near the gym, this two-story brick structure was in the best tradition of the Baltimore row house, and it allowed married instructors such as George Chandlee, Jack Garver, Reg Tickner, Ned Thompson, Joel Lorden, and Jerry Downs to live on campus with their families at minimum cost.

Unable to break the race barrier by adding a minority teacher, Callard moved to bridge the equally huge but more subtle barrier of class instead. Determined that Gilman students should not be quite so sheltered from the real world, he recruited Nick Schloeder from Calvert Hall in 1958 to be a social studies teacher, a coach, and a resident gadfly. Schloeder accepted the challenge, and the fact that this newcomer immediately assumed a mythic role among students suggests the narrowness of the Gilman mold. Schloeder was a Bucknell grad, who had been a boxer and a long-shoreman; he loved to tell stories about labor unions and democratic politics. Soon everyone knew that the new end coach, guarding the scrimmage line in gray sweat pants and a green windbreaker, was married to a former Miss New Jersey. When a helmet chipped the coach's tooth one day during a blocking drill, he spat it out silently and continued practice. "Mr. Schloeder is *tough*," was the whispered message in the locker room.

Schloeder was also an exceptional teacher—for students and faculty alike. Loyal to Mr. Callard and fully conscious of the unusual role he had been brought in to play, the craggy blond instructor with the Jersey accent set about his appointed task. In the summer he ran a community tennis camp on the Gilman courts, and in the winter he sparred with the well-to-do students in their coats and ties, egging them on to think more broadly. When the old guard assigned him to teaching First Formers instead of senior history students, he took it in stride. "They thought they had buried me," he told me later with a wink, "but I like to get to kids while they're young. It's easier to open up their eyes."

If Schloeder introduced a social dimension that other young teachers such as William Crawford, C. A. Porter Hopkins, and Reddy Finney could not provide, he was joining a faculty that commanded tremendous respect from students and parents alike. These imposing adults, with chalk on their coats, seemed almost universally knowledgeable in their fields, tireless in their dedication, and supportive in their manner. At Gilman a poor teacher was the short-lived exception. The rule was Bill Porter punning his way through a difficult science lesson, Richard O'Brien relating a scarcely comprehensible story in perfect French, Jerry Downs soliloquizing about an impenetrable English poem, or Ludlow Baldwin clasping his forehead in amazement at the sheer glory of ancient history. Even when they lost it momentarily—the icy glare of Miles Marrian, the reddened face of Roy Barker, the multilingual outbursts of Mr. Rasetti—these teachers were broadening our education, imparting lessons about high standards and honest emotions.

Impressive in the classroom, they were even better—and more three-dimensional—when out from behind the desk. Boys whose fathers were often away from home too much watched curiously as Mr. Woodworth led hymns, Mr. Porter repaired cars, or Mr. Garver created watercolors. We worked with them on Saturdays to put together the annual "Circus" in the musty old Cage, and we listened attentively on the athletic field to their various quixotic schemes, gruff reprimands, and occasional kudos.

If we stopped to think about it, we appreciated Dr. Firor taking time once a week to come teach a religious class, or "Nemo" Robinson driving over every after-noon to coach basketball. We marveled, and chuckled, at the all-too-human sight of Mr. Hausmann donning a referee's jersey at football games, Mr. Townsend shov-eling snow on a winter morning, or Mr. Downs driving a Coca-Cola truck during the summer vacation. Few kids grow up with such a rich array of uncles living so close to home.

In later years we Gilman students would marvel in disbelief at the tales of col-lege classmates who had had only one or two good teachers in their first 12 years of school. We had had so many extraordinary mentors that we had taken many of them for granted. It was their diversity of personality, their collective force of char-acter, and their overwhelming commitment to their task that made the school a remarkably open and challenging environment, despite all constraints. Isolated and homogeneous, narrow and demanding, pious and self-absorbed, Gilman in the 1950s still proved a fascinating land to inhabit and a good country to be "from."

Peter Wood '60 attended Gilman 1955–60 with his primary scholastic interests being history and English. He was on the student council for four straight years. By his senior year, he was president of the Sixth Form Committee, sports editor of the *News*, and a member of the Literary Club and Athletic Association.

Wood played varsity football (captain senior year), basketball, and baseball. At graduation, he was presented with the Fisher Medallion. He was a co-winner of The William Cabell Bruce, Jr. Athletic Prize (with Tim Baker) and was presented the Armstrong Prize for Poetry. He also received The Culver Memorial Football Trophy and The Alumni Association Baseball Trophy.

At Harvard, Wood majored in history and played three years of varsity lacrosse—captain of the '64 team. He studied history at Oxford University on a Rhodes Scholarship and earned his doctorate from Harvard. He is currently a Professor of History at Duke, special-izing in Early American history. His recent books include *Winslow Homer's Images of Blacks* (1988) and *Strange New Land, African Americans, 1617–1776* (1996).

The Urge to Help Others

WARREN BUCKLER '53

My time at Gilman began in the fall of 1945, just after the two nuclear bomb blasts that ended the war in the Pacific, and lasted until graduation in 1953, a month before the ceasefire that ended the Korean War. I cherish these years for many reasons, but mainly, I think, because I felt the school valued me as an individual and student even though my family's political and social views were very much at odds with the attitudes that prevailed during this difficult time in the student body and among some in the faculty. This was an era, remember, when Gilman was still determinedly uni-cultural. Many of my classmates came from families who accepted the two-party system only in the abstract.

In many respects, these were good years for most Americans, and for most of us in the Class of 1953, all the more so since we missed, by the skin of our teeth, reaching draft age when American soldiers were engaged in combat overseas. Our country had become the world's preeminent military and political power by virtue of its triumph over forces that were indisputably evil. There was nothing like a victory that was as morally unambiguous as it was militarily decisive to persuade us of our exalted position in the hierarchy of nations. The prosperity that lasted well into the 1980s had its origin in the post-war boom, and an avalanche of material goods seemed to be our birthright.

But it was also a time, paradoxically, when the country was consumed by fear and suspicion of "alien" philosophies, which were thought to infest every important public and private institution. Demagogues railed against any idea that deviated in the slightest from the narrow orthodoxy of "Americanism." Our class, which seemed to have so much to look forward to, was part of what became known as the Silent Generation, one that has been slow to take its place in the forefront of national leadership.

While there was reason enough for anxiety about Soviet intentions, claims of internal subversion more often advanced political careers than national security.

Congressman Dick Nixon and his ilk rose to power by glibly calling opponents "pink down to their underwear." Politicians eager to bag a "Communist stooge" ruined the careers of many decent citizens.

Baltimore found itself uncomfortably near the center of this destructive maelstrom. Alger Hiss, convicted of perjury, had been a distinguished native son. The famous (or perhaps infamous, in light of recent information) "pumpkin papers" were hidden on a Maryland farm. Owen Lattimore, a Johns Hopkins scholar, was falsely accused of being an accomplice in the "loss of China." Ugly redbaiting ended the distinguished political career of Senator Millard Tydings, a conservative Democrat.

Nor did the stresses and strains of these times spare my family. My father, an ardent New Dealer, early civil rights agitator, and sometime politician, ran successfully for the City Council as a reformer, a word not often heard in a city once content to leave municipal politics to the professional "bosses." In the heat of a debate one evening about the route of a new sewer line, another councilman denounced him, in the spirit of the times, as a "fellow traveler." The charge made headlines in The *Sun,* and some readers concluded that the Kremlin was using him as a tool to manipulate a Baltimore public-works project.

If my father's leftist leanings made me something of an oddball at Gilman, my mother's peculiarities brought me notoriety. For one thing, she preferred intuitive to formal book-learning. She couldn't understand why Ludlow Baldwin made us read musty volumes of *Plutarch's Lives* instead of urging us to grasp the unknowable through the use of dietary, breathing, and meditation techniques she was exploring at the time. Studying Latin, she thought, was as useful as learning to keep house in a cave. She viewed sports, which Gilman pursued with such high seriousness, as barbaric when they weren't boring. She and her coven of parental critics, including Peggy Waxter and Carrie Ramsey, mercilessly badgered Mr. Baldwin to modernize the curriculum. How she shrieked with outraged delight when I brought home an algebra book published in 1895, confirming her view that whatever happened in Gilman classrooms had little relevance to the contemporary world.

For its part, Gilman had reason for misgivings about my mother, or at least about her baleful influence on the young men whose values it was trying to mold. Few things amused her more during the after-school rush than pulling up beside the cars lined up at Roland and Belvedere, like competitors in the Daytona 500, and gunning her engine, a challenge to a drag race. Of course, her lowly Studebaker was no match for Fred Klaunberg's four-holer Buick or Frank Carozza's palatial Lincoln, or even for Eddie Dunn's Chevy Estate Wagon, which was a little the worse for having been driven too fast over rutted Howard County roads. But she was certainly game, and to my everlasting mortification became known to budding Al Unsers around Gilman as "Hot Rod Patty."

So it was presumably no surprise to anyone when in 1948, as we entered the Second Form, that my family supported the re-election of Harry Truman, or that I joined a handful of other boys in daring to wear a Truman button to school. This was in shocking defiance of the conventional wisdom that Tom Dewey was not only a sure winner, but would bring Republican common sense and a safe, comfortable mediocrity back to Washington after so many unsettling years under the New Deal.

Truman may be revered today, and politicians of both parties try to claim his mantle. But in 1948, sophisticated folks reviled and ridiculed him, much as they did Dan Quayle during his vice-presidential years. When he appointed Dean Acheson his Secretary of State, Bryn Mawr girls thought it witty to chant "Truman! Acheson! Hiss! Hiss!"—as though the president who stood up to communism in Greece and Turkey and persevered in his support of the Berlin Airlift was somehow part of a plot to turn us over to the Reds.

Months before the election, the pollsters and press routinely referred to Dewey as the next president. Only my mother, with her otherworldly resources, knew what the result would be, so I was prepared. The smugness I felt the day after the election made it possible to endure forever after the withering scorn that Bill Myers—our class's answer to Rush Limbaugh—and a Republican chorus that often included Jimmy Turner and H. Brooks Baker heaped on the New Deal and the Fair Deal.

Harry won, of course, and with the help and encouragement of Roy Barker—who deserves to be admired for his no-nonsense instruction of boorish adolescents, but also for motivating and inspiring them—the President and I went a long way together.

Mr. Barker was famous for his intense and sometimes fiery approach to teaching English to upperclassmen. If he was merely impatient when I was slow to grasp what Keats' "realms of gold" were all about, and disdainful when I sniggered while reciting Caesar's plea "to let me have men about me that are fat," he fairly exploded when I (or anyone) misapplied one of Gilman's sacred punctuation rules (which still rattle about my brain in the throes of composition). There may have been a couple of things you could get away with in Mr. Barker's class (though I can't remember what they were). Misplacing a comma wasn't one of them.

But nothing could build self-esteem quite like Mr. Barker's approval. I remember when Don Hoffman, the track coach and a likeable and entertaining character, died unexpectedly. Editor Tom Perkins assigned me to write about him for The Gilman News. I was manager of the track team that year, and my chief responsibility, along with hauling the shot and discus to meets and reminding Mr. Hoffman to bring his starter pistol to practice, was to listen with rapt attention to the coach's endless preposterous tales about his guns and his adventures while pursuing big game. So what I wrote for The News was more an appreciation than a conventional obituary and included the story about the hole in the ceiling of his apartment. He lived, as I recall, in a couple of rooms above the gymnasium lobby. The hole was created, or so he claimed, by a bullet that exploded when he inadvertently dropped it in the bowl of his lighted pipe.

Anyway, Mr. Barker sent a note that I kept for years and probably still have someplace. He congratulated me on my recollections of Mr. Hoffman, which he said were affectionate and respectful without being "mawkish" or "maudlin." (By coincidence, those last two adjectives were on the vocabulary list we had to memo-rize that week.) It was a huge morale booster, strengthened my still-tenuous inter-est in a career as an ink-stained scribe, and made me a lot less anxious about work-ing with him on one of the major events of our school careers.

In our Fifth-Form year, Mr. Barker guided us in choosing topics for our Sixth-Form speeches and then in writing the initial drafts. It was a signal we were nearing the end. For years we had sat and listened while student orators declaimed on an extraordinary variety of subjects—and gave us a few extra moments to prepare sur-reptitiously for our first class. Now *we* had to think about standing in front of the entire school and talking about a subject on which, thanks to relentless research, we were knowledgeable if not necessarily expert.

I resolved to speak on a question of public policy. That was, after all, a family tradition. And I was eager to argue the virtues of my old friend Harry Truman (who by that time was nearing the end of his term and still unpopular). At home I found a book about Truman's "Point Four Program." Hardly anyone had heard of it then, and only historians mention it now. But it *was* important, even more so in retro-spect. I told Mr. Barker I wanted to speak about it, and he gave the topic his whole-hearted endorsement.

The title referred to the fourth point in Truman's 1948 inauguration speech, which focused mostly on foreign policy and was farsightedly internationalist in tone. He rejected communism as an empty promise and committed the United States to support of the United Nations, the Marshall Plan, and the alliance that became NATO. Then he put forward a new proposal to share our "imponderable resources," technical knowledge, and the "vitalizing force" of our democratic system with underdeveloped nations, helping them defeat "their ancient enemies—hunger, mis-ery and despair."

Then as now, this seemed to me the right description of what America's role in the world ought to be. Point Four was the perfect marriage of idealism and prag-matism. For once, a Western power would seek unselfish relationships with poorer nations instead of grabbing their natural resources or profiting from their cheap labor. By helping poor people satisfy their wants, we would do away with the pre-texts or inducements for war, or so I figured back in 1952. And it seemed certain that countries uplifted with our help would be our friends.

As eagerly as I urged my thoughts on the student body after the usual hymn and Bible reading that morning, my expectations were way too high. Efforts to share our resources and political system have too often misfired or become the in-struments of ideological warfare. Still, the spirit of Truman's plan, the urge to help others join in reaping the benefits of democracy and free markets, continues to re-assert itself and to dignify a foreign policy that has a way of turning cynical.

The speech was not, however, an oratorical success, although I was greatly flat-tered that Mr. Barker had the text printed in *The Blue and The Gray*. ("Our readers ought to know about this," I remember him saying.) Compared, for instance, to the fevered histrionics of my friend and future college roommate Reza Alavi, who described with tremulous voice the life and thought of Jean-Jacques Rousseau—and all but convinced the younger boys that Molotov cocktails would start flying any minute—Point Four was bland stuff indeed. But even if I didn't win any converts, the speech helped me articulate a still ill-defined bias in favor of politicians who actively seek to make the world better.

I also drew much satisfaction from being able to make a case for a "liberal" program and for a president who was the target of many of my classmates' contempt—although I doubt most of them would admit it 40 years later.

As I look back over the scrawled comments of my classmates in my 1953 *Cynosure*, I find several urging me to see the light politically and others warning of Communist influences at college. Only Hugh Nelson signed himself "a fellow Democrat." But all are meant in good humor and written in a tone of gentle irony. Many other Americans my age were not so fortunate. They tell of parents and teachers and schools caught up in the hysteria of the time, of worries about saying something that could be labeled un-American.

I have many reasons for positive memories of Gilman. I had many splendid teachers, including Mr. Pine, Mr. O'Brien, Mr. Gamper, Mr. Chandlee, and, of course, Ed Russell, who all but became a third parent during the year I was manager of his wrestling team.

Classmates at Gilman remain among my closest friends. But I most admire the school for not giving up one bit of its integrity during a period when many other individuals and institutions lost all sense of perspective.

Warren Buckler attended Gilman 1945–53. His favorite teacher was Ludlow Baldwin, who taught him ancient history and Bible, and his favorite coach was Ed Russell, for whom he managed the wrestling team. Interested in history and English, Buckler was feature editor of the Gilman *News* and a member of the political club his senior year. At graduation, he received The Dr. John M. T. Finney, Sr., Essay Prize and the Mason Faulconer Lord prize.

Buckler majored in English at Harvard. He then spent four years with the Army in intelligence and a few semesters at Göttingen University in West Germany. Starting as a reporter, he worked at the Bennington (Vt.) *Banner* for six years before moving to the Louisville *Times*, where he worked as a reporter and editor 1968–86. Until retirement in 1995, he was an editorial writer for the Louisville *Courier-Journal*, to which he continues to contribute, specializing in the environment, Indiana politics, and foreign affairs. The father of two children, Buckler hopes ". . . to have my wife (associate professor at Purdue University North Central) bring home the bacon, cultivate a little piece of ground, and become a volunteer for a do-gooder organization."

May Holmes
and
Helen Stevens

REG TICKNER

Two Gilman stalwarts, the likes of whom may never again grace the halls of this 5407 Roland Avenue institution—May Holmes and Helen Stevens! Together they served the school for a total of 115 years: 66 and 49 respectively.

It was the spring of 1951 that my wife and I first met these two Gilman immortals. The cherry blossoms along the front drive of the school were in bloom. We had just driven down from Long Island. I had an appointment to interview for a teaching position.

The first Gilmanite we met was May Holmes, Headmaster Henry Callard's secretary. A short, gray-haired woman whose appearance exuded friendliness, she was the perfect one to put visitors at ease. She knew who we were. Soft-spoken and sincere, she created in the minds of a couple of strangers a highly favorable impression of Gilman School. She welcomed us as though we were old friends and escorted us to the small waiting room just inside the front entrance of the Upper School building—where she chatted amiably with us for a few minutes before going to inform Mr. Callard that we had arrived. After a pleasant and productive interview with Mr. Callard and Roy Barker, we were escorted to the second floor of the Upper School building where we were provided with sleeping quarters.

That evening, at dinner in the dining room—which today is the Fenimore Memorial Library—we met Helen Stevens, who, at that time, had living quarters in the Upper School. Miss Stevens was a formidable-looking lady, considerably larger than her close friend, May Holmes. She was outgoing and confident. We learned that she had already been at Gilman for many years, that she taught the First Grade, and that anyone who had the opportunity to teach at Gilman was indeed fortunate.

These two ladies—along with Headmaster Henry Callard—were highly effective in convincing strangers that teaching at Gilman was comparable to working in paradise. Miss Stevens and Miss Holmes continued to be positive forces in the lives of the Tickners for many years. They helped a rookie teacher and, later, a veteran teacher, understand both parents and students, and they helped launch, among many others, two Tickner boys on successful academic careers.

When we returned to Baltimore in early September of 1951, it was comforting to know that we had two friends. One of my immediate duties was that of being the homeroom teacher for 80 Seventh Graders. Now among eighty 13 to 14-year-olds there are always a few who like to play games—especially in the late afternoon study halls. When I encountered a seriously difficult situation, I would often consult with one of my advisers—or both of them. More often than not they knew the parents and the history of the student. Armed with the new information, I was generally able to improve these situations. These two ladies were highly instrumental in making the formative teaching years of a World War II veteran more productive—more effective—than they otherwise would have been.

By 1960, I felt like a veteran teacher, little realizing that I was about to become a rookie again. In the summer of that year Mr. Callard asked me to take the position as Head of the Lower School. Knowing that I had a good friend and adviser in Miss Stevens, I accepted.

Lower School parents are, as I quickly found out, emotionally involved in their childrens' successes and failures in school. I often relied on the advice of Miss Stevens to handle delicate situations effectively. She taught me to be understanding and straightforward in my conferences with parents. Whenever we had a parent conference scheduled, Miss Stevens and I would get together in advance to discuss the issues that were involved—behavior, abilities, preparation-performance. Miss Stevens was an expert at analyzing youngsters—both their strengths and their weaknesses.

We'd meet in my office or in the teachers' lounge. Only after initiating the meeting on a positive note would Miss Stevens then introduce the nature of the student's difficulty and suggest remedies. And she always made certain that those who were in need of greater challenges got them. By placing her students in different reading or arithmetic groups, she would ensure that they had positive experiences, experiences that would help them develop their self-esteem. Parents appreciated Miss Stevens' efforts to help the student improve and succeed; she was one of the chief reasons the Lower School always had a multitude of applicants.

In those days I often thought of the Helen Stevens-May Holmes DUO. However, each was a distinct individual. Miss Holmes was small, quiet, understanding, and kind—a favorite of students, faculty, and parents. Physically, Miss Stevens dwarfed her close companion. She was more outgoing, more likely to express her opinions, ready to extend herself to help her students and teaching associates. The Holmes-Stevens friendship was a close one. As different as they may have been in personality, they were one in their love for and admiration of one another.

Even when I left the Lower School to head the Middle School in 1970, I relied on Miss Stevens and Miss Holmes for guidance. Miss Stevens was always a source of helpful information about Middle School students who had graduated from the Lower School. It was not unusual for me to walk over to the Lower School to discuss a student with Miss Stevens. I would return and share her suggestions with fellow faculty members. As a result we were better able to help those who experienced difficulties and also those who were in need of greater challenges. And Miss Holmes, as always, was an encyclopedia of information on any matter having to do with the school and its students.

When Miss Holmes retired in 1982, Gilman faced the challenge of replacing a lady who had been an integral part of Gilman's history, a lady who was loved by all who knew her. When Helen Stevens retired in 1984 Gilman lost the second member of an unforgettable duo, a duo that is a rich part of its past. It was certainly appropriate that in 1993, Miss Stevens received the May Holmes Service Award. Both of these ladies will always be an important part of Gilman's history. They spanned the years that included a depression, a World War, and a recovery that resulted in the school's becoming an institution that serves all segments of the community.

The entire Tickner family, along with many other families, owes these ladies a debt of gratitude. Today, as a retired Gilman teacher, when I think of the 41 highly enjoyable years I had the pleasure of serving at Gilman, I always think of Miss May Holmes and Miss Helen Stevens, both of whom were vital forces in our landing and in our remaining in the green pastures of the Gilman School. Thank you, May; thank you, Helen.

 Reginald Tickner did it all at Gilman and he did it all well. The positions he held cover an unusually wide range of activities in teaching, administrating, and coaching. Tickner's 41-year teaching career at Gilman included service in all three divisions of the school: English teacher and football and wrestling coach in the Upper School 1951–60; Head of the Lower School 1961–70; Head of the Middle School 1971–80; and Assistant Headmaster in the Upper School from 1981 until his retirement in 1992.

Lower Schoolers of the 1960s remember Mr. Tickner as a barrel-chested dynamo of positive energy who taught geography with passion and coached football with concern, and even tenderness.

On he moved, from Lower School head to Middle School head, bringing with him his love of the *boy* in the Gilman student, and his identification with the daily adventure of a Gilman boy's life.

Continuing to grow and develop, Tickner became head of all summer school programs, coach of varsity football and varsity wrestling, and assistant headmaster. He accomplished a rare feat in education, graduating into upper administrative positions, and operating with efficiency, imagination, and excitement, while continuing to bring to the classroom, as an

English teacher, and to the field as a coach/athlete, a contagious sense of fun and positivism and humor, always building up the Gilman scholar, the Gilman athlete.

Tickner grew up on Long Island, New York, and entered World War II upon graduation from high school. From 1942 to 1946, he served with the Navy in the Pacific and was involved in combat. After the war, he attended Franklin and Marshall College, and then earned his Master's in English at the University of Pennsylvania. Headmaster Henry Callard lured Tickner away from the book publishing business, hiring him in 1951 as a teacher/coach.

As much as any of his coaching and teaching techniques, it was Tickner's active participation in the fields of literature and writing and sports (marathon runner, fitness guru, tennis nemesis of colleague Anton Vishio), that inspired thousands of Gilman students to push hard in their chosen fields. He also remained an active mentor to many after graduation, including, in particular, Doug Becker '84, entrepreneur and president of Sylvan Learning Centers, the largest after-school tutoring company in the country.

Tickner often returns to the campus for literary and sports events, as do his two sons, Robert '70 and David '73.

A Most Unusual Admission

HAL WHITAKER '54

Back in February of 1948 my older sister Carolyn was dating a young man named Preston Scheffenacker. Since Preston had a younger brother exactly my age, they hit upon the idea of introducing us, and invited the two of us to a movie on a Friday night.

David and I hit it off immediately, and he invited me to come up to his school the next day to shoot baskets. As a student at Roland Park Public School, I was curious about Dave's school, Gilman, and I asked him to show me around. As he did so, I decided that I really liked Gilman.

On Wednesdays, Roland Park Public ended the school day early, so I walked up to Gilman and into the front door asking to see the 'Principal.' Mr. Callard came out, and I told him that I was interested in enrolling in his school. He showed me around and cracked open the door to the Sixth Form Lower School, giving me a glimpse of the group of boys whom I hoped would soon become my fellow classmates.

Mr. Callard must have been somewhat intrigued by the hubris of this young 12-year-old; he called my parents that evening. He somehow convinced them that it was a good idea for me to become a student at Gilman and asked them to stop by to see him the next day. That Thursday they went up to discuss details, and they came home and announced to me that I would start Gilman on the following Monday.

Mr. Callard never let me forget our first meeting, and whenever I was struggling he would remind me that it was MY idea to come to this school, and that I couldn't let him down. I managed to graduate in the class of 1954, with those boys that I saw through the open door that day in February. I look back on my years at Gilman as some of the happiest of my life and am grateful to Mr. Callard for his magnanimity in encouraging my aspiration to come to Gilman, and once there, to graduate!

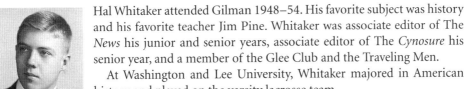

Hal Whitaker attended Gilman 1948–54. His favorite subject was history and his favorite teacher Jim Pine. Whitaker was associate editor of The *News* his junior and senior years, associate editor of The *Cynosure* his senior year, and a member of the Glee Club and the Traveling Men.

At Washington and Lee University, Whitaker majored in American history and played on the varsity lacrosse team.

Currently vice president of sales for White Rose Paper Company, Whitaker is married and has two daughters, one of whom, Molleson O'Donovan, is married to Charles O'Donovan '80, the son of Whitaker's classmate Charles O'Donovan '54.

In the future, Whitaker hopes to find more time to sail on the Chesapeake and off the coast of Maine.

Et in Arcadia Ego

SCOTT SULLIVAN '54

A dolescence is a miserable stage of life. Acne and agony of soul, loneliness and careening hormones, instant exaltation and chronic heartache—all of us who have made it through the minefield of the terrible teens deserve a pat on the back. So, too, do the institutions which, like Gilman, stand *in loco parentis* to recurring swarms of the anguished and self-centered young. Still more do the saintly men and women who shepherded us through our awkward age and sent us out into the world, physically whole and spiritually as little scathed as possible.

Gilman and its faculty have been performing that thankless task for a century now, and doing it—considering the odds—extremely well. I love my old school simply and undemonstratively, as a son a mother. Had my own children been boys, and had they lived in Baltimore, I would have sent them to Gilman without a second's hesitation.

Gilman made me. Who I am. And what I am. (I write this in my Paris flat, between trips to Romania and Armenia, after a week of more routine reporting in Hamburg, London, and Brussels. Dick O'Brien gave me the French to do the job I do; Jim Pine, the passion for Europe and its history; Roy Barker and Jerry Downs, the basics of my writing craft.) Along with the intellectual tool-kit the school provided, however, it instilled another, occasionally awkward, trait: a Quixotic absoluteness for truth. Nobody can sign the sentence, "I pledge my honor as a gentleman, etc." more than 2,000 times in seven years without something rubbing off on his soul.

So when Patrick Smithwick recruited me to write this piece, I had only one question for him: Do you want a pretty picture postcard or a stab at recalling the truth? Patrick swallowed hard and replied, as any real Gilmanite must: Go ahead and tell it like it was.

There are two vital differences between Gilman today and the school I attended from 1947 to 1954. The students are different. So is their achievement, at least as measured by the iron standard of college admissions.

Evidence for the first great change jumps out at you when you compare class pictures across the 40-year divide. In my time, we were, all of us, white. A tiny vanguard of Jewish Gilmanites was present in the school, but not in our class. In our tweed jackets, regimental ties, and (usually) well-ironed chinos, we were extraordinarily homogeneous. An authentic, if not specially interesting, sample of the WASP-and-assimilated-Irish Baltimore bourgeoisie. We were not long graduated, of course, when Reddy Finney set about the long-overdue task of opening the school up to Baltimore and the world.* It has been, and still is, a struggle. But a glance at a current *Cynosure* indicates it has been largely successful so far. Black and Asian faces grin out from class pictures; the dress code seems more honored in the breach than in the observance. Gone are the days of splendid isolation when Gilman boys lived very much like medieval monks, within the precincts of the secular city, but not of it.

Gone too are the astonishing successes Gilman once had in placing graduates in the best American colleges and universities. My class of 1954, one of the smallest in the school's history, graduated 40 boys. More than half of us went on to Ivy League schools, including eight to Yale, eight to Princeton and one to Harvard. Proportionate to its size, Gilman was beating the Saint Grottlesex biggies hands down, year after year. Here again, recent *Cynosures* indicate the measure of the change. From classes more than double the size of those in the 1950s, only a quarter as many Gilman graduates now make it to Ivy League or equivalent colleges. The very long list of schools they do get accepted in suggests that a robust pluralism has taken over in this area of Gilman life, as in all others.**

A certain kind of traditionalist would argue that the two phenomena are linked as cause and effect. Enlarge the school, seek out minority students, they would say, and quality will fall. We knew it all along.

But the story is not quite so simple as that, at Gilman or anywhere comparable. A contemporary school that continued in the 1990s to maintain de facto the exclusive standards of the 1950s would fly in the face of four decades of American social progress. It would probably be in violation of the law. It would, at any rate,

---

*See pages 180–183 of Peter Wood's "Gilman in the 1950s" for a look at how Headmaster Henry Callard set the foundation for the opening up of Gilman under Headmasters Baldwin and Finney.

**When asked to comment on the changes in Gilman's college admissions program over the past few decades, A. J. Downs, college admissions counselor 1963–80, notes, "A study of the records indicates that Gilman and 'the biggies' all did very well with the Ivies until around 1960; then, all began to reach out to other parts of the country at about the same time. A development that Scott and his contemporaries would find almost incomprehensible is that significant numbers of middle-class families choose not to accept Ivy admissions offers on the grounds of expense. The real cloud on the horizon for the Ivies—and for schools like Gilman, for that matter—is the possibility that we will all become schools for the very rich and those poor enough to qualify for financial aid."

have lost touch entirely with the spirit of the nation, the society and the city. Even if Gilman had found a way of legally excluding students and teachers on the grounds of color, race, and religion as well as sex, it would by now have lost its appeal to well-meaning parents and prospective pupils. It would wither and soon die.

For the fact is that Gilman, throughout its century of existence, has broadly conformed with, and reflected, the decent, mainstream views of Baltimore's upper-middle to middle-upper classes. (Gilman has never been a school for the local aristocracy; as often as not, Carrolls, Stewarts, and Garretts boarded at Exeter, Lawrenceville, or Episcopal.) The hothouse atmosphere that reigned at Gilman in my time, and my brother's, precisely suited the doctors, lawyers, and businessmen who paid the school fees. They wanted a socially prestigious institution that, also, maintained towering educational standards. In the 1940s and 1950s they could still have their Lady Baltimore cake and eat it too.

In retrospect, the degree to which the Gilman of those days operated as a mechanism for exclusion is simply breath-taking. Blacks, of course, did not apply. Jews, our parents patiently explained, felt happier "among their own kind" at Park or Friends. The fantastically ample and valuable chunk of real estate on which the school sat amplified its distance from the city outside and manifested the extraordinary privilege involved in being part of it. (I still recall moving from the Roland Park Public School next door to the Sixth Grade, with all the diffidence of a peasant lad transported to Versailles.) Anyone who failed to profit from this geographic largesse, the body language of our teachers and parents implied, had to have something wrong with him. And they were, of course, right on the money.

But Gilman's remoteness from the world was much more than simply a matter of turf, important as that was. The curriculum, grounded in ancient and modern languages, American and European history, English and the sciences, practically never intersected with the tougher, grayer world outside. At 17, I knew far more about Bismarck's era in Berlin than about Tommy D'Alesandro's stewardship at City Hall. (In the summer after my Fifth Form year, I began to report for the old Baltimore *News-Post*. I got to know the D'Alesandros, father and son, as well as the businessmen and crooks, hookers and cops who made up a—to me—new and utterly unknown universe). Gilman did not sponsor outings, except to sports matches and concerts.

To the degree to which the school articulated itself on any outside institutions, they were safe as houses. The girls we dated were from Bryn Mawr, Roland Park, and Garrison Forest. We swam at the Elkridge and L'Hirondelle Clubs. To be on the Upper School roster was to be automatically on the guest list for an endless round of debutante and sub-debutante parties. (I found much later that we had missed out on a good deal of the popular culture of our age-group. Real music for me was Buster singing "Cut down the Old Pine Tree." I caught on to Elvis Presley only after freshman year in college).

But Gilman left few of its inmates much time for exploring other worlds. Indeed, for students from the Third Form on, the school exercised a kind of benevolent totalitarianism. Classwork and three hours of sports daily, combined with Gilman's scores of extra-curricular activities, overloaded the sensory circuits. As a senior in Sixth Form, my own Gilman day stretched from 8 a.m. till 10 p.m. Play rehearsals and literary club evenings, getting out the *News* and the *Cynosure*, singing with the Glee Club and the Traveling Men consumed every minute upperclassmen could spare from study. And a night off very often meant still more school: basketball games, wrestling matches, school dances, and the rest. For students of my era Gilman was not so much a school as an all-encompassing way of life.

This self-preoccupation had some very ugly sides. Anti-Semitic jokes and cruel slurs on blacks were common currency among my classmates. (I like to think it was the stupid boys who practiced this, but I'm not quite sure they were the only ones). Girls who did not attend the appropriate private schools—and even a few who did—were sneered at as fast or frigid. Nasty bullying was commonplace, and worse perhaps than in other schools because of the fantastic length of the school day, which gave the tormentors all the time they wanted. (In the First Form, I was young for my class and very cocky, and so a perfect bullies' target. After months of taking beatings from a trio of teenage sadists twice or more a day, I finally turned on the ringleader and nearly maimed him with my fists and feet. That settled that).

We were a silent generation, the children of a smug and affluent society (Truman and Eisenhower were our presidents, the faraway war in Korea the only distraction from American inwardness), mindlessly snobbish, with scarcely a grain of charity among us. Like Arnold's Rugby, our Gilman was a tough and remarkably intolerant environment. Those who flunked or seriously rebelled left the school. The 40 graduates of my class were the survivors of 80 or more who entered along the way. Counseling was a virtually unknown art. Boys, in the Upper School at any rate, were expected to deal with the agonies of adolescence off their own bat. Lapses produced demerits, which were handed out with cheerful abandon.

The school ethos, though nominally Christian, was in fact profoundly pagan. Most of the teachers were agnostics and made no effort to hide the fact. The warmed-over Emersonianism doled out in what passed for Bible classes for the Protestant majority had no more to do with Christianity than it did with Zen Buddhism. (The Catholics, served by a seminarian from Saint Mary's across the street, presumably got something more like the real article). If the school was concerned with values, they were civic, not spiritual: honesty and plain dealing, physical courage (on the athletic field), and the elusive "gentlemanliness" evoked in the ubiquitous pledge.

And yet, and yet.

Like Goethe, I can claim: I too was born in Arcadia.

For all its foibles and flaws, Gilman in the 1950s was very heaven for most of those lucky enough to attend it. A feast for the mind, a daily challenge to the growing body, a place of warm friendships and equally formative hostilities, Gilman removed us from society the better to launch us back into it. The school equipped us with a splendid education, a sharp awareness of our specialness (We were Gilman boys after all!) and, paradoxically, a keen sense that much would be asked of us to whom so very much had been given.

Like most human institutions, Gilman had the virtues of its defects. By sequestering us and monopolizing our every waking minute, the school maximized its ability to inform and mold our minds, toughen our bodies, and shape us to its—after all, mostly admirable—values.

In this process, the vast physical plant played a central part. Gilman was literally large enough to encapsulate the world. As students there, we lived with the seasons—the autumn scarlet of the great oaks along Roland Avenue, the winter whiteness on the football fields, the spring splendor of azaleas. Teenage boys don't think about nature much, except for those heart-stopping little epiphanies that from time to time steal up on the adolescent soul and snatch it out of time and space. But the shaded path to gym, the dreaming green vistas outside every classroom, the fake-Colonial solidity of the noble Upper School building, the unforgettable scent of freshly waxed linoleum along the corridor to "A" Study Hall, all combined to create and sustain the atmosphere of Arcady.

We were safe in the school. Literally safe from theft and assault, from the troubling company of our female contemporaries, from the drugs and violence that so badly mar the atmosphere of our own children's schools, even "exclusive" private ones. (Gilman, of course, had its own vices: Saturday night booze in epic quantities and a higher than average incidence of in-the-closet homosexuality; they were tolerated precisely to the degree that they never intruded on the school's jealously guarded tranquility.) But the security Gilman offered went far beyond the physical. Just because it was so private an entity, it offered extraordinary opportunities for improvisation and experiment. Our teachers taught as they saw best, with scarcely a thought for conventional pedagogical models. Good students were constantly encouraged to push to their limits. Mr. Barker's literary club, for example, achieved a level of sophistication and originality that few adult societies of the same type ever attain. It was partly Roy's genius, of course, but it was also the standardized dress we wore, the homogeneity, the unspoken expectation that we would do it better because we were Gilman boys.

Out of vague reverence for the great English public (*i.e.*, private) schools, out of the deep American yearning for structure and regularity, out of its own half-century of history, Gilman wove a web of ritual that would impress a thirty-second degree Freemason. From morning chapel with its virile Anglican hymns ("Once to every man and nation comes the moment to decide") to coat-and-tie lunch in the dining hall, with a master at every table, to the unmissable postprandial milling-around on the front steps from 2 to 2:15, Gilman life was shot through with artificial but charming and deeply significant formal structures. We called all masters Sir, odd as that may seem in the second half of this century. (Of all the *little* things that Gilman gave me, this habit was perhaps the most valuable and one of the longest-lasting; I maintained it very happily in my post-Gilman life until very recently, until, in fact, there was nobody left in my office who was old enough for me to say Sir to). Like life itself, Gilman was hierarchized and absolutely unbending about it.

One of the central rituals was, of course, the pledge and the honor system generally. Forty years down the line, I'm still not sure whether the system was a good or a bad thing. It certainly did not eliminate cheating; on several occasions in my Sixth Form year, I was detailed along with a school officer to reprimand an underclass boy caught copying from a neighbor. These were heavy-handed and embarrassing sessions, replete with weeping by the offender and threats of instant expulsion if the offense were ever repeated. Nobody emerged enlightened or enhanced from the experience. And the literal-minded application of the idea behind the pledge could do real harm. In the central drama of my Sixth Form year, a class officer felt obliged to report half the varsity baseball and lacrosse team for breaking training by smoking and drinking beer in the wee hours of a spring Sunday morning. The offenders were duly suspended from the teams. And they in turn ostracized the boy who had reported them—the honor system was accepted by most of us in a general way, but this was puritanism and snitching, grave offenses in the parallel value system of student solidarity. (The hostility, thank God, dissolved in the bibulous conviviality of graduation week, but it tore our class apart as long as it lasted).

What is unarguable is that the pledge exerted a constant moral pressure on everyone in the school. Two or three times a day, in writing, one was obliged to assert not only one's honesty but one's adherence to the rather foggy code of the "gentleman." In the end, of course, the act of pledging became banal, almost automatic. But the issue was omnipresent, and it lasted. Even now, I catch myself reciting the pledge like a beloved old snatch of music: a tattoo on the soul.

No doubt the least ambiguous element in the old Gilman was its sports program. Like many other phases of Gilman life, it was Pharaonically ambitious. A school would have to be crazy to require every single student to practice a serious sport for two hours every day of the year. A school with graduating classes of 40 or 50 boys would be crazier still to play against massive public schools with classes of thousands. Gilman did both things and carried them both off. I can recall one efficient shirker in our class who managed to secure medical excuses most of the time. But he was the only one. (Consider our surprise, on arriving at Yale, to learn that "intellectuals" from Exeter looked down on their school athletes as "sweaty jocks.") At Gilman in our time, acceptance of the value of sports was nearly universal. And the results were near astonishing. Our football and baseball teams were regularly shellacked by the competition. But Ed Russell's wrestlers were still among the best in the Maryland Scholastic Association, and George Chandlee's lacrosse teams won championships as often as not.

For me, whom God made weak and ill-coordinated, Gilman sports were something of a life-saver. I competed fiercely and unthinkingly, avid to compensate for my natural inaptitudes with sheer heart. I still treasure my Varsity "G" above most of the scholastic and professional awards in my closets. Playing one particular football game against McDonogh (who whipped us, 19–7) was a high point in my Gilman life—in my life, period. Those endless afternoons on the football field and tennis courts hardened our bodies and honed our competitiveness. They forged tight links among us. And they taught us how to lose. For, except in our two specialty sports, Gilman lost and lost. Year after year, we went out to get pounded by hulking giants from Patterson Park and Poly, and went again the next year. Such practically inevitable humiliation was a marvelous corrective to the arrogance in-built into the Gilman mentality.

In the end though, the school was about what happened in the classroom. The faculty, especially the senior teachers and the headmaster, set the tone, made the school. And they were, to a man, exceptional in every sense of the word. They were hilariously eccentric, every one, a collection of originals as colorful as Mister Pick-wick's companions. About the only trait they had in common was a dogged dedication to teaching, and a surpassing skill at doing it. They were not particularly scholarly, in the university sense. But they were superb at the job they did.

Jim Pine with his gimpy leg and extraordinarily mobile face imparted his Germanophilic view of European history with such unflagging determination and enthusiasm that I can recall by heart complete passages of some lessons. I can hear him as if he were in the room with me, pronouncing the magical word "Zollverein" (customs union) like a barrage of machine-gun fire. Courtly, southern Tom Lipscomb drilled us in the lower forms in the intricacies of English grammar, giving us grounding that few of our university classmates could touch. Year after year, precise, elegant Dick O'Brien introduced his mostly unmotivated charges to the mysteries of French, enunciated with fanatical, lip-pursing accuracy. (Much of O'Brien's brilliant teaching went for nothing, of course; at least Tom Fenton '48 and I got plenty of mileage out of Gilman French as Paris-based correspondents and husbands of French wives). Red-faced, choleric Roy Barker cherished an almost religious veneration for great English literature (and of course tennis). He pressed his literary passions on generations of students, pushing most of them—certainly me—to read and enjoy texts way beyond our years, prodding, challenging, never accepting a lazy answer. Then there was Ad Hausmann, who taught Latin and German but lived in a world of ancient Sanskrit inscriptions, a curiously European figure in Gilman's very American halls, an inspirational symbol of the disinterested life of the mind. And Ed Russell, more at home among his wrestlers than his Latin authors, but a model of geniality in what was otherwise a rather earnest faculty. And Charlie Gamper, a mid-Atlantic Casey Stengel, a born-in-the-wool teacher-coach, a Christian and perhaps the closest approximation to that elusive ideal—a gentleman—that Gilman had to offer. Among the younger faculty, Jerry Downs stood out as a merry megalomaniac intent on shaping Gilman-Bryn Mawr theater to Broadway standards. (Jerry Downs' wish was almost fulfilled when Robert W. Corrigan directed a lavish, long-rehearsed, and sumptuously costumed "Merchant of Venice" that would have honored almost any repertory theater in the land.)

And finally, of course, there was Henry. Henry Callard was Gilman's soul and conscience in those days. A man of titanic moral sensitivity, he was and remains to me utterly opaque. For, as a Harvard graduate with a distinguished academic career before him, Callard chose to devote himself with a passionate singleness of purpose to running what was, after all, a small provincial private day school. He ran it, of course, extremely well, choosing his variegated faculty and leaving them leeway to go about their teaching as they saw fit, while he looked after what it is hard to find another term for, Gilman's "moral tone." It was a high tone, austere, New-Englandish, and Callard imposed it not through exhortation but through a kind of implicit moral blackmail. Everything that was done at Gilman, or left undone, was motivated by the unspoken premise that it would please, or pain, Mr. Callard. The result of this approach is what we have seen throughout this essay: a truly exceptional school, with unusually high academic standards and success, but a school that nonetheless conformed to and supported a class-and-race-based status quo.

Gilman was to change with the times and the country. Change began with the suave and worldly Ludlow Baldwin, the necessary and graceful transition figure between the saintly Callard and the charismatic Reddy Finney.

On the face of it, Reddy's Gilman of the '70s and '80s was worlds away from the school I attended, as is Arch Montgomery's Gilman now, approaching the millenium. It is bigger, richer in buildings, faculty, and programs. It has preserved and better exploited the school's magnificent physical setting. It has engaged with the city, not only seeking out students from previously unrepresented constituencies but sending Gilmanites out to study and to work in the larger community. It is almost certainly a happier and less stressful environment to grow up in. The needs of students in academic or psychological trouble are catered to, not summarily dismissed. Diminishing pressure to place a majority of graduates in Ivy League schools is good pedagogy and sound common sense. Students who would have been flunked out without fuss, and without appeal, are kept, cherished, and benefit—perhaps more than others—from the rich Gilman experience.

Yet, for all the differences, there are strong links between my Gilman and Gilman today. Reddy Finney is one such link; he had just arrived as an English and Bible teacher (and, of course, assistant football coach) in my last year. Though retired now, his influence still echoes in the hallways and on the playing fields. And there are scores of others at Gilman today, alumni, parents, and friends, who have helped Gilman move, sometimes enthusiastically, sometimes painfully, into a new and different era. They have preserved some of the most vital principles: a local boys' school devoted to academic excellence and to the forging of strong, responsible character. Modern Gilman serves its old community as well as exciting new ones.

That is no mean achievement.

Entering Gilman in 1947, Scott Sullivan quickly established himself as a gifted writer. Literature was soon a favorite subject and Roy Barker a favorite teacher. In his senior year, Sullivan was president of the literary club, editor-in-chief of *The Blue and The Gray*, associate editor of the *Cynosure*, co-editor-in-chief of the *News*.

History, French, and Latin were other subjects most enjoyed, with Mr. Pine (history) and Mr. O'Brien (French) teachers well remembered. Sullivan had a busy day on graduation from Gilman, pulling in a total of ten awards, including The Elisabeth Woolsey Gilman Prize, Douglas Huntly Gordon Prize, two speaking prizes, two debating awards, the Latin prize, and both the prose and poetry divisions of the Armstrong Prizes for Prose and Poetry.

Sullivan earned a B.A. at Yale, an M.A. in European history at Cambridge University, England, and then studied for two years at the University of Paris. He joined the Baltimore *Sun* as a local reporter, moved to city editor and Paris correspondent before joining *Newsweek,* where he is currently European editor. He is the winner of many journalism awards, including the Overseas Press Club's Ed Cunningham Award for Magazine Writing and is the author of two books, *The Shortest Gladdest Years* and *The Lerner and Loewe Song Book*. Sullivan lives in Paris with his French wife, Hélène. The Sullivans have three children and two grandchildren.

A Jewish Experiment

GEORGE B. HESS, JR. '55

The walk up the driveway to the Hess house at the end of my first week at Gilman left me in tears. I felt behind *everyone* else in Mr. Goodwin's Fifth Grade section. I didn't know how to write. (My former school only taught us to print.) My reading was slow; my knowledge of science was zero. Other than the guys who had attended the party Tommy Swindell's parents had had for me in that summer of 1947, I didn't know anyone else in the class. It was overwhelming, but thanks to wonderful support from teachers and my parents, the adjustment to the more demanding Gilman program was relatively smooth.

Social adjustment was something else again. Tommy Swindell, Pete Powell, Josh Harvey, Butch Michel, and others were all friendly at school. As I didn't live anywhere near Gilman or in "The Valley," I had a very different group of friends on the weekends. In those days Jews could not own homes in Roland Park, Homeland, or Guilford, and that created a sort of ghettoization west of Falls Road. It wasn't very common (for 10 or 11-year-olds) to have friends in Roland Park if one lived in Pikesville. It also was unknown at that time for a Jewish boy to go to Gilman. I was a "Jewish experiment" for Henry Callard and my parents.

My dad had initiated the experiment when he and my mom realized I was not challenged by the unstructured school I attended before Gilman. Before becoming headmaster at Gilman, Henry Callard and my father had gone to Hopkins together. When my dad approached Mr. Callard about my attending the school, Mr. Callard embraced the idea warmly. Throughout the eight years I spent at Gilman I felt that Mr. Callard kept a special eye on me. He and Mrs. Callard always recognized me, and their sons, David and Francis, became friends I could count on. I remember sharing in the Callard family's grief after Francis' premature death, which occurred shortly after we graduated.

But the architects of Gilman's experiment with a Jewish boy were not concerned with my social life. They assumed the social life would take care of itself. It did in a curious way. The Jewish kids who lived near us in northwest Baltimore were my friends during the weekends.

There were few incidents of blatant anti-Semitism at Gilman, but it wasn't far from the surface in those days. I'll never forget a disagreement I had with my classmate, Pit Johnson, in my first year at Gilman. The part I remember was his calling me a dirty Jew. Even in those days I outweighed Pit by a lot. It didn't take long before I was sitting on top of him, hitting him until he promised never to call me that again. This was one occasion when a fight led to a wonderful and lasting friendship. Pit and I developed a mutual respect and friendship that has been important to both of us throughout our lives. When Pit became a dentist and hung out his shingle in Anne Arundel County, I drove the 25 miles from where I lived and became one of his first patients. More than 25 years have gone by, and he is still looking after my teeth. We have shared most of the important events of our respective lives, and those that have been missed have been reviewed while I've been in his chair for my semi-annual checkup.

But there was another incident when I was in the Upper School that ended in the reverse way. A guy with whom I had been very friendly was sitting next to me in the dining hall at lunch. He was talking about how awful the Jews were. I told him that I was Jewish, and he said that he didn't believe me. I told him to ask Reddy Finney, who was the master in charge of our table, if he didn't believe me. He did, and after Reddy's affirmation that I was Jewish, the guy avoided me during the rest of that school year. He did not return to Gilman for the remaining years before graduation.

Enough about the "experiment." The most important purpose of the school in my life was to teach me the three "r's" and above all to be interested in learning. In that regard, I had an extraordinary experience.

Whether it was Dick O'Brien teaching me how to pronounce French words with his fingers under my jaws, Roy Barker challenging me about my dull Sixth Form speech on Johns Hopkins, or Miles Marrian smacking my hands with a ruler, I was stimulated to the fullest at the Gilman School. I could go on and on about Gilman teachers: Jimmy Pine would on occasion get so excited about his subject matter that he was oblivious to our talking or doing other things in the back of the room. But history came alive for us because of him. And Bill Porter was a great teacher. Whether it was teaching a science course, physics, or just orchestrating the Circus at Halloween, Bill was creative. He made you realize that "God is in the details."

As a somewhat corpulent and uncoordinated guy I saw another side of these men when I participated in athletics. They were patient with me, but they wanted to win. In this regard, the transition of Ed Russell and George Chandlee from the Latin and math classrooms to wrestling and lacrosse was remarkable. Both had a history of producing winners. They did so with a cold objectivity that was just as important a learning experience for me as my time with them in the classroom.

As the years progressed, I developed a fierce pride about Gilman with my Jewish friends. I was going to the hardest school, I thought, and I was passing. I was never flip about this, but within myself I knew I was working harder and learning more than most of them. They knew where my priorities were when I couldn't talk on the phone in the evening because I had too much work or when I had to work on some school extracurricular activity on a weekend. Gilman had to come first in my life or I wouldn't have made it through!

As I look back on it, the only part of the Gilman experience that was strange was my reaction to daily chapel. While it was only 10 or 15 minutes a day, the regular recitation of the Lord's Prayer and singing of Christian hymns left me confused about my Judaism. As a result, when I was at Dartmouth College I majored in religion. I was serious enough about my studies in the field to consider going into the clergy (not the Rabbinate.) Early in my junior year, I spent a week at Union Theological Seminary. During that week I realized I couldn't accept the deity of Christ. Ever since, Judaism has been the religious answer for me. I directed my vocational interests away from religion and toward business. Soon I was enrolled in Dartmouth's Tuck School of Business Administration.

As our three sons came along, I insisted that they have the Gilman experience if the school would accept them. It is noteworthy that all three had a great experience. As I write this, the oldest is completing his ninth year at Gilman teaching Fourth Grade; the second has paid all his bills with the sales of his sculptures since he graduated from Dartmouth nine years ago; and our youngest has just received his masters degree in biomedical engineering. What is important is that each of the three spent 12 years at Gilman and the school had the breadth and strength of teachers to stimulate each to go into a unique and different field suitable to his talents and interests.

 George Hess came to Gilman in 1947. He has so many favorite teachers, he prefers not to attempt to narrow down the list. His intellectual interests as a student revolved around math, French, and English. A member of the Glee Club and the Christian Association, he was also a two-year man on both the varsity wrestling and lacrosse teams. Spare time went to his hobbies of woodworking, sailing, hunting, and riflery.

Hess earned his undergraduate degree at Dartmouth, where he focused on the study of religion and business administration. He attended the Amos Tuck School of Business Administration at Dartmouth.

From 1960 to 1989, Hess held virtually every type of job Hess Shoes has to offer. He currently works with Magna Properties and the Joseph Meyerhoff Fund, providing the Meyerhoffs with "creative ideas about how they might give their money away," and advising them on investments. "I'm having a good time with my job, and I hope to continue to do it as long as I am able. I'd like to keep on helping others less fortunate than I, to keep playing and doing sports, and to travel and study."

Hess is the father of three Gilman graduates, Michael '80, David '82, and Bill '86. He served as president of the Board of Trustees 1990–94; vice president 1985–90; treasurer 1980–85; and has been a member of the Board since 1968. Among the committees he has served on are: the Budget and Finance, Faculty and Staff, Executive, Primary School, Tri School Coordinating, Financial Development, Trustees, and Investment Committees.

Ludlow Baldwin:
Master of the Socratic Method
and the Personal Touch

AMBLER H. MOSS '56

T
he decade of the 1950s was a transitional one. After it would come the various revolutions of the 1960s—the completion of desegregation, the protests against the Vietnam War, Woodstock, and a host of other metaphors of upheaval. Yet, all the seeds of the '60s were clearly present in the '50s and even permeated the walls of our very traditional institution. The complete picture of the '50s, as well as Gilman's place within it, is an important part of the subjective consciousness of each of us.

The strongest and most important of our recollections from that era have to do with people. Classmates, of course, come to mind. Surely each of us can remember the personalities of the majority of his classmates as well as those of the occasionally awesome characters several classes ahead of us.

Looking back, however, I realize that we were, intellectually at least, shapeless raw material. Its shaping was accomplished by the faculty—those who taught us to think (or, as some would say today, to think critically). So, logically, the faculty stand out as what I personally remember most of Gilman in the '50s. Whether we appreciated it or not (probably not), they were directly or indirectly responsible for setting the course of the rest of our lives. This is not to say that we students were like pieces of iron, passive objects to be seized by blacksmiths and hammered into standard products. Rather—and this is the mark of a fine school—the faculty responded to the initiatives and interests of students as individuals, beyond certain threshold standards, and helped them to develop their best potential in their chosen areas of particular fascination.

It was of crucial importance, for example, that Roy Barker led us beyond the front page and sports section of Sunday newspapers to the book and theater reviews. He, and Jerry Downs, and Alexander Armstrong brought alive Aristophanes, Shakespeare, and T. S. Eliot. They and others obliged us to adopt positions, and then defend them in writing and in speech. How many inarticulate people were we to meet in later life who never received such benefit!

Were the space unlimited in this personal history, I would dwell at some length on the indelible influence of many members of Gilman's faculty on my personal formation. Instead, however, I will focus on one master in particular, Ludlow H. Baldwin. It is not a random choice. Not one of the many truly superb professors under whom I have studied had as great an influence on my education.

Ludlow Baldwin came to Gilman in the aftermath of World War II, in 1946, having distinguished himself as a naval officer.* His academic and professional training was in the law and in business, but his real love of life was history. He would be a part of Gilman until 1968, dedicated to teaching and, from 1963, to serving as headmaster. He also filled in as acting headmaster during two absences of Henry Callard, in 1952–53 and in 1960–61, and was Dean 1955–63.

Ancient history, of the Near and Middle East, was a subject of particular fascination to him.** He brought alive the Sumerians, Chaldeans, Assyrians, the Sphinx, and the Pyramids, as if he had lived among them all. His sense of modern history, in which he was also expert, benefited from his appreciation of ancient peoples. Yet he was, at all times, keenly tuned into contemporary issues; his course on modern American history was the first experience of most students of the era in political consciousness-raising. At his behest, for example, many of us went down to the Fifth Regiment Armory to serve as ushers in both the Stevenson and Eisenhower campaign speeches.

Personal qualities which made him a great teacher were to contribute to his

---

*Ludlow Baldwin served 46 months in the Navy in World War II, from January of 1942 to 1945. He first served as an enlisted man, Aviation Ordinance, 3C, on the Aircraft Carrier (CV) *Wasp.* He then became a Lieutenant, USNR, on the escort carrier (CVE) *Nassau,* as Flight Deck Officer and Watch Officer. He finally served as Lieutenant Commander on the cruise carrier (CVL) *Independence,* as Assistant Gunnery Officer and Senior Watch Officer.

Baldwin accumulated five Campaign Ribbons: American, European-African, Middle Eastern, Asiatic-Pacific, World War II Victory, Philippine Liberation; 12 Battle Stars: Solomons, Attu, Gilberts, Marshalls, Leyte, Luzon, Iwo Jima, Okinawa; and retired with the rank of Commander, USNR.

**For his first 17 years at Gilman, Baldwin taught ancient history at the Second Form—Eighth Grade—level. He notes, "There was nothing like ancient history for forming the minds of boys 12 and 13, for teaching morals without coming head-on at morals or ethics. You can get it all out of Plutarch, the life of Pericles or Caesar or any of them. And you can get it by bringing in the Bible as history. I must have taught 500 boys, and I loved it. I thought I was doing something: preparing their minds in ways of research, in writing, and in other scholastic ways. It was a great age, 12 to 13. They don't know everything and they are willing to take advice and guidance. I think it was the most wonderful experience I've ever had."

success as a headmaster. It is an advantage, then as now, to conduct a class of teenage boys with a booming, clear voice and a steady gaze. What I was to discover years later in law school was that he was a master of the Socratic method, eliciting information and opinions from students by peppering them with difficult questions. It is, among other things, a technique which makes one reluctant to be caught unprepared.

I would be remiss in not recalling that Mr. Baldwin had, as seemingly did all Gilman masters, a trademark mannerism. He would, several times during a lecture, scratch the left side of his face or his left ear by reaching across the top of his head with his right hand, or vice versa. (Try it; it's not that easy.)

His personal interest in a student's development ran to great lengths. I had the good fortune to have him as a faculty adviser. Because of a particular interest in Spanish, I had exhausted the Gilman offerings. Mr. Baldwin arranged for me to take a graduate course at Johns Hopkins and to use his own car to get there. When I was working on a term paper on the nature of the U.S. presidency and its possible restructuring, he sent me to Washington to interview a Massachusetts senator who was conducting a study of that subject. He was John F. Kennedy. I won a prize with the paper.

It is a tribute to Ludlow Baldwin and to other Gilman masters of the '50s that they were able to engage our interest in contemporary problems and give students the analytical tools to deal with them without injecting the partisanship which characterizes a less professional teacher. Perhaps that is why, as creatures of that distant and transitional decade, we were able to adapt to the shifting rounds of the decades to follow.

Attending Gilman 1951–56, Ambler H. Moss, Jr.'s favorite teacher was Ludlow Baldwin (ancient and American history); his main intellectual interests were history, Spanish, and Latin. Moss was known for being courteous and unflappable as the following anecdote, related by English teacher Alex Armstrong '33, exhibits: "In Ambler's day the English office was on the second floor at the head of the back stairs, just two rooms. One day Ambler had an appointment with Roy [Barker]. Roy met him at the door. 'Ambler, would you mind waiting in the hall a few minutes? I have a disciplinary matter to attend to.' Roy shut the door. Then Roy, Jerry [Downs], and I created the sound effects of a terrific scuffle: fists smashed into palms, grunts, groans, objects knocked to the floor. We stopped. Jerry and I half-sat half-lay on the floor. Roy opened the door, apologized to Ambler for the interruption, and invited him to the inner sanctum. Ambler said not a word and never changed expression. With the briefest glance at Jerry and me on the floor, he carefully stepped by us and followed RCB into the other room. Imperturbable. There, had we but known, went the future Ambassador to Panama."

At graduation, Moss was the valedictorian and was awarded six prizes in the categories of reading, writing, debating and history. In the fall, he moved on to Yale where he concentrated his studies on Latin American history and U. S.–Latin American relations. He then served in the U. S. Navy (submarines) before attaining his J. D. in International Law from George Washington University in 1970.

Moss is currently Director of the North-South Center and Professor of International Studies at the University of Miami. He was the founding Dean of the Graduate School of International Studies at Miami, and served as dean 1984–94. From 1977 to 1978, Moss was involved with the negotiations of the U. S.–Panama Canal Treaty and was Deputy Assistant Secretary of State for Congressional Relations. In 1978, he was appointed Ambassador to Panama. A member of the career Foreign Service, Moss has received decorations from the governments of Spain, Panama, Argentina, and Catalonia. He is fluent in Spanish, French, and Catalan.

Moss is married to Serena Welles Moss and has four children.

On Learning
about Learning

JOHN DORSEY '57

Frequently on summer Sunday afternoons three friends and I take a bike ride from Bolton Hill to points north, and it often happens that on our way up Roland Avenue we drift into Gilman for a drink of water at the fountain by the gym. Standing there for a few minutes, looking around at the playing fields and the modest cluster of buildings called Gilman, I am likely to feel a brief twinge that I can only define as a blend of nostalgia and regret. For I now remember my Gilman years with considerably more fondness than I felt for them when I was living them, and wish I had spent those years more wisely, more happily, more fully.

Gilman and I were something of a mismatch, and looking back now I think Gilman knew that; but, like a fond parent with a recalcitrant child, it did its damnedest for me nevertheless. I only came to realize gradually and over a long time how much that was. Of all that Gilman gave me, three things stand out in my mind today, all associated with learning and each associated with a different teacher.

One of those teachers was Richard O'Brien, who taught French probably as well as or better than any high school French teacher in America ever has. Totally dedicated, completely disciplined, with a knowledge that comes of a lifetime of learning, he was a quiet man who could not by any stretch of the imagination have been called boastful. But I remember one day he mentioned that the great French scholar Henri Peyre had called him from Yale to ask if there was a French word for skyscraper. There was, and Mr. O'Brien knew it—*gratte-ciel*, a literal translation from the English. (The word is by now in French dictionaries, but back in those days the concept of the skyscraper was considerably less than 100 years old, and we all know how strict the French are about letting new-fangled terms into the language.)

Day by day and year by year Mr. O'Brien patiently and persistently built up our knowledge of French, like a mason building a wall brick by brick, until you knew more than you knew that you knew of the language—from the spelling and grammar to the literature and the oh-so-important pronunciation. I remember spending an evening in Paris some years ago among a group that included someone who had graduated from one of the other good Baltimore schools and who spoke French by pronouncing everything exactly as it would have been pronounced in English, so that *veuillez* came out something like *view-lay*. I thanked Gilman for Mr. O'Brien that night.

At the risk of sounding grossly self-serving, I want to relate something that happened once in Mr. O'Brien's class. One of the things we did was read French aloud. Mr. O'Brien would assign, say, a poem, and on the appointed day he called on each member of the class to read a few lines. That was the part of the class I liked the best, and I practiced those assignments with a diligence I rarely bestowed on any other assignment of any kind. One day the assignment was a poem by Lamartine, "Le Lac," of no fewer than 16 four-line stanzas. When the time came to read, Mr. O'Brien called on me first. I read the first stanza, and paused briefly, but Mr. O'Brien didn't call on anybody else, so I went on to the second stanza. Still Mr. O'Brien didn't call on anybody else, so I went on to the third stanza, and the fourth, and the fifth, and the sixth, gradually beginning to realize that he was going to let me read the whole poem. Imagine, if you will, that you catch a pass on your team's 10-yard-line, and charge down the field dodging everyone in your way, until at last you're in the clear and headed for the touchdown, and you will have some idea of how I felt as I read on and on with growing confidence and elation, all the way to the end. After which Mr. O'Brien said, "That is the way that poem ought to be read," and we went on to something else.

Of course it is only years later that one identifies certain things as having been important in one's life; but I think Mr. O'Brien taught me something in those few moments that my gradual recognition of his own lifelong and unassuming devotion to his subject only reinforced: that learning is only secondarily a stepping stone to some tangible reward such as a degree or success in one's career. Learning is first and foremost an end in itself, and its own reward.

The second teacher I especially remember is Ludlow Baldwin, for the American history course he taught my senior year at Gilman. Mr. Baldwin's was an American history full of facts—so full that I carried the fat loose-leaf notebook from that course all through college with me, and it helped me on many a paper in preparation for many an exam. But Mr. Baldwin's was also an American history full of life, the life his enthusiasm brought to it. There was a sense of competition and excitement in that class, especially when Mr. Baldwin, as he did frequently, put his head down on his arms on the desk so that you couldn't tell whom he was going to call on, and formed a question followed by the bark of a name. If the name was yours it was almost like being hit in the chest, and you had better have the right answer right away or Mr. Baldwin would bark out another name and you'd have lost your chance. This method might sound intimidating, but actually it was exhilarating; it was like a game, with teacher and students all in it together, and you loved being in the game partly because he so obviously loved it too. I don't think I've ever known a teacher who got so much sheer enjoyment out of teaching as Mr. Baldwin did, and that sense of enjoyment was so infectious that it determined my college career. I majored in American history. Mr. Baldwin taught me the joy of learning.

Finally, there was Jerry Downs, to whom I owe so much in so many ways. As my advisor, he was gently encouraging. As the guiding light of the theater group, he *at last* was able to get me interested in some sort of extra-curricular activity not long before I graduated. But it was as my English teacher for four years that he gave me the greatest gift a teacher can give a student. I don't remember much of what we read in those years, but I do remember the discussions. Mr. Downs weaned his students, especially as they got older, from simply listening and taking down what he said, and encouraged them instead to develop their own points of view and even to challenge his. One's own opinion might be looked on as ridiculous and even embarrassing later—I confess to once arguing that Poe was greater than Shakespeare (well, I was only 16)—but that mattered less than the fact that the opinion was one's own. And Mr. Downs, as I remember, never took the line that, well, discussion was to be encouraged and so forth but in the end his opinion invariably ruled. He introduced us to the possibility that the teacher might, on occasion at any rate, be wrong and the student might be right. (He was wrong, I thought then and still think, in preferring Sibelius to Tchiakovsky, but I won't press him on it.) He taught me that the essence of learning is not to receive knowledge but to think for oneself. He gave me the gift of independent thought, and to do that a teacher must have those rare qualities, true generosity of spirit and a genuine respect for the other individual. Those have always been Jerry Downs' hallmarks, as a teacher and as a person. I owe him.

I owe Gilman, too.

John Dorsey is a 12-year Gilman man, attending 1944–57. In the Upper School, he was a member of the Dramatic Association, Political Club, and Christian Association. His favorite teacher was A. J. "Jerry" Downs. At graduation he won the Armstrong Prize for Poetry. His principal interests throughout his years at Gilman, and then Harvard, were history and American literature.

After graduation from Harvard, Dorsey signed on with the Baltimore *Sun*, and has been there ever since, as a feature writer, book review editor, restaurant reviewer, and currently as the art critic. Dorsey won the A. D. Emmart Award, the first one given, in 1974, for excellence in writing in the humanities, and is the co-author of *A Guide to Baltimore Architecture* (1973, 1981), the editor of *On Mencken*, a collection of essays on Mencken and selections from his writing (1980), and author of *Mount Vernon Place, an Anecdotal Essay* (1983).

Chapel, Mr. Callard, and a Cherry-red James Dean Jacket

FRANK DEFORD '57

I t certainly never occurred to me back then, but Chapel was an ideal way to start the day. It provided time for you to get squared away, to catch your breath and (optional) listen up to what was going on. Since I departed Gilman, I have found, in life at large, that mornings are different. Post-Gilman, the days just sort of come upon you. A bell rings or the boarding gate opens or someone says, "You can go in now." Chapel was just right for getting the cobwebs out, a quasi-spiritual coffee.

Looking back, it seems so wonderfully quaint. In fact, I think it was quaint to us, even then. Chapel was held in "A" Study Hall, which I always thought was a pretty insipid name—couldn't they do any better than just "A" Study Hall? "A" Study Hall housed the Third, Fourth, and Fifth Forms. For Chapel, the members of the First, Second, and Sixth Forms would share seats with those permanent denizens. Since there was an abundance of First and Second Formers, some Sixth Formers had to sit on the ledges around the sides of the room, which was the most prestigious place to be.

The devotional part of Chapel was but a modest part of the whole program, lending itself to the name—Chapel—more so than in spirit. There was a Bible passage and a prayer, and since virtually everybody in those days was Protestant (let alone Christian), the scripture had a familiar drone to it.

But there were also, on many days, secular divertissements. In fact, if Chapel lasted into overtime, the whole school simply went on "late schedule." This meant everything was pushed back, with a little chunk sliced out of each class period. If you think about it, this was a wonderfully civilized way to run things.

215

But then, there was a lot of quaint stuff at Gilman then.

I may be a little hazy on exactly who ran Chapel. I believe it was something like this: Mr. Callard two days a week, Mr. Russell one day (usually Fridays), other faculty members one day, and members of the Christian Association or class officers or other student muckety-mucks one day. Does that seem right? Some teachers never seemed to run Chapel. I never knew whether they didn't want to, whether they demurred for religious reasons, or whether it was a clause in their contract not to have to. Mr. Marrian, for example. I don't believe he ever hosted Chapel. But then, I don't believe Mr. Marrian did anything outside of the math classroom. He was a specialist.

There were three things that dragged Chapel out and tilted us into "late schedule." These were: 1) Sixth Form Speeches, 2) Leo Collier's mother's string quartets, and 3) Mr. Russell, who loved Chapel more than anyone. Mr. Russell came from the Cotton Mather School of Devotions, which believed that windiness is next to Godliness. Mr. Russell was genial enough, pretty much off-the-cuff, and would have been perfect for public access cable TV, only it hadn't been invented yet. But Chapel was, under Mr. Russell's aegis, a sort of "Wayne's World" ahead of its time.

Sixth Form speeches were something you had to endure; the greater interest was whether the speaker would screw up, rather than anything he might actually say. The only Sixth Form Speech I ever remember that anybody talked about ahead of time was Cotton Fite's. Cotton stuttered terribly, especially when he had to make even an informal address in class. It was assumed that Cotton was going to create a late-late schedule.

But Cotton was an extremely popular fellow, and this was the one time that everyone in "A" Study Hall was actually rooting for the speaker *not* to make mistakes. We were all breathless, when Cotton stood up to the podium, looked over the throng and began: "Mr. Callard, members of the faculty, and fellow students." Not a hitch. We sighed. It was all downhill from there. Cotton never blew so much as a syllable. Got a standing O.

It was one of the finer days I ever had at Gilman, and about the best Chapel of all, the morning Cotton Fite gave his Sixth Form Speech, flawlessly.

But then: poor Leo Collier. He lived way up in Aberdeen, and the story was that sometimes Leo would sneak onto the Proving Grounds and ride around in the tanks. I don't know whether this was true, but it certainly impressed me.

But: poor Leo Collier. His mother was determined to improve the Vulgate musical taste of Gilman boys. So, she was always dragooning string quartets and foisting them on us in Chapel. Mandolins and flutes and cellos and oboes—oboes!—and Leo was mortified because he had to take crap all day from everybody on account that his mother made us listen to "fairy music."

Actually, everybody rather liked the music. Well, we didn't like the *music*, but we liked it that it always took up a lot of time, the oboes, and put us on late schedule.

Now, Mr. Russell: he was at his best on game days in Chapel. He would lead cheers for the teams and have the varsity boys pick up their books and walk out while we all clapped for them. McDonogh really got Mr. Russell worked up. He had a thing for McDonogh. He called them "The Farmers." It was written on a lot of signs, too: PLOW THE FARMERS, stuff like that. In fact, in normal, everyday conversation nobody ever referred to McDonogh as "the farmers." It was just something that had been made up for effect—probably in Chapel, probably by Mr. Russell himself. Everybody called us "the Gilman fairies" all over Baltimore, so that probably inspired us, "the fairies," to get back at McDonogh. It was pretty weak, but it was all we had.

McDonogh—excuse me, The Farmers—were our traditional rivals, our arch rivals. I never knew why. Nobody did. I didn't even know where McDonogh was, except it was somewhere out in the sticks. I didn't know anybody who went there. Worse than farmers, too, McDonogh was actually a bunch of little soldiers. Who, in their right mind, would want to go to a military school? Or, even worse, who would want a military school as an arch rival? There were ten other schools around town I had more interest in, but Mr. Russell told us in Chapel that McDonogh mattered, so he would get up and stir us into a frenzy, have Walter Birge lead cheers—the works—and we would all go along and scream bloody murder about the Farmers.

Late schedule.

As it mirrored his personality, Mr. Callard ran a subdued Chapel. Even if he was addressing the whole school, jammed two to a seat, he had a wonderful way of making it sound like an intimate conversation. You had to strain just a tiny little bit to hear him. Sometimes, though, he would talk very frankly—if, for example, he had had to kick somebody out, and he wanted to explain his reasons. Other times, there would be homely little anecdotes.

One in particular I remember was about honor, and about how honor was not just something you had to attest to at the end of every test and every quiz. Honor was something you had to live up to for yourself, within yourself. If anybody else had framed this topic—especially someone from the Christian Association or the Student Council—that's it, lights out in the minds of everybody in "A" Study Hall. But we all kept on listening to Mr. Callard. I know, because we talked about it later on that day.

To illustrate his point, Mr. Callard told us about how, early one morning, he was driving to Penn Station to catch a train, and he knew it was going to be a close call, but still, it wouldn't be right to exceed the speed limit. And right away, we all nodded. We could *see* Mr. Callard's car limping down Roland Avenue at six o'clock in the morning, hardly a car on the road, sticking at 25 miles an hour.

Everybody just looked at each other, amazed. But nobody did one of those things where then you had to stare down at your shoes and hold your breath to keep from laughing. Because everybody believed Mr. Callard. Everybody could visualize him, crawling down by the Water Tower at the crack of dawn, not another car in sight. We kept talking about it all day. In awe. Nobody doubted him for a minute.

Mr. Callard said he missed the train, too. You see, that was the real point. That was the price of honor that you paid to yourself. To be honorable, you had to miss trains and go onto your own personal late schedule in a world that didn't accept that.

So, that was another Chapel I remember vividly. In fact, sometimes I think about that when I speed when nobody else is around. I guess it doesn't stop me from speeding, but at least I know I'm wrong and I have to deal with that myself.

Mr. Callard and I finally came to a collision of sorts over Chapel—well, a glancing blow. Now, of course, everybody had to wear coats and ties in Chapel. But there was no rule *written down* that you couldn't wear anything *over* your jacket. Like, for instance, another jacket. A different jacket. After all, who in their right mind would want to wear anything over a sport coat in a room stuffed with 350 boys, a number of whom probably didn't bathe daily?

But then, there was James Dean. *Rebel Without A Cause* had come out during my junior year, and it had made an impression upon me the likes of which had nothing since *Catcher In The Rye*. If you will recall, James Dean—by now, in 1956, the late James Dean, which added to his mystique (the good die young)—wore, throughout the movie, a cherry-red jacket. When I discovered that such jackets were available at a store in Pimlico, near where the Gilman *News* was printed, I bought one. The cost was $19.95. The only other vanity purchase I ever made for such a huge sum of *my own money* was the Charles Atlas Dynamic Tension muscle-building mail-order course.

I wanted desperately to be seen in my James Dean jacket—and where better a place than "A" Study Hall, at Chapel, where the entire Gilman universe was gathered together? So, I wore it over my standard-issue tweed coat. Every day. I worked it so that I would arrive in Chapel at the last second, as if I just hadn't had time to remove my cherry-red James Dean jacket. Probably this was transparent. Certainly, though, it kept me within the letter of the law and left me terribly smug. In those days, the '50s, the idea was not to break the rules; it was to stretch them as far as you could. Kids battled authority with their wits, not with confrontation; victories were small, but the satisfaction larger, I think.

Then one day I was elected president of the Student Council for the next year, and my first responsibility in this new position was to go down to the Lower School and address the boys in the Sixth Form there who would be moving up to the Upper School next September. Mr. Callard told me about this and what day I was supposed to make the speech. I started to leave his office. "Oh, Frank," he said softly, and I turned back.

There was a little smile on his face.

"Yes sir?"

"Now, you won't wear that red jacket of yours when you talk to the Lower School, will you?"

I hesitated for a moment. He had caught me completely off guard. "No, sir," I said, and I grinned—probably foolishly—and then we both laughed a bit. I got the picture. Mr. Callard never said another word. And even though it wasn't actually against the written rules, I never sullied Chapel again with my cherry-red James Dean jacket.

 Frank Deford came to Gilman via Calvert School in the First Form, Upper School. His main interests throughout his six years were English, history, drama, and basketball, and his favorite faculty members were A. J. "Jerry" Downs (English) and John M. Robinson (basketball). By his senior year, Deford was student council president, editor-in-chief of the *News,* president of the Dramatic Association, president of the Literary Club, editor-in-chief of the *The Blue and The Gray*, and a member of the varsity basketball team.

Winner of the Fisher Medallion at graduation, Deford was also awarded the Sixth Form Speaking Prize and the Armstrong Prize for Prose. He was a co-winner of the Class of 1939 Basketball Trophy.

Attending Princeton, Deford majored in sociology and history, and was chairman of T*he Daily Princetonian.* He started at a lowly editorial position at *Sports Illustrated* in 1962. By the 1980s, The National Association of Sportscasters and Sportswriters had voted Deford Sportswriter of the Year six times, and the *Washington Journalism Review* had chosen Deford Best Magazine Writer in the country twice.

Frank Deford is known for bringing a warm, personal, empathic tone to his writing. This was especially true in his book *Alex—The Life of a Child*. Deford wrote *Alex* after his daughter, Alexandra, succumbed to cystic fibrosis. As the Chairman of the Cystic Fibrosis Foundation, Deford looks forward to the cure for the disease.

Currently, Deford is a contributing writer at *Newsweek,* has a weekly sports commentary—punctuated with wry observations of ironic circumstances and four and five-syllable Latinate words in which he seems to take glee—on National Public Radio, and contributes to HBO television and ESPN radio. He continues to push the boundaries of his oeuvre, in 1993 completing the historical novel *Love and Infamy.*

1960s

1960
Family Day is inaugurated.

1960
Headmaster Henry Callard attends two-month European conference on a Fulbright grant.

1961
Standing behind the podium on the stage of the Alumni Auditorium, Pope Barrow '61 commences his Sixth-Form speech on Pablo Picasso. The curtain opens for the showing of slides and neatly enwraps the presiding and seated Ed Russell, leaving nothing visible except Mr. Russell's feet. Pope Barrow—the only person who cannot see what is happening—is baffled as his audience goes into paroxyms of laughter over the same speech no one had found humorous during dozens of rehearsals.

1962
The Science Building and Lower School addition are built.

1963
Henry H. Callard retires; Ludlow H. Baldwin '22 succeeds him as headmaster. May Holmes retires, only to return to Gilman yet again in 1965. Large contingent of old guard retires, including Tom Lipscomb, Richard O'Brien, Ed Russell, and Al Townsend.

Charles C. Emmons '23 is appointed director of development.

1964
Charles F. Obrecht '52 is appointed first general chairman of the Annual Fund and sets up detailed fund-raising organization.

1965
The Gilman Circus provides funds for Upper School library renovation, incorporating the student mailbox corridor and old Sixth Form room to which a balcony is added, doubling library capacity.

In a faculty softball game, Reddy Finney breaks up a double play, plowing up a 30-foot strip of sod and sending faculty member Dimitri Manuelides to the emergency room.

The Class of 1966 joyously assembles on the steps outside the Cottage in 1960. As the "Sixth Form" of the Lower School, this was their year to be top dogs. Just to assert this point, the class mascot proudly sits in the middle of the bottom row. For more about this class and life in the cottage, read Tim Baker's "In the Custody of Strong, Nurturing Men."

1966

New construction links the Cage and the Gymnasium.

Headmaster Ludlow Baldwin asks Latin and Greek teacher Anton Vishio to begin special community service program to be coordinated with Echo House Foundation. The resulting program is named Operation Greengrass.

1967

Mathematics teacher Ned Thompson '45 teaches the use of Gilman's first computer, a closet-sized machine, on the second floor of Carey Hall, in the Alumni Room.

With the strong support of Headmaster Ludlow Baldwin, Operation Challenge, known today as Upward Bound, is founded by faculty members William B. Campbell '52 and Redmond C. S. Finney '47 to assist disadvantaged students.

Sherm Bristow '67 is named one of the Outstanding High School Basketball Players in Baltimore by area coaches, The *Sun*, and The *News American.*

Under the coaching of Redmond C. S. Finney, with Nick Schloeder as one of the assistants, Gilman's football team has an undefeated, and untied, season. Stars include fullback Stuart Simms '68, running back Allen Kirby '68, and quarterback Dennis Malone '68.

"Latin Day" is officially begun. Latin and Greek teacher Anton Vishio expands the annual Latin Declamation Contest to include a full day of Latin skits, trivia contests, model contests, a Latin play, and the notorious Chariot Race, for which students make their own chariots.

1968

President of the Board Dr. Ridgeway Trimble announces in morning chapel that Ludlow H. Baldwin will retire after graduation and Redmond C. S. Finney '47 will become headmaster.

Dennis Malone '68 is named one of the Outstanding High School Basketball Players in Baltimore by area coaches, The *Sun*, and The *News American.*

1969

Bill Campbell and Headmaster Finney persuade Bill Greene to work at Gilman full-time; Greene becomes the first African-American to join the Gilman faculty. In 1970, Greene succeeds Campbell as director of Gilman Upward Bound, a position he holds with distinction into the '90s.

In order to strengthen Anglo-American cultural bonds, Thomas G. Hardie II '39 establishes the Harry Hardie Anglo-American reciprocal student exchange program with St. Edward's School in Oxford, England.

Opposite: After studying art with Jack Garver 1961–62, eight members of the Class of 1963 formed the non–self-perpetuating Art Club in 1962 and supported projects such as Eat Jello with Humility Week and Garver Yo-Yo Industries. Top to bottom: Mitch "Mitchelangelo" Miller, Club President "Mumblin" Dick Small, Craig Woodward (Small's interpreter), John Loeb, Tom Chase, Jimmy Rouse, and Vice-President Peter "Picasso" Rodman. Not shown is Terry Mudge.

Above, it's a ragtop kind of day in the 1960s, and tailfins are in.

Left, Upper Schoolers dine formally in the Fisher Memorial Dining Hall. A few may be planning to catapult pats of butter to the ceiling. Perfectly aimed butter pats would stick to the ceiling, gradually melting, and splatting on the head of a teacher.

High-scoring varsity basketball player Tim Baker '60 dunks one.

Below, seniors are rather remarkably calm and studious in this shot of the senior room, 1963.

Opposite at top, coaches Nick Schloeder and Reddy Finney talk strategy with John Claster '63, captain of the varsity football team.

Below, cheerleaders of 1963 show off their clean-cut look and well-synchronized moves. From a Lower Schooler's point of view, watching the cheerleaders in the Sixties was almost as exciting as watching the football games—or even starting up a touch football game.

FOLLOWING PAGES:
Fresh-soph wrestlers Tom Whedbee, Brent Whelan, and Trey Sunderland yell encouragement to a fellow wrestler in this shot taken by a *Life* Magazine photographer. By their senior year in 1969, Whelan, as captain, and Sunderland were two of the top wrestlers in the MSA, while Whedbee switched his winter athletic interests to skiing and outdoor pursuits of the Hoffman Club.

Opposite, L. Bruce Matthai congratulates Headmaster Ludlow Baldwin after Gilman won the Gilman-McDonogh Football Trophy on November 18, 1966. During his six years as headmaster, Baldwin had the best athletic record of any Gilman headmaster.

Above, Graeme Menzies and Major General Warren Magruder were favorite teachers of Lower Schoolers in the 1960s. Many students left the two in the Sixth Grade, only to happily return to them as JV lacrosse players in the Upper School. (Magruder is not photographed in his typical Gilman teaching/coaching attire.)

Left, Dawson Farber '35 has been one of Gilman's most active and influential trustees for almost half a century, from 1964 through the 1990s.

Right, Meredith Reese, teacher at Gilman 1950–79, talks to Jack Harvey '69, student council member and perennial class officer. Harvey and the Student Council of 1968–69 had an especially busy year handling all the changes brought in with the new and youthful Headmaster Reddy Finney.

Lower School Head Reg Tickner works with a Lower School student. Tickner, who taught, coached, and served as administrator at Gilman 1951–92, was known by students and faculty for his boundless positive energy and his love of the Gilman boy.

Below, the Class of 1969 in 1963 as Sixth Form leaders of the Lower School. First row: Libbey, T.; Clinnin, D.; Sunderland; McCardell; Speed; Buck; Harvey, John; Simmers; Torrance; Baier; Danzer; Lynn, W.; Slaughter. Second row: North; Lambert; Smithwick; Iglehart, T.; Lewenz; Dunn; Novak; Burghardt; Milnor; Koppelman, M.; Whelan; Franke; Deford; Boyce. Third row: Machen; Curtis; Eager; Gamper, D.; Herrmann, W.; Koppelman, L.; Rohrer, R.; Huppman; Somerville; Purnell; Proutt; Rice; Bradley; Goldsmith; Whedbee; Marshall.

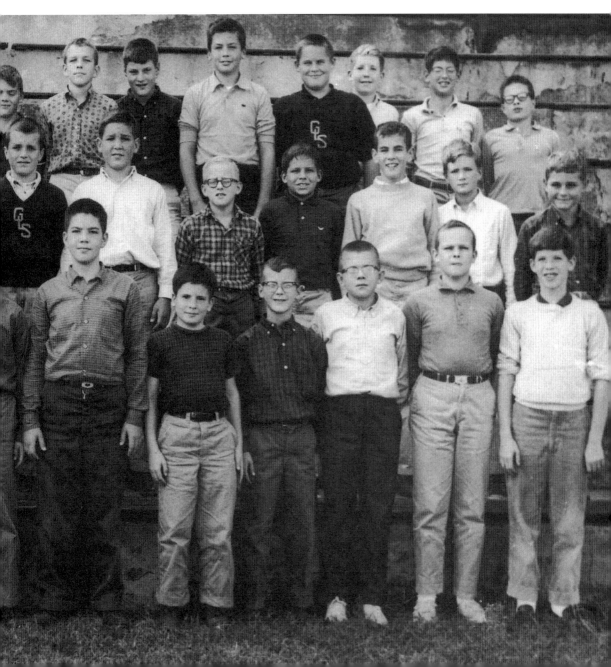

Gilman in the 1960s:
A Commitment to Change

NICK SCHLOEDER

The Fifties are thought to have been the decade of the center—quiet, conservative, uninteresting. I'm not sure I agree with "uninteresting," but "quiet and conservative" fits the Gilman I came to in the fall of 1958. And if the decade of the Sixties is thought to have been a decade of reform, activism, and change, Gilman was bubbling with all three when I arrived on that September morning. Gilman was a place where people cared and people valued a commitment to service, a commitment to change what was not right in society by working to make things better. So while the Sixties were a decade of change, at Gilman the fundamental values were all in place. The players changed, the union broadened, that was all. As they might say on the street these days, the "motion of the ocean" was always there.

The Sixties began with the comforting sleepy reassurances of the Fifties, and Gilman was as reassured as any place. I remember asking a senior that year where he was going to college the following September. He told me that he hadn't really thought about it, but he guessed Princeton, Harvard, or Yale. Knowing something about his academic performance, I asked him where would he go if he didn't get into one of those schools. He looked at me as though I were some alien being who hadn't quite connected with Earth after leaving the spaceship. It was not an unfamiliar look during my early years at Gilman. After a moment or two of hesitation, the senior said he guessed he would *have* to go to Amherst or Williams. The teacher-alien felt even more unconnected when the lad ended up at one of the Big Three. (I've learned enough in my 30-odd years at Gilman not to say which one of the Big Three.)

When Anne Carey came up with the idea of a Country Day School for Boys in the 1890s, it was to be an alternative to sending the sons of the Baltimore establishment away to boarding school at an early age. In Brad Jacobs' wonderful piece that begins this book, he quotes Anne Carey: ". . . sending a nine-year-old boy to boarding school and then to college, and perhaps to Harvard Law School, meant that when he came back to Baltimore to make his living, *he was never exactly of us.*" The decade of the '60s saw the composition of the pronoun "us" change dramatically. By 1970 Gilman would still be a great school, but it was a very different school than it was in 1960 and moving quickly toward even greater changes.

Integration came to Gilman in 1962, eight years after the Baltimore public schools. There had been emotional opposition to integration from some alumni. This reached a crescendo at an annual alumni banquet meeting at the Maryland Club at which the vote was two to one in favor of integration. The president of the Alumni Association resigned. Another alumnus asked that his name be expunged from the school records. One can only imagine the pressure under which Mr. Callard worked.

There were a great many in the faculty who supported integration with varying degrees of ardor, and there were no "segregation now, segregation forever" types, but caution was still the dominant point of view on the faculty. Henry Callard was the key. If anyone personified the art of "gentle persuasion," it was Henry Callard. In his quietly dogged way he brought people around to his way of thinking—and I think it really took its toll on him.

I often wondered why he wouldn't call more openly for support. Out of admiration, respect, and even love, I think he could have "made the call" on the faculty support at almost any time, but his technique with the faculty was to listen and to listen some more and to gently nudge, and even more gently bump or even spin you until you came to his side of the issue believing that is where you always had been.

There were only five African-American applicants in the first three years of integration. Hardly the massive influx that some people expected. But it was a beginning. The first Asian-American was also admitted during these years.

The Sixties were a turnabout time of unforeseen challenges and change. Fortunately for Gilman, it was also a decade of three remarkable headmasters: Henry Callard, Ludlow Baldwin, and Redmond Finney. They were different, but there were traits that linked all three. Each was a man of the highest character, with a rigorous intellect, a constant caring and concern for all the young men in his charge, and finally, a deep and abiding love for Gilman.

In the summer of 1958, I received a call from Mr. Callard. It seemed there was an unexpected opening on the First Form faculty, and he wanted me to come to the school for an interview. It was a most unusual job interview which lasted well over four hours and consisted of a long discussion of philosophy, politics, economics, and just plain life, as well as a long walk around the campus with stops along the way to weed a flower bed or two and pick up the odd piece of paper. We returned to his office where he offered me a job for the coming year.

I had one nagging worry. The previous winter I had brought an opposing basketball team to the Gilman gym to play a very good Gilman team. During the entire game one of our fans seated directly behind our bench had loudly berated me and my players for our mistakes. Close to the end of the game after one particularly obnoxious outburst, I got up, found him and very loudly, clearly, and graphically told him what I would do to him if he didn't shut up. I reminded Mr. Callard of my unseemly outburst and wondered if there was a place at Gilman for someone like me. He assured me there was, adding that he remembered my outburst and while he might quarrel with my choice of words, he thought the fan was obnoxious and deserved to be reprimanded.

I have always been impressed that Mr. Callard's office was a large open room where the door was never closed and traffic was constant throughout the day. It was located next to the Gilman Room, at the top of the stairs, across from the student mailboxes. I don't even remember there being a door to his office. Every single kid had to go into the Headmaster's Office at least once a week to pick up his edition of the weekly *Bulletin*, which was one sheet listing all of that week's homework and class assignments. When a student walked in, Mr. Callard would look up from his desk and ask, "How're you doing?" There he had it—an automatic weekly meeting with each Upper Schooler.

Mr. Callard spent a good part of the day roaming the building and grounds talking to students, teachers, staff, or anyone else who happened to be there. He had a wonderful ability to make you feel that when you talked to him you were completely enveloped in his world.

In the first weeks of my stay at Gilman, he arrived at my classroom door and asked if he could talk with me a moment. As we walked back to his office, he told me he had the father of one of my First Formers on the phone and the father was complaining about the length and difficulty of my homework assignments. Mr. Callard asked if I thought the assignments were too hard. In reply, I stammered all over the place not so much in fear of losing a job as in embarrassment for having let him down in some way. He said very gently, "No, do *you* think they were too hard?" I said, "No, I don't." He picked up the phone and told the parent that he had Mr. Schloeder right there and Mr. Schloeder had assured him that the assignments weren't too hard and as far as he was concerned that finished the matter. I recognized the prominent name of the parent, and I was most impressed with Mr. Callard's handling of the matter.

During the Callard years, the faculty was almost in a cocoon; you were protected from parents, alumni, and trustees. There was a change in this that began during the Sixties. The change in the role of the teacher was much more a reflection of societal changes than anything that reflected on the subsequent headmasters. The changes also reflected the attempt to open Gilman up to students from very different backgrounds.

It became apparent in the Sixties that the best way to diversify the school was to make it larger. This would mean that the school could still accommodate its traditional clientele as well as add students from non-traditional communities. To do this, the school would have to be enlarged in every way: more faculty, more staff, more buildings. Money would have to be raised. I have from the beginning been impressed with how the entire Gilman community—alumni, parents, trustees, friends—rallied to the task. Prior to this time Gilman had no real history of major fund raising. I remember being told that the auditorium wasn't begun until all the money needed was raised. In this time of corporate, personal, and governmental borrowing, this approach is mind-boggling. The Gilman community put all that behind them and went out to raise some real money the same way everyone else did.

A Development Office was begun in 1963 to raise money for the many changes that were to occur. Money was raised for endowment that would be used to increase teachers' salaries and offer more financial aid for deserving students. In 1964, the Gilman Summer School opened its doors for the first time. The Summer School with all its academic and non-academic programs provided opportunities for students to make up courses or to build their academic experience. It gave "at risk students" a chance to fortify themselves before entering Gilman for the first time. Finally, it provided added income to Gilman teachers and their families.

A new science building was built in 1962, and in 1963 the Lower School was made larger to allow Gilman to expand its student body. The athletic facilities were upgraded with the addition of three new fields and the refurbishing of the Cage into new basketball courts, along with the linking of the Cage with the main gym. New faculty housing was built, as well as many other capital improvements. In the early Seventies, the boarding department was phased out, and the boarding corridors became a series of classrooms to accommodate the expanding student body.

There were many people from Henry Callard on who wanted to bring diversity to Gilman, but until Reddy Finney and Bill Campbell made the cause their own, its success was not inevitable. The original vehicle for Gilman's wider commitment to a larger community was Operation Challenge, which came to Gilman in 1967. It came because Finney and Campbell *willed it* to come. They secured a grant from Upward Bound, a federal educational program for disadvantaged urban children and a part of Lyndon Johnson's War on Poverty, to begin a program at Gilman called Operation Challenge with 50 young people who had just completed Eighth Grade. They were students who had academic potential but had not been producing up to this potential. In other words, they were all academic risks.

The program, which has since become known at Gilman as Upward Bound, was a six-week summer session followed by a full academic year follow-up. It was, and still is, a fantastic success decades after its beginning in that summer of 1967. I remember a sign one of the first-year teachers brought with him into the classroom: "We Do Not Care Who You Are, Or Where You've Been. We Only Care What You Are And Where You're Going." The sign-bringer was Bill Greene, who in 1970 became director of Upward Bound, and, later, assistant headmaster. The national Upward Bound program remains one of the few existing War on Poverty programs, and Gilman's chapter is one of a handful still being operated in a secondary school setting. It is a truly wonderful program that has added a great deal to Gilman.

I remember being very surprised when Henry Callard announced in January of 1963 that he was planning to retire at the end of the school year: he was so full of energy, so much on top of his game. To many at the school, he *was* Gilman. His spirit and presence fairly overwhelmed the campus; he personified what Gilman was all about. What would happen to the promise of change, openness, and liberalization now that Henry Callard would not be there to lead us through the tangles of change? On top of his leaving, some of the "Old Guard" were announcing their retirement. Such "venerables" as Ed Russell were leaving after only 48 years of service to the school, Miss May Holmes after only 47 years, Al Townsend after 44 years, Tom Lipscomb after 43 years, and Dick O'Brien after a mere 41 years. Together that was 223 years of devoted and exemplary service to the school. All leaving at the same time as Henry Callard.*

As a young teacher not yet conditioned or calloused by the changes of life, I was stunned. All these people had been kind and helpful to me in my first years at Gilman and to me they were irreplaceable parts and indeed they *were* irreplaceable, but Gilman got new parts, different parts, wonderful parts, and continued. After my 38 years at Gilman, after the increasing contemplation of my own retirement, I understand what Callard, Russell, Holmes, Townsend, Lipscomb and O'Brien understood—we were good, we had had a great run, but it was time to go and make room for others to carry the banner. And carry the banner they did with Ludlow Baldwin—who, remember, had had experience as acting headmaster during 1952–53 and 1960–61 when Henry Callard was on sabbatical—leading the way. Mr. Baldwin continued the profound changes that Henry Callard had begun. During his tenure from 1963 to 1968, Gilman was firmly placed into the mainstream of Baltimore; it was truly an urban community school. By the end of his five years, almost 80 percent of the graduating seniors were involved in either Operation Challenge, the Hospital Project, the Tutorial Project or some other community service activity. The student body became increasingly representative of a larger Baltimore community.

The mid-Sixties were a time of great shifts and changes in the country, times of heightened protest, dissent, and political involvement. Under Mr. Baldwin the students were encouraged to join in these re-examinations. I remember the day after that tragic evening in Memphis, April 4, 1968, walking to chapel and seeing a sign written on one of the brick walls, "WAKE UP WHITE AMERICA." I remember Ludlow Baldwin's compassionate, caring plea for understanding, for unity, for progress that day in Chapel. It was a wonderful moment. Ludlow Baldwin, an old

---

*Ed Russell couldn't manage to fully leave Gilman. He continued to help coach the lightweights in varsity and J.V. wrestling for five or six years, including the editor of this book, and in the late fall to give his annual morning-chapel prognostication, derived from the Hagerstown *Almanac*, on how badly Gilman would beat McDonogh. Flipping through the *Almanac*, he would pretend to find that the McDonogh game date was "a disastrous day for farmers," which would instantly bring howls of approval from the entire Upper School student body.

sailor, had the steady hand and clear eye to guide Gilman through the rocky shoals of the mid-Sixties.

There was in the United States a reaction, a backlash, after 1968 to the massive social movements of the Sixties. Richard Nixon became President of the United States, promising to "bring us together" and to end the war in Southeast Asia. Sadly, he didn't do that. Rather, the war was still going on five and a half years later when he resigned the office of the Presidency in disgrace, and the politics of racial division was the centerpiece of American domestic politics.

In July of 1968, Reddy Finney became headmaster of an urban community school just months after that cruel April when Baltimore had burned during the riots following Dr. Martin Luther King, Jr.'s murder. In the 24 years that Reddy Finney led Gilman School, enormous social movements—initiated by societal changes unleashed in the Sixties and exacerbated by the reactions of society to these movements—engulfed America. Wounds were rubbed raw by callous and inept leaders.

Throughout these 20-plus years, Finney was a rock that stood fast for what he believed in, taking the positive momentum of the changes and calming it, controlling it and moving it to a much more placid stream. He did it gently and constantly, often without seeming to be doing anything at all, but he was always in control.

But let me explain a bit more about Finney. Eddie Zanfrini, Princeton's athletic trainer, had grown up in my old neighborhood in North Jersey, and from time to time he would come back to the corner outside the 3rd Ward Democratic Club and tell me and Johnny the Mouse, Backstage Paulie D., Crash Heimbach, Woo-Woo Strella, Nuke Hogan, and the "fellas" about Princeton football and in particular about some guy with four last names who was this incredible football player. Eddie Z. invited us down to see Princeton play, and we all wanted to see this guy with the funny name play ball. We weren't disappointed; he was incredible.

I remember counting the blocks Finney would throw on a single play. On one long touchdown run he threw four of them. I've never seen that since. Reddy Finney was unique, but not just as an athlete. He was one of those rare and unforgettable people who became a part of your own history in a most positive way. As I write this, I haven't talked to Reddy in months, but his impact on me is as real, as current, as it ever was. I think that there are literally thousands of people who feel the same way that I do about Reddy. We carry him with us every day.

The 1960s saw a change in the make-up of the Gilman faculty. It was to remain overwhelmingly white and male, but it was to lose its predominantly Anglo-Saxon character.

There were Jack Bartkowski and Walt Kozumbo, two wonderful science teachers, Jack becoming chair of the science department and currently retired; Walt eventually earning a Ph.D. in biology and doing research at the National Institutes of Health.

Christy Maltas, a Greek from Alexandria, was a wonderful teacher, film buff, and accomplished soccer player. Anton Vishio, irrepressible and unique, is still going strong in the 1990s as a master teacher and wonderful influence on all.

Bernard Bichakjian, French teacher and bachelor extraordinaire, is now married with children and teaching at a university in the Netherlands.

One of the most remarkable of the 1960s influx was Claude Edeline. Claude fled Haiti with his wife and young children under threat of death from "Papa Doc" Duvalier, the worst of the Haitian dictators. The Edelines arrived in New York with the clothes on their backs and $27 in their pockets. Somehow they made it to Gilman, where Claude helped begin the soccer program and taught French and Spanish.

The Gilman faculty also included Mlle. Mireille Bertrand, Ms. Gertrude Erichsen, Jose Ribas, Joaquin Roy, Ed Villamoore, and Marcelo Zambrano. Zambrano was a World Cup soccer player from Ecuador, a national hero in his home country, who would do things with a soccer ball not seen since.

Bob Fitzpatrick, who retired in the early '90s as head of Euro-Disney, was chairman of the Modern Language Department during the late '60s. Bob was a dynamic teacher as well as a leader of the anti-war movement in Baltimore. He was also elected to the Baltimore City Council running on the first racially integrated ticket ever for that office.

Another Irish-American, Joe Carroll, added diversity to Gilman during the '60s. Joe had been a legendary athlete at both Calvert Hall and Georgetown and has remained close to the school since leaving to pursue a career in law.

A number of nationally known men such as Buzzy Krongard, head of Alex. Brown & Sons, and Ben Civiletti, former Attorney General of the United States, had brief stints on the Gilman faculty during the '60s. Henry Ciccarone, who later coached Hopkins to four national lacrosse championships, put in a stint as the fresh-soph basketball coach. Willie Scroggs, who coached three national lacrosse championship teams at the University of North Carolina, taught history, and coached football and wrestling as well as lacrosse. He was also the first Gilman teacher with Polynesian blood.

Bill Greene, now assistant headmaster, as mentioned earlier, came to Gilman to teach math and head the Upward Bound program. His contribution to Gilman in the 25-years-plus he has been here is immeasurable.

The Sixties was a time when Gilman took on a much more ecumenical flavor. Roman Catholic priest Larry LaPointe was school chaplain and counselor for a number of years and still returns to Gilman on visits from his parish and teaching duties in Connecticut. Rabbis Howard Simon and Martin Weiner taught on the faculty, as did The Rev. Wendell Phillips, one of the great leaders of the civil rights movement in Baltimore. My apologies to the many others I've failed to list. This is just a flavor of a very colorful, diverse, and accomplished faculty who would help lead Gilman into the next decade.

By the end of the Sixties, there was a tangible and exciting sense in Gilman's halls and on Gilman's fields of unrealized possibility; unrealized, yes—but still very much a possibility.

Hired in 1958 by Headmaster Henry Callard, Nick Schloeder has taught at Gilman over five decades and under four headmasters, and for most of that time coached varsity football, varsity basketball, and varsity baseball, winning numerous championships in each sport. He has been awarded the Ed Russell Award and the Class of 1947 Award; in 1990, he picked up the new position of dean of faculty. From 1971–76, he served as executive committee chair for the history department. Over the 1996–1997 academic year, Schloeder was still carrying a full load, teaching history and coaching football.

Brought up in North Bergen, New Jersey, Schloeder's own early high school career was a bit checkered. He was once suspended from Fulton, the local high school, for shooting baskets in the schoolyard on a pretty spring day rather than attending classes. The suspension may have been one of the luckiest breaks the youthful Schloeder would experience. Soon afterwards, he was awarded an athletic scholarship to attend The Peddie School, where he played football, basketball, baseball, and tennis. He also boxed as an amateur, but that was mainly at home in the summers, and for a while without his parents' knowledge. Schloeder was all-county in football and basketball, and all-state in basketball. He left Peddie for Bucknell on a basketball scholarship; he earned his bachelors in history and played basketball, baseball and tennis, and then earned a masters in clinical psychology.

After a two-year stint in the army, three years of teaching and coaching at Calvert Hall, Schloeder was lured away to Gilman by Henry Callard. Able to offer only a minimal salary, Callard gave him carte blanche use of the Gilman tennis courts, and thus Schloeder launched a secondary summer career as a tennis pro. Iconoclast, individualist, raconteur, and athlete, Nick Schloeder is one of Gilman's all-time great motivators. A liberal Democrat with a strong involvement in Maryland politics, he is the founder of the political consulting firm, Grassroots Associates.

Yes, his wife really was a contestant in the Miss America contest.

No, he never threw a student out a classroom window; "but there was one time when I did open a window—and I'm talking about a ground-floor window; this is no second or third story window!—and I did *assist* the student in making a quick exit from my classroom out the window."

Schloeder's son, Nicholas C., is a 1985 graduate and teaches in the Lower School.

In the Custody of Strong, Nurturing Men

TIM BAKER '60

I t was the fall of 1952. Fifth Form Lower School. In the Cottage. Someone in the next classroom pounded on the wall. "Bang. Bang. Bang-Bang-Bang."

Mr. Goodwin stopped his American history lesson in mid-sentence. He spun around toward the sound, put his hand to his ear, and listened with exaggerated attention. The banging came from the Sixth-Form room next door, where Mr. Robinson was teaching math.

As a new student at Gilman that fall, I had no idea what was happening. I sat wide-eyed at my desk and listened while Mr. Robinson repeated his coded message.

"Bang. Bang. Bang-Bang-Bang."

Mr. Goodwin went over to the wall and pounded out an answer.

"Bang. Bang-Bang-Bang. Bang."

The other boys around me began to laugh. We could hear Mr. Callahan start to bang on the wall in the other Fifth-Form classroom across the hall. Then more banging came from Mr. Ackley's section of the Sixth Form at the other end of the building.

The four teachers continued to pound on the walls for another minute or so. Then Mr. Goodwin concluded their communications with three final funeral blows.

"Bang. Bang. Bang."

He shook his head. "It's Schmick," he informed us. "Hacking round again." He lowered his eyes at the thought of the Sixth Former's punishment. "Poor Schmick." He ran his finger across his throat.

The uproar in the Cottage came to an end as suddenly as it had begun. Mr. Goodwin resumed his American history lesson as if nothing unusual had happened. Whatever they'd done to Schmick couldn't have been too serious. He looked okay when I saw him at recess.

At dinner that night, I breathlessly told my parents the whole story. That first year at Gilman I came home with a lot of stories.

Mr. Goodwin had stood on top of his desk to re-enact the Battle of Bunker Hill. Mr. Ackley had drawn a map of medieval England on the blackboard and labeled one of the towns "East Jockstrap." Mr. Robinson had sunk a set shot from half court. Mr. Callahan kept a stack of erasers on the corner of his desk. His aim was deadly. If he caught you whispering, he'd bounce one of them off your head. I can still sing the song he taught us: "C-A, double L, A, H-A-N spells Callahan." Joe Callahan. Shang Goodwin. Nemo Robinson. Bill Ackley.

Later I had wonderful teachers in the Upper School. Then I went on to Williams College and Harvard Law School, where I was taught by some of the finest professors in America. But that team in the Cottage was the best I ever had.

We had to work hard. Much harder than I'd ever worked in my old schools. But with my new teachers, learning was fun. Exciting. We never knew what they'd do next. Neither did they. They made it up as they went along. Each day sparkled with their spontaneity. I couldn't wait to get to school in the morning. When my birthday came in May, I asked my father for what he thought was a peculiar present. But he gave it to me. That morning he dropped me off in front of the Cottage at seven o'clock, an hour and a half early.

Gilman was so much fun that the Lower School's disciplinary system lacked a credible deterrent. If I got a demerit for "hacking around," all I had to do was come back to school on Saturday morning and help clean up litter for an hour. Gilman was the only place I wanted to be anyway. When we'd finished picking up paper, the teacher on duty would usually start a touch football game. No N.F.L. quarterback has ever called audibles at the line of scrimmage like Mr. Goodwin.

"98-left-Alamo-shift-47-flanker-A-Simon Bolivar-Rochester. Hut. Hut. Hut."

Monday in school we'd tell the other boys what Mr. Goodwin had done. Someone else would have a story about Mr. Robinson.

"*Mister* Goodwin." "*Mister* Robinson." Even among ourselves, we never referred to our teachers as "Goodwin" or "Robinson," let alone "Shang" or "Nemo." It was always "Mister." And "Sir." When you spoke to a teacher, you said, "Sir."

Before I came to Gilman, I had gone to schools in which all of my teachers had been women. But that fall in the Cottage, suddenly all of my teachers were males. They were well-trained and dedicated educators. They were good coaches. They worked hard. But for a 10-year-old boy, the most important thing was that they were men.

The men who taught me in the Fifth and Sixth Forms of the Lower School played a crucial role in my life. They guided me through the first stage of my male initiation into the world beyond my family. In those two years, Gilman began to replace home as the central focus in my life. As I began to move out from under the protective wings of loving parents, I passed into the custody of special men.

Strong men. Warm men. Men who smiled easily and laughed often. Men who encouraged and supported boys as well as taught and disciplined us. Men who won our affection as well as our respect. Caring men. Nurturing men.

These days we don't often hear "nurturing" associated with maleness. The word itself evokes images of breast-feeding. But women aren't the only sources of human nourishment.

The ability to nurture is one of a man's natural endowments. Yet, in many of us it lies undeveloped. It won't flower on its own. Like any other talent, it requires a sense of purpose and a willingness to work at it.

Most of us won't apply ourselves to that task unless we see nurturing men whom we admire, men whom we want to be like. We need models. I can go back a long way to find some of mine. Back to the Fifth Form. Back to that group of warm and wonderful men who taught me a lot more than math and American history.

Tim Baker attended Gilman 1952–60 with his favorite course being history. By his senior year, he was co-business manager of the *Cynosure*, and a member of the Athletic Association and Sixth Form Dance Committee. He played three years of varsity football, three years of varsity basketball (captain his senior year), and four years of varsity lacrosse (co captain junior and senior years). At graduation he was a co-winner, with Peter Wood, of The William Cabell Bruce, Jr. Athletic Prize. He was awarded The Tyler Campbell Lacrosse Cup and The Class of 1939 Basketball Trophy.

A 1964 graduate of Williams, Baker served in the Peace Corps in Ethiopia 1964–66. He graduated from Harvard Law School in 1969, was Assistant U. S. Attorney for Maryland 1971–74, U.S. Attorney for Maryland 1978–81, a partner at Piper & Marbury 1981–86, and a candidate for Attorney General of Maryland in 1986.

From 1972 to 1982, Baker served on the Board of Trustees for Gilman. The father of Richard '92, and two daughters, Baker lives in Columbia, Maryland, with his wife Betsy. He works as a writer. Among his literary marketplaces is The *Sun*, for which he writes as a columnist, and in which a version of the above essay was published in January of 1993.

Appropriations

MITCHELL MILLER '63

Gilman is its teachers. I myself have now been teaching philosophy in college for over 20 years, and my memories of Gilman faculty, surprisingly sharp and vivid, serve me as resources and standards. There are many I could cite, but here are several that are particularly dear to me.

Chalk in hand, standing silently at the blackboard, Mr. Marrian could transform the classroom with his gray-eyed gaze; in the distilling anxiety he generated with that gaze, we became quiet and lucid, our powers concentrated, open, miraculously, to mathematical reason. Outside the classroom, none of us, I think, knew just how to interpret the experience he enabled within it; we spoke of him as "strict" and "hard," as a severe taskmaster—but what he was showing us, giving us an inner place to go back to and cultivate over the years, was the total attention that allows the pure logic of number and proportion to reveal itself.

In every superficial way, Dimitri Manuelides was quite the contrary. Imagine the cheerful chaos of a classroom in which the teacher once strode late into class wearing a friar's cassock or, on another occasion, a medieval lancer's helmet (with the mouth guard locked down, turning his exuberant words into a muffled roar). In his passion to elicit a feeling for history, he rushed upon our sleepy adolescent minds with all the weapons of evocative rhetoric, storming about the classroom, haranguing and joking, falling suddenly silent to let some significant point sink into us. With laughter and temper and, most of all, surprise, he wakened in me my first concrete sense of historical difference.

Mr. Callard never taught me in a classroom setting; he was headmaster during my early Gilman years. What I somehow learned from his sheer presence came home to me in a very peculiar way several years ago when, far outside my competence, I was preparing a lecture on the political wisdom of Taoism. The *Tao te ching*, as I read it, was suggesting as an exemplary political leader someone wise enough to temper authoritarian action with the impartial spirit of the law, and to temper that spirit, again, with a benevolent heart, and to temper that heart, finally, with a resolute withdrawal into inconspicuousness. My Western sensibility protested at this. How could there be such a man? And if there were, how could he actually lead a community? I came across this passage:

> Hesitant, he does not utter words lightly.
> When his task is accomplished and his work done,
> The people all say, "It happened to us naturally."

Many who remember Mr. Callard will understand already why it was the example of his moral depth that let Lao Tzu's obscure words suddenly make concrete sense to me.

Oddly, the impressions I carry with me of the man who was, most of all, my mentor, Roy Barker, are different in kind. As I sit here writing, I have The *Sun* obituary photo in front of me—but I find it distracting. Mr. Barker dwells within me not as a face but as a voice, as words. Moreover, he is not a voice that reminds me of him; on the contrary, he is present as a voice that relates me to myself. Will it make sense if I say that rather than ever really knowing him, I feel *known by him*? He dwells within me as, in the richest possible sense, an editor's voice, examining my thought for style, for logic, and for its openness to its own subject matter. Right now, in fact, he is warning me not to be "repetitious" (I can see that rounded red-ink scrawl, drawing my attention from my text to its margins, setting my words in a new light), and he is giving my punctuation a meticulous going-over. I have come to realize that these are far from trivial services he has performed for me these many years.

My own philosophical work has taught me that searching for fresh language is not just looking for the best way to express oneself—as if the self to be expressed were there in advance, already formed. On the contrary, to search for words is to explore what forms oneself can take; it is to let the possibilities implicit in one's thought emerge, and this, in turn, is to let that thought itself expand and complicate itself. In an analogous way, Mr. Barker's insistence on those notorious "Gilman punctuation rules" turns out to have been my first systematic lesson in logic. Remember the rule that requires a comma before a clause beginning with "and, but, for, or . . . ?" Or the insistence on putting commas both before and after parentheticals and appositives? Those rules encode the basic distinctions between conjunctive and subordinative relations and, again, between defining and inessential properties; these distinctions, in turn, are basic to all argument and conceptual order. When my inner Mr. Barker requires me to discipline my writing by means of those rules, he is, therefore, requiring me to examine my thought for its rationality. He makes this requirement, moreover, not because he insists on conformity to the rational; he is, after all, an editor of stories and poems as well as of essays. On the contrary, he requires this examination as the best way for me to position myself to decide for or against the rational; he requires it as a means to self-knowledge.

As I understand them now, these two editorial demands, to search for fresh language and to be accountable for the logic (or illogic) of what I am saying, flow from something still deeper. It is true, as The *Sun* obituary reminds me, that Mr. Barker was notorious for his bursts of temper when students failed to meet his high expectations. It is also the case that he could marshal an irony, even a sly gaiety, that left you (especially if you were an earnest 16-year-old) uncertain just what he meant. But I can never remember feeling put down or dismissed by Mr. Barker. Thinking back, I marvel at this. Could *I* have sat straight-faced through all the baseball stories and moral allegories I inflicted on him in our Literary Club sessions? His criticisms of my work, always painstaking and extensive, were also always encouraging. As a classmate, Tommy Chase, remarked to me recently, "He always let us be our age." What sustained him in this Socratic patience? I am sure he took genuine pride in the effort he could elicit from his students. And I imagine this pride taking the form of delight as, reading our work, he would come across the exceptional moments of grace and clarity in which, touched by the powers of language, we grew. But beneath this, I think, it was a pleasure in the world itself, a pleasure quickened by those moments of grace and clarity, that moved and sustained him.

There is a piece of advice Mr. Barker once gave me—not as English teacher but, rather, as coach of the tennis team—that has lingered for years in the back of my mind, his odd way of putting it asking for interpretation. Transposed from the context of ground strokes to that of language, it makes me believe that he took deep joy in the thought that his students might come, through the development of their way with words, to share in his sense of the beauty of the world. "Use the whole court," he said. "It's *a better game* when you use the whole court."

Would Mr. Barker recognize himself in this interpretation or, more generally, as this editorial voice in which he so often speaks to me? It is a teacher's fate to be appropriated by his students, and in these appropriations the teacher's intentions are often taken in surprising ways. Perhaps Mr. Barker would tell me that he was just talking tennis or, again, that I am over-interpreting the "Gilman punctuation rules." But I doubt it. It is truer to his generosity of spirit, I think, to imagine him deflecting the question of his self-recognition and raising, instead, the question of mine. The rounded red scrawl might read: "I wonder how fully you understand what you are getting at. Expand and clarify."

 Mitch Miller entered Gilman in the Fourth Grade, 1954. By the time he reached the Upper School his main scholastic interests—especially writing, history, literature, and mathematics—had begun to emerge. A. J. Downs and Alex Armstrong (English), James Pine and Dimitri Manuelides (history), Ellery "Woody" Woodworth (music), and Fred Williams (biology) were all influential in Miller's student life. It was Roy Barker, however, the teacher/coach, who had the greatest impact. Barker taught Miller English, coached him for four years on the varsity tennis team, and advised him in his work as editor of *The Blue & The Gray*.

By Miller's senior year, he was serving as editor-in-chief of the *News* and *The Blue and The Gray*, and he was president of the Literary Club. He was a four-year member of the varsity tennis team, and with classmate John Claster, won the Maryland Scholastic Association doubles title several years in a row.

In one of the few times in Gilman history, in 1963 both the Armstrong Prize for Prose and the Armstrong Prize for Poetry were awarded to one recipient—Mitch Miller. He was also given the C. David Harris, Jr. Tennis Award. And along with Tom Chase, he was a co-winner of the Sixth Form Speaking Prize.

Miller majored in German at Stanford University, and he continued his interests in fiction, history, and poetry. He received his doctorate in philosophy at the State University of New York, Buffalo, and in 1973 began teaching philosophy at Vassar College. Miller has written two books on Plato, *Plato's Parmenides: The Conversion of the Soul* and *The Philosopher in Plato's Statesman.*

Miller continued to send his mentor, Roy Barker, copies of his work right up until Barker's death September 12, 1993. Reminiscing about teaching and old students in a 1992 letter to the editor of *Gilman Voices,* Roy Barker wrote in his firm script, "*The Parmenides* is considered to be Plato's most difficult dialogue. Mitch's book is ten thousand leagues over my head. But then, one has to face the fact that the pupil often outstrips the master, as I discovered when my son first started to beat me in tennis. One faces this sort of thing with mixed emotions: pride in the winner but a certain sadness that the loser cannot any longer keep up with the winner."

Gilman in the Kennedy Years

THOMAS CAPLAN '64

Baltimore in the early Sixties was a city of poignant autumns hesitant to give way, of Thanksgiving blizzards and long over-ripe springs. Even more than it is now, it was an oddly self-referential (and, more than occasionally, self-reverential) town, especially when one considered its geographical situation along the Washington-New York axis. Gilman sat at its familiar, but then quiet intersection, its neo-Georgian buildings and green playing fields nestling in a hollow of dogwood, cherry blossom, and time. Until recently, it had been known officially as The Gilman Country School for Boys, and it still retained many of the bucolic elements which that name conjures. Every day boys and masters walked outdoors: to class from morning chapel in the auditorium, from afternoon study hall to athletics in the gym, to and from the Science Building, which opened in 1962. The driveway, which one entered on a slope from the south side of Belvedere just east of Roland, was unmarked, suggesting the certitude of the proprietors that those who might need to know would find it.

The Sixties, of course, were not one era, but three. First—beginning with the election year that saw John Kennedy into the White House and ending, if not with the November Friday of his assassination then with the arrival of The Beatles in New York the following February—came the era of J.F.K. This was succeeded by a long period of national gestation from 1964–1967 whose key public events, such as The Gulf of Tonkin incident and Resolution, Civil and Voting Rights legislation, NASA's Project Gemini, and the enlargement of the Viet Nam War and draft, seemed either coda to the previous epoch, or else significant largely in retrospect. Our wornout mask of innocence had slipped in most cosmopolitan centers by 1967 when The Beatles released "Sgt. Pepper's Lonely Hearts Club Band." By the next year, "Sgt. Pepper" was universally an artifact and the frantic/antic Sixties of long hair and free love, of mind-obliterating music and substances subsumed large parts of our culture, lasting well into the subsequent decade—until the end of the war in Asia and even the resignation of Richard Nixon. A snapshot of what is now commonly supposed to have been the 1960s could have been taken on most American streets in 1972, but, excepting in a few enclaves of the *avant garde*, not before 1967.

Nor could it have been on the Gilman campus during the early years of that decade, when the culture we as students imbibed was lineally descended from the atmosphere and assumptions of the Fifties. That culture still presented its heroes, albeit soon to be simplified of subtlety and cartooned in the persona of James Bond, as realistic and feasible models: Cary Grant as the sophisticated ex-cat burglar, at home with the sybaritic ways of Europe in "To Catch a Thief," for example, then as the superbly tailored, utterly confident New York ad man in "North by Northwest," accepting, with lighthearted resignation, the grave responsibilities which accidents of fate have forced into his hands.

Though it would have been loathe—far too self-effacing—to advertise the fact, such quietly wielded but absolute competence seems an accurate description of the quality Gilman sought to develop in its young charges. In consequence, the school placed a strong emphasis on decency and honor; on sportsmanship, sound minds, strong bodies, the quest for and occasional attainment of excellence, if rarely the nourishment of genius. Decades later, these seem not merely noble ideas, but noble in the very innocence of their context: a world in which it was assumed that such values could be transmitted from one generation to the next without much interference from the general culture. These goals were espoused in a moral climate that had just begun to bestow hospitality upon the perspectives of others, to draw in those of disparate backgrounds, but which also had yet to become embarrassed about itself.

There was an obligatory chapel of a very low church Episcopalian sort: predictable Bible readings; familiar, rousing hymns: "Once to Every Man and Nation," (No. 519); "Eternal Father, Strong to Save," (No. 512); "The Church's One Foundation," (No. 396); "Dear Lord and Father of Mankind," (No. 435). The enthusiasm or indifference with which they were sung had more to do with the mood of the school (pre-exam or pre-game) on any given day than with faith, lyric, or melody.

The old oak-paneled dining hall still functioned, producing the intermittently edible cuisine traditional to such venues and somehow conducive to indelible memories of them. The upper three forms lunched at 1:30 precisely, the lower three earlier. Each long table was headed by a master and included at least two members of every class. Seating assignments were obligatory and rotated every six weeks. The resulting proximity fostered friendships, many of which have proved remarkably durable, across then otherwise impassable barriers of age. Boys served as waiters, two at a time, for a week. One stood behind one's chair until the headmaster had offered grace and he and those at his table, which was platformed a few inches off the main floor in a style derivative of high tables at Oxford and Cambridge colleges, had been seated. "Lord, help us to act, in Thy sight alone, as though all the world were watching," Mr. Callard would frequently pray, and a moment of camouflaged frisson would pass among the members of the school. More than anyone, he had a way of articulating a profound moral vision, of stripping it of piousness so that young men could grasp it without embarrassment. Henry Callard's essential goodness—his capacity, even in his snow-haired years, to display in his blue eyes the reflection of ourselves we privately hoped to see was the force which animated Gilman in those days. His was the "long shadow" which defined the institution in Emersonian terms. His, the moral weight which ultimately tilted the school from reluctance to eagerness to face a new era.

Its stairwells draughty, its Common Room austere, the school might have struck a visiting Englishman as an outpost of empire. Truth be told, it had stirred aspects of the South into the style of St. Grottlesex, just as the boarding schools of the North had stiffened their English model with Puritan/Yankee starch. Maryland may have been a border state, but its gentry was predominantly Confederate; even an adolescent boy could feel a residual languor about the campus, especially between April and early June.

Of course, as a boys' school, it was the domain of gods, at least as beheld by those a year or two behind them. Football, lacrosse, and wrestling established the loftiest heroes; academics secured a sufficient brand of success; but there was probably not so much validation—much less *kudos*—as there ought to have been for any but the most assertive eccentrics. Scott Fitzgerald, who knew the type as well as the archetype from which it was drawn, wrote of "that most limited of all specialists, the 'well-rounded man.'" Rather too often in our community, and with hardly any appreciation of the implicit ironies, it seemed that this was the standard elevated before us.

The school's emphasis on rigorous mastery of basics translated variously into: (1) well-mastered computorial skills, verbal conjugations, and other bodies of knowledge; or (2) episodic, if inevitable boredom. Among the best conceived courses, in my own view, were a Fifth-Form term paper—executed to the standards of most universities—on an original topic, which would subsequently be turned into a Sixth-Form Speech to be delivered to the assembled school during chapel, and a semester spent memorizing and dissecting "Hamlet" in Fifth-Form Honors English. The latter was one's first prolonged, intensive exposure to greatness.

Among the weakest aspects of the school seemed its tacit acceptance of a culturally prevalent dichotomy which insisted that mathematics and science, on the one hand, and imaginative natures, on the other, were axiomatically unreconcilable—that the former province properly belonged to "engineering types" whilst the latter nature would inevitably do best in the arts or humanities. It is difficult to estimate the costs or consequences to students for whom vocations may have been foreclosed in later life as a result of this undemonstrable, yet apparently unquestioned cliché.

The era of automatic admission to Princeton and the Ivy League had collapsed against the sheer numbers of the baby-boom generation and our parents' post-war prosperity. So, we sat uncertainly for P.S.A.T. examinations in Junior year, then for the S.A.T.s themselves during a fraught Saturday morning of our last autumn. The notion was abroad—as it had been all our lives, since early applications of the Stanford-Binet I.Q. test—that one was simply bright or not; that each of us occupied a predetermined position on a fixed scale of cleverness. Of all the suppositions taken for certainties in those years, this was patently the most absurd and trouble-causing.

In a bright ground floor warren that overlooked the terrace and, beyond it, goal posts and gridiron, "Dr." Pine, whose "Ph.D." had been affectionately conferred by his students, taught the history of a Europe as courtly as he. Large Repogle maps on blind-like sprung cylinders behind him, he was able to reach over his shoulder without turning to fix his long, wooden, rubber-tipped pointer automatically upon Metternich's Austria or Bismarck's Germany even as he kept eye contact with his students and continued his lecture.

Because we were young, milestones such as the Congress of Vienna seemed lost in the mist of time, distant from, if in any way relevant to the central concerns of our time. Still, when the Cuban Missle Crisis disturbed the peace of October 1962 and we emerged from our air raid drills (We made pilgrimages to the ground floor or beneath our desks, hands clasped tightly over our necks, heads bowed in our squat, cross-legged laps, the better for weathering falling rubble) nothing on the planet seemed so vital, so indispensable as American military power. Like the British of a hundred years before, we were the scions of empire. Our embryonic solipsisms still clothed forgivably in adolescence, we blithely confronted a future in which, if one excepted annihilation, nothing terribly bad could happen to us.

Or so, in those idyllic days, it seemed. Indeed, an accident had served to connect a number of our lives to the very center of the larger world 40 miles to the southwest. At 14, I had been an eager volunteer—even, eventually, president of the Teen Democrats of Maryland—in the Kennedy campaign of 1960. On forays to the national headquarters in Washington, I had met not only Senator Kennedy and his brother Robert, but some of the senior members of his staff. In school, after the election and inauguration, I had felt an inevitable let-down, but when the Peace Corps was launched and my father happened to suggest the possibility of a junior companion program under whose auspices young people might correspond with their contemporaries in what were then quaintly called the "underdeveloped countries," I decided to put the idea into action.

A number of us, including Jimmy Hardesty, Bobby Locke, John MacLean, Stevie Mason, Bobby Pine, Steve Scott, Kemp Slaughter, and Fife Symington, launched the Youth-to-Youth Pilot Project, which soon had members in Forms III through VI writing to and receiving letters from teenagers in Senegal, Mali, and other newly independent nations. Inevitably, it wasn't long before we had embryonic parallel programs in operation at Garrison Forest, Bryn Mawr, and Roland Park.

The project was private, but it had the eye of the Kennedy White House and so provided a reason for some of us occasionally to come and go from that heady place. In consequence of it, Ted Sorensen, President Kennedy's Special Counsel, met with a number of Sixth Formers who were then shown around the Oval Office in the spring of 1962. Andrew Hatcher, the deputy press secretary, came to the campus one evening to talk to a special meeting of the Political Club. Then, in the summer of 1963, Bonnie Miller (sister of Mitch Miller '63 and a student at Garrison) and I appeared on the "Today Show" to explain Youth-to-Youth.*

The assassination of the President, early on the afternoon of the McDonogh Game in our senior year, shook the Gilman community as profoundly as it did the rest of the country, though, at first, not so obviously. A hasty decision was made to play the traditional game, but I left the McDonogh stands early and, returning to Gilman alone, brought the flag to half-mast among the stark shadows of the almost leafless trees.

*The tradition of a Sixth Form trip to the White House continued in 1964, under the auspices of Major General C. V. Clifton, President Kennedy's military aide, who had stayed on briefly under President Johnson, and Mrs. Evelyn Lincoln, who had been President Kennedy's personal secretary and was then beginning to archive his papers and possessions.

Roy Barker inspiring him in English, and James Pine in history, Tommie Caplan graduated from Gilman in the spring of 1964. He entered the Georgetown University School of Foreign Service where he majored in international relations. Holding an MBA from the Harvard University Graduate School of Business Administration, Caplan is the author of three novels, *Line of Chance* (1979), *Parallelogram* (1987), and *The Reluctant Ex-Patriate* (1997).

A Small and Silent Symbol of Audacity

TIM BAKER '60

"L ean forward," Gibbs whispered. The pat of butter sat poised on the end of
his dinner knife. "But remember, Baker, don't look up."

Several times a year a boy at Gilman committed a perfect crime and
lived in legend for a day. Someone must have first performed this particular exploit years ago. By 1957, however, no one remembered that first boy's name.
You couldn't find it chronicled in *Gilman Walls Will Echo*. But word of the hero's
feat had passed from generation to generation and inspired daring efforts to duplicate the deed.

The other boys at the table stole admiring glances at Gibbs. He proceeded with
a casual disdain for the school's disciplinary system. We all knew if he were caught,
his stunt would cost him at least three demerits.

In the fall of my Third-Form year, I sat next to Gibbs every day at lunch. We
ate at one of the long wooden tables which lined the old dining room. A teacher
presided at the end of each one. The dark wood-paneled walls rose 25 feet to the
arched white plaster ceiling high above us.

Gibbs was a Fourth Former that year. The collar on his charcoal sports jacket
stood up behind his neck, and the knot on his tie hung loose at the throat of his
shirt. He looked past me to check Mr. Chandlee at the end of our table. The teacher
was busy eating the meat and potatoes on his white china plate.

I pushed the food around on my own plate while Gibbs completed his prepa-
rations. He had placed a pat of butter near the end of the handle of his stainless-
steel knife. He had selected the pat carefully. It had to be hard enough so that it
wouldn't cling to the knife and yet pliant enough so that it would stick when it
struck the target. Otherwise, it would bounce off.

He wedged the blade end of the knife into a horizontal slit between the table top and the leg. The handle end stuck out parallel to the floor. He pressed down with his thumb and bent the knife until he couldn't hold the tension any longer. The knife snapped back and launched the butter pat into a towering trajectory above our table.

We all wanted to look up and follow its flight. But we busied ourselves with our food instead. Otherwise we would have given Gibbs away. The seconds passed by one after another. Finally, Gibbs looked up. Then I did. Then the other boys at the table. No one pointed. But there it was. Gibbs grinned in triumph. He'd done it.

The yellow butter pat shone like a little star up among the intricate designs in the arched white plaster ceiling high above us. The news raced around the dining hall. Boys at other tables began to point. At the far end they stood so they could see. The laughter built and rolled across the room. The headmaster rose to his feet and banged his knife against his glass until the teachers had restored order.

The next day, and for days thereafter, we could see the little butter pat on the ceiling, far above the administration's ability to retrieve it. It hung there, an assertion of our independence, a small and silent symbol of audacity. At lunch we entertained ourselves by guessing when it would fall and where it would land. Then one day it was gone.

A profile of Tim Baker appears on page 243 following his essay, "In the Custody of Strong, Nurturing Men."

Learning to Spit

WILLIAM DEBUYS '67

I remember my years in the Upper School at Gilman as a period of nearly continual embarrassment and social confusion. It seemed to me in those days that personal Apocalypse was always near at hand and that its horsemen numbered many more than four. Indeed, my hormone-plagued existence, like that of my friends, seemed to hold more dread riders than Attila's horde. Among their ranks were the inevitabilities of pimples, proms, and pretty girls; they included whole mortifying calvaries of fashion misstatements, such as too-short trousers, pink shirts, and neckties with gastrointestinal motifs. And then still others: dead batteries on crucial dates, beery proofs of manhood and idiocy, bad hair months that stretched into years, and again and everywhere the opposite sex, pretty and otherwise. But for pure, unredeemed humiliation, there was no evil more Manichean or implacable than ordinary dental braces.

I wore those gleaming tooth jackets for most of my Upper School years, and thanks to the grinning, moon-faced orthodontist who wrenched my tooth roots on Tuesday afternoons, my braces manifested such marvels of oral engineering as circumferential wires, sliding caps, rubber bands, and molar springs. Painful, too. I remember a Thanksgiving dinner at home with my parents and sisters around a table festive with bright linens, glittering serving dishes, the red of wine and cranberry, and a great bronze bird gleaming in the middle, yet because most of my teeth were slowly, excruciatingly in transit to new locations in my gums, all of my turkey and most of my vegetables had to pass first through an old-fashioned, crank-driven meat-grinder affixed to the table beside me.

The single positive virtue those braces possessed became known to me during Mr. Bichakjian's French class. I recall Mr. Bichakjian with fondness and his tall French wife with awe. She was dark and elegant—or am I making this up? I hardly know anymore, and know still less whether the truth or falsehood of the matter is important. But the Madame Bichakjian of my memory had piercing eyes and straight, night-black hair. She bore no resemblance whatever to the tightly permed

255

matrons in wood-paneled station wagons who collected my surly companions and me after each day's final bell. She belonged to some other splendid species. The time or two I saw her caused me to believe that Mr. Bichakjian was not the simple caricature of accent and foreignness that we students generally made him out to be.

As I recall, Mme Bichakjian rarely visited the campus; in fact, she may have lived in another city, or moved away from Baltimore in the several years her husband was at Gilman, which may have accounted for the aura of loneliness that surrounded him.* He was short, swarthy, altogether Armenian, and during athletic periods his unenviable domain was the cindery field within the oval track where boys in shorts kicked soccer balls. In those days the world's most popular sport was scarcely recognized to exist at Gilman, let alone to be a legitimate athletic pursuit, and Bichakjian and his spindle-limbed charges were long gone each day by the time the cleat-clacking endomorphs of the varsity and J.V. football teams trotted homeward across the oval to the gym.

Bichakjian, among the Gilman faculty, seemed always outcast—foreign, small, perpetually alone. So deprived seemed he of adult scale and so cut off from general acceptance that except for his dark beard and the age and experience in his eyes, one might have mistaken him for one of us. Perhaps he too sensed our common predicament. It seemed at times that Mr. Bichakjian, in his restrained and dignified way, looked for friendship among us, his mainly unwilling and uninterested students. It did not help his cause that the courses he taught—all French—were among the most hated in the curriculum, yet on he drove us through thickets of irregular verbs and the featureless banalities of plays like *Topaz*, whose name is welded into memory because even in French I could grasp how bad it was. Still onward he drove us to *Vol de Nuit,* whose elegance was as clear as mountain water, but though Bichakjian led us to it, we horses would not drink.

Instead we threw spitballs, doodled mazes and monsters, or passed messages to our friends that were variations on precious few themes of insult, of which Bichakjian, often as not, was the target. What he needed was an overhead projector so that he might show his writing large upon the wall and still keep an eye on us. What he had was a blackboard—and pandemonium each time he turned his back.

Matters were never worse than on the day Twig, a classmate whose nickname derived from his bony frame and squirrelly ways, mastered the art of folding the smallest paper airplane yet devised at Gilman. The inch-long missiles could be cupped between two fingers and launched with a certain overhand throw that was occasionally, if accidentally, accurate. Throughout class, whenever Bichakjian turned to the board, Twig pivoted in his seat and shot airplanes at enemies in the back row. His victims, naturally, reciprocated at every opportunity with fresh volleys of spitballs and retrieved airplanes. None of this occurred in silence, and after half an hour, the drone of disorder had risen to a low but constant roar, and Bichakjian's temper

*In fact, Mme Bichakjian was teaching half a mile away at Bryn Mawr.

was as frayed as a battle flag. You could feel him, with all his soul, willing the bell to ring, the class to end, his hyena-like tormentors to run off to haze some other stolid beast.

As I recall, I sat close to the door in the second row. I held back from the warfare of spitballs and airplanes not because of goodness and still less for love of French, but out of pure, unsmiling misery. My braces, tightened the previous day and equipped with new devices, caused all my teeth and both jaws to ache. Small, stout rubber bands now linked my uppers with my lowers so as to draw the former in and pull the latter out. The consequent tectonics caused my jowls such pain that only vigorous yawning gave relief. I was in the midst of one such protracted and, sadly, uncovered stretching of oral ligaments when someone from the back of the room launched an errant airplane, which flew straight and true, high over Twig's head, past the front row, past the teacher's desk, past Mr. Bichakjian's right ear, and directly into the back of his writing hand, which at that moment was scripting the pluperfect conditional.

Bichakjian whipped around. "Who trew dis ting!" he shouted. His eyes blazed, and he held his long stick of white chalk the way Lizzie Borden must have held her axe. At this crucial instant, God chose to frown upon me. The commotion had broken out as I in mid-yawn, explored my braces' right-hand rubber band with my tongue. Perhaps I probed too hard. Perhaps Bichakjian's outburst caused me to flinch. Whatever the case, my tongue jarred loose the rubber band from its lower anchor so that it snapped with an audible thwack and shot out my gaping mouth. Like a glistening meteor, it described before the attentive eyes of all present a mathematically correct parabola linking point A, my mouth, with point B, the left lapel of the sports jacket Mr. Bichakjian was wearing. Having landed, it stuck, glued by saliva, and all of us stared at it in horror.

In the crystalline, crotch-tightening silence that followed I was chiefly afraid that either Mr. Bichakjian or I would begin to cry. Instead Mr. Bichakjian pulled himself to his full height, mustered his considerable dignity, and, as he brushed the offending item from his jacket, muttered, "Dis is no good." His fingers kept brushing his lapel as he searched for words, for grace, for a path toward physical and moral escape. Mercifully, the bell rang. Seconds later, as last among the students I left the room, I noted that Mr. Bichakjian was peering intently into his cavernous briefcase as though he had lost something in there and knew he would need a long time to find it.

An hour or two later, I had recovered the greater part of my nerve and exhausted most of my supply of rubber bands. I'd learned to shoot them with fair accuracy by pulling back my cheek and flicking the right-hand band loose with my tongue. My classmates found my new talent revolting, which was to say that it was impressive and exceedingly enviable. At last I'd found redeeming value in my braces.

On the way to lunch I went into one of the giant bathrooms of the main building to take a leak. Cold and white-tiled, those washrooms echoed with the solitary drip of water—up to the moment, that is, when they resounded suddenly with a mighty, explosive flush and hurled some confused-looking kid out from a stall with his pants askew. Looking back, I suppose teachers must have had their own rooms of rest, for as I recall, they rarely shared the horse-high urinals and dank stalls of the main bathrooms with us. Thank goodness for that. To be an adolescent is to feel awkward, continuously, for years. Having teachers in the room while you relieved yourself was no relief at all.

So I felt nothing less than terror when, as I stood before the porcelain amphitheater of the urinal, Mr. Bichakjian entered the room. He paused a moment, seeing me there, then strode forward to stand at the urinal next to mine, unzip, grope, and stare nearsightedly at the tiled wall the same as I was doing. I shuffled a little closer to the urinal, seeking protection in the nearness to its fouled surfaces. After a silence, Mr. Bichakjian turned and looked down at me, though short as he was, the angle was not very steep. His eyes were dark as an elk's, soulful even, and it occurred to me that these eyes must have been what attracted his sleek and beautiful wife.

"What for do you trow such tings at me?" he demanded.

"I didn't mean to," I said. "It was an accident." The plea hung in the air, as worthless as the smell of urine. I tried to look contrite, and no doubt looked the guiltier for it.

"I should give you tree demerits."

He peered disdainfully down his long nose at me, exacting his revenge as he made me squirm. I finished at the urinal, which gave me reason to break free from his gaze. While I zipped and rearranged, I mumbled something about the new braces, how they hurt and why I yawned, and how surprised I was when the rubber band flew off. When I looked up again, Bichakjian, who now refastened his belt to the jingle of pocket change, regarded me with a wry and quizzical smile.

"I never heard of such a ting," he said.

I pulled back my cheek to show him, then shot a rubber band into the urinal. "With you it was an accident, but that's how I learned to do it."

Bichakjian's smile blossomed to a grin. He seemed relieved. Then he turned back to the urinal he had just used and spat vigorously.

It was a curious kind of spitting. Nothing came but sound, but the sincerity of his hacking and expulsion could scarcely have been greater. Now that I was exonerated, I felt bold again. "What did you do that for?" I asked.

"What?"

"Spit like that."

Bichakjian seemed surprised. "Don't you spit when you smell someting foul?"

"No, not particularly. Is that something they do in France?"

"Well yes, perhaps. It is something very natural to do, nothing more." Now Bichakjian seemed a little flustered. "Actually, it is done in many places. Now, come on. We will be late for lunch." Out the door and down the corridor we marched together, almost friends.*

When Gilman walls echoed in the 1960s, they mainly echoed with orthodoxy. Even so, there were moments when one glimpsed in small ways, at odd angles, the hard kernel of individual aloneness, when one sensed the gulf of foreignness that separated each person, place, and group from every other. No matter how big one's world might grow, one had to sense that other worlds lay beyond. They were distant by thousands of miles, yet vast as skies.

From the day of the errant rubber band onward for many years—even to the present, in a way—I marveled that somewhere out in Armenia or France or in some third unnamed land there existed a society of people who compulsively spat at foul odors. Perhaps lions roared in their night, or packs of lean gaunt wolves howled. At 13 or 14 years of age, I expected no less.

Bichakjian was not Gilman's only infiltrator from the world beyond. There was also Nick Schloeder, an arrival from nearer lands, whose lethal chalk throwing and seeming readiness for violence made his the most peaceful classroom on campus. When he called himself "apostle to the privileged," he used his best Hoboken accent and set his shoulders as though to bear a load of chips. We his catechumens listened up. J.F.K. was warm in his grave, and the South still shook with racial revolution, but most of us carried to Schloeder's government class the sense that society's affairs were safely in the hands of good-hearted clones of Spencer Tracy and Jimmy Stewart. What we carried away, after a semester with Schloeder, was different indeed.

Bichakjian and Schloeder, however, were exceptions. Mostly at Gilman one steeped oneself—and stewed—in orthodoxy, embodiments of which, admirable in the extreme, were never lacking. There was Reddy Finney, not yet headmaster but already the most indisputable Mr.-All-Everything-All-the-Time any of us would ever know, who ranged the halls in giant strides, his head forever wobbling on a neck so thick with muscle it didn't seem to need a bone.

There was A. J. Downs, ruminating with his pipe, as calm as the smell of good tobacco. No paradox unsettled him. "Yes, this is an absurd place," he would say, "absolutely crazy. Unreal. Isn't it wonderful?"

There was George Chandlee, who brooked no sloppiness when it came to proving geometric theorems—or tucking in a shirt-tail. Perhaps no man who ever lived gave the shirt-tails of teenagers more attention.

There was Charles Gamper, the dean we called the Duck,** who enforced the

---

*Bernard Bichakjian taught French and some Spanish at Gilman 1961–68. He was head of the language department and was instrumental in bringing a language lab to the school. In 1968, he was offered a teaching fellowship at Harvard while he worked on his Ph.D. Upon receiving his doctorate, he left the States to teach at the University of Nijmegen in Holland.

**This nickname in part derived from Charlie Gamper's habit of barking out "Quiet!, Quiet!" in study halls, classrooms, and hallways in such a way that it sounded like "Quack!."

demerits for dangling shirt-tails that Chandlee handed out. As a student, I never sensed what a leader he was, or how he revolutionized high school athletics in Maryland.

There were apostles of literature, like the good Frank Andrews, the only westerner at the school. There were more than a few apostles of the gentlemanly way, led by Russell and Lipscomb, old men in flannel shirts, whom even the most irredeemably sullen of us could find no reason to dislike. There were apostles of snobbishness and apostles of sportsmanship, apostles of music and art and religion. Among the adults, there was no apostasy.

There was the graceful Henry Callard, no longer teaching and old when I knew him, who seemed as gray and noble as R. E. Lee, and I recall his thoughtful wife as no less substantial, a woman who troubled to observe much about us boys yet did not trouble us with observations.

There was Ludlow Baldwin, headmaster in my years, with a voice like a president and much hidden humor. I always suspected that after growling at us for one infraction or another, he withdrew to his office and roared with laughter.

Among all that reliable, predictable, estimable and, yes, insular faculty, none was more the apostle of orthodoxy than Roy Barker, head of the English department and a veritable archbishop of punctuation. He caused us, on pain of severe penalty, to learn his dozen or so rules of punctuation, not in spirit but to the letter, mark by mark, even to the pixel, and he graded us down if we deviated in our written regurgitation by so much as the substitution of a new word for its synonym. No matter that the world, if not literature, was full of obscene dashes, rebellious colons, and periods of outright chaos. In Barker's class, and at Gilman in general, order ruled.

Yet it ruled incompletely. From my day with Bichakjian onward, many a faint rank smell that rose to consciousness carried a suggestion of distant realms where orders and disorders outside my ken held sway, worlds beyond the horizon, where I hoped one day to go, where in my adolescent imagination lions roared and wolves howled, where every outcast felt at peace, and tall exquisite women smiled enigmatic smiles.

"Interested in just about all subjects," William deBuys '67 was a 13-year man at Gilman. During his senior year, he was chairman of the Judiciary Committee and, as noted in the *Cynosure*, the "driving force behind the Tutorial Project." He enjoyed playing football, wrestling, and playing lacrosse, "mostly J.V. stuff." On Founders Day, he was presented with The Daniel Baker, Jr. Memorial Award given to a senior who "through thoughtfulness and by reason of his character, has contributed to the general welfare of his fellow men."

Attending the University of North Carolina on a Morehead Scholarship, deBuys majored in American Studies while devoting most of his energies to the study of literature and creative writing. Then it was off to the mountains of northern New Mexico, where he served as a research assistant for Harvard child psychologist Robert Coles. Eventually, he made his way to the University of Texas, Austin, where he earned an M.A. and a Ph.D. in American Studies. Since his student days, deBuys' career has taken two intertwined paths: one, following his passion for environmental conservation, the other, his passion for writing.

From 1982 to 1986, the former Nick Schloeder catechumen was executive director of the North Carolina Nature Conservancy. Since 1986, he has served as senior associate and New Mexico representative of The Conservation Fund, and since 1989, as editor of *Common Ground*, a bimonthly newsletter published by The Conservation Fund.

The one-time initiate into the sacred punctuation rules of Roy Barker has been publishing a constant flow of short stories, including "Dreaming Geronimo" and "Devil's Highway," in literary journals, as well as articles and reviews centering on conservation and the West, such as his review of *Beyond the Four Corners of the World* in The *New York Times Book Review*.

In 1991, deBuys' *River of Traps: a Village Life* won the Evans Biography Award and was one of three finalists for the Pulitzer Prize in general non-fiction. In 1987, his *Enchantment and Exploitation: the Life and Hard Times of a New Mexico Mountain Range* won a Southwest Book Award.

William deBuys lives in Sante Fe, New Mexico, with his wife and two children.

Gilman Days and
Outlaw Ways

PATRICK SMITHWICK '69

For years after graduating from Gilman, I sometimes had nightmares about the place—all of them having as the common denominator that I am unprepared for an event of momentous importance. (Look at that! Immediately I fall into using a favorite expression of Gilman Upper School teachers: "the common denominator.")

For instance, I'd be rushing around, up on the third floor of the Upper School building, where I once boarded, looking for my notes, having been up all night—off somewhere—and just gotten back to discover I have a huge math or history or BIOLOGY (as in "Bugsy" Williams) test. I'd rush and search, the clock ticking away, the interstice between the present and the time for the test narrowing, shrinking, as I race faster and faster until there I am, in a sweat, in the capacious "A" study hall room, sitting at my desk, feeling defeated, trying to pull myself together, what will I do, there's no time left—the situation worsening until finally, as in a dream where one is about to drown—I burst out of the surface of the dream, suck in the oxygen, awaken, roll over, assert to myself that I now have a son the age of myself in the dream, and try to shake it off.

Or, I'd be trying to *get* to the auditorium, where I am due to give my Sixth-Form speech, in my old beat-up black 1966 Ford Falcon, "totaled," but its powerful V-8 still roaring, flying from my life (without the common denominator) in the country, into the city, and, as I near Roland Park, getting a flat, and having to run the rest of the way—then I'm in the Senior Room, searching for my notes. . . . And in these dreams, when other students are around, they are tranquil, in control, unperturbed, confident, holding their common denominators close to their vests.

I've also had pleasant and rewarding dreams about Gilman. Sometimes, when I was holding a job of which I was not fond, I would dream I was back at Gilman, ensconced in its protective, familiar, familial walls. A few times, when troubled, I would dream I was in the hallway outside our Upper School mailboxes, headed back with Mr. Gamper, dean of students, to his office, and I'd feel this glow of comfort, of being part of a family, assured that all would be all right.

While working on making a big decision, post-Gilman, on two separate occasions I dreamed I was speaking to Ludlow Baldwin (headmaster most of my time at Gilman). The day after each dream, I had forgotten all about the dream, and was walking through the campus of Johns Hopkins, and suddenly, there Ludlow was, healthy, vigorous, asking what I was up to. Both times he was excitedly preparing for a trip abroad, and had a word of advice for the interior trip upon which I was embarking.

I've survived a few serious car crashes, came within seconds of meeting my maker on a motorycle, have had some close calls on horses, and came close to becoming crab bait while dredging for oysters on a skipjack out on the Cheseapeake Bay—yet I never had recurring nightmares about those events. They didn't mark my psyche the way Gilman did. I have always felt a special—this is hard to say— spiritual-like connection with the paradox that is Gilman.

What I will attempt to do in this memoir is show my love as a student for Gilman on one side—through sketches of great teachers, most of whom have not been mentioned elsewhere in this book. On the other side, I will voice the difficulties many of us as students had with the rigidity and conformity and pressure-cooker that was Gilman by using my experience as an "outlaw" or "outsider" as representative of the experience of some of those students who did not possess the Gilman common denominator.

LOWER SCHOOL GLORY DAYS:
MESSRS. VERNER, MENZIES, MAGRUDER, TICKNER

I was introduced to the toughness of Gilman on my first day there in the Fourth Grade. Out on the lawn during recess, I asked a classmate if I could try using the strange-looking stick-net contraption in his hand. "Sure," he said. I approached, and he delivered a powerful and accurate right to the jaw, laughed, and walked away. I remember his face and name perfectly—he was an early Upper School casualty. And I remember the exact spot of geography, a grassy downhill slope now covered up by the expanded Lower School building, where it happened.

I thought I was coming into the Fourth Grade, but I quickly noticed that all of our books had "Fifth Grade" printed on them. In effect, I had to skip a year, and that year may have been the toughest one in my school life. Only Elliot Verner, the tall, lanky, Dick Van Dyke-like, flamboyant, positive and energetic classroom teacher, could have gotten me through that year. "Ye-gads!" My favorite memory of Mr. Verner takes place at a class picnic. It was a clear, sunny spring day. We were playing baseball and Mr. Verner and I were on first and second. He was coaching me, spurring me on, *teaching me how to steal* (so un-Gilman-like!). There we were,

together, no longer teacher and student but teammates, laughing, conspiring, steal-
ing our way, base by base, around to home. I was part of the team—that's the feeling the Lower School engendered.

In the Fifth Grade I ended up over in "The Cottage" with the fatherly, round-
faced Mr. Magruder—who we all knew was an Indian chief and was on his way to
becoming a general. Like a good chief, or general, he was calm, unflappable, well-
grounded, giving. The day after one of his history essay tests, he'd read from a few
of the essays to the class. An 85–88 was a high grade from him, and I can today *feel*
the glow in my chest when I recognized my words as he read, without singling out
the author, a section from one of our essays. If he had read from your paper, he'd
give you a conspiritorial wink as he handed it back—always folded in half, verti-
cally, with the honor code written on the outside. You'd feel this private connection
with him, one that I still feel today when I see him. Modesty was stressed. The competitive element was downplayed. He had read your paper as a model.

I can remember someone bringing in a record player and a stack of "Forty-
fives" one morning, playing Chubby Checker's "They're twisting, they're twisting,"
and all of us ecstatic in Mr. Magruder's homeroom twisting away moments before
the first bell was to ring. Dickie Gamper sat near me in that class; he was as sharp as
could be, often our class president, and it amazed me how for such an athlete, class
leader, A-student he was such a caring, modest guy, interested in *others.*

By the next year—Sixth Grade, the equivalent of being a senior in the Lower
School—I had caught up academically. I had learned what a lacrosse stick was. I
had made some good friends, in particular, Tom Whedbee, Reed Huppman,
Teddy Rouse, Trey Sunderland. And childhood friends Tom Iglehart and Rob
Deford were still at Gilman. Most importantly, I had for a classroom teacher the
wily, fun-loving, black-haired, broad-shouldered Graeme Menzies, who understood some of my horsey heritage.

Early in the fall of that year I rode a horse called Crag in the Elkridge-Harford
Hunter Trials, a mile's ride from our farm in My Lady's Manor, out near Monkton.
My father, A. P. "Paddy" Smithwick, a legendary professional steeplechase rider, had
ridden Crag—and won—in both hurdle and timber races, and now, here I was, just
a kid, riding a horse, not a pony, in what were to me THE Hunter Trials. He was a
small horse with a long flowing stride and the biggest heart in the world.

Going at an open gallop around that course over good-sized post-and-rail
fences, we pulled in one ribbon after another, until finally we were awarded the
trophy for champion. The next morning, to my surprise, Mr. Menzies explained to
my homeroom what Crag, with me in the stirrups, had accomplished the day
before. This nod by Mr. Menzies helped bring two divergent—often conflicting—
parts of my life together, the world of horses and daring and risk at home, and the
world of intellect and books and security at school.

I had my first "college-like" course with Mr. Menzies. It was on English history.
He taught it in such a way that none of us thought of it as a "course." We read from
a serious, darkly-bound little hardback—not a textbook type—every night, and the

next day we discussed the reading in class, Mr. Menzies leading off by asking genuine questions. And then he *listened* to us!

One afternoon Mr. Menzies walked into class alongside another man whom he
introduced as an expert on city design. The next thing we knew, Mr. Menzies had
let this man *loose*: the visitor was pacing in front of the class, talking about the lay-
out of the streets of Paris with great enthusiasm, explaining why the many circles—
so artillery could be positioned in the centers of the circles and then blast away,
down the spokes, breaking up any barricades. He leapt to discussing the planning
behind Washington, D.C., and he and *our teacher* were suddenly rushing down the
straight rows of desks, and rearranging them into what at first looked like a big
mess, the kind of thing we might do, and then suddenly the two of them were in the
center of a wheel of desks, grinning, and aiming their imaginary guns down the
spokes.

In the afternoon, with the light shining brightly through the many windows,
Mr. Menzies surrendered his homeroom to The Geography Teacher. In he walked,
barrel-chested, grinning, a primal force—Mr. Tickner. Studying all those countries
and their capitals, having those weekly tests, working on projects, turning in the
maps we so painstakingly drew, learning about mining, coal and iron and minerals,
and the timber industry and hydroelectric power and mountains used for centuries
as defense and great rivers creating valleys so fertile they'd fed huge sections of
Europe and Asia and Africa for thousands of years—what a class! We soaked it up.
Everything was so clear. Each day, like emissaries from Gilman, we toured a different region of the world. And this man leading us—his craggy forehead, his funny
accent—he injected everything he did with such enthusiasm and energy and power.
He was so *positive*.

Learning with Mr. Menzies or Mr. Tickner was nothing but a wonderful
time—with the only downside that year being the pall that hung over us, the occasional last-resort comments made by one or two teachers: "Next year, when you're
in the Upper School, you won't get away with that." Or, "And *you* think you're going
into the Upper School next year." These few teachers painted the Upper School as
dark, Dickensian. I had only been in its high-ceilinged halls once or twice with the
older Dickie Small (another country boy) and I'd been petrified, though I certainly
didn't tell Dickie. I had heard parents speak in reverential terms of the headmaster,
the great Henry Callard—and I had heard some of these adults talking in low voices
about something seemingly shady that Mr. Callard was doing that they were not so
certain about (leading the school toward integration). The parents seemed per-
plexed, confused, hurt, as if Mr. Callard had let them down. I don't recall Mr.
Callard ever visiting us. No one in the Upper School condescended to visit us. There
was no gentle initiation, indoctrination. No visits to the spooky, other-worldly,
sprawling Upper School building. The Lower School, First through Sixth Grades,
was on its own. But in those days of being a "Sixth Former" the next year seemed an
eternity away and we lived and learned and had fun being top-dogs.

HALCYON DAYS OF HOOT OWL

Before I'd reached the more impersonal Ninth through Twelfth Grades of the Upper School, I, along with fellow country boys Tom Iglehart and Rob Deford, had the good luck to have been given most-favored-student status for a year in the Eighth Grade by Percy Meredith Reese, our homeroom teacher. (Tom, who didn't like the "brutality" of Gilman, and Rob, who was simply told he was going, both headed off to St. Paul's School, Concord, New Hampshire, for the Ninth Grade—thus depriving me of some common denominator material. Up to Concord and into the Sixties they went, with modern curricula, hip classmates, and teachers who knew the difference between The Doors, The Stones, and The Beatles while we in Southern, Behind-the-Times Gilman kept twisting away to the Fifties beat of Chubby Checker.)

As Seventh and Eighth Graders we still had homerooms, unlike the lordly Ninth through Twelfth Graders. Our base of operations consisted of two connected old classrooms jammed with desks on the dungeonesque basement floor of the Upper School building, directly beneath the majestic, cathedral-like space of "A" Study Hall—domain of the Upper Formers.

Trip Maumenee or Blake Goldsmith would get in trouble in study hall with Mr. Reese, but his punishment would be just what you wanted in the first place: he'd put you up in front of the class—holding an eraser up against the wall with your nose. If you let it drop, you supposedly got a demerit. You had to pay attention, keep just the right pressure against the eraser. (Lord help you, if the chalk dust made you sneeze.) If you started to daydream, it would slip from your nose and you had to catch it with your hands while the class watched and rustled—stifling laughter, or pretending to stifle laughter, depending on your current status—and you quickly put it back up while Mr. Reese kept his nose in his papers, pretending he hadn't noticed all the commotion.

Mr. Reese, receding hairline, a cheerful expression on his owlish-looking face, and able to move that pudgy body more quickly than it appeared possible, was the greatest history teacher I ever had at Gilman or Johns Hopkins. Hooter, Old Hoot-Owl: he could make Ancient History come alive. He didn't joke around with his history; if he wanted you to know that the Assyrians were relentless with their foes, and wanted their opponents to be terrified of them before they even picked up their swords, he gave you specific examples, in graphic detail, of the tortures they were infamous for giving. As Eighth Graders, this was all fascinating to us.

It was by taking Mr. Reese's tests that I began to learn how to write under pressure of the clock—a lesson that served me well in later classes, particularly in Alex Armstrong's English class a year or two later where we often spent an intense full class period writing a timed essay. Both these classes helped me when the stopwatch was ticking in college and later, when as a neophyte newspaper reporter, I sometimes had to pound away on an old Royal manual with an editor standing beside me counting down the seconds before he would rip the sheet of paper out of my typewriter and run it to the typesetter.

Each of Mr. Reese's tests was an artistically designed labyrinth of a race course, with all kinds of hurdles to cross—including the renowned date box where you didn't have to know the exact date of an event; instead, you had to arrange all the events, in a dozen boxes running horizontally across the page, in the correct order. When the tests came around, I went for broke and was one of the last to leave.

There is one event that stands out with Mr. Reese. I am riding a young black pony called Twinkle in a show, and up there in the judge's stand, with his judge's pin in his lapel, is Hoot Owl. The class is a timed pick-your-own-course: a maze not unlike one of Mr. Reese's tests. Twinkle tries to prop and stop—"refuse"—going into the spooky-looking fences, and I have to ride her every step of the way, pushing, squeezing with my legs, feeling the exertion in my lungs.

After the class, Twinkle and I are called into the ring, awarded a ribbon—I can't remember what color, but I remember who patted my pony on the neck and hooked the ribbon onto her bridle.

A DOUBLE LIFE

The riding was not done for kicks: As children, my sisters and I "made" ponies and sold them, and we helped my mother teach riding.

From the age of 14 up, I went to the track—Delaware Park, Belmont Park, Monmouth Park, and Saratoga Springs—with my father every summer, worked every morning. I was out in the real world, one minute standing in the paddock at Saratoga talking to Alfred Vanderbilt or Ogden Phipps or Willie Shoemaker or Eddie Arcaro or Winston Guest, the next sitting in a tack room after work sipping a Heineken and eating a roast beef sandwich along with jockeys and trainers, and watching retired fighter Jack Dempsey pace the shedrow, and the next, standing in line at the racetrack cafeteria alongside drunks and con-artists and gamblers—one, a Jackie Gleason-sized avuncular racetrack mentor, murdered by the Mafia the day after we had split a two-dollar bet, and he had placed it for me. I would take in this life over the summer, and then, when I returned to Gilman in the fall, it was another world: unreal, cocooned, insulated.

I received no big G for my sweater for spurring and whipping a bucking, wheeling, flipping-over-backwards rogue across the asphalt at Pimlico at 6:00 a.m. on a finger-numbing February morning, and then, lungs bursting, legs burning, *riding* him every step of the way around the track in the dark. My riding was something I had to sneak in; it was outlawish—I began to feel like an outlaw, and I began to act like an outlaw.

Those last few years of Gilman were the tough ones for me, starting with the Ninth Grade when my father—then the all-time leading professional steeplechase rider in America—had a bad fall over a hurdle at Monmouth Park and was paralyzed. I was 14 and had driven him down from Belmont Park, down the Jersey Turnpike at 90 m.p.h., to the race that ended his riding career. The first word I heard was that he would die, then, later, that he would be paralyzed for life. I lived a daily nightmare. When I visited him a week later, hooked up to wires and pulleys in a New York City hospital room, he was 90 percent paralyzed. (My mother had also had a bad fall at this time. She had broken her leg in a horse show and was in traction in a Baltimore hospital.)

I remember trying to study late one evening, the autumn after Pop's fall, when he was fighting his way out of the paralysis and had started training. I wanted to quit school, ride, help my father begin his training career. This—studying, going to classes, engaging in boyish pranks, playing on sports teams—all seemed irrelevant.

As a Fifth and Sixth Former (junior and senior) at Gilman, I hopped in my old Ford Falcon out at the farm at 5:30 a.m., raced to Pimlico. My father was 75 percent recuperated from the paralysis by this time and I'd get a leg up on a few of his tougher horses. In the winter, in the dark, the cars accelerating down Northern Parkway, Pimlico—the track being up on a hill—is a cold place to gallop a horse. Once off the last horse, I'd hop in my car, roar down Northern Parkway, across the Jones Falls, and back up to my other institute of learning. Between shifting gears I'd be unlacing my riding boots, left hand on the steering wheel, right on the laces, head part way under the dashboard. Enjoying myself thoroughly, I'd rumble onto the campus, sweater pulled half-way over my head blocking my vision, feet tangled in boots between the brakes and clutch. Pimlico and Gilman, like the two lenses of a pair of glasses joined by the nose-bridge, are forever linked by Northern Parkway in my view of life.

THE HONEYMOON'S OVER

It was after the honeymoon Ninth Grade that our class started to split into sects; suddenly so-and-so was an athletic hero and was in "a whole different ball game"; suddenly so-and-so was in advanced such-and-such and you never had him in one of your classes again. We splintered. Old friends flunked out, were kicked out. A kind and gentle member of our class became weaker and weaker. He went into the hospital. We gave blood for him. He had an insidious disease none of us understood. Soon we were attending his funeral. It was a cavalry charge and fellow warriors were dropping on either side. You held on tight and rode straight into the barrage.

On the playing field we were forced to knock into each other until we saw stars. I couldn't see the point. At least when I got on a tough horse, it put food on the table. We studied until 2 a.m. We were immersed in a pressurized cauldron of conformism—where the students who were the jocks and/or who did all the right things in class and who wore the right shoes (Weejuns loafers—more expensive than the hardier thicker-soled brands my grandmothers purchased for me) and full suits to school were the ideal, even in those late '60s, and where we weren't meant to come up with our own interpretations and ideas about the previous night's reading—as in Mr. Menzies' or Mr. Magruder's classes—but were instead ordered to memorize long passages of Shakespeare, spit out grammar rules on command, and thrive in a climate where there wasn't a female in sight.

There were classmates and Upper Formers (one rarely condescended to speak with someone in a lower form, unless on a team with him) who were supposed geniuses and it sucked the confidence out of you when word filtered down about their totally unimaginable, stratospheric S.A.T. and achievement test scores. Or when they were accepted early-decision to Harvard or Yale or Princeton. We were judged, compared, sorted, classified, categorized, accepted or not accepted at our college choices—and towards the end, you felt stuck in Gilman's grid-of-life, as if these scores, grades, judgments sealed your fate. We were judged by brain power (determined by I.Q. tests, P.S.A.T.s, S.A.T.s, Gilman grades, Gilman awards), and by athletic power—the latter insofar as as it contributed to the glory of Gilman. Your overall make-up as a person came less and less into play. If you didn't fit the bill, you didn't get the attention. It was best to be either a brain who rocked the Upper School with incredible numerical scores or a football player who knocked opponents into the stands. Artists, athletes interested in other sports, eccentrics—these were barely tolerated; rarely were their differences celebrated.

Most who did not fit the bill were squeezed out, but some stayed on, endured, and for many, it took a while to recuperate from the battering. I am reminded of *Cool Hand Luke*, and his warden saying to him, "What we have here is a failure to communicate." Classmates who were "different" in one way or another, and had gotten down on their luck—most of whom have gone on to stellar careers—were unmercifully picked apart, some by teachers, others by students, day after day.

The common denominator thread was woven through the academic as well as the social threads of the school. I remember returning on a bus filled with classmates late one night from a field trip to New York—adrenalin and testosterone pumping—and pouring out onto paper a picaresque tale for an English assignment. The next day, filled with hope and excitement, I handed it in. It was an account of a long ride on ponies Tom Whedbee and I had taken. We'd gotten caught in the dark in the Griswolds' Woods in a thunderstorm, and ridden home while sheets of rain poured down, thunder crackled all around, limbs crashed to the ground around us. Arriving home, how we had appreciated the warmth and dryness of the barn as we grabbed fistfuls of bright clean straw and rubbed our ponies down before we jog-skipped through puddles to the house for steaming baths and hot soup.

I got the paper back the next day, and it had hemorrhaged. It was covered with red ink. Grammar and punctuation errors had been slashed, circled, and categorized, and I'd gotten a horrible grade—and that did it for me.

From then on, for English classes, I took no chances. I wrote in short simple sentences. I regurgitated what the teacher wanted. I didn't explore. I kept things at the common denominator level. I didn't try to make anything different, unique, to put my stamp on it. A side of me shut down. I'm thankful it opened up again once I got into college, and out into the world.*

*See Clapham Murray's "In Pursuit of Matters Cultural," page 143, for the totally opposite effect occurring through a teacher's generosity of red ink.

LEGACY: HARD WORK AND DISCIPLINE

One attribute Gilman stamped onto one's very core was how to work hard. It gave you good work habits. But the pressure. Was it worth it? The competition? The vigilance with which constant day-by-day judgment was pursued, leading to a lifetime of incessant, hammering judging of oneself?

The sports instilled a discipline, an ability to withstand pain and discomfort, a stoicism, and the faith that you could overcome the most insurmountable odds—if you tried hard enough. This has come in handy over the years. Wrestling, in particular, was the sport where when we were younger, say on the J.V., and we practiced with the varsity, we were pushed to the limit. We'd have a long practice at the end of a long day in that stifling, padded room. Most of the practice would have been fun—we did have time to goof around. Classmate Ken Marshall (how he could hold those leg lifts forever) and Teddy Rouse (his speed and flexibility combined with an occasional ferocity) were among the Merry Pranksters at my weight and age. And we felt honored and privileged when this gentle, devoted, feathery old man called Mr. Russell would come down to the end of the room and work one-on-one with us welterweights, including later varsity star Trey Sunderland and future MSA champion Brent Whelan.

It was at the end of practice, when we were worn out, that the killer came. We'd line up against the wall, and, like soldiers rushing into battle, one wave, one weight-class at a time, we would sprint for the far wall. Then stop, turn around, wait for the other weight classes, sprint back. Stop, turn, sprint. Stop, turn, *race another weight class*—older guys—*sprint.* Stop, turn, *sprint.* Stop, turn, *sprint.* The coach yelling to go faster, push harder.

I didn't realize then how well this would prepare me for the many sprints that would make up the marathon of life.

NED THOMPSON AND CHARLIE GAMPER

And then again—there were the uncommon denominators in the upper forms: especially math teachers Ned Thompson and Charlie Gamper. They had a way of treating and respecting you as a young man, as an equal.

I hadn't liked math much in the Upper School. I had been miserable in an earlier math class where we had all these long, lugubrious word problems and where the teacher physically intimidated George Fenwick and me. We watched one afternoon as he grabbed a student in the second row by the front of his shirt, lifted him out of his chair, and shook him. In a later class, where the teacher exhibited no control over his irrational temper, we sat there scared and bone-stiff-quiet while an old basement pipe overhead dripped lukewarm water onto us. A hint of possible violence pulsated through the thick air of these teachers' rooms, and occasionally exploded.

Not so with Mr. Thompson! Quick-moving, quick-witted, one glass eye, mischievous, capricious—I realize now that he had been during his youth, was as a teacher, and still is, a rebel. You had to be on your toes when you entered his room, ready to banter, to duel, ready to answer questions about the homework as well as the latest rumor going around about some escapade. Mr. Thompson made math fun. He *read* my rebellious side, and played on it. "Smithwick, now that you're so famous—or perhaps *infamous* would be a better adjective—would you mind gracing our presence with an explanation of the different permutations and combinations available to us through problem seven in last night's homework?" The class would snicker, the game was on, and we'd all give it our best shot.

I had Ned Thompson up in a small, second-story classroom with worn, dusty, concave, wooden floor boards, off the beaten track, near where he had his computer—a big, intimidating, closet-sized machine, which he told us doubting Thomases would be so important in a few years. We'd been studying something new and had just had a big marking-period test. I hadn't been the model student for that marking period, but for the few days before the test I'd immersed myself in math. A group of us, led by math wizard Thomas Courtenay Whedbee, practiced homework problems in the Common Room every day after lunch. We weren't so concerned about our upcoming grade. We wanted to do well, for Mr. Thompson, to thank him for his style, to *show* him. We were competing with him, in a fun way.

I took that test the way I'd once skied a race. I was on the verge of falling the entire time, through one gate, then another, pushing as hard as I could go, risking everything, leaning forward, reaching.

The next day, before handing the tests back, he *roasted* an anonymous student for doing well, waving the test paper around, pointing out that the student's reputation as a rebel might now be diminished. With a big grin he slapped the folded sheaf of papers onto my desk, and on it was written "100" with "Congratulations!" scrawled in large letters underneath. He ribbed me about the grade—What kind of a rebel was I anyway?—and announced to all not to worry (taunting me, provoking me, *spurring me to prove him wrong*), the bubble would soon burst.

Charlie Gamper was another Upper School teacher who appreciated the uncommon denominator. I had Mr. Gamper in a math class down in the basement, stuck under some stairs, with one window, the pipes clicking and clanging all around us. Mr. Gamper had an unusual teaching methodology: Short, stocky, a gruff exterior camouflaging his warm interior, he'd come storming into the class late, from what we assumed was an important administrative meeting, and without consulting notes or textbook, having been born with all this in his head, attack the blackboard with a rapid fire, rat-tat-tat-tat of white chalk hitting black slate, immediately launching a fast-paced class during which we would be totally immersed in the language and precision and imagination of mathematics, with a few good laughs for breathers. I will carry one of his sayings to my grave. A student would say, "I think I have an easier way of solving this problem." And Mr. Gamper would reply, "Page," (He always called you by your first name—in contrast to many teachers and students who called you by your last name. When Mr. Gamper said, "Patrick," I felt he was communicating with the interior, real me.) "Page, I think you mean a *simpler* way, not an easier way. Don't you?" As with Messrs. Menzies, Magruder, and Thompson, you forgot you were taking a course with Mr. Gamper. You felt this was where you belonged.

NICKED

It was Nick Schloeder—a history teacher—who got me started in what would eventually become one of my careers: journalism. I was in an Eleventh-Grade history class of his, and we had to write two research papers. Mr. Schloeder had a sense of my personality, although, I was often irritated with him because he, the self-proclaimed "Apostle to the Privileged" who thrived on breaking the Gilman student's inherited Gilman/Princeton/Roland Park/Republican/Alex Brown iconography, stereotyped me as being a scion of the horsey set who had been brought up in a mansion in the Worthington Valley and after college would retire there to hunt foxes and drink mint juleps and open monthly envelopes from The Mercantile Safe Deposit and Trust.

Mr. Schloeder could see that we needed to get out into the world for some primary sources. He also was a believer in getting involved locally, waking up and examining life right here, in Baltimore. I wrote two papers—this was in 1967—one on air pollution, one on planned parenthood. I can still feel the excitement of hopping in my little Corvair right out in front of the main building in the light of day!—*legally*—and driving over to Towson to interview some important county personage on air pollution, and then later, driving down to Baltimore to interview the head of the Planned Parenthood office. Mr. Schloeder did not mindlessly cover the papers with red ink. And he truly employed the Socratic method in his class, pushing and prodding us to think—even to act—and not just regurgitate textbook material. He unleashed power in us, made us feel we could make a difference, in our future adult lives, yes—but also right at that moment while students at Gilman.

CYCLES

The ever-spiraling, changing, developing cycles of many of our lives and careers lead to the return of confidence, the building up of self-esteem. Confidence post-Gilman was bestowed on me by horse trainers, jockeys, editors, professors, writers, readers who valued one precisely because one *did* possess an uncommon denominator. (One noticed in a jarring, and for me, releasing way, that the rules leading to "success" in life-after-Gilman were often the opposite of those during life-at-Gilman.) I have heard this story, of having to go about re-gathering confidence post-Gilman, in different versions from hundreds of alumni.

A decade or two off the campus, we can see what Gilman did for us, and feel the pride in having absorbed, endured, prevailed over the rough-and-ready Country School atmosphere of Gilman and can celebrate the memories of playing keep-away on the endless fields at recess, of running and throwing the football, the lacrosse ball, the baseball with Larry Koppelman and Pearce Johnson and Braxton

Andrews and Bruce Rice and Page Boyce and Chip Tompkins. We can take joy in the memories of epic snowball battles waged on the steep slope between the Upper School terrace and the fields and lasting into the next class period where we would finally arrive, splat down in our seats, laughing and together, steam rising up around us, the barnyard smell of sheep seeping out of our soggy, Gilman-blue wool sweaters, and the teacher, a fellow male, scolding us out of one side of his mouth, and grinningly, conspiratorially, even enviously, identifying with our boyish excitement and energy out of the other.

The camaraderie then, and the connection now: when a member of the class of 1935 or 1995 tells me he is a Gilman alumnus, or a youth informs me he is a Gilman student—it forms an instant positive impression. This gentleman has an immediate leg-up in my estimation and in what I will do for him. I feel a brotherly bond with him, no matter what his age or looks or personality: we have been through the same rite of passage.

The kick, the click, the common denominator I feel with a Gilman alumnus is something I treasure. I love Gilman the way one loves a childhood friend with whom he has shared life-forming experiences, both good and bad. When trouble occurs, right or wrong, no questions asked, I will be there.

 Patrick Smithwick galloped half a dozen race horses at Timonium Racetrack the morning of his graduation from Gilman. He rushed home, changed into his white pants and shirt, and headed into town in his banged-up Ford Falcon. On Charles Street, he picked up a hippie hitchhiker. Past the Greater Baltimore Medical Center, rounding the sharp curve by the entrance to Sheppard Pratt, the Falcon blew a back tire. The deadline for graduation approaching, the graduate-to-be wrestled the car to the shoulder, jacked it up and changed the wheel in Indy time while the hitchhiker stood a few feet away with his thumb out.*

Once at graduation, Smithwick *sat* all of the time—with the one moment of exception—while other fellow late-alphabetters, with whom he had been bound since Fourth Grade, were practically doing squat thrusts. Graduating in the first class to have Reddy Finney's signature on the diplomas, Smithwick worked his way through Johns Hopkins by exercising thoroughbreds at Pimlico, Bowie, Timonium, and Delaware Park racetracks in the early mornings before classes and riding steeplechase races in the summers. Two scholarships awarded for character and individualism helped with the tuition.

Out of Hopkins in 1973, Smithwick worked for a year on *The Dorchester News* in Cam-

---

*Smithwick's father, Paddy '46, and uncle, Mikey '47, had a simpler commute to Gilman during WW II: they rode the Ma and Pa in from Hydes in the Long Green Valley every morning, and in the afternoons, chased after the caboose, back where the tennis courts are now, and jumped on board. The engineer—unwilling to fully stop the train due to the steepness of the incline—would yell at them to hurry as they threw the football back and forth one last time. Paddy Smithwick's classmate W. Boulton "Bo" Kelly has since confessed to soaping the tracks so that once the train slowed, its wheels would spin and spin heading up the steep grade.

bridge, Maryland, as reporter, photographer, editor before being accepted into the Graduate Creative Writing Program at Hollins College, Roanoke, Virginia. At Hollins, he wrote fiction and met his wife-to-be, Ansley Dickinson.

Receiving his master's from Hollins in 1975, Smithwick focused on writing short stories, memoirs, and magazine features while holding down positions as a newspaper feature writer/photographer, Chesapeake Bay waterman (oystering on a skipjack, a member of the only working sailing fleet in North America, crabbing on a Bay-built deadrise), English teacher, freelance rider of race horses, freelance college writing instructor (Goucher College, Johns Hopkins Continuing Studies), and publications director for St. Paul's School. In the 1980s, he earned a Master's of Liberal Arts from Johns Hopkins. He has won awards in the writing of newspaper features, short stories, and investigative journalism pieces, and in the editing of school magazines as well as fund-raising publications.

Smithwick was first interviewed to write and edit the history of Gilman by Headmaster Reddy Finney and Director of Development David Drake in 1991. In 1995, Headmaster Arch Montgomery hired Smithwick to direct Gilman's publications and public relations, and to teach an English class.

Smithwick lives on the campus of Oldfields School in Glencoe, Maryland, with his wife Ansley, who teaches French at Oldfields, and their three children, Paddy, Andrew, and Eliza.

Saint Nick

ALLEN KIRBY '68

I t is the early 1990s, and I am standing at the top of the concrete slab of bleachers on a fall day, staring down at a Gilman football game, now in time-out, and a familiar figure jogs onto the field. A hefty, blond, scar-tissued gentleman enters the defensive huddle. The blue-clad players surround him; then suddenly there is a terrifying yell: "Shut up!"—audible even 50 yards away where I stand. Almost immediately, a player, his head dangling down like a scolded puppy, runs off the field.

Nick Schloeder—veteran coach, teacher, molder of tender psyches—has struck again.

I laugh—and remember.

It's almost 30 years earlier, spring of 1965, and I am walking onto the Gilman campus for the first time in my life, going to take a math entrance exam, escorted by a Gilman student down the path in front of the main building. Suddenly, through an open first-floor window, a young lad about my age comes flying head-over-heels, falling onto the thick green grass.

"That's Mr. Schloeder," my escort says, referring not to the boy who is scrambling to his feet, but to the faceless force that had apparently propelled the lad outward. "But don't worry, he only teaches freshmen. You're going to be a sophomore."

We walk a few paces up the brick steps almost into the Common Room, and my escort pauses and looks at me.

"Oh," he says ominously. "You play football and basketball, don't you?"

I remember that moment and then wonder if it is accurate or not. Had I really seen Nick toss a boy out the window, or had the legend impressed itself so much on my consciousness that it had become inseparable from fact? It is hard now to separate the apocryphal from the genuine, but in the long run, it doesn't make any difference. The legends of Nick Schloeder are as compelling as the historical facts.*

August, 1965, and Lyndon Johnson is in office, the Vietnam War is ongoing, and we are daily reminded by the number one song of the summer that we are all on the "eve of destruction." I can't speak for the universe, but for the 40 or so boys that August, summer football practice was a reasonable facsimile.

I can remember nearly fainting going through the physical tests and examinations on the first day and being outfitted in heavy archaic equipment and ill-fitting uniforms. (My pants would hang loose for three days until I procured a belt.)

Names were taped to the backs of helmets, and I can recall them now, with respect and awe: Campbell, Wasserman, Boland, Anderson, Beadle, Legg, Fisher, Simms, Malone, Cooper, Reilly, and a guy named Bristow. And plenty of others with whom I would sweat and bleed and taste victory.

Hovering above us all though, head bobbing, mammoth arms and legs restraining their strength, veins in the neck popping, is the head coach. Deadly earnest, he will speak of "reckless abandon" and "wars of attrition" and "going into the arena." He is bigger than life and seems in perpetual motion; he is Redmond Coningham Stewart Finney. In the next three years his teams will go 8-1, 8-1, and finally, in the fall of 1967, 9-0—the only undefeated, untied football team in the school's history since the team of 1921. In the fall of 1968, he will relinquish his coaching duties and become headmaster. In his heart of hearts, he probably regards it as a demotion.**

But on those first days of August 1965, someone is missing. The other boys speak of the absence in a hush; the word is that the missing man's wife is having a baby. They cannot imagine how such a minor event could deter the backfield coach from administering torture. What delights can a newborn offer Nick Schloeder when he could be at the Gilman athletic fields on hot summer days, making sure his charges start the practices off with seven-minute miles?

And then he returns; it is like Patton or Napoleon entering the fray. I can remember holding my pants up, jogging around the track in full uniform on a 90-degree day, listening to the manager count the time off. Next to him, the squinty-eyed blond man on the track observes all. After the ordeal is over, Nick speaks to one of us: "You're in awful shape. I mean awful. Didn't you work out at all this summer?"

He is a demanding man. For the next two years on the football field, he times our movements, requiring excellence, punishing us for laxity by running us "up to Belvedere," the road that has now become Northern Parkway. Of course, he gives a

---

*Nick Schloeder notes, "Look, it was a basement ground floor window. It was a spring day. This student was being very noisy so I lifted the chair and the student, together, and set them outside. I wasn't angry. I said to him, 'You're being a little noisy. You just take your notes out there.' It was all in good fun."

**Dr. Ernest Cross '33 reports that his son, Sam Cross '67, told him, "Gee Dad, you wouldn't think he'd give up being Head Coach just to be a headmaster."

time limit; if we don't make it, we try it again. And again. Until we learn to do it right, to operate more quickly and efficiently.

He has even invented a special routine for the backs, a pleasant exercise called the "Labor Day Special": we are paired off, set at opposite ends of the track, and told to run in the same direction until we catch our mate. All this is after practice, of course, and performed before an audience of linemen sitting, drinking ice water out of rusty buckets.*

One day he is directing a defensive back retreating drill, and he runs me from the practice field back to the front of the old gym, a hundred and fifty yards away. For a moment, I think he is going to demand I run through the wall; and I would have, the alternative being to suffer in another more painful fashion. But finally he beckons me back, and I find out that I had been turning my back on my retreat, a cardinal sin for a defensive back.

Then one day, a year later, in a running drill, I am tackled, and the defensive player clings to my lower leg while I pull futilely to get away. Nick takes the ball from me, assumes the same position I had been in, and proceeds to stomp firmly on the tackler's midsection to get away. In time we learn that Nick hates tape and analgesic heating salves; one day he asks a player wearing wrist bands if his arms will fall off without the added support.

It is ironic that Nick is absent for the undefeated, untied season; he has decided to take on the Maryland state constitution and is away on leave with fellow scholars while we go through the season winning by an average score of 41–9 and earning a number one ranking in the state—one of the first polls ever established in the area for high school athletics.

I can recall the Gibbons game. On the Thursday night prior to the game, spray-painted predictions of a Gibbons victory are discovered in our end zone; in the game on Friday we pummel them 54–6. Against Curley I am poked in the eye so severely that the swelling prevents me from seeing; in a panic I turn to Bobby Green on the sideline and ask if he can still see my eyeball.

It is an awesome year; we are called the "machine" for our ability to function without errors. But we are greater than that really; many of our games are blowouts by half-time and our substitutes play much of the second halves. Reddy has established the tone of the season by posting words of the week—determination, dedication, concentration, etc.—on the varsity locker room wall. One day, Nick pays a visit from Annapolis, and we point to the words on the wall. He slowly examines them, nodding his head. Then he turns towards us and says, in his Jersey accent: "You gotta do more than just read them."

---

*At the end of the Saturday morning practice before Labor Day, Schloeder would tell the backfield, "Whatever you're doing over the weekend—going to the beach, traveling—I just want you to be thinking about what you will face when you get back at the end of a long Tuesday practice: The Labor Day Special."

He's right; you have to do a lot more. In the basketball season, Nick is head coach, and in one of my first scrimmages with the big boys my lip is split wide open, the blood dripping out. He is the referee, and I glance over at him to see if he will stop us, but we go on, my lip swelling and the blood congealing.

Two years later, I am playing with a sprained ankle, and I'm on the bench next to him and he asks how my ankle is. I tell him that it's sore; later, in the locker room, he explodes: he doesn't want to know if my ankle really hurts; he wants to know that I want to play, that I am willing to play.

One day during scrimmage at Christmas time (we are in the infamous hair-shirt sweat suits), another player goes down. He is writhing with apparent cramps near the foul line, but Nick-the-referee continues the scrimmage and we play around the injured player. Finally, Nick blows the whistle and says to the kid: "Do you think you can crawl off the court?"

But Nick is more than a disciplinarian; he is a story teller whose reminiscences resonate with emotions and convictions. And we hear much about them in a small dusty room off the lobby of the old gym: golden-glove bouts; pick-up games against Bob Cousy; being knocked cold as a kid by Tommy Heinsohn, the future Celtic forward; how Nick stood up with his chin held high as his high school coach demeaned him in front of the whole school; and how, while at Bucknell, in an away-game against Navy, a black Bucknell player had endured racial taunts the entire game. After the game was over, when the black player had headed into the Navy locker room to claim some justice, Nick and his teammates were right behind him.

One day, during a championship game played at what is now called the Baltimore Arena, we are down to the last few minutes against Park School. Nick gives a few of us permission to shoot; the others he wants to freeze the ball completely. One of the others, however, decides to take an easy shot while he is under the basket. He misses. In the timeout following, Nick says: "Do you know why I told you not to shoot? Because I knew you'd miss it." Twenty-five years later that same player tells me that every Gilman student should have the privilege of having Nick as a teacher or coach.

These memories flit through my brain on this lovely fall day, almost 30 years later. Nick is on the sidelines coaching, a subordinate to one of his former players, Sherm Bristow. But it is still the same Nick—at least if the voice that resounds across the field is any evidence. It is still the same Nick Schloeder who is instilling, in his own distinctively ungentle style, qualities of manhood and honor.

Allen Kirby turned the passion for sports he exemplified at Gilman into a passion for literature, writing, and teaching. Attending Gilman 1965–68, Kirby was a two-year varsity football ball player, three-year varsity basketball player, and three-year varsity baseball man, co-captain his senior year. He also found time to work for Operation Challenge and in his senior year serve as Athletic Association secretary.

Attending Rutgers, Kirby majored in English. He received his master's from the University of Denver. Kirby has taught English, literature, and writing at independent schools and colleges in the Baltimore metropolitan area, including Calvert Hall, Severn, Essex Community College, and Catonsville Community College. Through Essex Community College he has taught dozens of courses in developmental writing at the Maryland House of Correction in Jessup. Over his teaching career, Kirby has taught just about every type of writing, including journalism, business writing, creative writing, and, his favorite, expository writing. Planning to continue teaching, Kirby is also working on a novel. He lives in Baltimore with his wife Felicity and three sons, Ryan, Dan, and the youngest—Nick.

1970s

1970

The George E. P. Mountcastle Memorial Lecture series is begun.

The Harry Hardie Anglo-American Prize is awarded for the first time to John N. Renneburg '70.

1971

Encouraged by the success of *The Mikado* in March, producers Barry Talley and Jerry Downs, and most of the cast, establish the Gilman Summer Theater. The first production, *Iolanthe*, in the newly air-conditioned auditorium, is a success, and the company goes into another season. Out of this beginning grows the Young Victorians, still going strong a quarter-century later, albeit at Bryn Mawr School.

1972

The Fisher Memorial Dining Hall becomes part of the Edward R. Fenimore, Jr. Memorial Library. Gilman students form a line from the old library, currently The Gilman Room, to the new library, and transfer the books, box by box. Author and historian Walter Lord '35 buys ice cream for the entire school.

A new wing is constructed east of the library, housing study carrels and open stacks on the upper floor, a cafeteria and language labs on the middle floor, and a lecture hall and industrial arts center on the ground floor.

The boarding department is closed, making Gilman exclusively a day school for the first time in its history. The phase-out of boarding is a difficult decision. Limitations of property and buildings make it difficult to meet rising demands for a Gilman education from the greater Baltimore area. Demand for out-of-state boys to attend Gilman are handled on a case-by-case basis by placing students with a teacher or with a Gilman family.

Gilman celebrates its 75th anniversary. Eighty-two students graduate. A pictorial history of Gilman's first 75 years, 1897–1972, is published. Edited and written by English teacher Alex Armstrong '33, the history displays Gilman's collection of archival and contemporary

Bob Thomas '76 breaks away from Eagle tacklers to score a touchdown as Mike Austin '76 (#43) watches.

Gilman goes high tech—soon earning it the sobriquet "Gillie Tech" and "The Tech" from neighboring schools—as this shot of William S. Brusilow '71 and William L. Scherlis '71 working in the physics lab shows.

photographs. May Holmes teamed with Armstrong in locating and identifying the photographs; Armstrong wrote the text.

Speakers and panelists for the September 29th and 30th 75th Anniversary Program include Jim Rouse, president of The Rouse Company and father of two graduates; Page Smith '36, American history professor and author; Mebane Turner, president of the University of Baltimore; and Roger Howell '56, president of Bowdoin College.

Construction of John M. T. Finney Hall, a one-story "open-classroom" Middle School building, is completed.

Chaired by Richard Thomas '43 and with strong support from President of the Board Owen Daly '43, The Challenge of Leadership Capital Campaign is completed, having raised $6 million for new construction and new endowment for faculty salaries and financial aid.

1974

Coordinated classes with Bryn Mawr School begin.

Henry Blue '74 and Guy Phelan '75 are instrumental in forming the varsity golf team. Frank "Bill" Andrews is the coach.

1976

May Holmes breaks ground for the swimming pool. It is dedicated on Friday, October 29, Circus Day. Profits from ten Gilman Circuses helped fund the pool. Special gratitude is extended to Bill Porter, science teacher and Gilman Circus czar, "whose vision, enthusiasm, and leadership kept alive this dream and brought it to fruition."

Led by Tim Holley '77, the varsity baseball team wins its first "B" conference championship.

282

A. J. "Jerry" Downs taught English at Gilman 1950–89. Downs once told a *News* reporter, "I always felt like Peter Pan. It was a continuing source of astonishment that I was paid for doing something that is so much fun." Read Downs' "Three Titans" in the 1990s section.

Left: Father-son Fisher Medallion winners William H. Mueller '70 and William R. Mueller '35 pose at the conclusion of the 1970 Founders' Day.

e 1970 production of "The Petrified Forest" was met with unanimous approval.

Class of 1972 members Tom Porter, Alan Kaufmann, and Ted Trimble triumphed in scholastic competition over 81 area high schools to win WBAL-TV's "It's Academic" championship. Through their appearances on the program they earned cash awards to be used by Gilman's scholarship fund to help deserving students.

Below, the Areopagus Debating Team in the mid-70s shows off its checkered presence: Messrs. Carpenter, Nicholson, Benninghoff, Smith, and Meyer seated; Messrs. Wong, Wolff and Mathews standing.

Opposite: the Gilman championship varsity lacrosse team of 1973.

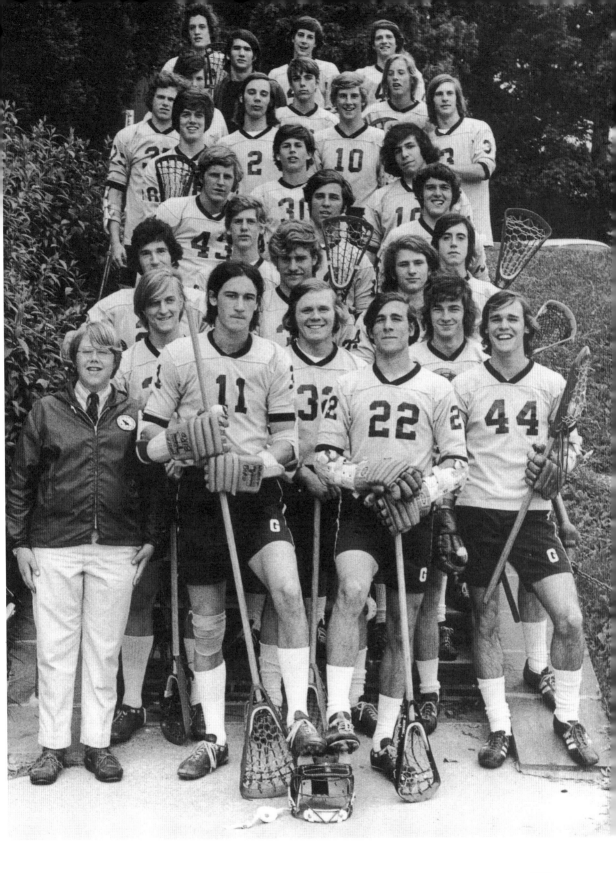

285

Bill Campbell '52, standing, taught and coached at Gilman 1961–74 and 1984–85. Campbell played a key role in the diversification of Gilman; he and Reddy Finney founded Gilman Upward Bound in 1967. Read Finney's "Reflections Upon Gilman Headmastering" in the 1940s section for more on Campbell and Upward Bound.

Below, teacher/coaches Joe Duncan (in hat) Jack Thompson (in middle) and Jerry Thornbery (far right) have made dramatic contributions to Gilman over the decades in the language, math, and history departments. Here, as coaches in 1980, they celebrate a victorious cross-country meet with Ian Liska '82, manager; Steve Levin '82, and Robbie Harrell '81. The three teachers are still coaching cross-country together in the 1990s.

Above, the varsity cross-country team of 1972. Front row, Henry Rinder '75, Giovanni Prezioso '75, Douglas Nelson '74, Tom Gamper '74, Joseph Carton '73, Chris White '74. Back row: Richie Blue '73, J. T. Christmas '74, Courtenay Jenkins '74, Howard Hill '74, William Reese '73, James Lynn '74, Christopher Phillips '74.

Left, from 1946 to 1984, Charlie Gamper was a forceful presence everywhere on the campus as a teacher of math and French, dean of students, athletic director, and assistant headmaster; he was especially influential in revolutionizing high school athletics in Maryland through the Maryland Scholastic Association. From Scott Sullivan's "Et in Arcadia Ego": "And Charlie Gamper, a mid-Atlantic Casey Stengel, a born-in-the-wool teacher-coach, a Christian and perhaps the closest approximation to that elusive ideal—a gentleman—that Gilman had to offer."

Headmaster Reddy Finney is caught during an athletic event in a rare moment of stillness. Finney is known to be one of the most vociferous and physical of Gilman sports fans in Gilman history, i.e. don't sit next to him at a football game.

Left, the varsity basketball team of 1975. Bob Ehrlich '75, #32, is the third man from the left. Ehrlich went on to Princeton and law school, and served eight years in the House of Delegates before being elected to the U. S. House of Representatives in 1994. Read his "Life Change."

Gilman in the 1970s:
A Period of Transition

MICHAEL A. SARBANES '82

"Whereas the founders conceived of Gilman as a community school, the community to be served today must have a far broader base and representation. This is not only dictated by the make–up of our community and the greater mixture of peoples from all backgrounds in every segment of life, but it is important for the educational climate within the school. A true sense of the dignity and worth of all human beings can only be fostered in an educational environment where peoples from different backgrounds associate with one another in a variety of experiences."

(Philosophy of Gilman School as revised in 1968.)

Gilman in the 1970s had an aspiration to change and a plan to realize that aspiration. In the rapidly changing world of the late '60s and the '70s, Gilman determined to be a "community school," which according to William McCarthy, Chairman of the Board of Trustees in 1977, was:

"an educational institution which realistically offers the same possiblity of admission to all candidates who choose to apply. A community school also is one that is in contact with its neighbors and not an isolated island set off from the mainland."

In some respects, the community school which took shape in the '70s would have been unrecognizable to a visiting alumnus from an earlier era. Its student body and faculty were larger and significantly more diverse—racially, ethnically, religiously, and socioeconomically. Upward Bound, the Tutorial Project, Operation Green Grass, Encounters and other programs involved Gilman in the world beyond the school's grounds. Ancient practices were reconsidered and new experiments attempted, including coordinated upper school classes with Bryn Mawr and Roland

Park Country School students, the "open" classroom in the Middle School, and pass–fail grading for second–semester seniors.

Yet, for all the innovation, the school would have still seemed familiar to an alumnus from an earlier era: There were many familiar names on the school's rolls, as another generation of longstanding Gilman families filtered through Anne Carey's country day school. The faculty was exceptional and demanding as ever, and some of them were ripening into Gilman legends. And, the school held true to its core educational philosophy which sought to educate the "whole boy." As summarized by Headmaster Redmond Finney:

> "The basic goals of the School, to promote the best development of each student's intellectual capabilities, to develop the whole person and strong character, and to encourage a commitment on the part of each individual to something far greater than himself, are forever true."

Gilman remained self-consciously dedicated to educating its students to be leaders in their society. However, now the society which Gilman students were to enter and in which they were expected to be leaders was changing dramatically. The comfortable days when the society that mattered was Baltimore Society were fading fast. Changes and movements which had simmered in the post-War period erupted in mass movements which challenged deeply-rooted hierarchies. The Civil Rights Movement, Women's Liberation, the Vietnam War, and a host of other movements for social change began to reshape the social and political landscape. To provide the education in values and character on which Gilman had traditionally prided itself, the school had to change while maintaining a path of continuity. Leaders routinely appealed to the traditional purposes of the school to justify significant changes in the composition of the student body and practices of the school, spawning a period of feverish activity.

Beginning in the mid-'60s, Gilman's student body became more diverse. However, the vast bulk of Gilman students continued to come from economically privileged white families. For these boys, Gilman became the place where they encountered some degree of diversity. For the relatively small group of non-white students and the even-smaller group of students from poor or working class backgrounds, Gilman became a place where they encountered a "preppy" world for the first time.

An analysis of school records and available census data for the '60s through the '90s reveals several interesting developments. Gilman could scarcely have become less diverse than it was in 1962—when all students were white. Virtually all students came from census tracts with less than two percent African-American populations. None came from census tracts where the median income was less than 120 percent that of the Baltimore region.

From 1962 to 1992, as one might expect from demographic shifts in this period, the school moved from being a school of city-dwellers to one of county dwellers. Simultaneously, the proportion of the school which was non-white increased steadily, from two percent in 1968–69 to 28 percent in the '90s. The growth in Asian-American students was particularly dramatic, from less than one percent in 1971–72 to 11 percent in 1992–93. The increase of African-American students was more gradual, from six percent in 1971–72 to 11 percent in the '90s. These statistics highlight the school's function as the major place where students encountered peers from different backgrounds.

Finally, most Gilman students continued to come from economically privileged neighborhoods. The proportion of students from neighborhoods where the median income was equal to or less than that of the region has remained stubbornly consistent since 1970.

These statistics do not capture some of the most significant changes in the composition of the student body. In religious affiliation, the school began to include far more Jewish students. The presence of Jewish students was a dramatic aspect of the diversification of the school from the '50s. Changes in the language and life of the school reflected this development.

Also absent from these statistics is the arrival of coordinated classes. The official reason for this change was that it allowed Gilman and Bryn Mawr students to access a richer set of curricular offerings. While not explicitly part of the "community school" idea, coordination had the unprecedented effect of bringing Gilman boys into contact with girls as peers in the classroom. The arrival of this new era was neatly captured in the Winter 1974 Gilman *Bulletin* which featured Bryn Mawr student Kathy Martien on its front cover. The same picture gave a hint at how much of a change in attitude this new era might require: the caption to the picture described her as "Gilman's first cover girl."

Of overriding importance in Gilman's becoming a community school was the admissions process. Admissions policies were based first on academic achievement and potential based on testing, grades and recommendations. Added consideration was given to qualified sons of alumni and to qualified brothers of Gilman students. In addition, beginning in the Callard years, Gilman teachers and administrators looked for students from neighborhoods and families with which Gilman had no prior connection.

Even with this more open admissions process, the school still drew most of its student body from its traditional sources of students. Financial aid was concentrated in grades seven through twelve, making scholarships in the earlier grades relatively rare. In 1974, 70 out of 95 slots for the Seventh Grade were taken up by the Gilman Sixth Grade class and what the Gilman *News* called the "de facto quota" from Calvert School. After the Seventh Grade, about another 20 students entered the Upper School. Diversification of the student body thus had to be achieved within a small segment of the school.

With the move to diversify the student body, financial aid became of unprecedented importance. In earlier decades, financial aid, as stated in a 1977 report on the scholarship program, had been mostly for "sons of alumni who had encoun-

tered difficult times economically, and a modest number of youngsters from families of low-level income." Since the Board had a longstanding policy of not paying
for financial aid out of tuition incomes, financial aid had to come from capital cam-
paigns and annual giving. The school set a long-term goal of raising sufficient
endowment for financial aid to serve 25 percent of student enrollment—12.5 percent for full scholarships and 12.5 percent for partial assistance. By 1977, 10 percent
of the students received financial aid; and by 1994–95, 20 percent.

The community-school idea required a determined leadership, a committed
faculty, a supportive Board of Trustees, and a major infusion of money. To make the
school more diverse, it had to increase in size and accessibility. With faculty and
plant already at peak capacity, money was needed for major physical improvements
and faculty salaries. Money was also necessary for a serious financial aid program
to make the promise of more open admissions a financial reality.

In 1970, Gilman launched a $6 million Challenge of Leadership Capital Cam-
paign, a goal ten times higher than the largest previous fund drive in the school's
history. This stands out as a remarkable collaboration of alumni, Board, and faculty
who had attended or taught at the old Gilman to make a new, more diverse Gilman
possible. The campaign was as lofty and ambitious in its social objectives as it was
in its dollar totals. The school was worthy of support not merely because of its history and old school ties, but because it had an essential function in the emerging
world. A proposal seeking support for Gilman's Challenge of Leadership campaign
states:

> Today major roles related to population growth, technological advance, and suburban-
> ization, have greatly complicated the challenges facing public education. Public schools
> are facing overwhelming problems of increasing depersonalization, de facto segregation,
> a continuing exodus of more affluent citizens to suburbia, and an onslaught of detri-
> mental influences. These problems are causing a progressive polarization of social, eco-
> nomic, and ethnic groups at the very time when our nation can least afford it.
>
> It is our contention that the Gilman School and others like it, located within the metro-
> politan area of one of the nation's largest cities, is fulfilling a vital educational role. Not
> only is the educational program which is oVered one of proven excellence, but personal
> contact and the development of the unique talents of each individual continue to be
> emphasized. The opportunity to develop and maintain a challenging educational pro-
> gram and to innovate, experiment, and change, while at the same time promoting a
> community atmosphere of mutual respect and responsibility, makes the independent
> community day school one of the most viable educational forces within our nation
> today.

The $6 million campaign provided the underpinnings of the community school
idea. It enabled Gilman to set up the financial aid program discussed above. It
allowed the school to increase the faculty from 65 in 1969 to 84 in 1976, while maintaining competitive faculty salaries. And, it provided the lion's share of the funds

needed for many physical expansions and improvements which occurred in the 1970s:

The John M. T. Finney Middle School was completed. The Fisher Dining Room became part of the Edward R. Fenimore, Jr. Memorial Library. The Cochran Study Area was added to the library. The Lower/Middle School dining area, the David K. E. Bruce Language Center, a 120-seat lecture hall, and an Industrial Arts center were all completed in the '70s. Major renovations were made to the Upper School, now called Carey Hall. An art center and a computer center were completed; and in the fall of 1976, the pool— dedicated to Harry Wilson, the gym superintendent 1946–75—and the Edward T. and Florence C. Russell wrestling room were finished.

By the conventional measures of standardized test scores and admissions to prestigious colleges, Gilman continued to perform well throughout the '70s, and was assisted by the scholarship students whom the community school concept brought to the school. The more difficult challenge of this era came from changes in the broader culture. Vietnam, Watergate, the anti-war movement, the Civil Rights movement, and a wide "generation gap" posed trenchant critiques of various official hypocrisies and of an Establishment which Gilman in some respects epitomized. These changes posed continuing challenges to the very basis for authority of the school and of parents. At the same time, rapidly evolving technology—the early phases of the electronic age—increased the information, influences, and distractions to which students had access. The headmaster's annual reports were preoccupied with achieving a balance in a polarizing time. "Schools must preserve and promote freedom of inquiry and the opportunity to challenge traditionally accepted beliefs. At the same time, schools must not abrogate their responsibility to foster the development of self-discipline and a concern for the groups and community."

Gilman approached these problems through three paths: dialogue, community engagement, and faculty. The sheer amount of dialogue and number of meetings, committees, task forces, associations, and forums was striking. From dialogue over the Vietnam War, to political debate, to the honor code, to the ever-present dispute over the dress code and hair lengths, students, faculty and administrators talked. As Mr. Finney wrote, "One of the most exhausting, yet vitally important, responses to student concern has been the increased amount of time devoted to student-faculty discussions and to listening to student concerns. . . . This trend has been accompanied by greater participation of students in the governing process, a development which requires large expenditures of time, but which has a real educational value and, in the long run, serves the best interests of the School."

This dialogue also focused explicitly on how members of the Gilman community treated one another. In 1974, a human relations committee was formally created, composed of alumni, parents, teachers, and students. Some of the issues among students were longstanding—particularly the bullying of non-athletic students.

Other issues were a direct result of a more diverse student body. While incidents of open bigotry were rare, there were occasional manifestations in school life of the same prejudices and insensitivities which were at work in the larger society. A racially offensive word was scrawled on the back of a car on the school grounds. In one Lower School class, the entire class was invited to a boy's birthday party, except the lone African-American. Anti-semitism was present in some degree beneath the surface of school life; I heard an anti-semitic remark for the first time in my life from a group of fellow students in my first year at Gilman.

A more diverse student body also meant that students had to confront issues, perspectives, and experiences which did not exist in the Gilman of the '50s or earlier. From the earliest days of diversification, the details of daily life raised basic issues about individual and group identity, and about how a majority and minority should interact. Was the student body a "melting pot" in which all ethnic, religious, and racial differences should fade? Did African-American students have to become "whitewashed" to be at Gilman? Several years after he graduated in 1968 as one of Gilman's first African-American students, Stuart Simms wrote, "Gilman was no 'melting pot' and there were those who subtly reminded me I was not going to 'blend in.'" The Gilman *News* talked about "de facto segregation" in the lunchroom and editorialized anxiously about whether the formation of a Black Awareness Club might increase divisions in the student body. A full-day discussion of the Holocaust, sponsored by the Human Relations Committee, evinced some tense moments charged by religious differences.

Like institutions in the broader society, the Gilman community dealt with these issues with varying degrees of success. However, unlike many institutions, the official environment of the school did stress the importance of the issues raised by these differences and strongly encouraged dialogue about them.

Dialogue about human relations within the school was enhanced by engagement with the wider community beyond the school grounds. In the community school ideal, the school and its students should be enmeshed in, learn from, and serve the society around them. The Upward Bound program became an established and highly successful Gilman institution over the course of this period.*

Operation Green Grass, inspired by Thomas G. Hardie '74, brought students from poorer neighborhoods in Baltimore City to the Gilman campus for sports and other activities. The Tutorial Program paired Gilman students with students from the Lexington Terrace housing project and the Franklin Square community. Encounter offered seniors the opportunity to spend several weeks at the end of the year working off campus in projects of their own choosing.

Ultimately, the emphasis on faculty is the most distinctive aspect of Gilman's response to the social upheavals of the '70s. If there is a common Gilman identity

---

*For more on Upward Bound, founded by Bill Campbell '56 and Reddy Finney '47 under the headmastership of Ludlow Baldwin, see Reddy Finney's "Reflections Upon Gilman Headmastering," and Nick Schloeder's "Gilman in the 1960s."

which pervades the chapters of this history, it is in the interaction of the students and the faculty. So many of the faculty in the '70s were on their way to becoming long-term institutions. Graduating in 1982, I was taught, coached, or scolded by Mr. Porter, Mr. Williams, Mr. Schloeder, Mr. Barker, Mr. Downs, Mr. Reese and others who began teaching at Gilman long before I was born. More importantly, the daily interaction with teachers and coaches was the primary means by which the school's culture rubbed off on the students. This was the essence of the school's response to the challenges of the '70s. Mr. Finney wrote,

> *"Although we have always accepted the importance of close personal contact between students and sympathetic teachers, this aspect of our experience in a private school setting is more important than ever before, and we are redoubling our efforts to achieve the openness and mutual trust which develop from close personal relationships. Only through this process does it seem that we can give our young people a sufficient sense of their uniqueness and importance as individuals and, at the same time, provide further means for the School to weigh constructive and significant change."*

The faculty were intended to be "a company of giants" who provided "living examples of the kinds of qualities to which we want our students and children to aspire." But now it was essential that these giants be comfortable in the more student-centered, interactive classroom and that they exhibit with students and with each other the "mutual respect" which was the credo of a more diverse Gilman. The faculty also had to become more diverse. In this respect, progress in the '70s was slow. In 1976, A. J. Downs, English teacher and college counselor, noted in the Alumni *Bulletin* that the faculty was the least diverse component of the school, with students and Board including more Blacks, Jews, and Catholics.

Pervading all aspects of this process was Headmaster Redmond C. S. Finney. Finney played the unique role of embodying the vision of what the school was and how it could and should change. A son of one of Gilman's oldest and most distinguished families, his traditional Gilman credentials were beyond cavil and helped to reassure some alumni who were uncertain about the changes the school was embarking upon. He was able to retain and nurture the loyalty of the alumni to the school and to harness that loyalty to a vision of the school which was very different from the one they attended.

At the same time, he believed passionately that the school had to become something other than an exclusive preserve for privileged people—or else it should "go out of existence." In daily interaction, he personified the mutual respect which the school sought to inculcate. To us students, Finney meant something quite fundamental. He was the living incarnation of the idea that the school—whatever our complaints about it—cared about all of its students, and he insisted that we should be and could be at our best. He had the unique ability to impart this sense to virtually every student in the school. We all were personally concerned that we not "disappoint" Mr. Finney. He communicated this sense more by casual interactions in the hallway than by speeches in chapel. Yet, his chapel speeches about the three types of citizens and the parable of the talents will be remembered by any student who heard them at least several times each year.*

As in the society at large, there were tensions and discomforts at Gilman in the '70s. The school was attempting to address some of the most deeply rooted and explosive divisions in American society. Mr. Finney's genius was that he was able to recognize these divisions, transcend them in his person, and communicate to others the highest standards of how people should treat one another. Regardless of background or of status within the school, each of us knew that the school belonged to Mr. Finney. And therefore, it belonged to all of us.

---

*"Third class citizens throw trash on the ground, second class citizens only take responsibility for their own trash, and first class citizens clean up whatever trash is there." So familiar was this refrain that there were occasional pieces of trash found on the campus with the scrawled message, "Congratulations to a first class citizen from a third class citizen." Mr. Finney inherited this parable from Ed Russell, one of his own favorite teacher/coaches.

Michael Sarbanes graduated from Gilman as the school's first National Football Foundation, Greater Baltimore Scholar Athlete. Among the prizes Sarbanes won at Gilman during his senior year were two debating prizes; the French prize; the Latin prize; a public speaking prize; The Daniel Baker, Jr. Memorial Award; The Alex Randall, Jr., Memorial Prize; The Culver Memorial Football Cup; and The William Cabell Bruce, Jr., Athletic Prize.

As an athlete, Sarbanes led the MSA "A" Conference football league in pass receiving and was named 1st team All-Metro by every newspaper in the Baltimore area. In basketball, he co-captained the varsity team. As a top varsity baseball pitcher, Sarbanes was known for "setting up" the batter and for throwing with precision.

Sarbanes earned a bachelor's in public and international affairs from Princeton in 1986 and a bachelor's in ancient and modern history from Oxford in 1989. He received his law degree from New York University in 1992.

At Princeton, Sarbanes earned the highest general distinction presented to a Princeton graduate, the M. Taylor Pyne Prize, for his unequaled contributions to the university. (His father, U. S. Senator Paul Sarbanes, won the prize in 1954.) At Oxford, he received the George C. Marshall Scholarship, and at New York University he earned a fellowship for public interest law, and the Award for Excellence in Advocacy.

Sarbanes worked at the Community Law Center in Baltimore, before going to work in 1995 for the Mayor's Coordinating Council on Criminal Justice for the City of Baltimore, focusing his time on helping communities organize to reduce drug-related violence. In 1996, he was appointed director of the Governor's Office of Crime Control and Prevention.

A Warm Welcome, Generous Friends, and A Prank on a Thief

BY BOB ISAACS '71

At first glance my primary and secondary educational transcript must look like a) I was a serious discipline problem, b) someone in my family was running from the law, c) my parents were in the military, d) the truth, that my father, a physician and scientist, was always willing to move to seek what was on the other side of the hill and my mother was good at organizing our family and making our many new houses into good homes. I was enrolled in five schools and was fortunate to be a member of the Gilman graduating class of 1971. In fact all my siblings were graduates of Gilman, Jimmy '64, John '67, and Billy '73. (This familial trend of the same schooling continued after Gilman as we all, including my mother and father, received degrees—four doctorates and a dietitian degree—from Johns Hopkins.)

I began my secondary education while living in Atlanta, Georgia, at a private school, my fourth school, for grades 7, 8, and 9. While my admiration for the faculty and the administration was high and my educational opportunies excellent, I had a difficult time in a social climate I could not understand. This was a society school where the clothes you wore were more important than what you were.

I tried to fit in. I played football, soccer, and wrestled; I was on the Honor Roll, but that was not enough. Clothes were Number One. I remember I just had to have a genuine Alligator belt. Everyone else did. Izod golf socks were a must, and I know from personal experience that these socks were definitely not made to fit a Seventh Grader. They always ended up balled up in the toes of my obligatory polished tasseled Weejuns. 1966 was before manufacturers placed labels on the the outside of their clothes. Thus, it was necessary for classmates to pull your shirt collar inside out to verify your social status. This was a common lunch room pastime. I was destined for social mediocrity as I could make the grades, play the sports, and match the wardrobe, but I could never compel myself to check my classmates' collars. Fortunately, my family moved back to Baltimore in 1968, and I enrolled at Gilman as a sophomore.

My first memory of Gilman is sitting in "A" Study Hall as everyone around me introduced themselves with smiling faces and warm handshakes. As far as I could determine, there were no pretenses here, not one Alligator belt except mine, a vestige of my southern training. It seemed I was truly being welcomed. This was so remarkable that I can remember in detail the warmth I felt sitting in that great open room with the old comfortable desks, the large plentiful windows filling the room with light, and my new classmates wanting to know me. Some of this group seemed to have been born at Gilman, and yet there was no hesitation to include me as one of them. Here I could be myself. Even though I was not very sure who I was, here at last I had the opportunity to find out not what my clothes label said I was, but rather who was the person inside those clothes. I never wore that belt again.

It was about this time in study hall that Bill Campbell came up to recruit me for his J.V. football team. In his vigorous manner, he said he knew my older brothers, Jim and John, and their athletic talents, and that he would appreciate my trying out for his team. Did he know I only weighed 110 pounds? Although I was sitting down, it was obvious that I was little, but he too was welcoming me to Gilman and including me in his game plan. Mr. Campbell phrased my tryout as a suggestion, but I instinctively knew that he expected me to be there. I soon learned that he always expected the best from everyone, and his encouragement and coaching were rewarding. As it turned out, I played on Ed Brown's and Mr. Campbell's team for two years and we were undefeated in 1969, with combined scores of Gilman 238, Opponents 6.

My initial impressions of Gilman as a welcoming place were never proved wrong. As I spent more time in Baltimore I realized that it had as strong a social elite as did Atlanta; yet, there were major differences. Here I was at Gilman, the most prestigious school in Baltimore, and on me the pressure to be accepted was absent. I could be friends with anyone, and it was easy.

An example of how open and sharing my classmates were with each other involves an Oldsmobile station wagon which belonged to Pete and Geoff Menzies. This car, like others back in the '60s, did not need a key to start up. This fact, along with the gregarious nature of Pete and Geoff, made their Olds Vista Cruiser the communal class car to be borrowed by all with or without their knowledge. One Monday evening after athletics Pete and Geoff waited patiently for their car to be returned by its anonymous borrower. It never appeared. This was sad news for the entire school. It had been stolen.

Two nights later was the appointed rendezvous of the Wednesday night sneak-out club. Unknown to my parents and several other classmates' parents until they all read this confession, on Wednesday nights around one a.m. I would borrow my parents' car and drive around town picking up assorted classmates for a night out. Our activities included exploring abandoned Nike missile silos, haunted houses,

Dunkin' Donuts, and if enough people came out—sometimes I had 15 students at one time piled into my car—we would go to Green Spring to play ice hockey without skates and a coke can for a puck. We did not go out to drink or smoke; we just had a lot of extra energy that I guess ten hours of school and sports plus homework could not exhaust. On this particular Wednesday night my first stop was for Bo Carey and then on to the Gilman boarding corridor to pick up the always-faithful Mike Karas and Jeb Byron.

Now as fate would have it, the Menzies' Oldsmobile had idiosyncrasies other than no key. The fuel gauge did not work. As we were driving west down the Northern Parkway hill at 2:00 a.m., there on the opposite side of the street was the Olds apparently out of gas with no one in sight. Quick thinking and as foolish as 16-year-olds are, we decided to steal it back. I dropped off Bo and Iron Mike beside the Olds, along with one hockey stick as support, while Jeb and I drove back to my house for some gas. When we returned, Mike, Bo and the car were still unmoved. We poured in the gasoline, turned the ignition, no key needed, and sped off with our hot car. As both cars were cruising back down Northern Parkway and off to the Menzies', we saw the original thief hiking back up that long hill with his gas can. We honked and yelled as we passed him and he yelled right back.

It was a glorious moment to sneak into the Menzies' house, roust Pete and Geoff out of bed, and walk them out to their car which sat bathed in morning mist and moonlight. Our evening activities were all but completed with the exception of Mike and Jeb sneaking back into the boarding corridor.

I am married now, living in northern Baltimore County, and have two beautiful daughters. Who knows—for them maybe Gilman will be coed in ten years. I hope not. But maybe one of them will meet an energetic, sincere gentleman who had the good fortune of attending Gilman. I would be grateful.

 Bob Isaacs is one of the four Isaacs brothers—Jimmy, John, Bobby, and Billy—who swept through Gilman in the 1960s and '70s. Throughout his Gilman years 1968–71, Bob Isaacs leaned toward an interest in the sciences, and yet his favorite teacher was Willis Spencer, history.

Isaacs was on the 1970 varsity football team and was a two-year varsity wrestler. His favorite coach was Bill Campbell '52, who coached J.V. football. Following the medical bent in his family, Isaacs worked on the Hopkins Hospital Project during his senior year at Gilman, and then attended Hopkins, where he majored in Natural Science. Graduating from Hopkins, he worked four years as a carpenter.

In the early '80s, Isaacs enrolled in the University of Maryland, Baltimore College of Dental Surgery. Isaacs is now an orthodontist, married and with two daughters, and has not withdrawn from his love of building and carpentry. On any Sunday afternoon, whether 98 degrees or 28 degrees, he can be found, saw and hammer in hand, building a balustrade around the second floor porch of his Monkton home, up on a ladder putting in an Isaacs-built window frame for his daughters' bedroom, or inside the house, re-finishing the floors.

From the Dark Ages
to the Renaissance

CHARLES B. DUFF, JR. '71

English literature is full of stories about boys in schools. At least two of them were required reading at Gilman in my day. They all seem to have the same plot. A small boy—David Copperfield, say, or Robert Graves—is bundled off to a big school with bad food and brutal schoolmates. He feels tiny. He withdraws. He ekes out one or two friendships, usually with outsiders like himself; otherwise, he lives on books and dreams. Then, suddenly, he's in the Sixth Form, and everyone respects him. He isn't sure why, but classmates elect him to school office. Bullies get out of his way. Some girl smiles at him. Then it's over. He goes off—maybe to Oxford, maybe to London, maybe to the trenches; and the book either ends or turns out to be about something else.

As I look back over my 12 years of school, nine of them at Gilman, I find that my school career fits the pattern of these classic stories. David Copperfield and Robert Graves are my brothers. But I still don't understand the process, any more than they did. How did the tiny, terrorized boy become the masterful Sixth Former?

For me, the tiny, terrorized phase lasted eight years. The first three, at the public schools of Mount Washington and Roland Park, sapped the joy of learning. I responded by biting my nails and eating myself into obesity, and I still regard public education as a personal enemy. Gilman, which I entered in the Fourth Grade, was my third school in three years, and I was a bit shell-shocked on arrival. The Lower School teachers were the first good teachers I had ever seen. They had real zip and bounce. But the verve of those few visible adults paled beside the unexpected and altogether tireless cruelty of my schoolmates. I would still like to know why my new associates at Gilman were so much harder to get along with than my old ones at two obviously inferior institutions. At any rate, the opening months of the Fourth Grade set a pattern of good teaching and chronic low-grade fear, and that pattern persisted, with improvements in detail, for five very long years.

But something amazing and delightful happened on the first day of Third Form. Suddenly, with no apparent preparation, on the first day of what might have been just another dreary year, I opened the same old door and walked straight into the Italian Renaissance. The world was suddenly big and brilliant, and Gilman was at the center of it. Everything was different. There were so many things to learn, and so many wonderful people. Within a week, John Merrill had me whistling a catchy tune by a man named Haydn, and suddenly there was music in the world. Within a month, Anton Vishio had me believing, by the example of his astounding Romans, that I had what it took to attain glory. By Christmas, there were boys in my own class who were the most interesting human beings I had ever met. By Easter, I had lost thirty pounds without really trying, and I had learned the names of four girls at dancing class, one of whom was the only girl in the world. I was still a long way from masterful, but I was infinitely less terrorized—and thirty pounds tinier.

Not that my last four years at Gilman were constantly happy. I have known long periods of sustained happiness, and the last four years of Gilman were not like that. They were full of stress; the difference was that much of the stress was now joyful. Most of the pains were clearly related to growing, and I bore them with my head high. For the first time in my life, I cared deeply about most of the things I did, and cared passionately about most of the people around me. For the first time in my life I felt fully alive.

It was at Gilman, in those last four years, that I first allowed myself to think that there might be others like me—and not just individuals, like the wonderful friends I was making, but whole organized groups. In Third Form I picked up the idea that there was an organized group of people who were dedicated to reading hard books and saying what they thought without fear of getting slugged. They were called Intellectuals. I resolved to find them and join them. Later, probably towards the end of Fourth Form, I picked up the idea that there was another organized group of people who were dedicated to kindness and duty, and to maintaining the disciplined Georgian elegance that kindness and duty entailed. They were called Society, and everybody said that they were threatened on all sides. I resolved to ride to their aid and raise the siege. It was some years before I had to face the fact that intellectual and social eminence were different things, that scholars were not often gentlemen, nor gentlemen scholars. And it was a profound shock for an old Mount Washington boy (though a gentile) to find that Society was for the most part closed to Jews. But that was a college crisis, not a Gilman stress. Gilman, for all its jock roughness, made the union of mind and manners look more attainable than it has ever looked since.

One day in the spring of my Fifth Form year, as I sat idly in the Publications Office on the second floor of the main building (idleness and an office were signs of the masterfulness already somehow gathering around my friends and me), it occurred to me that my life was a scale model of western cultural history. Early childhood had been Classical Antiquity, an easy yoking of grace and common sense under the auspices of my parents. Then came school, the Dark Ages, eight pointless years of migrations and violence. And then, suddenly, on the first day of Third Form, I walked into the Renaissance.

As I sat there in that office, 25 years ago, I already understood that the first flush of the Renaissance was over for me. In two and a half years of rapid advance I had claimed and surveyed an immense new territory—Haydn and Cicero and Dickens, Vishio and Schloeder, Kopper and Blum. Now I had to buckle down and farm it. That would be hard work. The law of diminishing returns was already setting in. But I knew that I had taken the one decisive step. I had put the Dark Ages behind me, albeit unawares. I had entered a big, bright world, and I was living life with a vibrancy that I knew I would never wholly lose.

And I knew that I would love the Gilman School for the rest of my life, simply for being the place where this miracle had occurred. I suspected that I would be angry at Gilman from time to time—if not for the topical stresses of that season, then certainly for those first five years. But I knew that love and gratitude would win out in the end, as indeed they have.

 Charlie Duff attended Gilman 1962–71 with his main intellectual interests being the study of the classics, literature, history, and music. The teachers who most inspired Duff were Anton Vishio (Latin), Nick Schloeder (history), John Merrill (music), and Bill Merrick (Lower School history). In his senior year, Duff was president of the Pnyx Debating Club, editor of *Vantage*, secretary of the Political Club, and vice-president of the Literary Club. At graduation, Duff won all three debating awards, plus the Herbert E. Pickett Prize for General Proficiency in History and one of the Edward T. Russell Latin Prizes.

Majoring in English and French, Duff attended Amherst. Upon graduation, he taught Latin at The Boys' Latin School for three years, and then enrolled in graduate school at Harvard to study city planning. Duff is currently president of Jubilee Baltimore, Inc., a nonprofit housing development corporation specializing in mixed-income housing and historic preservation.

Three Generations

DEE HARDIE

My grandson Albert Birney, a member of the class of 2000, once gave me a Gilman baseball cap for my birthday. I wear it backwards, the same way he does, but that is the only thing backwards about Gilman. I should know. My husband Tom is the class of '39; our son Todd, '71; our son Tommy, '74; Bill Isaacs, our son-in-law, '73; and now there's Albert, '00. You might call it a family circle.

To think I never even heard of Gilman School in my twenties before moving to Baltimore! Incredible! And I never even thought about it seriously until I was in my thirties, half a life ago. What woke me up, quite honestly, were country car pools. Our sons had to get to school on time—down Falls Road, left on Belvedere, right on Roland Avenue, then hang a left into the school of brick buildings with a cricket on top of the roof.

Every school morning a small herd of station wagons would gather at Sam Adams' grocery store in Butler. These Gilman car pools, besides being our sons' chariots to education, were a common denominator. We were a team. Maybe sometimes even a Mafia. We got the job done. For me, it was even more. As a new girl in town, these car pools to Gilman helped me become part of the gang. The mothers I knew then, I know now: they're my best friends. And those boys have grown into men.

Way back then I wasn't sure how my passengers were going to turn out. They were a lively group. When they were discussing sports, especially lacrosse, things were relatively calm. But I still remember the morning when they were so distraught because they had heard the wooden lacrosse stick was going to be replaced by a synthetic one. And what's more, they were going to come in colors! All those boy-years of putting an old flat iron in the cradle, night after night, to make a proper pocket were soon to be only a memory. We all know Gilman lacrosse teams survived the new wave, but that morning there were almost tears.

Driving home in the afternoons, I still had a spirited cargo. For a few months I had two young members combing the back of my head while I was driving, for a penny apiece. It sounds crazy now, but I was desperate to keep them occupied, out of trouble. John and Wicksie loved describing my hairs' country texture. "Like hay," they'd say, "or maybe straw." They were probably right. This hair care scheme worked until a visiting school psychologist asked our daughter Louise what her mother did, and she said, "She has little boys combing her hair in car pools." The taxi hair salon immediately stopped. Oh how I miss those Gilman car pools, especially those boys who kept my hair, at least the back, so very tidy. And at such a price!

Our first child, Todd, entered Gilman in the Fourth Grade. At the same time our second son Tommy entered the First grade. We were thrilled to have two sons under the same roof of education. They did well, and we thought we did too. Every night we helped them study long lists of spelling; every year we manned booths at the Circus. Then one afternoon Todd, or maybe it was Tommy, brought home a note from Mr. Tickner, then head of the Lower School. He politely suggested that our sons needed haircuts. I immediately took them to the local barber. In those days I did *everything* I was told. But I couldn't resist writing back to Mr. Tickner. I told him, "You cannot make a silk purse out of a sow's ear." Reg and I have been pals ever since. I had dropped a motherly gauntlet, and he accepted it with grace.

Even with the unregulation hair, our two sons graduated from the Lower School to the Upper. In those days there was no Middle School. But before doing so we had several Sixth Grade projects. One day Tommy and I rushed into a hardware store, and I said, "We'd like some gray paint, please."

The man asked, "House paint?"

"No," I said, "castle paint."

And that brief dialogue was the beginning of Tommy's most important Sixth Grade project. He was going to build a castle. When Todd was the same age, he hero-ically erected Nelson's Column in our bathroom. Can you imagine constructing the Washington Monument, a shape similar to Nelson's Column in London, out of plaster of Paris as high as your knee bone? Well, Todd did. Anything, it seems, for Gilman. This school is a builder of men, but it also expects its men to build, espe-cially in the Sixth Grade.

Before Tommy decided to build a castle, he planned to do Agincourt. I was thrilled thinking of all those stirring, colorful banners and striped tents. But Tommy's teacher, Graeme Menzies, thought Agincourt was perhaps a little too ambitious.

Tommy had other choices from his history book. Would you believe? . . . Cae-sar lands in Britain, Birth of Christ, The Black Death, Magna Carta, Wars of the Roses, and Vasco Da Gama sails to India. I personally thought Wars of the Roses had some marvelous decorative possibilities. But of course I didn't tell him. And since his friend Jimmy took the Battle of Hastings and friend Chris took Hadrian's Wall, Tommy took a castle.

Or perhaps I should say the castle took him. He was back in the Dark Ages for days. He enclosed himself in what he called a "donjon," previously known as his bedroom. And from all those various-sized tin cans, popsicle sticks, corrugated cardboard, and gobs of gray paint, a castle was born. King Arthur may have pulled a sword out of a rock, but Tommy made a castle out of soup cans.

Then there were the terrors and traumas of giving a Sixth Grade speech. Todd's speech was on Mountain Dew, the great Maryland steeplechase horse owned by a neighbor, Mr. Janon Fisher, Jr. '16. Todd and I walked the Maryland Hunt Cup course, then drew a large sketch of the double oval. Mr. Fisher even loaned him the large silver trophy, The Maryland Hunt Cup, to bring to school for his speech. The night before Todd hardly slept. Not just because of the upcoming event, but because of the glistening prize sitting close to his bed.

When it was Tommy's turn, he talked and showed slides of his beloved St. Bernard, Tuffy. Somehow that speech didn't give us as much concern. We knew more about dogs than we did about horses.

Those Sixth Grade speeches, as frightening as they were to think about, were Gilman steps in the right direction. Our two sons, for the first time, were standing on their own two feet addressing a large peer group.

It also helped them prepare for the Upper School, helped them assume the ties of early manhood. And that's exactly where my husband's ties went—to the Upper School. In those days a tie, shirt, and jacket were *de rigueur*. And the boys daily tapped their father's tie rack. I liked the look, I still do.

Tommy first dressed in this uniform for his Sixth Grade graduation. I'll never forget it. A sea of gleaming, freckled-faced boys walked into the auditorium to "Pomp and Circumstance." During the actual graduation they sang "America the Beautiful" and "No Man Is an Island." Believe me, it was a touching moment. Then these young cubs walked out of the auditorium, as manly as possible, to the tune of "The Triumphal March" from *Aida*. I know because I still have the program. And if that wasn't a class act, I don't know what is.

Todd went away to school when he was 16, but Tommy was at Gilman for all 12 years. And I believe they were the best, happiest years of his life. When he was a sophomore, he became assistant manager of the Gilman football team. Then in his junior year he became chief towel carrier. Tom and I went to every football game. Not to see a quarterback throw the winning pass, but to cheer the manager who carried a little black bag full of bandages and served Gatorade to the team.

There was a time, I must admit, that I was jealous of Gilman. Once Tommy was old enough to drive the family Land Rover, we hardly saw him. He was always at Gilman. In his senior year I even worked as a volunteer in the school library, thinking I would see him on his own ground. Ha, I thought, I'll outfox him. I soon discovered that as a senior he wasn't obliged to have supervised study halls in the library. But everything has its gift. How else would I have gotten to know JoAnn Davison and Ursula Murray?

There were good reasons why we didn't see more of our son. At Gilman he started the Ecology Recycling Center, a work-day to clean up around school, and he started a project called Operation Green Grass, which brought children out from the inner city. On Saturday mornings he tutored those children from the inner city.

At graduation when Tommy won the Fisher Medallion, I forgave Gilman for monopolizing him. I was delirious with joy. Tommy was in a daze. He never expected such an award. He even let me kiss him. "He must be in shock," laughed Chris and Jimmy, who knew him well. They knew a kiss in public, especially from a mother, would otherwise never be allowed.

Now that Albert, our grandson, is at Gilman, I can go home again. And that's how I feel about Gilman School. I've always felt comfortable and welcome there, even when Tommy made it his priority rather than us. And I met a man I shall never forget, shall always honor and respect, my forever friend, Redmond Finney.

The blue and gray ties even grow stronger with Archibald R. Montgomery IV as the present headmaster. Archie, as we called him then, and our son Todd were good friends when rambunctious teenagers.

Gilman School helped make my husband the person he is; it made men of our boys. And now there is Albert. In the Fifth Grade he asked me if I knew what a thesaurus was. Thesaurus! I didn't use one until I was an English major at college. Albert knew all about the impressionist painters in the Fourth Grade and used a computer for years as if it came out of the womb with him.

The night he gave me my Gilman baseball cap, he sat next to me at the birthday dinner table. Out of a clear blue sky he turned to me and said, "Momma Dee, I love you." Such an unexpected gift. "Albert," I said to him, "why did you tell me that just now?" He quickly replied, with a big grin on his ten-year-old face, "It's part of my job!"

Well, to this wife, mother, mother-in-law, and grandmother, Gilman School has always done its job. And for that, I shall be forever grateful.

Dee Hardie entered Skidmore College in 1944 and was soon writing for the college newspaper and literary magazine, becoming editor of the magazine, PROFILE. After graduation, she wrote for *Vogue* out of New York, London, and Paris, as well as for The Baltimore *Sun*. More recently, she has written a monthly column for *House Beautiful*. With her husband Tom, Class of 1939, Dee writes a syndicated column on grandparenting for over 60 newspapers.

The mother of Todd '71 and Tommy '74, Mrs. Hardie has heard many a story about her husband's favorite teacher/coaches: Miles Marrian (math, baseball), Richard O'Brien (French), and Tom Lipscomb (English). Tom Hardie '39 played football, basketball, and lacrosse, and in 1935 was the center on the great 118-pound football team coached by Marrian. Led by Captain Howard Baetjer, they won all 20 games, scoring 410 points to their opponents' 0.

The Hardies sponsor Gilman's Harry Hardie Anglo-American Exchange with St. Edwards School, England, and the Tommy Hardie Outward Bound Project. They can be found in the car pool line picking up grandson Albert Birney '00.

Building Characters

EDWARD L. TRIMBLE '72

He who writes memoirs of Gilman has several choices of tone. He can be maudlin, with reminiscences of the flowering cherry trees, the friends made for life, the school ties that bind, the life lessons learned at the feet of Mr. Finney. How clearly I remember winning the Maryland Scholastic Association wrestling tournament, publishing my Fifth Form paper in the *The New Yorker,* playing the role of stage manager in the senior production of *Our Town*, dating Bess Armstrong, going directly from Gilman to Oxford as a Rhodes Scholar.

Or he can be bitter, with acid-etched reminiscences of juvenile angst beneath the leafless elm tree, the friendships forsaken, the school ties which choke, the dry platitudes of chapel. My three divorces, my heart attack, my failure to write the great American novel despite my clear youthful promise, can all be blamed on the blighted days, my prison sentence, at the Gilman School.

Neither of these approaches seems appropriate. Let me focus, perhaps more objectively, on what happened at 5407 Roland Avenue, Baltimore, Maryland. At Gilman we began the process of becoming adults, differentiating ourselves from our peers and our families. We were aided in these efforts by our classmates and our teachers. In the best of our classes we learned to think for ourselves, to write down our thoughts on paper, to argue for what we believed. And we continued those arguments between classes, on the playing fields, on evenings and weekends, and on through the years since graduation.

The rest of this essay chronicles a few of the arguments which occupied our time as we hurtled from adolescence on the way to manhood, between 1966 and 1972. The first concerns the question "Does athletics build character?" We learned early in our Gilman careers that building character was the leading purpose of the school. Academic studies, although important, seemed to have little impact on building character. Homilies at chapel, the athletic awards ceremonies held three times a year, and Mr. Finney's paternal squeeze of the biceps informed us that athletics builds character.

The hoopla surrounding football, wrestling, and lacrosse made it clear that these sports built character better (or perhaps faster) than such endeavors as soccer, tennis, baseball, or track and field. Those of us for whom catching a lacrosse ball, getting a tennis ball over the net, or putting a basketball through the hoop was a rare triumph of the will were condemned to "Special Exercise." This consisted of running and going to the weight room on a self-imposed schedule. "Special Exercise" built little character. But what about editing the school newspaper, producing the school play, working in a political campaign? Did they build character? We debated the issue for six years then and 20 years thereafter. We have concluded that any activity which subsumes a person, which demands thought and determination and cooperation, builds character, with or without the award of a Gilman "G."

We debated the dress code. In those days, even if we could grow facial hair, we could not sport it. We could not have hair below the back of the collar. We had to wear dress shoes, dress pants, dress shirts, and ties. At chapel and at lunch we had to wear sports coats. Athletic shoes were only permitted in the gym. Dungarees and blue jeans were not allowed during regular school hours. As might be expected, we rebelled, with string ties, hair just over the collar, a beard painstakingly nurtured over summer vacation. We protested and petitioned and argued. The student council spent much of its time debating amendments to the dress code and submitting them to Mr. Finney and the faculty for review. We asked to wear open-collar sports shirts in the heat of May and September. We requested permission for neatly trimmed beards, mustaches, and sideburns, for hair below the collar. We argued that a coat and tie were not essential to education or discipline. Despite our eloquence, our determination, our passion concerning this issue, we lost every battle. It is possible, however, that the great dress code debate, despite its failure, may have built character.

Formally and informally, we debated many other things, the war in Vietnam, the draft, the environment, communism, Humphrey versus Nixon, Nixon versus McGovern. The most enduring debate, however, was over girls. We knew they existed. Bryn Mawr and Roland Park were close by. Western, Garrison Forest, and St. Tim's were a little farther away. We knew about the mechanics of sex. Amid our embarrassment, our school chaplain, Dr. Alfred Starratt, had taught us sex education. Among other things, he told us that one generally did not smile during intercourse. We even had a few co-educational classes, "Marriage Seminar" with Reverend Wendell Phillips (and girls from Roland Park), "Writing Short Stories" with Roy Barker (and girls from Bryn Mawr). But how exactly did one become friends with girls? What did one do on a date? We expected that we would marry after college; we suspected and hoped that we would experience sex before then. How did one discuss sex with a girl, much less do it? We had heard of sexually transmitted diseases, which in those days of innocence consisted of gonorrhea and syphilis. We knew about birth control pills and condoms. My own mother, a gynecologist who was a medical director of Planned Parenthood of Maryland, had been interviewed on TV advocating the availability of condoms in gas station rest rooms. But how was one to translate all that knowledge into action? Would going off to college doom a promising high school romance? Just what was the relationship between sex and marriage? This issue of "girls" continues to be a subject for debate to this day, although it now has been renamed under the rubric of "women and marriage."

There is not world enough or time to review the debates which have surfaced since that time. Can one feel allegiance to any professional football team after the departure of the Colts for Indianapolis? Is Barry Levinson's portrayal of Baltimore more accurate than that of John Waters? Will John Scherlis ever return home from Cambridge, England? Did Mama Cass really choke to death on a ham sandwich? But in the fervor of these arguments, in the logic and emotion we have learned to harness, I can see the stamp of Gilman, the character built by stubbornness and tribulations, by good luck and bad luck, and by just plain growing up.

 Entering Gilman in 1966, Ted Trimble soon discovered an interest in writing. At graduation, he was awarded the Armstrong prize for "Best Imaginative Prose," as well as the Daniel Baker, Jr. Award given to a senior who "through thoughtfulness and by reason of his character, has contributed to the general welfare of his fellow men." He also was awarded prizes in reading and Latin.

Trimble most enjoyed Roy Barker's English class, Nick Schloeder's history and government courses, and Anton Vishio's Latin class. His favorite sport was soccer.

Attending Harvard, Trimble majored in history and literature, returning to Baltimore to receive his medical degree from the Johns Hopkins School of Medicine in 1984. Married and living in Baltimore, Trimble specializes in gynecologic oncology at the National Cancer Institute.

Theater and Gilman Culture

JAMIE SPRAGINS '73

While I was a Gilman middle schooler in the late 1960s, I was fortunate to have had the opportunity to spend several summers at Hyde Bay Camp in Cooperstown, N.Y. The camp was run by a rare collection of Gilman characters: Herb "Mouldy" Pickett, Hunt Hilliard, Alton Davison, and in earlier years, George Chandlee, Edward Russell, and the Commodore, Walter Lord.

These gentle men created an environment in which boys could thrive both physically and imaginatively. Hyde Bay featured intense team sports, individual tests of strength and ability, big woods mountain and river expeditions, ghost stories and Leatherstocking lore, even work—all activities to be expected at any good camp. But what made Hyde Bay special was its cherished tradition of theater.

We didn't just do theater at Hyde Bay. We lived it. The distinction between reality and the imagination had been refined out of existence. The buildings themselves had all been painted by scenic artist Jack Garver with visions of camp life from years past. Wandering the grounds made a 12-year-old feel like a character in a vibrant adventure. Word play, nonsense rituals, and role playing were a natural part of daily life. Not only did every camper perform in an original play, but most counselors did too. The theater gurus (Josh Shoemaker and John Schmick) wrote and staged 30-odd plays each summer. The whole community gathered on Saturdays to watch.

The routine of daily life was enlivened by a superb sense of the grand gesture. Anything could happen. On one occasion, a 12-foot fiberglass sailboat had recently been given several coats of fiberglass so that it would stop sinking. This rare event called for a formal boat launching with full pomp and circumstance: muscle-bound oarsmen marching synchronized routines, dancing flower girls, the boat itself festooned like a Mardi Gras float, and finally a coach drawn by lackeys carrying the sailing staff in full regalia, accompanied by the Commodore himself in a rare *pro tem* appearance. His ceremonial dunking climaxed the ritual.

There is a photograph of me taken as I gaped in astonishment at this spectacle. My eyes still sparkle.

I first came to appreciate the meaning of tradition at Hyde Bay Camp. Tradition is not simply a set of values or manners. It is a gift for living kept alive from generation to generation. A major part of my responsibility as a teacher of English and drama at Gilman is to pass this gift for living on to the young. To imitate the style of 30 years ago would be pointless, impossible to accomplish. But the spirit which inspired those gratuitous gestures—that cannot be allowed to pass.

The Hyde Bay tradition of theater grew out of Gilman's early culture—still vibrant in the late 1960s. The school reveled in a love of language as intense as its love of football, wrestling, and lacrosse. The late 1960s at Gilman, far from being a time of violent dissent, was a time of neo-Victorian form and Imperial manner. Theater fit naturally into the life of the school.

Latin Day was celebrated in the grand, mock-heroic fashion with mandatory togas, ivy garlands, and reckless chariot races, all interspersed by mighty feats of grandiloquent oratory: poetry recitations and contests, debate between the Areopagus and the Pnyx. In those days the Gilman Circus was a huge extravaganza which the whole school helped create and sell. The Spring Art Show took over a full wing of the cage. Traveling through it was a strange fun-house adventure. McDonogh Day was the occasion of bonfires, chicanery, and song climaxed by the ceremonial reading of the Farmer's Almanac by Mr. Russell in his aged, quavering voice. Tradition was palpable because its energy found vibrant form not only on special occasions but also in the rituals of our school day.

Rhetoric was in our blood. Each morning at Chapel we'd sing one of the Protestant Dirty Dozen hymns, chant the sonorous rhythms of the King James version, and listen to the schoolmasters—Mr. Finney most memorably—solemnly sermonize. The Senior Speech was the most decorous and mannered of rites of passage. A tidal wave of language enveloped the classroom experience. Everyone imitated the grand style. Teachers lectured. Students were regularly assigned speeches in history as well as English and Latin classes. We studied Cicero and J.F.K.'s inaugural address. We memorized Shakespeare, studied parts of speech and diagrammed sentences. We wrote massive research papers. Life was dominated by daily rhetoric and ritual. We even sat down to formal lunch in an ornate dining room, prayed, watched our manners, and wolfed the horrible food.

The theater in those days reflected the WASP male culture of the time. The style was neo-Victorian; plays like "The Barretts of Wimpole Street," "Arsenic and Old Lace," and "The Madwoman of Chaillot" predominated. "The Caine Mutiny" was out on the cutting edge because it featured a central character who was Jewish. Student enthusiasm and talent brought into being a summer repertory company dedicated to producing Gilbert and Sullivan operettas. The Young Victorian Theatre Company came into being in 1971 (the year of the invasion of Cambodia), and it is still going strong. The theater at Gilman was palpably connected to the school's rhetorical excess and its grand sense of WASP pomposity. Despite its biases, Gilman's culture was vigorous and lively.

Thankfully, Gilman has undergone vast changes in the last 25 years. Our community's demographics now reflect the reality of society at large. We have assumed a new responsibility. We model for the city how a community of diverse backgrounds can function creatively and responsibly. Extensive coordination with girls' schools has encouraged a new open-mindedness and tolerance. The ongoing renovation of the school's physical plant is indicative of Gilman's effort to re-define and re-shape its image while maintaining its traditional identity.

The administration cherishes and protects a core program: rigorous academics, competitive team sports, and a devotion to an open society founded on the principle of honor. These aspects of Gilman have not changed, but the school is still groping to find a way to leave its patrician past behind and embrace a vastly different student body. The only common denominator which exists to unite our student body is the predominant culture of sports in America. It is my hope that the theater can play a role in helping Gilman refine and reshape its identity to be more inclusive.

Happily, the school's administration is open to innovation. The leaders have taken a *laissez-faire* attitude toward change. If students or teachers want to try something, typically they are encouraged. This open-mindedness reflects a sea change in educational philosophy. Instead of force-feeding students information, the teacher now encourages the development of independent thinking. The seminar style has replaced the lecture in most classrooms. Student ideas drive classroom discussions. We don't test memorization skills as much as we encourage students to sharpen and revise their own responses to the text. Texts no longer express one point of view. Students see life from many cultural, gender-inclusive perspectives. Students learn how problems have various solutions and how collaboration is frequently necessary to uncover the "truth."

Our assemblies, like our classrooms, are no longer occasions for lecturing and sermonizing. Instead, our most successful assemblies have taken on the form of a Quaker meeting where anyone can speak if the spirit so moves him. Students no longer observe the rigorous coat-and-tie rule of the patrician dress code. More often the sports culture dominates dress. The school's atmosphere is more relaxed and egalitarian, less patriarchal and upper class.

This new atmosphere of openness and flexibility, this new receptivity and spontaneity is indicative of an ambiguous emerging style profoundly different from the Gilman style of yesteryear, and that is good. But something vital has been sacrificed in the process. Sadly, our banquet of the arts and love affair with language have gone the way of formal luncheons. We no longer have a taste for ornate speech or the grand gesture for fear of appearing overbearing or incorrect. There is no obvious performance analogue, no formal ritual to our daily interaction. The consequence is an uneasiness and tentativeness which typifies our relations. We err on the side of politeness rather than risk offense by showing our true selves. The end result is that the vibrancy of true cultural interaction fails to take place. Only on the athletic field do we truly overcome our differences, but that activity excludes a sizable percentage of our school's population.

It is my belief that the theater program will play an integral role in helping Gilman follow through on its commitment to model a healthy, open society which celebrates diversity. Instead of promoting assimilation, the theater can celebrate difference and teach empathy. It can help Gilman find a style which facilitates student expression and interaction. Performance art—pervading all three school units—could be the new rhetoric which invigorates and gives form to the school's daily life. And this performance art, this theater program, will continue to be based upon the same principles which I absorbed as a Gilman middle schooler at Hyde Bay Camp: a dedication to universal participation and an encouragement of the grand, gratuitous gesture.

With major inspirations being Roy Barker ("Hamlet"), Alex Armstrong (theater), John Merrill (music history), and Edgar Boyd (modern European history), Jamie Spragins has focused on the teaching of English and drama since his first year of working at Gilman in 1987. While a student at Gilman, he was a member of the Dramatic Association, Areopagus–Pnyx Debating Society, Hoffman Club, and the Gilman Bavarian Band—a rhythm section which performed at sporting events. Graduating Cum Laude, Jamie moved on to Williams College, majoring in English with a specialization in Shakespeare, modern drama, and James Joyce.

Spragins has a burgeoning interest in multi-media education and hopes to help students create projects in a performing art/multi-media facility: a full theater with a shop, radio station/recording studio, video soundstage, and computer room.

Reverse Assimilation

HARRY B. TURNER '71

If I had my childhood to do over, I would still want to grow up in the Roland Park of the 1950s and '60s. Falls Road and 40th Street were perfect protective barriers that insulated youth from "outside" influences and helped to make childhood innocent, easy, and happy. And for me, such idyllism also made later introductions to new brands of person, to fascinating discoveries of unknown worlds.

The young Roland Park male in the '60s was attending Gilman or, if his parents fancied themselves enlightened, Friends. Prior to Gilman he had gone to school with girls: either six years at Calvert, or three years at Roland Park Country School (RPCS), where he learned everything there was for an eight-year-old to know about classical Greek architecture from Miss Jose. (For some reason RPCS thought it unwise for its girls to be exposed to nine-year-old boys and forced us out after Third Grade. In 1961, RPCS was unmanned entirely.)

Gilman Lower School let out early on Wednesdays, which suspiciously coincided with the timing of Mrs. Farber's dancing class at the Elkridge Club, where the face of the Roland Park boy would contort in pain whenever Mrs. Farber or my Aunt May forced him to dance with the freckled, homely "chubbette" in the corner. He didn't know then that he'd give his right arm to dance with that same comely brunette in a coffee house ten years later. He bought his baseball cards at The Morgue (Morgan & Millard's) and fireballs at Doc's (Tuxedo Pharmacy), and terrorized crotchety neighbors. Whatever he did, he did it in Roland Park with other Roland Parkers. (Most of the boys back then are still there and still the same, except now they terrorize neighbors into buying insurance.)

The Lower School seemed to foster Roland Park's insularity. The only observable blacks were those found in the photographs of the *Weekly Reader*. And, we mused, what did those poor African kids want with the pencils and erasers we sent them in those CARE boxes? Wouldn't they be happier with a box of Hydroxes? Knowledge of the Civil Rights movement was limited to the shock of the family

maid's preëmpting of *Pete the Pirate* on TV to watch Dr. King's speech on that
Wednesday afternoon in August 1963.

Gilman seemed to keep us safe from the world. We were protected against
polio by "cubes" of sugar administered to us in the Lower School auditorium. The
Cuban Missile Crisis didn't phase us. How could it? Our school was on such safe
ground that Gilman didn't make us dive under our desks for air raid drills as we had
to do at RPCS. At 1:00 Monday afternoon when the sirens sounded, we might be
found in Hunt Hilliard's shop making "skyhooks" or rehearsing our centennial
production of the Civil War—the whole war in 30 minutes with John "Abie Baby"
Deford in beard and stovepipe hat. (The sympathies of the boys definitely ran in
favor of the Stars and Bars and my R. E. Lee.)

Our occasional glimpses of a troubled world beyond Roland Park were rare.
Our knowledge of other locales seemed, instead, confined to our summer camps
and, as required in Fourth Grade, memorization of the names of the county seats
of all 24 political subdivisions in Maryland.

We only began our growing up and a real awareness of a larger world that Friday afternoon in November 1963 when Reg Tickner unexpectedly entered our classrooms to announce that the President (whom most of our parents disliked) had
been wounded in Dallas.

In First Form my homogenetic nurturing was radically interrupted by my discovery of Jews. They were new and strange: they came to Gilman each morning
from that faraway, unknown world on the other side of the JFX; they didn't leave
school early for Mrs. Farber's; they never received demerits in study hall, always did
all their homework, and they were never seen on Saturdays swimming at the clubs
or loitering outside the drugstores on Roland Avenue. Thinking now about that first
influx of Jews into Gilman, I wonder whether we seemed as novel to them as they
did to us.

In First Form I was a closet Gilbert & Sullivan freak (SWM into G&S) who
would never dare sing my patter songs anywhere but in the seclusion of my third-
floor room at home. When I discovered, however, I had a classmate at Gilman who
knew every word from every song from every operetta, had even played Ko-Ko in a
Mikado at Pikesville Elementary, I came out of my G&S closet.

Chip Manekin and I became fast friends, obnoxious Savoyards who got on
everyone's nerves, and great jokesters who were always on the brink of receiving that
dreaded third demerit. Chip could confound teachers out of demerits by sheer
illogic. Me? Whenever I really got on Herbie Dresser's nerves in English class, I would
be ordered to the headmaster's office. Schlepping myself out of class, I'd strut into
Ludlow Baldwin's office, take a seat, explain to him that I was only visiting, and then
spend 15 minutes regaling him with stories of Turner goings-on. To this day I don't
think Herbie Dresser ever realized that Ludlow Baldwin thought my mother a saint,
and that sons of saints could do no wrong.

Spending time with Chip Manekin, one couldn't help but notice other differences: his absences from school on odd days to miss when not sick, the matzo he'd

carefully unravel from saran wrap in the dining hall during Passover, and the Hebrew books he'd sometimes carry and study from right to left. Chip was brash and didn't care what others made of him or his curious outlook on adolescence: "Someday I'm going to be Orthodox, but right now I want to have fun!" This was all alien to me. To sing *Pinafore* with Chip was also to receive an intro course into the Hebraic mysteries.

One thing led to another. Chip led to Ray Bank and Larry White, to Marvin Miller and Michael Blum. . . . I noticed something inexplicable happening to me. For almost six straight Saturdays I found myself at friends' bar mitzvahs instead of with family and friends at my brother's Severn lacrosse games. If my parents were alarmed at all my new Jewish friends, they never betrayed any such feelings. The doors of my parents' house were always wide open to the comings and goings of Blums, Banks, and Manekins as well as Gampers, Smalls, and Defords. Mom never balked at having to drive me over to spend weekend nights on South or Labyrinth Roads, and Dad enjoyed priding himself on his recollection of G&S as he chauffeured Chip and me to Mergenthaler to worship our idol, Bruce Baetjer, as he wowed 'em in the Comic Opera's latest Gilbert & Sullivan. In fact, Mom would take extra care to stock the fridge for the advent of Michael Blum and his somnambulant tours of our kitchen in search of individually-wrapped slices of American cheese.

With my discovery of Jews came my first consciousness of anti-Semitism (more often than not from my Jewish friends). One of the most impressive talks I ever heard Ludlow Baldwin make came not when he was lecturing about the Fertile Crescent, but when he was livid on discovering penciled Stars of David next to each Jewish name on the Honor Roll in the common room.

There had been a few Jews at Gilman before my time, but nothing like the numbers enrolling in the mid-'60s. For those of us who entered the Upper School from Calvert and from the Gilman Lower School, the presence of so many boys who seemed so unlike us was bewildering. Attending six bar mitzvahs, getting to know Park Heights Avenue as well as I knew Roland, having friends who couldn't or wouldn't be my guests at the pool, loosening ties to some of my boyhood chums, and awakening to anti-Semitism caused anxiety that combined with other adolescent tensions to produce a somewhat mixed-up kid. By the end of Second Form I wanted out of Roland Park, out of Gilman, out of the house. I insisted on packing myself off to boarding school. Though I left Gilman, I did not leave behind what my experiences there had taught me, nor did I leave behind my friends, almost all of whom were Jewish.

At an Episcopal boarding school I was lectured that Jews and blacks weren't the problems. What we really had to worry about were those Catholics. How the *Book of Common Prayer* and Archbishop Cranmer were relevant to the dangers in dating Catholic girls, I'll never understand. I could stand only one year of boarding school. My last day there I was awarded the prize for excellence in Ninth Grade English—a copy of the then-current best seller, Chaim Potok's *The Chosen*.

Back home I became a sort of Dickensian orphan who belongs nowhere and so can move freely from one world to another. I'd go chug beers at the Hunt Cup with fellow WASPs and act in community theater with Jews; date debutantes from Bryn Mawr and Deborahs from Park. In step with the times, I became "anti" any established group whose exclusiveness hindered my freedom to move with whom I wanted.

I rejected as élitist certain fraternities and organizations at college. Rather, I pursued my chosen course at the University of Pennsylvania by acquainting myself with as many different types of people as I could. I celebrated seders with Sue Schwartz and brunched at The Newman Center with Mary Van Metre. I would masquerade with Manekin on Purim in the Kosher Kitchen at Yale and imbibe with Ned Grassi at swanky parties in Princeton. I once gained admittance to a small, private reception for Hubert Humphrey at Hillel by merely assuming the name of my Gilman friend, Michael Blum. Poor Mike. He had such a bad reputation at Penn and he didn't even go there.

Rather than relegate myself to any social sect, I have grown comfortable being in between. The personal advantages of being betwixt outweigh the guilt associated with betraying feelings and values for the comfort of acceptance. I'm way too goy to be Jewish and not faithful enough to the old boys to be a true-blue WASP. I would feel as uncomfortable wearing a yarmulke on my head as I would a duck-laden belt round my waist.

Increasingly, I find myself a go-between for those who have relegated themselves to their own too-narrow spheres. I cast no malicious stones at either the old-boy or old-Jew but, rather, have come to believe that most ugly social and religious prejudices are by-products of the natural, strong prejudice both have in favor of their own and by which they believe their traditions, values, and respective societies are safeguarded. This doesn't make things such as anti-Semitism or extreme ghetto insularity right, but for me it does make them somewhat understandable.

My wife went to Princeton and to Harvard Medical School, but she never went to Mrs. Farber's or the Hunt Cup. Not making a debut at Baltimore's annual Anglo-ethnic folk dance (a/k/a the Bachelors' Cotillion) is of little consequence in the grand scheme of things. Our feelings of pride and joy when our daughter was given her Hebrew name "Daniella" at the Hillcrest Jewish Center in Queens were no less true than those universal feelings of Pride and Joy all peoples share.

I never disparage my childhood neighborhood or what it did for me. I am thankful to have had a father who introduced his son to the absurdity of Gilbert & Sullivan and to have had a number of years at a school which, to its great credit, parted the waters of the Jones Falls and lured parents into sending their sons across and into the wilderness that was Roland Park.

Harry Belt Turner attended Gilman 1962–67 before moving on to St. James School in Hagerstown, and St. Paul's School, MD. At Gilman, Turner's favorite teacher was Willis Spencer, who taught him ancient history.

A member of the political club and astronomy club, Turner picked up a passion for theater—acting, directing, attending performances—and in particular for Gilbert and Sullivan, while at Gilman. This passion was further inspired by Turner's eight summers spent at Hyde Bay Camp in Cooperstown, N.Y., a camp founded by Gilman history teacher Herbert Pickett.* Turner received his undergraduate degree from the University of Pennsylvania, where he majored in English. He taught English at Maryvale Preparatory School for two years, and was an actor/director with the Young Victorian Theater 1971–81.

Turner received his law degree from the University of Maryland School of Law in 1981 and currently has his own legal practice. He is married to Dr. Beth Schwartz, and has two children, Danielle and Jeremy.

*For more on Hyde Bay Camp, see Larry Pickett's "Memoirs of a Faculty Child," Cooper Walker's "Of Ed Russell and Wrestling Reminiscences," and Jamie Spragin's "Theater and Gilman Culture."

Life Change

BOB EHRLICH '75

I remember the night my father informed me that I would be attending Gilman the following August.

Gilman?

My thoughts turned to preppies, khaki slacks, homework, a foreign neighborhood, and no girls—all of which seemed like a mighty high price to pay, particularly since I had just graduated from a junior high where I walked to and from school. It was equally hard to believe I had passed Gilman's difficult entrance exam, the likes of which I had not seen prior to that time.

Gilman?

It was odd I had not been provided a choice in the selection process. My father merely told me I would not be attending our local school (Lansdowne High), nor would I be playing football, baseball, and basketball with the friends I had played with during my youth on the sandlots and hard courts of southwestern Baltimore County. I was a big kid for my age, a 14-year-old sophomore with an "attitude" about my new surroundings (coats and ties, "chapel," homework, interscholastic practices, and a pressurized academic environment), and a silent but, nevertheless, real fear of failure. These initial observations are still fresh 20 years after my first visit to the Common Room with my parents, and Messrs. Schloeder and Campbell.

In retrospect, these changes were relatively easy compared to the more profound changes occurring in my mind, for although I quite correctly expected that athletics would provide a vehicle whereby I could achieve acceptance in my new environment, it soon became apparent I was now *expected* to achieve, academically and athletically, to a degree I had not thought possible.

Whenever a graduate of my generation begins to discuss Reddy Finney's contributions to Gilman, he is invariably assured by older alumni that previous headmasters similarly evoked the kind of universal admiration and respect accorded Reddy:

"You could have heard a pin drop in chapel when Mr. Finney spoke."

"Mr. Finney bit a guy so hard during a game that he drew blood *and* the officials had to wrestle him away from the poor fellow."

"Mr. Finney was going to become a minister after graduating from Princeton."

"Mr. Finney never took a drink during his four years at college."

"They talk about Jim Brown and Reddy Finney in the same breath at Princeton."

"Did you see Mr. Finney picking up trash around the campus last night?"

"Mr. Finney found some guys drinking in their car last night, you should have seen their eyes when they realized it was HIM."

"Mr. Finney wrote a note on my report card telling me how proud he was of my 87 in chemistry."

The moral leadership Reddy Finney provided left an indelible impression on many young Gilman students. We all competed for grades and athletic honors; we also competed for Mr. Finney's approval. In my mind, Reddy Finney's greatest accomplishment was to encourage a group of boys to *think* about the morals, values, and sense of individual responsibility first ingrained in us by our parents. A difficult task indeed for children raised in post-1960s America!

Thousands of Gilman graduates owe a large debt of gratitude to Mr. Finney. Of those thousands of men, however, I would most likely find myself near the top of the gratitude scale since (unbeknown to me at the time) it was Mr. Finney who located the financial support that allowed me to attend Gilman. I can only guess how many other young men benefited from this underpublicized aspect of Mr. Finney's tenure at Gilman.

The task of instilling the values, discipline, and work ethic it takes to succeed in the classroom and on the athletic field was not the task of one man alone. It was also the Schloeders, Sotirs, Tickners, Browns, Bristows, Neales, and so many others who played such a large part in developing the skills it would take to achieve success far beyond the closed, protected environment of Gilman. Indeed, my initial attempts to come to grips with this new world soon became linked to the men who taught and coached in the Upper School. The memories of these teachers are forever etched in my mind: Nick Schloeder's history class, where it seemed politics and sports were the focal point of every discussion; Alex Sotir's fanatical preparation and attention to detail on the football field; Sherm Bristow's self-assuredness while playing sports trivia games with a bunch of seniors; Jack Thompson's patience with a struggling sophomore in geometry class; Cliff Taggart's smooth delivery in the classroom; Reg Tickner's unbridled enthusiasm for every Greyhound athletic team; Cary Woodward's love of Shakespeare; Anton Vishio's annual pitch for my participation in his Latin class; and Mercer Neale's gentlemanly manner.

Gilman boasts a beautiful campus, the latest in high-tech classroom aids, high ratings from the country's most prestigious colleges, and a sustained reputation for turning out high-caliber students. Yet, beyond the bricks, mortar, computer screens, and athletic fields are the unique men and women who choose to teach and coach a few hundred boys each year. These dedicated educators continue to make Gilman a unique place to learn, play, and grow.

My professional career has allowed me to meet thousands of the sharpest minds in law, business, and government. Yet, the group of men who taught and coached at Gilman stand out from the rest due to their commitment to the intellectual, athletic, and social development of young men.

I cannot help but compare these educators to today's athletes and entertainers, who complain when informed that their actions set an example for a generation of young people who seem to have gone mad over Hollywood stars and professional athletic teams. Many Gilman teacher/coaches gave up the possibility of substantially higher incomes and more prestigious careers in order to contribute to the successful development of the young men who are fortunate enough to attend Gilman. *They* are indeed the true role models because they touch lives and make a difference. I, for one, will forever remain indebted to them.

 Robert L. Ehrlich, Jr. entered Gilman in the Tenth Grade, making an immediate impact as an athlete. By graduation, he had played three years of varsity football (captain, senior year), two years of varsity basketball, and three years of varsity baseball (captain, senior year). Ehrlich's strongest intellectual interests were in the study of history and politics. His favorite teacher/mentors were Nick Schloeder and Reddy Finney. He holds fond memories of being coached by Alex Sotir (football) and Sherm Bristow (basketball). Hobbies while at Gilman: golf, tennis, weights. At graduation, Ehrlich was presented with The Culver Memorial Football Cup, The Alumni Baseball Cup, and the school's highest athletic award—The William Cabell Bruce, Jr., Athletic Prize.

Attending Princeton, Ehrlich majored in politics, concentrating on Russian history, U. S. history and politics, and economic theory. Captain of the varsity football team there, he considered a career as a professional athlete.

After receiving his law degree from Wake Forest University School of Law in 1982, Ehrlich joined Ober, Kaler, Grimes & Shriver (first as an associate, then "of counsel"), remaining there until 1994. Running as a Republican, he was elected to serve as State Delegate for the 10th District of Baltimore County in 1986. He served eight years in the House of Delegates.

On November 8, 1994, Ehrlich was elected to the U. S. House of Representatives (2nd Congressional District). He was swept into office along with the much-ballyhooed class of 73 freshman Republicans who championed House Speaker Newt Gingrich's "Contract with America." In his campaign, Ehrlich focused on his working class background. He and his father often credit Gilman, and in particular Headmaster Reddy Finney, with opening the doors to Ehrlich's career.

The Team

CHARLES HERNDON '78

T he first swing came the way wiry teenage boys throw them—wild and fast and looping. Out of control. You could tell in the delivery: there was rage behind it.

Milton's head snapped back; the fist missed. But it didn't matter. The fight was on.

Only I wasn't part of it. As the three Patterson High boys hurtled into Milt Boone and David Robinson with a flurry of punches, the rest of us on Gilman's track team—their teammates—stood, stared, and did nothing.

This sort of thing didn't happen in our world, and certainly not at a track meet. Across Patterson's grimy fields, our coaches had finished with the last events. And in the parking lot, we'd come to board the bus to take us home.

It was obviously racial, that I knew. Milt and David were black. Those who taunted them were white, and when they spit out an insult, it was easy to hear the hate.

That day, David and Milton gave as good as they got. Finally, a bulky Gilman shot putter waded into the fray. Surely the fight would end now, I thought. Instead, he grabbed Milton, and then others pulled David back, all in a well-intentioned effort to throw our teammates onto the bus and out of harm's way.

But as we held our friends back, the Patterson boys, unfettered, renewed their attack. This time, they brought their lacrosse sticks into it, slamming poles down across Gilman backs and shoulders.

It has been almost two decades since that day, but I still remember the fury of that sweet spring afternoon. I remember how Milt and David stayed behind with Coach Thompson, black and blue and telling their side of it through broken teeth and swollen eyelids.

And I remember how difficult it was to sleep that night. I'd been raised to turn away from violence and fighting, but this had been different. Where was I when Milton and David needed me? Where were the others? Why had we done nothing?

Gilman's track team through the mid-1970s was like that. It seemed a place not only to grow physically but an ethical proving ground as well, a crucible of tiny moments that somehow even years later revealed larger lessons.

It was not lacrosse, Gilman's money sport. It was not baseball or football or even cross country. Track was a singular sport where black boys met white boys on equal footing in the purest of competitions. And while we ran alone, we ran together as well in those years, so well that in 1978 our effort won Gilman's first track championship since World War II.

We were coached by a white man and a black man. Jack Thompson led with amiable enthusiasm and grit and a genuine love for the sport. Bill Greene led with a sly smile and fierce determination, a sprint specialist who knew wits were as important as wind in races with little time to think.

But as a unit, we were all in it together. With each test, whether it be a relay or a riot, we learned a little more to rely on one another, to realize the importance of teamwork in a sport of individual merit, and to overlook entirely the color of our skins.

For me, that lesson came early and easy—but I had good teachers. As a J.V. runner, I watched varsity men like Carl Combs and Mike Austin with awe and admiration. I wished to run as they did and studied their grace and strength and style with the devotion of an acolyte. I watched once how Carl collapsed in agony on the track, his leg knotted in a cramp, and recognized the pain of those who were truly good at what they did.

And I took on a mentor. Spencer Johnson, older by a year and faster by a mile, became my secret source of inspiration. A generalist like me, he encouraged me to run faster and jump longer. I admired the way he let his running talk for him; his quiet, almost bookish intensity seemed as crucial to his success as moving fast.

Never once did I think of Spencer or Mike or Carl as black, or of myself as white. They were teammates. They were runners. They were friends.

During my sophomore year in a meet at Southern, I remember once drawing the unenviable spot of anchor leg on Gilman's J.V. mile-relay. The day's last race, it determined that day which school would win the meet.

Coming into the final lap, our runner was even with theirs. The handoff, the slap of the baton in my palm, yelling all around, silence. First turn. I was a step behind.

Think. I had a good kick for the finish, but what did this guy have? He looked faster. He seemed smoother. Into the backstretch, I moved closer, so close our legs meshed. I wanted him to sweat, to hear my breathing in his ear.

"Do it NOW!"

It was Mr. Greene's voice from across the field.

"Come on, PASS HIM!"

Was he talking to me?

"NOW HERNDON, NOW!"

Against my better judgment, I stepped out, I passed, and I cut back in front, fouling the other runner's stride as we headed into the back turn. Now I led. Now I worried what he would do. 200 yards. 175 yards. 150.

Both of us gutted out that agonizing final sprint, churning our leaden legs as best we could. I saw Mr. Greene at the line, yelling, "RUN HERNDON!"

And so I did. We won that day by inches, me, my teammates, and Mr. Greene. He was happiest of all.

It all came together my senior year, 1978. The team raced through the year winning meet after meet, thanks in large measure to Chris Ewart, a Welsh national champion runner who spent the semester at Gilman as part of an exchange program. Mr. Thompson argued to the league that Chris should be allowed to run, and did he ever. I don't think anyone ever beat him.*

McDonogh on a cool and clammy day. It was the last meet of the year, and we knew that losing meant a three-way tie for the conference championship. If we won, we won it outright.

Too neatly, it came down to the final event to determine the winner, a nail-biter of a high jump between McDonogh's star jumper and Gilman's own, Stanley Ruff. They dueled for more than 30 minutes, and with each successive attempt, the bar inched higher.

Stanley made it.

The other guy made it.

Stanley missed it.

The other guy missed it.

I never saw Reddy Finney more anxious than he was that afternoon. He and the hundreds of others that came that day cheered and gasped and whooped. And in the end, we all held our breath as Stanley Ruff and the McDonogh jumper leaped higher . . . and higher . . . and higher.

Until Stanley finally won.

Our team ran its victory lap around McDonogh's track with a sense of history on our shoulders, the tangible feeling that we had accomplished something no one else had in more than 30 years.

At the time, I don't know if any of us really understood that we had become more than an athletic machine then. We had come together as comrades and friends, too, linked by victory and bonded by pain and sweat. The moment was sweet. It is no less sweet today.

For our championship, we got letter jackets. I'd never even thought about wearing one before; to me, they'd always seemed the accouterment of lacrosse or football lettermen.

---

*Chris Ewart was a Hardie Scholar. The Harry Hardie Anglo-American Prize was established by Thomas G. Hardie '39 to encourage Anglo-American student exchanges. The prizes, in the form of grants, are given each year to one junior at Gilman and one junior at St. Edward's School, Oxford, following a competition and selection by committee. A list of Hardie Scholars from Gilman is given on page 406 at the end of Joshua Civin's "A Wonderful Present."

But when the jackets arrived, they dazzled us all. They weren't the heavy dark wool coats like the football players wore, but handsome, shinier jackets, embroidered with our names and, after our mothers finished with them, festooned with Gilman "G's" sewn onto the backs and shoulders and breasts.

I still have mine, a little ragged and tighter than I'd like. But those jackets still seem to me now a fitting memorial to our efforts back then.

For they were neither black nor white.

They were blue and gray.

Charles Herndon has spent much of his life writing for newspapers, specializing in features that focus on ordinary lives, " . . . on the ordinary things people do that are, upon closer examination, extraordinary." This interest in the lives people live began at Gilman, where Herndon's favorite teachers were Ned Clapp (ancient history, anthropology), A. J. Downs (English), Mercer Neale (American history), and coaches Jack Thompson and Bill Greene (track). Editor of *Vantage* and president of the Literary Club his senior year, Herndon won the Alexander Randall Prize for Literature.

Running—track and cross country—was a passion of Herndon's. He ran on J.V. teams 1974–76, and on varsity teams 1976–78, winning several MSA track awards for the mile relay, 880-yard dash, 440-yard dash.

Majoring in Journalism/English at the University of North Carolina at Chapel Hill, Herndon studied North Carolina history, American literature, and writing, graduating in 1982. He reported for the Statesville *Record & Landmark* in 1981; the Wilson *Daily Times* in 1982; the Greensboro *News & Record* 1982–86; the *Virginian Pilot & Ledger-Star* 1986–88; and the Charlotte *Observer* 1988–91. In 1991, Herndon moved back to Maryland, writing for the *Towson Times* before becoming supervisor of communications for the Baltimore County school system, and then communication specialist for the State Department of Education. Among Herndon's journalistic achievements are several environmental coups, including helping to save Buxton Woods on Hatteras Island, N.C., from development.

Herndon has in mind a coming-of-age novel set in 1970s Baltimore that he would like to find the time to write, and he hopes to return some day to the coast of North Carolina, writing and editing for a newspaper. He is married to the former Neaville Christian of Searcy, Arkansas.

In Thy Light—Light

ARCH MONTGOMERY '71

Great schools—schools that have a significant and permanent influence for the good of their students—are distinguished by remarkable people. Redmond Finney put it simply: "The true measure of any school is the quality of character of its members." Every boy at a great school has a relationship with and is influenced by a noteworthy and admirable figure. The complex web of relationships at schools defines the quality of the experience for each boy and determines whether he will be genuinely reached by his educational journey. This premise forms the foundation of my educational philosophy and influences my approach to every school issue. I believe *In tuo lumine lumen,* "In your light—light," that the light of a school emanates from relationships between people who care about each other and about fundamental truths—intellectual, physical, and spiritual—that will shape boys into responsible, moral men.

Without question my boyhood Lower School experience at Gilman was influenced by people whom I remember well and fondly. Boo Smith was one. He was an aggressive Third Grader who introduced me to Gilman with a quick pummeling. I had made the mistake of retaliating when he made fun of the name "Archibald." "Well, Boo," I said, having been told that his given name was Francis, "at least my name isn't Francy." I spent some wonderful weekends out at the Smiths' farm and remember exhilarating moments racing through his fields and unsuccessful attempts to shoot squirrels from Boo's bedroom window with a .22 caliber bolt-action rifle.

Fred Brune and I became fast friends playing in the dirt with match box cars and trucks, crawling through underbrush pretending to be soldiers. Fred cultivated awe-inspiring poison ivy blisters between his fingers that I could never duplicate, and we played endlessly with his giant, gentle mastiff, Hilda.

It took me two tries to escape Graeme Menzies and the Lower School. After my appointment to become Gilman's eleventh headmaster, Graeme wrote me a friendly note insisting that I had not stayed back. Instead, I had been red-shirted for a second crack at Calvert.

Few people who have not undergone it can possibly understand the humiliation of repeating a grade at Gilman. I hope very much that my memories of what seemed at the time like a terrible failure and permanent blemish on my personality give me a useful perspective on the problems of little boys. I believed in Sixth Grade that my good friends who were now Upper Schoolers while I remained behind would no longer be my friends, and I was convinced that my new classmates thought of me as "that dumb kid who flunked." Every eye was on me, I thought at the time. Thanks to Jim Fusting, the only new Sixth Grader in Graeme Menzies' class, there was someone else who felt a little out of place. We became good friends, and I was introduced in short order to many other friendly boys.

It was the kindness and understanding of Graeme Menzies and Reg Tickner that really made a difference to me during my second Sixth Grade year. They were the light that I basked in, the reason that my Lower School experience was worthwhile.

My second Calvert game was at home on the varsity field. What a thrill it was for Lower Schoolers to be on that field. Frank Davis was our three back, Ned Grassi the two back and Hugh McCormick the one back. I was the four back, asthmatic as ever and running a fever. We won, but the memorable moment for me was the embarrassment of my mother wrapping my shoulders in her overcoat late in the game. Oh the shame for a manly Sixth Grader.

Two other Lower School experiences stayed with me indelibly. The Sixth Grade speech was one. The unmitigated terror of standing behind a podium to make a speech before the assembled Sixth Grade and then the sense of delightful triumph and relief when the ordeal was accomplished are unforgettable. I remember the terrified looks on classmates' faces; I remember Charlie Duff's flawless presentation (we called Charlie "Blake" back then); I remember Reg Tickner's congratulations.

The other experience was raucous afternoon Lower School carpools. We'd pile into Mrs. Dobbin's, Mrs. Davis's, Mrs. Hardie's or some other beleaguered mother's station wagon and begin misbehaving. There was cross seat wrestling, pummeling a momentarily hapless victim, and general unruliness. Mrs. Morton once refused to drive us home and hauled us in before Reg Tickner for a stern lecture. Another time she scared us half to death by taking us to the police station and threatening to leave us there as criminals. How the long-suffering mothers tolerated us, I don't know, but whenever I am tempted to criticize the behavior of children at Gilman today as hopeless and unprecedented, I think back to those station wagons full of squirming, shouting incorrigibles and their white-knuckled moms.

Seventh and Eighth Grades were once the First and Second Forms of the Upper School. Those two wild years in the basement of Carey Hall! Handful-sized spitballs hurled against the study hall walls and left to dry into a disgusting white crust were only possible if Mr. Reese left the room or was momentarily distracted. Overcooked

Brussels sprouts could be smeared into a paste on the underside of the dining hall tables in order to avoid having to choke them down. Carefully placed knives wedged into the table were perfect launching platforms for pats of butter that would catapult toward the plaster ceiling. I believed for years that the whole ceiling had to be replaced because of our butter pats. A teacher, disgusted by our antics, had overstated dramatically the dastardly damage we were doing.* I remember a brave Ned Grassi trying valiantly and failing miserably to get us to behave ourselves and to treat one another with respect. He was the first example in my life of a peer adhering to a code of honor no matter how much scorn and abuse was heaped in his direction. Ned took the job of Class President seriously and received nothing but the disdain of his classmates (especially me) in return. That sticks with me.

Another particularly memorable moment was John Kopper's extraordinarily brilliant and precocious speech during a debate in Nick Schloeder's history class. Despite the rather thick callus I had managed to cultivate around my thinking muscles, I was appreciative of John's precision and thought. Equally impressive were the entertaining debates between Nigel Ogilvie, a Goldwater man, and "Blake" Duff, a Johnson supporter. Such passion, such hyperbole, such red faces and noise!

The single clearest memories for me are the wrestling matches in the old gym. It seemed that the whole school turned out to cheer for Charlie Fenwick, Chris and Ben Legg, Bill Groff, Jack Harvey. The noise level was indescribable, and every student seemed to writhe and jump with the wrestler's moves. Howls of glee greeted every Gilman success, and short lapses into silence followed any reversal in fortune. I remember leaving the gym in a euphoric state ready to wrestle senseless any imaginary opponent who dared challenge me! Such was my Eighth Grade imagination.

Despite the vibrancy of my classmates, for reasons not completely clear to me even now, I never connected with any teachers during my Seventh and Eighth Grade years. I know only too well as an educator that those two years in the grips of puberty with hormonal explosions, extraordinary growth spurts and mood swings make it hard for many boys to connect with anybody outside their own skin. I languished, and my parents recognized that I needed a change to help me flourish as a student and as a person.

I left Gilman after Eighth Grade in the belief that the school did not know me very well, that it was not a particularly warm place, that the teachers probably did not care whether I was there or gone. The irony is not lost on me that I now sit in the headmaster's chair at the school that seemed a bad fit many years ago. It is interesting to note, however, how very flawed my Eighth Grade perceptions of Gilman were. I discovered my yellowed, dog-eared student record just a year after becoming headmaster. It was full of teacher comments, but one letter in particular, written by Ludlow Baldwin to the Admissions Director at Westminster School, where I would spend my high school years, was particularly telling. The letter had me

---

*For more on butter catapulting, see Tim Baker's "A Small and Silent Symbol of Audacity," p. 253, and Alex Armstrong's "The Lighter Moments," p. 86.

pegged. It described in accurate detail a vigorous sometimes obstreperous boy who was not flourishing as he should. Gilman knew me well even if, as a self-absorbed teenager, I didn't recognize it.

My return to Gilman as headmaster in 1992 was not only ironic, but also a process of transition and clarification for me. My educational philosophy was distinctly "boarding school." That a teacher could really get his hands on a student and help shape him in mind, body, and spirit, was the central idea in my educational philosophy. Boarding schools, I believed, were uniquely situated to accomplish that mission. Moreover, my memories of Gilman, however mistaken, were of a highly academic school that had been unable during my Seventh and Eighth Grade years to connect with me. Consequently, when a Gilman School teacher and former colleague at the St. George's Summer School, Burke Rogers, told me that Mr. Finney was retiring and that I should consider applying to become Gilman's next headmaster, I was amused, flattered, and adamantly uninterested. But I knew that Burke was a boarding-school product. I knew that he believed strongly in the idea that teachers can and should have a direct, personal impact on the lives of students, not merely in mind but also in body and spirit. He suggested persuasively that I at least learn more about Gilman. "You'd be surprised," he said, "about what kind of school Gilman is." My meeting with Burke was the catalyst for a careful scrutiny of what Gilman was, and, consistent with my belief that the most telling aspect of any school is the quality of the people involved with it, I allowed myself to be influenced by the people I met during the search process.

Redmond C. S. Finney. The myth does not do the man justice. It is true that Gilman had become under his guidance a truly Baltimore institution, one that served a broad community of boys from every nook and cranny of the city. I was delighted with the diversity and energy of the place, something that no school I knew of had been able to achieve to such a degree. Many other things are true about the Finney myth, but one thing became indelibly clear to me during my conversations with him about Gilman. Simply stated, Mr. Finney gave to his boys his total, unqualified faith and love. "Faith" and "love" are two anachronistic words that seem hollow to late 20th century ears but best describe Finney's perspective. Could a school under a man like that, I remember thinking, do anything less than care about and nurture its students?

George Thomsen, former president of the Gilman Board of Trustees, alumnus, Gilman parent, prominent local attorney, and chairman of the search committee, seemed to me at first to be a forbidding figure, but he and his wife Mary Ellen helped persuade me that Gilman's philosophy was almost identical to my own. Although mildly intimidated by George's stern demeanor, I was captivated by the effervescence of his wife, Mary Ellen. It was interesting and telling to hear them speak about their three sons, all Gilman graduates, each with distinctly different personalities and strengths, and each of whom had flourished under the guidance of Gilman teachers. Below the surface, George Thomsen is a sensitive, warm family man who is passionate about education and articulated to me very effectively his firm belief in the power of teachers to influence students. During the search process he took time with my wife Phyllis and me to ensure that the interviewing ordeal was as hospitable as possible. He could not have known whether we would be chosen for the job, but he cared that we left the experience with a warm feeling about Gilman School. We did.

The chairman of the Board, George Hess, walked Phyllis and me back from the Finney Center to our car after the final meeting of the search process. I had just finished addressing and fielding questions from the Board. Dr. Ted Woodward had asked me what the single most important decision of my life had been, and other Board members had asked equally daunting, revealing questions. I was tired. George was carefully and sensitively probing for my reactions to my day at Gilman. His obvious concern for us and for the school was palpable and helped to crystalize my evolving picture of Gilman School. Here was the president of the Board of Trustees, a long-time trustee who had served Gilman well, one of the first (if not the first) Jewish boys to attend Gilman, the former president and chief executive officer of Hess Shoes and the current executive director at the Meyerhoff Foundation, and a man extremely active in Baltimore metropolitan community affairs, taking the time to walk us to our car. He spoke eloquently about Gilman's role in helping to solve the problems of Baltimore City, about the duty of all institutions to make significant contributions to the communities that support them. This seemed to me to be the kind of school of which I wanted to be a part.

My first few years at Gilman confirmed for me that it is, indeed, the kind of school at which I want to be. Although those early years were hectic with school-wide self-evaluations, centennial planning, substantive technological and curricular changes, and construction projects, people—students, teachers, staff, and friends of the School—are what I remember about Gilman.

Dawson Farber had greeted me during the search process with an ominous remark, "You know, there are people around here who remember you!" I was too startled at the time to notice his eyes, which are a dead give away when he is giving someone the needle. Shortly after my arrival in Baltimore during July, 1992, Dawson invited me to join him for lunch, during which he provided me with "Gilman According to Farber," a loving and detailed account of more than 60 years of Gilman history. Dawson's limitless affection for Gilman School became increasingly apparent during his story. He spoke about Gilman's integration process, about Ludlow Baldwin's extraordinary contribution to the school, and about the importance of the Gilman faculty. Although few teachers know about it, Dawson might be called the tiger of faculty salaries. "We've got to get 'em and keep 'em," he is fond of saying.

My ongoing relationship with Dawson has become symbolic for me of Gilman's respect for its rich legacy without a trace of complacency. There is simply nothing complacent about Dawson. His love for Gilman School motivates him to be a school gadfly, constantly reminding me and others that it is the teachers and the students—the people—who have distinguished Gilman in the past and will do so in the future. He knows that they are Gilman's light from the past and beacon for the future.

Another individual who made an appointment to see me early in my time at Gilman was Josh Civin '92. He was graduated from Gilman and on his way to Yale when he made an appointment to see me in early July during my very first week on the job. He spoke with genuine feeling about the importance of the arts at Gilman, and his hope for Gilman's future as a place more hospitable during its second century to boys whose talents lay in areas other than the playing fields. Although my observations of Gilman have not all squared with Josh's thoughtful remarks that day, I was interested in and touched by his willingness to take time to speak to the new headmaster about a school he had left but about which he cared deeply. And Josh was not alone. A host of graduates spoke with me that summer, all from personal perspectives, all about a school which seemed to have provided a special light in their lives.

Sherm Bristow, Class of 1967, has personified the Gilman teacher/coach philosophy for over two decades. He was, when I came to Gilman, associate headmaster, English teacher, athletic director and head football coach. I worried that it might be difficult for Sherm to embrace enthusiastically a young, inexperienced headmaster, having served as an integral part of a successful, experienced administration. I knew that Sherm's support would be critical to my success as a headmaster and that it could be natural for him to maintain a distance, a reserve from the new guy. Our first meeting during that summer of 1992 convinced me that my worries were unfounded. He articulated beautifully his commitment to the "whole boy" approach to education. Even when he addressed issues touching upon possible Gilman weaknesses, he approached the subjects with sensitivity and thoughtfulness.

Sherm had the self-assurance to allow me to assist him with the varsity football team, and I have come to appreciate the warmth, humor, and insightfulness he offers the students. His pre-game remarks to his players before all contests, big or small, are simple and direct. "Be Gilman!" he says. And every boy understands exactly what their coach means because they know that to Sherm "Being Gilman" means simply: Be your best, in body, mind, and spirit. It is a matter-of-fact, direct statement of the Gilman motto. Because Sherm lives it, the boys understand it. "In thy light—light."

I remember and am grateful for the service of several students during the early part of my term as headmaster. Michael McWilliams '93 was the president of the Senior Class during my first year as headmaster. He should have been an adjunct faculty member, given his mature and careful handling of several sensitive issues. We had, for example, an unfortunate and rare incident of covert anti-semitism. Since we had no suspect but wanted very much to end some intolerable behavior, it was a tricky problem to approach the students effectively without alienating the innocent majority. Michael, along with David Shapiro, Dave Powell, and others, decided that an open forum would be the best method, and Michael spoke to our

Upper School in his quiet, forceful, and persuasive way about the impact of intolerance in a close community like ours. No person of any age could have spoken more eloquently and effectively, and Michael managed to turn a bad situation into a positive learning experience for us all.

School President Ted Lord '95 caught my attention when he won the Spiked Shoe Classic as a sophomore, exhausting himself in the effort and collapsing in his father's arms at the finish. More impressive than Ted's physical prowess, however, is his integrity and moral courage. He singlehandedly rescued Gilman School from an embarrassing incident when he was the lone boy to resist an idea involving production of an obscene T-shirt to be worn on McDonogh weekend. I walked into my office at 6:30 A.M., and there was Ted, sitting alone in the dark. "Mr. Montgomery," he said, "Do you know what's going on? Do you know that some students are going to produce a T-shirt that will seriously hurt the school?" Ted's simple act, which risked the possibility of peer censure and anger, seems to be in the tradition of Callard/Baldwin/Finney—that is, a highly developed sense of what is right and good.

Ted Lord, Michael McWilliams, Josh Civin, and Dawson Farber are only examples whom I have chosen among many from the Gilman family to illustrate the impact that the people of the school have had upon me during my short time as Gilman's 11th headmaster. They have confirmed for me my predisposition to believe that great schools are about relationships between people. The educational process is enhanced by constant elbow-rubbing between people of character who care deeply about important issues.

Teddy Roosevelt was right when he wrote, "To educate a man in mind and not in morals is to create a monster." Anne Galbraith Carey knew that, and her legacy is alive and well at Gilman—*In tuo lumine lumen.*

Archibald Roger Montgomery IV attended Gilman 1960–67, with his favorite teachers being Graeme Menzies and Reginald Tickner. For most of those years the young Arch lived on the campus of Garrison Forest School, all girls and with a strong boarding department, where his father "Tad" was headmaster. In 1967, Tad Montgomery accepted the headmastership at The Hill School in Pottstown, Pennsylvania, and Arch, going into the Ninth Grade, left Gilman and was enrolled in The Westminster School in Simsbury, Connecticut. Within two years he found his role as leader and athlete.

Junior and senior year, Montgomery was named Most Valuable Defensive Player in football. Senior year he was MVP and was named National Football Hall of Fame Scholar Athlete. He was All League Football in '69, '70; All New England Football, '70, and captain of the team; captain of the 1971 swimming and lacrosse teams; All League Lacrosse '69, '70, '71; All American Lacrosse '71; and in 1971 was awarded the Eversley Child's Cup—given to the best athlete of the school at graduation.

At Westminster, Arch Montgomery was inspired by history teacher Jacob Nolde, and became interested in U. S. history, politics, and drama. He majored in history and sociology at the University of Pennsylvania, specializing in Russian–American relations, and played lacrosse, again becoming captain. He was president of St. Anthony's Hall Fraternity, vice-president of Friars Senior Honor Society, and a member of Penn's Mask and Wig acting troupe.

Determined not to follow in the footsteps of his father as an educator, Montgomery served in the U.S. Army 1975–79, rising to sergeant, and representing the army across the country as a marathon runner. He graduated from the Army's Monterey Language Institute, with a major in Russian, in 1979. Financed by the army, he began classes at the University of Texas School of Law, where he was editor-in-chief of *The Review of Litigation* and captain of the Legal Eagles Football Team. Montgomery joined Venable, Baetjer and Howard in Baltimore as an associate in 1982. In 1984, after two years of legal work which he did not enjoy, Montgomery decided to go into education. He accepted a teaching/coaching job at St. George's School, Rhode Island, a boarding school of 325 students.

Montgomery was twice elected coach of the year by the St. George's students for his work as varsity lacrosse coach, and in 1990, after his team won the league championship, was elected coach of the year by league coaches. He served as headmaster of the St. George's Summer School and Chair of the history department.

In 1991, Gilman School conducted a nationwide search for a headmaster to succeed the retiring Reddy Finney '47. On December 9th of that year, Search Committee Chair George Thomsen '48, and Board President George Hess, Jr. '55 called Montgomery, asking him to be the school's next headmaster. Montgomery accepted and on July 1, 1992, became Gilman's eleventh headmaster. He lives on the campus with his wife, Phyllis, and their two sons, who both enrolled in Gilman in September, 1992—Gregory, '02, and Tyler, '05.

1980s

1981

The first class of 100 members graduates.

The Alumni Association establishes the May Holmes Service Award to honor outstanding service to the School. Miss Holmes, who worked at Gilman for 60 years, is the first recipient.

The Cotton Lecture series is begun. Alumni return to Gilman to speak on their vocations.

1982

Religion and history teacher David Neun begins working at Gilman and sets up the Upper School volunteer community service program.

1985

The Building Character Capital Campaign concludes. Chaired by Walter G. Lohr, Jr. '62, the campaign raises $6 million for endowment for faculty salaries, financial aid, and campus improvements. LeRoy E. Hoffberger, Robert G. Merrick, Jr. '50, and Thomas P. Perkins III '53 are among key campaign chairmen.

1986

An extension to the Lower School, including a multi-purpose room, is completed.

1987

The Gilman School Athletic Center Campaign begins to raise $5 million for the construction of The Redmond C. S. Finney Athletic Center. Campaign is chaired by Ralph N. Willis '49. Among campaign leaders are Earl L. Linehan, Thomas Schweizer, Jr. '62, and William J. McCarthy '49. President of the Board George E. Thomsen '48 and Executive Secretary Sherman A. Bristow '67 are active in campaign.

On the left, 15 members of the class of 1980, apparently inspired by Latin teacher Anton Vishio, have pulled on their togas and are preparing to ride through the campus in a chariot that will be lucky to survive the experience.

Classmates Rory Holley and Keefe Clemons '85 prepare to speak at a Middle School pep rally.

Right, Betsy McDonald, favorite Lower School teacher of many, reviews the alphabet. For a loving portrait of Mrs. McDonald, as well as a comparison of Headmaster Reddy Finney to Triceratops, turn to "First Grade" by Gregory Paul Lee.

The Middle School resumes publication of *The Blue and The Gray* as a news and literary paper.

Henry Franklin '87 wins his second MSA wrestling title.

1988
Community service becomes a requirement under the aegis of Director of Community Services David Neun. A minimum of 50 hours in one placement during one calender year is required for graduation.

Water polo is launched as a varsity sport.

1989
The Alumni Auditorium is renovated.

338

Right, Richard Ginsburg '85 was an MSA J.V. Diving Champion.

Below, tight end Matt Atkinson '83 leaps for a pass in the end zone leaving the McDonogh defender helpless. In "A Full Friendship: From Calvert through Gilman," classmate Jerome Hughes recreates the improbable catch Atkinson made that clinched the 1982 MSA "A" Conference Football Championship win over Loyola.

Left, Michael Sarbanes '82 and Matt Atkinson '83 pose as the first one-two winners in Gilman's history of the Greater Baltimore Chapter National Football Foundation and Hall of Fame Scholar Athlete of the Year.

Tennis coach Jim Busick began at Gilman in 1982 and as of 1996 had earned a 124–36 record, not far behind Bruce Daniels' 1964–81 record of 161–29, and surpassing Roy Barker's 1946–1963 record of 100–56.

Above, Assistant Headmaster Bill Greene. In 1970, Greene was the first African-American to become a Gilman teacher. He succeeded Bill Campbell as director of Gilman Upward Bound, a position he is still holding in the 1990s. For more on Greene's contributions to Gilman, read Reddy Finney's "Reflections on Gilman Headmastering, 1968–1992" in the 1940s section.

Above right, Harry Halpert '85 drives past his opponent toward the goal. Soccer gained popularity in the 1980s.

Below right, Chair of the Classics Department for 30 years, and Latin and Greek teacher, Anton Vishio is known for his wit, humor, and passion for the Classics. Vishio is a devotee of community service as well as a founder of programs such as Operation Greengrass and Special Olympics Day. His office is always filled with excited students. And, he has a cat called Caesar and a statuesque assistant called Mickey.

Far right, the special "shaved head squad" of the 1986 varsity football team. Top row: Joshua Freeman '87, David Levi '88, Pierre Silva '87, Charles Linehan '88, Jack Buchanan '87. Kneeling: Pete Kwiterovich '87, Todd Murphy '88, Clark Wight '87, Jack Cavanaugh '87, Joe Miller '87. The cool guy reclining: Stockton Williams '87.

Senior prefects of 1989 show off the stern dispositions that won them their positions of power. The six across the bottom are Andy Martire, John Snead, Alex Martin, Mark Burnet, Rob Marbury, and Jeff Zeitung.

Below, the senior room of 1989. On the couch are Jamie Hamilton, Alex Martin, and Lucas Scheps.

John "Doc" Merrill picks up the tempo in his renowned course, 9th Grade Music Appreciation. Merrill, who retired with a great surprise party thrown by past Glee Club members and Traveling Men in 1996, taught at Gilman for 34 years and was the inspiration behind many a Gilman musician's career.

Left, "The Youngest and the Oldest." The continuity of Gilman is symbolized in this planting of a Liberty Tree on Patriots' Day, April 18, 1975. Chi-Kai Chien '86 (six years old) is helped by May Holmes, 83, an indispensable Gilman resource for 54 years.

Gilman in the 1980s:
Reeling in the Years

J. B. HOWARD, JR. '81

"Gilman is one of the most important educational institutions in the country. Anything that improves Gilman improves Baltimore." The words of Baltimore Mayor Kurt Schmoke at the September 28, 1988 groundbreaking for the Redmond C. S. Finney Athletic Center defined and confirmed Gilman's stature, nationally and locally, as the school entered the final decade of its first century.

Likewise, Schmoke understood why the magnificent $5 million facility about to be built was so named: "Mr. Finney is one of the area's greatest educational resources. He has successfully expanded opportunities to kids in the area otherwise unable to take advantage of those opportunities, without sacrificing excellence. Mr. Finney—is Gilman."

If the 1960s and '70s were Gilman's time of experimenting, evolving, and establishing its new identity as a more diverse, connected "urban community school," then the 1980s were a time for consolidating and shoring up the positive changes of those more eventful decades.

The school had gone through profound changes under Mr. Finney's leadership since 1968, especially in the creation of what Schmoke had called "expanded opportunities" for students of varied socioeconomic, racial, and religious backgrounds—students from all over Baltimore who would not have found their way to Gilman but for Gilman's outreach efforts. Simply put, Gilman graduating classes in the '80s looked, acted, and interacted differently from the more homogeneous and culturally cohesive classes of earlier decades. The days were past when Gilman boys were neighbors in Roland Park, Ruxton, or the Green Spring Valley, when their families belonged to the same clubs, and when their parents grew up and went to college together.

A personal anecdote might illustrate how complete this transformation was by the mid-1980s. In 1985, I taught first-year Latin to a small group of Gilman fresh-men, all of whom were new to the school and needed to fulfill the Latin requirement that their classmates had endured in Eighth Grade. My students were Chinese, Indian, Korean, Jewish, Pakistani, female (Bryn Mawr girls) and black; not one fit the already-outdated caricature of the Gilman "preppy." As the year progressed, I watched as many of these new students matured intellectually and developed a seri-ousness of purpose that probably came with an awareness that the academic stan-dards they were now expected to meet were higher than what they had known before. Nine years later, I ran into one of the most obstinate and unruly boys in that class, one that I had had to refer for discipline problems more than once, primarily to impart that—whatever he had been used to before—at Gilman, respect for teach-ers and for other classmates who were trying to learn *mattered*. Now, in 1994, he was a second-year law student at Michigan, a highly sought-after recruit for the city's best law firms, and—a real gentleman. He was, in short, one of the many examples where Gilman's outreach efforts had demonstrably improved Baltimore, and the opportunities open to a worthy young man.

It is instructive to compare the trajectory of history at Gilman during the '80s with that in the country as a whole. The resounding mandate of the American elec-torate in 1980 had been for change, and it swept into office a President who, most felt, would look and at least act the part of a colossal leader—a presidential, Reddy Finney-type. Fed up with the ruinous economic consequences of double-digit in-flation and eager to shake off the malaise of the late '70s, the country was ready to feel good about itself again; in Ronald Reagan it found a leader who promised to return to a less troubled, pristine era—sometime before the '60s came along. The Reagan Revolution rejected the late '70s feeling of impotence and victimization, brought on by the day-by-day obsession with the Ayatollah's hostage crisis and the inability to respond to the Soviet Union rolling into Afghanistan. Ronald Reagan's radical spirit of change and redirection—"getting government off the backs of the people," cutting taxes sharply, deregulating industry, rebuilding the national defense—was a resolute break with the past.

Finney's Gilman in the '80s had no thoughts of breaking with the recent past and returning to less complicated times. In some ways, Gilman in the 1980s was beginning to live its golden years. Compared with the previous decades, the '80s were a more conservative period at Gilman—"conservative" in the core sense of that word meaning "tending to favor preservation of the existing order."

By the end of the decade, the national mood was souring. The unraveling of the booming success of the early Reagan years may have begun with the exposure of the Iran-contra deception, or the crash of the stock market in 1987, or the trickle that became a wave of savings-and-loan failures, or the arrest of Ivan Boesky, who during the 1980s merge-and-acquisition craze had argued that "greed is good." By 1990, renowned conservative Republican analyst Kevin Phillips would note in his seminal work, *The Politics of Rich and Poor*, that the "1980s were a second Gilded

Age, in which many Americans made and spent money abundantly. Yet, as the decade ended, too many stretch limousines, too many enormous incomes and too much high fashion foreshadowed a significant shift of mood." Whether the '80s were a return to the Gilded Age or not, one phenomenon is indisputable: as Phillips put it, ". . . the rich were getting richer, while the poor were fulfilling their half of the cliché." According to the Congressional Budget Office estimates, the top one percent in income—two and one half million people—doubled their inflation-adjusted, after-tax income. The top 20 percent gained 20 percent in pre-tax, inflation-adjusted income, while the bottom 20 percent actually lost six percent by the same measure, working five percent harder than they had in the '70s. The 60 percent above them— the middle class—did not do much better, working two percent harder, and gaining only five percent in income during the decade, compared with gains of 12 percent and 35 percent in the '70s and '60s. In short, the country in 1990 was politically, socially, and economically a very different place from what it had been in 1980.

Gilman was not. In fact, it was much the same, and edging closer to its ideal for itself. This can be seen perhaps most clearly in the Long Range Planning Report released by a committee of the Board of Trustees in 1988. That report, to which Mr. Finney contributed substantially, recommended not bold new initiatives, but a strategy of building on Gilman's strengths and consolidating positive changes. For example, coeducation, that perennial bugaboo, that spark for countless hours of dining room table debate in Gilman homes, was rejected as "not now a practical alternative." Stick with what worked and build on it, the report urged, recommending expansion of coordinated classes with Bryn Mawr and Roland Park Country School, Gilman's new neighbor with whom coordination started in 1986. Nor was it deemed wise to grow: the school should remain approximately 900 students, and the present 67-acre campus was quite adequate. But within those confines, substantial capital improvement projects were needed; plans for a new athletic facility and a more functional Middle School building were taking shape.

Instead of new directions, the course charted for Gilman was straight—the continuing fulfillment of its mission statement. The elements of that statement, set forth in full in the Long Range Planning Report, both characterized Gilman as it stood in the late 1980s and defined its ideals for itself. They were 1) dedication to "helping students prepare for college and a life of involvement and service"; 2) a strong tradition of academic excellence ; 3) a commitment to "seek to assemble a talented and diverse community"; 4) a curriculum intended to celebrate "the wonder of learning" and to foster "creative, critical, and independent thought and expression" and "an appreciation of the arts and our cultural heritage"; 5) "extracurricular opportunities" to "develop personal interests and talents," to participate in community service, and to promote "physical well-being, good sportsmanship, and teamwork" through an outstanding athletic program; 6) affirmation of "the spiritual and ethical values of the Judeo-Christian tradition"—character, self-discipline, integrity, confidence, compassion, respect for the dignity and rights of others— together with respect for other creeds and beliefs; and 7) the honor system.

The two *sine qua non* factors in the school's accomplishment of these goals were the commitment of a devoted, talented corps of career faculty members and the ability to offer student scholarships. Finances were critical to both, and from the perspective of 1979, the ailing economy posed a genuine threat to the maintenance of Gilman's excellence on these points. Finney emphasized that it was the "human resources"—faculty and students—who traditionally had distinguished Gilman; as he said in 1982: "We must maintain our superior level of faculty competence and dedication by means of more competitive salary levels, and we must also keep in mind that the quality of our student body has been greatly enhanced by our financial aid program. If we don't pursue and keep the best faculty and student body, we're moving backwards."

The Reagan Administration kept the lid on inflation, and Gilman clearly benefited. Faculty and scholarship financial needs were the impetus for the "Building Character" capital campaign. As Campaign Chairman Walter G. Lohr, Jr., '62, put it, "'Building Character' is the right name for the campaign because it suggests the human qualities that distinguish the school." The solid financial position of the school in the 1980s was substantially related to the campaign's tremendous success. Started in 1982 with a goal of $5.2 million, the Campaign had raised over $6 million by 1986. The Long Range Planning Committee could report, in 1988, that ". . . the school is currently in a strong financial position . . . and has adequate reserves" to meet foreseeable contingencies. And yet, there was much to be done.

The need to attract and retain talented young faculty was no chimera. By the end of the 1980s, many of the seemingly ageless Gilman teaching legends had moved on. Retirements included, in 1980, George Chandlee (44 years at Gilman as a math teacher and, for 23 years, head coach of varsity lacrosse); in 1984, Helen K. Stevens (49 years teaching in the Lower School, shaping its curriculum and the reading and study skills programs for the entire school); Charles R. Gamper (Renaissance man of 38 years, serving Gilman in numerous teaching and administrative roles—most notably for students in the early '80s as dean of students); in 1989, A. J. Downs (39 years as English teacher and, to many, the conscience of the school) and Edward "Ned" Thompson (35 years, first as science teacher, then anchor of the mathematics department). The school community also mourned the passing of legendary history teacher P. Meredith Reese (1979), Ian Jewitt (1984), former Headmaster Henry H. Callard (1986), and May Holmes (1986), who after 60 years of service to Gilman became in 1981 the first recipient of the Alumni Association's May Holmes Service Award. And Leonard Carter, with over 30 years of maintenance service at Gilman, retired in 1986.

The nucleus of a new generation of faculty and administrative stalwarts, however, was already evident by the early 1980s. In the Upper School, the unhappy few posted on the daily "Gamper's List" of study hall vagrants and off-campus wanderers no longer faced the good-natured scowl of Mr. Gamper; now they answered to John "Johnny Law" Schmick, a veteran Lower School teacher, who took over from Gamper as dean of students in 1983. Other long-time Gilman teachers assumed administration roles when history teacher Mercer Neale became the first head of the Upper School in 1984, and English teacher and football coach Sherman Bristow the first Associate Headmaster in 1988. Gilman's successes in college counseling and placement continued when the able Jeff Christ succeeded Jerry Downs as College Counselor in 1980. In the Middle School, math teacher nonpareil Ron Culbertson, winner of a 1983 Presidential Award for Excellence in Science and Mathematics Teaching, took over as Head in 1986, and in 1988 Jean Brune became Head of the Lower School after serving as interim head following the departure of Richard Snyder, head for twelve years.

In addition to those who rose to administrative positions, the foundation for the next group of potential long-term teachers was discernible in the arrivals of Jerry Thornbery and Peggy Wolf (1980), Doug Lewis (1981), John Xanders '77, Jim Morrison, and Peter Julius (1983), and Timmy Holley '77 (1984). A few of these had come to the school initially on a Michael H. Cooper Fellowship, a program created in the early 1980s to attract as teachers young people who might not otherwise enter teaching.

Mirroring the times, persistent socioeconomic and racial tensions bedeviled the school throughout the 1980s. Far from ducking these uncomfortable issues, Gilman squarely faced them, turning a critical eye on the attitudes and social constructs that generated them. Under the courageous moral leadership of the young chaplain, Chris Leighton, from 1979 to 1987, each year a school day was set aside for lectures and discussion groups on issues of collective responsibility for the Holocaust, racial divisiveness, and others.

There was also a feeling that Gilman was not fulfilling its promise to its artistically gifted students. While Headmaster Finney, in a 1988 interview, cited progress in the arts programs as a significant change at the school during his 20-year tenure, it is clear from the Long Range Planning report that a deficiency in the arts programs was a major concern; that view was reinforced by a teacher quoted in the 1988 Gilman *News* saying that Gilman's drama program was "light years behind" academic and athletic programs. Again, the school responded with action. In 1987, Gilman hired Jamie Spragins as its first full-time drama teacher.

Another area where the school was perceived to have fallen down was in its training of students for the practical realities of the business world. The ability to understand the economic dynamics of our society was surely part of the total preparation for "a life of involvement and service" that Gilman promised. Here, again, a need was addressed, if perhaps incompletely: the Douglass Cotton lectures were instituted in 1980 to "... instill in our students a better understanding and a keener interest in the world of business and economics."

The corrosive effects of substance abuse on spiritual and ethical values presented unique challenges. A disturbingly high percentage of Gilman students admitted abusing alcohol and drugs. Gilman *News* polls in both 1986 and 1989 showed that 80 percent of seniors drank on weekends. In various ways, the school struggled to address this phenomenon. English teacher Bob Bulkeley, a self-identified recovering alcoholic, served as contact for many troubled students. A major 1988 lecture focused on substance abuse. Still, many questioned the effectiveness of the school's efforts in a social milieu where alcohol consumption, at least, was condoned and even sometimes promoted by parents and much of the larger culture.

Finally, after faculty excellence and student scholarships, maintenance of Gilman's fine physical plant was considered an "essential need." In 1986, an extension to the Lower School, including a multi-purpose room, was completed, and a renovation of the Alumni Auditorium was undertaken in 1989. The crown jewel was the new Finney Athletic Center, on which work began in 1987. This new facility (actually a thorough renovation and extension of the existing 60-year old building) would house 1,000 spectators in a grand basketball and wrestling arena, with entrance through a spacious two-story lobby. Additional gymnasia and locker space were planned to accommodate the 900-boy student body that had, until then, made do with a facility built for 400.

How, ultimately, did the school fare during these years? There is no better evidence of Gilman's continuing excellence during the 1980s than the individual accomplishments, at Gilman and afterwards, of many of the young men who graduated during that decade. 1980 graduate Storrs Hoen went on to earn a Rhodes Scholarship. Michael Sarbanes '82, as a standout senior wide-receiver, earned Gilman's first statewide Scholar-Athlete Award; in 1986, he went on to receive Princeton University's highest award, and to study in England on a Marshall Scholarship. Jerome Hughes '83, served as a student ambassador to Japan, an event that was recorded in a memorable Baltimore *Sun* photograph of Hughes standing next to Ronald Reagan and other world leaders (and looking very much at home there!). Eric Becker and Chris Hoehn-Saric '80, along with Doug Becker '83, developed a "card" containing individuals' medical histories, breaking ground for the health security card President Clinton brandished as a symbol and cornerstone of his ill-starred health care plan; the young entrepreneurs went on to found Sylvan Learning Centers, which went public in early 1994.

Gilman's venerable track record of college placement—the lion's share to the premier Ivys, especially Princeton, a solid minority to "the public Ivys," Virginia and North Carolina—held steady during the 1980s, with some new twists. From classes of approximately 100, Princeton averaged about five boys a year; Virginia about three. Other southern alternatives also soared in popularity: Duke University, identified in a New York *Times Magazine* article in 1985 as a "hot college," became a huge draw to Gilman students, attracting ten in 1984, nine in both 1982 and 1985, and seven in 1981. The University of North Carolina averaged about four. Local schools Johns Hopkins (about four per year) and Maryland (about six) also were consistent favorites.

There were during the '80s the manifold athletic glories that mark each Gilman decade. The 1981 MSA "A" Champion Lacrosse Team gave Gilman its last lacrosse championship until 1994 and launched the spectacular careers of some future lacrosse Hall of Famers: the second-ever four-time first team All-American,

Del Dressel '81 (JHU, '85); college All-American, club lacrosse MVP, and World Games MVP Mac Ford, '81 (UNC, '85); and repeat All-American and NCAA Champion Joey Seivold '82 (UNC, '86), among others. Though Gilman lacrosse slipped from its championship perch during the 1980s, the program continued to churn out winners: a remarkable five members of the 1984 Gilman varsity lacrosse team were elected captains of their respective college teams in 1988: Ted Brown (UNC), Chris Coffland (W&L), Bill McComas (Brown), Chase Monroe (UVA), and Jim Swindell (Denison). Gilmanites also shone in the big-name revenue sports: Mark Agent '85 started at offensive tackle for the University of Maryland's football team, and Matt Eastwick '88 starred on the Pete Carrill Princeton basketball teams that became a national power in late '80s and early '90s.

At the end of the 1980s, it was not uncommon to hear talk of a national "hangover," a certain weariness born of the excesses of a decade that produced an unprecedented national debt, a costly savings-and-loan bailout, and a felt need for a "kinder, gentler" America. The combination of these and other complex forces would shortly plunge the country into a sustained economic recession.

Gilman, on the other hand, ended the decade in a position of strength and confidence, its place at the forefront of Maryland schools indisputable. To be sure, the next decade would bring its share of problems, and a dynamic new headmster to chart the course, but the legacy of Reddy Finney's 1970s and 1980s was a vigorous and proud school.

J. B. Howard attended Gilman 1969–81—covering a span of three decades. His main intellectual interests were English, Latin, philosophy, and history. Favorite teachers were Anton Vishio (Latin), Cary Woodward (English), and Chris Leighton (philosophy); favorite coaches were Bill Baker and John Schmick—both lacrosse. A member of the 1981 MSA co-champion varsity lacrosse team, Howard was First Team All-Metro Lacrosse. (He admits to being captain of the Sixth Grade football team that was "crushed by Calvert.")

During his Upper School years, Howard was editor-in-chief of *Vantage*, sang in the Glee Club, and was a writer for the Gilman *News*. Graduating Cum Laude, Howard received a Morehead Scholarship to the University of North Carolina.

At UNC, he graduated Phi Beta Kappa, winning the Albert Suskind Prize in Latin and the Atlantic Coast Conference Scholarship Award. He played varsity lacrosse, and was a member of the NCAA Division I Championship Team of 1982.

Howard was a Cooper Teaching Fellow at Gilman during the 1985/86 academic year, before entering the University of Virginia School of Law. In 1993, he began work as an assistant attorney general for Maryland.

A Full Friendship:
From Calvert through Gilman

JEROME HUGHES '83

IMPROBABLE.

Though it could not have landed in more fitting hands, it was improbable that it found its way to him on that October day. One second on the game clock. Score tied. The MSA "A" Conference Football Championship hanging in the balance. A Hail Mary from John Roe, our quarterback, to any eligible receiver downfield. Three Loyola defenders with an opportunity to break up the play.

Somehow the football bounced off their hands and into Matt's hands for the game-winning touchdown. And there was Matt, my good friend, at the receiving end, arms spread-eagle as though he were aflight, running through the end zone with mouth wide open but no words fitting for the occasion, until he was picked up, knocked over, swarmed by grateful teammates, until the entire end zone was one blur of blue and gray, tumbling, embracing, laughing, rising, falling, and rising again. As the Loyola scoreboard looked on, it grudgingly read "Loyola 14 Gilman 20 0:00."

The game was over, but the lesson lived on with a freshness which gave greater meaning to Coach Sherman Bristow's pre-game pep talk: "Don't quit. Just do your job. Give it all you've got for four quarters and then look up at the scoreboard." Clichés are stripped of their triteness when the bare truths which they harbor are experienced.

The Gilman experience for Matthew Smith Atkinson IV and me began in the halls of Calvert School. Those years paved the way for our enduring friendship. I remember Matt in primary school as a consistent student and a good athlete. Whereas I would often be scrambling in the few minutes before class to do my homework, Matt rarely came to class unprepared. Though he never had the reputation of a class "brain," he was bright, neat, and steady. Matt was very practical, even as a child, and practically impossible to hate. The closest I came to disliking him was in the Fourth Grade. Because he had such a close rapport with our Fourth Grade teacher, Mr. Gillette, I tried to label him the teacher's pet in an attempt to assuage my disappointment at my own lackluster academic performance. Isn't it peculiar how even a child can try to use labels to garnish his own mediocrity and failure? No labels stuck to Matt, nor did he label others. He never stroked people with obsequious flattery, nor did he project himself to draw such strokes from others. His accolades came from the strength of his own inner confidence. While I was trying to find myself, Matt was being himself.

Three symbols from the Calvert years encapsulate the broad, common ground which laid the foundation for our friendship: a low rim, a photograph, and a trophy. The basketball goal on the Calvert playground was just seven feet off the ground. Because Matt and I both hit our growth spurt at 11 years of age, we discovered that we could both slam-dunk the basketball on the low rim. The changes in our bodies brought a certain amount of embarrassment when our voices cracked in Mrs. Bannister's music class, but the added height advantage of early puberty made it all worthwhile. As we harmonized on that low basketball goal with in-your-face slams and three-sixty, double-pump jams, the sound of the shaking backboard and clattering rim blended beautifully with the melody of our unabashed laughter.

In stark contrast to our acrobatics on the playground was the photograph which John Patterson, our Sixth Grade teacher, took of Matt and me. Our anxiety to see the snapshot quickly turned to confusion when the film was developed. We had expected to see two young men standing robust and tall, but instead two awkward-looking stumps stared out at us with blemished faces which remarkably resembled our own. Our egos were quickly deflated when we realized that we were the stumps.

That photograph of Matt and me provoked an awareness in us which had puzzled us at first glance—people don't always see us the way we see ourselves. This awareness would eventually take us beyond the narrow corridors of self-centered thinking and would open the door for us to explore our friendship beyond the common ground we found on the athletic field. On that particular day, however, we were not looking for any deep meaning; that would come later, over a cup of orange juice the next day. The problem as we saw it then was that the photograph sure made us look bad. Thankfully, during recess, that low basketball rim "morphed" the photograph of The Two Stumps into the more favorable image of Air Atkinson and Air Hughes.

Public image was not the driving force of my friendship with Matt. He was never my "white friend," whose influential connections would one day help me to carve out my slice of the great American pie; I was never his "black friend," who would widen his cultural experience so that he could relate to people of all nationalities. We were friends. Period.

Before the age of political correctness, Matt and I shared the stage for one defining moment at Calvert School. During the graduation ceremony we were announced co-winners of the Sportsmanship Award. We accepted the trophy together, and then something unusual happened. Matt handed the trophy to me, and I handed it back to him, and then he to me. Back and forth the trophy went until, following an inner cue, we looked at one another, smiled, and walked back to our seats together, each holding one handle of the cup. The cynic might call this experience a well-staged photo opportunity. But we were too young to be cynical. Matt thought I was more deserving of the award so he gave the trophy to me. I thought he was more deserving so I gave it back to him. We realized that we had to compromise so we walked off with the trophy together. To this day I still think that I was right.

After graduating from Calvert School, we left the trophy behind to etch out our place at Gilman School. We found no low basketball goals on the Middle School playground. What we did find was a place where it was safe for us to study, to play sports, and to dream without being ridiculed.

During our six years at Gilman, we were never pressured to conform into the mold of the perfect Gilmanite. The strength of the Gilman experience was that the faculty and staff cared for the students. Redmond C. S. Finney, the headmaster, was a living example of what it means to be a compassionate human being. His influence on our lives was immeasurable. Matt and I drew from the strength of Gilman's nurturing faculty and administration, and added to it our own individual gifts, talents, and idiosyncrasies.

To the outsider looking in, Gilman sometimes took on the mystique of a sheltered bastion for privileged children—the sons of doctors, lawyers, and politicians neatly tucked away from the real world between the corners of Roland Avenue and Northern Parkway. In reality, Gilman was not an elitist school steeped in antiquated traditions. Most of the school's traditions encouraged diversity fortified by character rather than character fortified against diversity; like all established institutions, however, there were certain traditions that promoted uniformity. The dress code, for instance, helped to perpetuate the "preppy" look: polo shirts, Izod sweaters, and docksiders.

Matthew Smith Atkinson IV wore his docksiders well. His life represents what is best about Gilman School. Matt was a scholar-athlete who did not seek the limelight. His grades put him in the top quintile of our class, but he was never the type of guy who would go around after exams had been graded asking: "What did you get? What did you get?" Matt was an articulate speaker and a precise writer. He gravitated more to history and the humanities than to the sciences. In classes where seats were not assigned, Matt usually sat towards the back of the class. From that vantage point he would ponder the lesson and speak when he had something meaningful to ask or to say. He would engage in light conversation with teachers who were open to personal interaction, but his wit did not violate their authority or class rules. Even in the locker room, his sense of humor was never presumptuous, always respectful.

Matt was a gifted athlete and the type of player every coach wants on his team. He lettered in three sports: football, basketball, and lacrosse. Though his speed and quickness were just a little above average, his technique was exceptional. Many people remember Matt as the tight end with great hands who caught the last-second bomb to beat Loyola. He also was an excellent blocker who used technique and determination to drive much stronger and heavier opponents off the line of scrimmage. The spotlight shone on Matt at times on the sports field, but what made him such a great team player was what he did in the shadows: blocking downfield, setting solid picks, and going after ground balls in football, basketball, and lacrosse, respectively.

Matt's outstanding academic and athletic performance did not go unnoticed. In his senior year he was named the Greater Baltimore Chapter National Football Foundation and Hall of Fame Scholar Athlete of the Year. When he took the podium, some people in the banquet hall might have wondered if the Gilman connection had influenced the voting, especially since Matt was the second Gilman student in two years to receive the prestigious award. To compound the implicit skepticism, the Gilman student who had won the previous year was the son of a United States Senator. Always the master of the understatement, Matt began his speech by saying that he would not bore the audience with endless platitudes. The body of the speech was vintage Matt Atkinson: witty, enlightening, unassuming, and gracious. He thanked his teachers and coaches for instilling in him "the belief that achievement was secondary to effort and the will to improve." By the end of the speech the skeptics had been converted. Nobody in that room could ignore the simple fact that Matt had won the award on merit alone.

Matt and I were committed Christians in high school and we would frequently pray and study the Bible together. One summer we attended a Christian camp in Martha's Vineyard sponsored by the Fellowship Of Christians in Universities and Schools (FOCUS). Our in-depth discussions of our mutual faith were complemented beautifully by the tranquility of our favorite pastime, tossing the pigskin. Playing catch with a well-worn football was more than recreation for us. It was one of the simple pleasures which made life worth living. Often, in my adult life, I have longed to see that old football spiraling towards me. But would I be able to toss it back again?

IMPROBABLE.

Though it could not have landed in more honorable hands, it was improbable that it found its way to him on that September day. Six years since we had graduated from Gilman in the spring of 1983. Friday, September 15, 1989. Matt was just 25 years old. My father telephoned me at my home in Chapel Hill, North Carolina, to tell me that Matt had died suddenly of a heart attack. Later the doctor would reveal that Matt was born with a heart defect.

I drove to Baltimore numb. The last time I had seen Matt was on May 16, 1987, when he surprised me by traveling many miles to attend my wedding in Edenton, North Carolina. People can drift away from each other as their interests change, but true friends are always there for one another at critical junctures.

My family and several close friends went to the Atkinsons' home after the funeral to console the family. I knew their pain would be stronger than my own. Matt came from a close-knit family. He and his sister Katie enjoyed a special friendship. Matt was also fond of his older brother John and his older sister Martha. He and his mother were inseparable. In fact, the last thing Matt wrote on his senior page in the 1983 *Cynosure* was: "Most of all, thanks, Mom, for being the most solid, supportive, and caring person I know."

Their bond was so strong. What could I possibly say to the Atkinson family to console them? Hurt and awkward, stumbling for the right words, I approached Mrs. Atkinson. In spite of her own grief and loss, she was able to sympathize with my uneasiness. Before I could say what I had rehearsed, she asked, "What can be said?" Mrs. Atkinson's ability to empathize with my discomfort beyond the pervading pain of her own grief reminded me of Matt's sensitivity to the hurts of others. He was one of the most gracious people I have ever known.

Freed from the dreadful burden of having to say the right thing, I shared openly the memories of the good times with Matt. I was not surprised when Mrs. Atkinson told me that Matt took losses harder as a prep school lacrosse coach than he did as a player. Undoubtedly, he was feeling the loss for every one of his players. Maybe it was only fair that we should have the opportunity to feel a loss for him.

Family, friends, co-workers, classmates from Gilman School and Princeton University, teachers, and others attended the memorial service. As we left the chapel after the service, many memories converged in my mind: slam dunks at Calvert School, the trophy, the Awesome Foursome Sophomoresome, Friday evening FOCUS meetings, the summer at Martha's Vineyard, the 1982 MSA "A" Conference Football Co-Championship, college visits with our mothers, hours of fellowship. I wondered if those memories would ever pay sufficient tribute to the true character and integrity of Matthew Smith Atkinson IV. I wondered if my reflections on our times together could possibly compare to the simple joy of tossing that old pigskin back to my good friend.

IMPROBABLE.

 E. Jerome Hughes began a full career as a student/athlete and community activist at Gilman in 1977, Seventh Grade. Early on, his interests swirled around the Bible, the global political landscape, the Romantic writers (Wordsworth and Coleridge) and African-American literature.

Nick Schloeder had a profound influence on Hughes, teaching him history and coaching him in football and baseball. Reg Tickner (English) was Hughes' favorite teacher.

Hughes held leadership positions in the Student Council, Human Relations Committee, Fellowship of Christian Athletes, Black Awareness Club, and Operation Green Grass. He played three years of varsity football, two years of varsity basketball, and three years of varsity baseball.

In his senior year, Hughes was the U. S. Senate-Japan Youth for Understanding Scholar, a Morehead Scholar, and the U. S. Student Representative at the 1983 Williamsburg Summit.

He attended the University of North Carolina at Chapel Hill where he majored in English, "watched Michael Jordan sky, slam, and jam," and "dreamed that I could do the same."

Married and with two children, Hughes lives in Asheville, North Carolina, where he is pastor of The Lord's Church of Asheville. Hughes teaches the Bible, and engages in Personal Evangelism—talking to individuals about the saving grace of Jesus Christ—as well as Multicultural Ministry: "going out into the sea of humanity with a net to draw people from every nationality and socio-economic background, rather than with a line, targeting a certain group of people." He is a believer in outdoor evangelism—street preaching, community crusades, passing out Christian tracts, and ministering to the physical and spiritual needs of the lost and dying.

Hughes plans to continue loving God with all his heart, mind, strength and soul, and to love his neighbors as himself. His dream is to "birth" children of the ministry—apostles, prophets, evangelists, pastors, teachers and missionaries who will spread the Word.

Gilman and Memory

ANTON VISHIO '85

It all begins with Gilman—at least for me. By this I mean that my earliest conscious memories presuppose a Gilman context. This is unsurprising, since I was not quite two when my family—my father, entering his fourth year teaching Latin and Greek, expectant mother, younger brother, and I—moved on campus in 1969; but even with the best efforts of numerous baby pictures and home movies I have not yet been able to recapture, or indeed imagine, a life previous to that of our first campus home, 5407 B Roland Avenue, just behind Headmaster Finney's house. Nor do I remember seeing Gilman for the first time, although this experience certainly predated our moving there—but this is also understandable, because at that age one sees so much for the first time, not knowing what experiences to mark as valuable for retention. But these gaps in my self-history, these reference points lost, have conspired to give Gilman a peculiar pride-of-place in my psyche.

Simply put, Gilman marks for me not merely a plot of land, a bounded region of space, but also a limit to my memory; for me, beyond Gilman there is only not-being.

I do not mean for this recollection to seem hyperdramatized; we all have hazy limits to our memories. Yet, this is only a fragment of my story; here I want to provide a meditation on what it means to have an institution, particularly one as complex as Gilman—simultaneously school and playground, parochial neighborhood and broad-minded community, home and historic presence—as the backdrop and very substance of one's formative years. This leads to another aspect of my Gilman origins: growing up in, at, and around Gilman has prepared me for a life of negotiating personal definition from within institutions of one stripe or another. I am a classically-trained musician, and much of what I do—as composer or as interpreter of works in the classical canon—often seems impossibly burdened by the awesome weight of what has been accomplished before me.

One attempts to carve out a space for one's own creative work, but the tradition budges slowly, if at all; it is a challenge to develop a sense of self, to make a contribution which is identifiably one's own. This daily confrontation is far more oppressive than anything that has shaped my Gilman experience; nonetheless, these early interactions with establishment pressures have helped me immeasurably in understanding where the dangers of such encounters lie for the individual.

I have grown up with a childhood memory that is at once personal and reluctantly institutional. The slightest change in Gilman's geography is enough to disturb countless places in my remembrances, dislodging the meaning and substance of my past and therefore of my present. There is clearly a tension here between competing desires of continuity and invariance, between that which must adjust itself to match changing reality, and that which holds fast to unchanging identity. The source of the tension is this: Gilman evokes in me a timelessness.

It is no simple matter to describe exactly in what consists this impression—at any rate, a subjective phenomenon such as timelessness is hard to make precise. The school has, of course, always been extremely conscious of its own history; indeed, there is ample evidence for this preoccupation throughout the plaques and photos in the Carey Building, in the memorial to Lewis Omer Woodward affixed to the auditorium's front, in the numerous awards for athletic achievement that used to line the corridors of the old gym. But this commemoration of the past in itself is not sufficient for the aura I have in mind, since no archival display can faithfully convey the condition of that which it archives. The sober appearance of the buildings and the immaculate fields are more to the point, as these structures seem to be able to contradict the changing seasons of progressing years.

I admit that timelessness has its internal generators as well, and these are most important. For me, they include not just a literal sense of the word—what I might describe as "time-less-ness" or the quality of being without time—in that, as I have recounted above, Gilman is the point beyond which my memory will not go and thus my time sense will not carry me. Timelessness exists also in my perceptions and recollections of the ageless faculty members, friends of my family, who are integral parts of my past, one-time teachers or neighbors—Roy Barker, Charles Gamper, John Merrill, George Chandlee, E. E. Thompson, Redmond Finney, R. Bruce Daniels. These people contributed to my complicated picture of Gilman, and my notion of Gilman's timelessness, as composed of a plurality of aspects, of people and place and history.

It is this timelessness of Gilman that still affects me. Whenever I return to find a shift in the terrain, be it a newly erected fence, or a newly renovated building, the sense of timelessness has been violated; I am troubled by my resulting insecurity, stemming from the confusion of memory denied. Initially, the desire for continuity, seems to aright the situation; the novelty is quickly reined in, and my internal map of Gilman replaces the old with the new. The result, however, becomes stubbornly regimented. The change has, as it were, become the tradition, and the former state becomes irretrievable to the conscious mind, as if there never were a change, as if the current institution were as before. Thus, I know that the Middle

School was constructed in the early 1970s, and well I remember the noise and commotion of building that awoke us seemingly every morning before 6:00 one summer. Yet lost to me is the grove of trees that was there before; I've searched long for it within my memory banks and found it wanting. When we moved onto the campus, the modern Northern Parkway was still the dream of an urban planner, and the massive wall that stretches from the Lower School to the north entrance to the campus, the wall upon which we played hours of wall ball as kids, was not yet constructed; however, I cannot recall there not being a barrier there, so starkly it imposes itself as a boundary. Examples of the struggle over memory continue; with the recent construction of the Finney Athletic Center, I have found the need great to resist forgetting the structures which have been replaced, so as to safeguard more of my rememberings.

I want to point out this alarming power institutions can have on our self-histories—and it is indeed alarming the way I have let institutional concerns control my own perceptions. Nevertheless, I do not look upon myself as being in the situation of Dwight Robbins, the president of Benton College in Randall Jarrell's comedy *Pictures from an Institution*, of whom it was observed that he "was so well adjusted to his environment that sometimes you could not tell which was the environment and which was President Robbins." Nor do I have a desire to criticize Gilman for plotting to deprive me of my youth (although I can think of times not relevant to this essay—particularly those during frustrating homework assignments—that the thought had occurred to me . . .). Growing up on campus had its glorious side. There was the wonderful illusion that the fields and gym, when devoid of practices and games, were ours, so that I and my comrades among the campus kids—in particular my brother Alex, Jeff Taggart, Niki Greene, later David Neun and Anthony Pletcher (an honorary campus kid and fellow faculty son)—could while away the summer hours playing interminable three-on-two baseball games, the fall weekends playing touch football, the winter doldrums playing basketball in the gym. By pointing out the complex relationship between an individual and a multifaceted entity such as Gilman, I only wish that we should be aware of the dangers in the interaction, the need to keep clear where the boundaries between them lie—and then we might revel in our collective memories, made all the more fertile by the resultant diversity.

Entering Gilman in the Fourth Grade, Anton Vishio soon found his major intellectual interests to be music, French, Latin, and religion, and his favorite teacher (excluding his father, Anton Sr., Gilman classics scholar and teacher) to be music teacher John Merrill.

In the Upper School, Vishio belonged to the Band, the Fellowship for Christian Athletes, the Areopagus/Pnyx Debating Society, and the Human Relations Committee. He ran J.V. and varsity track and cross country.

As a junior, Vishio was a co-winner of the Caruso Music Award; in his senior year, he won it outright, along with the Daniel Baker, Jr. Award.

Vishio majored in music at Princeton, continuing his interests in linguistics and philosophy. He was awarded a Mellon Fellowship to pursue graduate study at Harvard University. He has been active as a freelance chamber musician. From 1993 to 1995, he played the organ and directed the choir at a Massachusetts church. Over the summer of 1996, he was finishing his thesis for his doctorate in music theory from Harvard and preparing to begin his first full-time teaching position at Washington University in St. Louis.*

*Anton Vishio notes, "I wish to thank Ellie Hisama and my classmate Steve Howard for their perceptive criticisms of an earlier draft, and my father, Anton Vishio, Sr., for that and the inspiration to write the essay in the first place."

First Grade

GREGORY PAUL LEE '86

With a focus of mind and purpose that would have rivaled that of the most anal-retentive of accountants, I hold my gaze steady and straightforward, careful to keep it intelligent, informed, yet obedient and properly respectful. My right hand presses flat against my left hand, each finger matching the other, hoping to realize a physiological symmetry. To an ignorant outsider, I am praying, but my straight back, perfect posture, and forward stare speak otherwise. I am one of 22 First Grade students in Mrs. McDonald's class 1A in the moments before being dismissed for lunch and recess. We are competing for the honor of being the first to be dismissed and the selection is based on nothing less than the maintenance of perfect posture, silence, and true academic poise. My best friend this week, Robby Frazier, whispers something to me. Of course I know better than to respond but, of course, I do.

"Yeah, I wanna play Four Square at recess."

"Gregory?" Inside, I panic and feel the pressure of stress such as a six-year-old can feel.

"Yes, Mrs. McDonald?"

"Is there anything which you would like to share with the rest of the class?" I do not see her bemused and benign smile; I am too busy swallowing the disappointment of having been caught by the Teacher.

"No, Mrs. McDonald." My conscience registers the first-grade equivalent of *mea culpa* (it is not until eight years later, of course, when the *sagita amicaque* Mr. Vishio leads us on Julius Caesar's romp through Gaul, that my super conscience replaces "caught" with the better-dressed Latin). Guilt is soon replaced by a sense of injustice. But, it's not my fault, it's Robby's fault, I think at her, but she does not hear my thoughts. Mrs. McDonald looks at me and for a moment, I feel that she has heard me and in fact understands what has happened.

It seemed that my First Grade time was like that. Mrs. McDonald was an all-knowing, caring, and communicating Adult. She helped me face certain issues that were to arrive in my life on a recurring basis, each time like a big wave that would sometimes catch me unawares and knock me down, and other times merely spray me with salt water.

"Mrs. McDonald?" It is minutes before the end of recess, and I am the only one back in the classroom. Before entering, I check my shirttail and my shoelaces.

"Gregory." It is a statement of assurance that said she knew from the look on my face and the tone of my address that although I thought that something was wrong, in fact everything was all right.

"Mrs. McDonald . . . "

"Gregory."

"Mrs. McDonald . . . " Speaking her name must be giving me strength. "*They* called me Chinese." I look at her defiantly. I am upset, though I am not sure why, other than that it was easy to tell that they were calling me names, and not just names, but names which were specific to me. I like to think that if they had called me "Stupid" or "Sissy" or "Dummy" I would be less offended, if only because I could easily rebut their insults with the like. "Oh yeah? *You're* a Dummy. Ha!"

Mrs. McDonald looks at me and says, "Oh, Gregory." She takes my hands and immediately takes measure of the extent of my pain. I bear no tears, but instead righteous anger and indignation.

"You are not Chinese, are you?" I do not think that her question is relevant. I am impatient for her to strike down the guilty ones with the wrath and thunder that can only belong to the Teacher.

"No, I'm Korean." I think about this for a moment. "I'm American also. But, Mrs. McDonald . . . " I struggle to get her back on track, focused on the real issue here . . . punishment. "Gregory, what other people call you is not important. What you call yourself is . . . " (In my mind, I understand what she is going to say and replay a recording of my mother's take on the issue: Greg, you are a very special boy and they are just jealous of you. "They are? Are you sure?" Their jealousy is not intuitive to me. Why would they be jealous of me?) ". . . what is important. Your Korean background gives you something special and unique which you should be proud of. There will be people in life who will not understand or appreciate this, and they may call you names. However, if you are nice and follow the Golden Rule and treat others with respect, then it doesn't matter what others say. A good person never has anything to be shamed about. I think that you are a good boy, and I am proud to have you as one of my students."

Just then, I hear a loud, thunderous rumble, which sounds to my ears like a stampede of Triceratops (my favorite dino at the time). A huge gray giant rumbles into the classroom. "Hello there, Mrs. McDonald. How are you doing? And, how about you, sir? How are you?" I recognize this man with the Superman build, the Hulk-sized handshake, and the big smile. He is the one who taught us about the differences between the First Class Citizen, the Second Class Citizen, and the dreaded Third Class Citizen. I know that I'm not a First Class Citizen yet (judging from the messy state of my room at home) and fear that he will ask.

"Hello, Mr. Finney. We are doing just fine here. This is Gregory Lee, one of my students."

"Well, hello there, young man." I know the cue and accordingly thrust out my hand only to see it and a good portion of my wrist and forearm engulfed by the giant's handshake.

"Hello, Mr. Finney."

The Head of the combined Lower, Middle and Upper Schools is an important Adult whose huge athletic frame seems appropriate to the Olympian task and duties of his job. Even as little First Graders, we are aware of the legends which surround Mr. Finney—a Gilman student himself, a heroic football player, wrestler, and lacrosse player, the kind of student who would always get check-pluses with stickers. Our contributions to the early deification of Mr. Finney are as natural to us as the natural acknowledgment of Brooks Robinson, Johnny Unitas, and Jim Palmer in the pantheon of our Heroes.

As Mr. Finney leaves and the sound of Triceratops rumbling through the Lower School fades away, I look up at Mrs. McDonald and wonder how she had treated Mr. Finney as a First Grader. No doubt that Mr. Finney was never called names and never needed recourse to the Teacher to resolve disputes with the other kids.

"Gregory, are you okay?"

"Yes, Mrs. McDonald."

"Always remember, Gregory, that you are what you make of yourself and no one can change that. I cannot wait until the day when you will come back and visit me as a tall, young gentleman who has done well in school, gone to college . . . "

"And medical school, too!" I interject as though some Pavlovian stimulus has prompted me to speak out.

"Yes, and medical school. I will be so proud of you, just as I am now."

Mrs. McDonald reaches into her desk and pulls out one of the treasures of the Realm, one of two currencies which had any value among my classmates and me, a Lifesaver candy roll, and offers me one (The other currency was a French fry from the cafeteria, and I am not sure Mrs. McDonald approved of that currency). I accept it, aware of the honor, and sense that the conversation is over. I do not feel so bad any more and in fact, feel no malice towards those who were my enemies only minutes before. In fact, I think that one or more of them probably filed their way into my best friend cycles at some point during the school year. The school bell rings and the other First Graders start to come in from recess. I excitedly tell them I had spotted Mr. Finney, and we attempt to outdo each other in extolling his strength. Meanwhile, our local Hero and surrogate Mother moves about the room admonishing us to tuck in our shirttails and tie our shoes. Noting the particularly dirty and sweaty-faced of us, she sends us to the washroom. My crisis seems to be over for now as my mind leaps to other issues.

Mrs. McDonald was always there for us. Five quick years later, when I was a big Fifth Grader in Mr. Schmick's class, she came and heard me deliver the graduation speech for Class 5B. "My, Gregory, you did a wonderful job. I am so proud of you.

Look how you've grown." It did not occur to me that she had taken care of four classes of First Graders since me. To me she was still the Teacher, the original Teacher who seemed to impart as much importance to us individually as students as we did to her.

In the 12 years of Gilman, four years of liberal arts at college, and seven-plus years of investment banking that so far have defined my learning curve of life, my mind and my heart point to the early, formative years of my education as the foundation of my belief system. Though it was a simple world of bad and good, heroes and enemies, the lessons first painted there for me have lasted and endured modifications, denials, yes even the liberal Eastern Establishment Elite and the stress of Wall Street.

Mrs. McDonald, whose responsibility it was to teach us our ABC's and 1,2,3's, cared for us and taught us far more. Mrs. McDonald retired in 1994, having shepherded her 24th class of six and seven-year-olds through their first year of the Gilman Experience.* Her dedication and her humanity were part of the Gilman Experience for everyone who had the honor of sitting in her classroom, and the extraordinary legacy of her love for students and Gilman will be part of the Gilman Experience forevermore.

*Mrs. McDonald's retirement did not last long. She was back in the Lower School classroom, working part-time, immediately after her retirement, and in the academic year 1996–97, was the favorite teacher of many a Gilman Lower Schooler.

Gregory Paul Lee attended Gilman 1974 to 1986. His main intellectual interests during those years were history, Latin, and math, while his favorite teachers were Mrs. McDonald in the Lower School, Mr. Culbertson (math) in the Middle School, and Mr. Vishio (Latin) in the Upper School.

Lee wrote for the Gilman *News* and was a member of the Student Council and Asian Awareness Club. He was inducted into the Junior Cum Laude Society, won the Brown University Book Award, received the Thomas Hardie Scholarship, and was a three-year member of both the varsity baseball and soccer teams, captain of the soccer team and winner of the Dr. Phillip Whittlesey Soccer Trophy his senior year. Weekends often found him wheeling and dealing in the baseball-card trade.

Attending Harvard, Lee majored in government while retaining the active interest in community service he developed at Gilman. He played on the varsity volleyball team. After graduation, he worked at TTG Capital in New York and Capstar Partners in Hong Kong in structural finance before moving on to Salomon Brothers Inc, where he is a vice-president in the Capital Markets Products Group, travelling throughout the United States and Europe. Lee married his college sweetheart, Gina, in 1996; they live in New York.

Gilman Changed the Course of My Life

KEEFE CLEMONS '85

Gilman was unlike anything that I had experienced in my brief life. The cute little brick primary school, the playground, the Country Store, the large green fields; all of these struck a sharp contrast to my Sandtown-Winchester neighborhood in West Baltimore. Gilman was a beautiful place, in the rather idyllic setting of Roland Park. While I did not realize it at age seven when I entered the First Grade at Gilman, this school would change the course of my life.

I spent 12 years at Gilman. Looking back, I have fond memories of my experience. Gilman, however, was not Camelot, or nirvana, or any other place that is totally free of troubles or worries. The Gilman I encountered in 1973 was a school that was struggling to adjust to its increasing diversity. The first black students did not graduate from the school until the late '60s, long after the Supreme Court decision *Brown vs. Board of Education.*

While integration at Gilman was not accompanied by violence or massive protests, there were hostilities which played themselves out at a more personal level. Having grown up in a neighborhood that was completely homogeneous, nearly 100 percent black, I had never been the target of racial slurs. This would change when I arrived at Gilman. A school-yard disagreement could easily end up with a classmate calling me "nigger." Ultimately, we would both end up in the principal's office, explaining what had happened.

What was impressive to me was the way in which the school handled these racial conflicts. While teachers and administrators emphasized it was wrong to fight, they made it clear that they would not tolerate racism of any kind at the school, and punished kids who used racial slurs, regardless of the target. The school, in my experience, was committed to achieving diversity, believed in educational equality, though it was by no means perfect. This was at once comforting and empowering to me. The school made it clear to me that I would be given an equal chance to achieve and excel there, and that its expectations for all of its students were equal. Because of the school's commitment, I was able to become a fully participating member of the student body, and contribute to it. A significant force behind the school's commitment to diversity was the leadership and drive of its headmaster at that time, Redmond C.S. Finney.

Mr. Finney was an impressive man. I first met him shortly after my arrival at the school. He was tall, slightly graying, athletic, and friendly. He emphasized the importance of a firm handshake and good eye contact. To a seven-year-old most adults are impressive, but my view of Mr. Finney would continue as I grew in to adulthood. It was rumored, and I have yet to confirm this, that Mr. Finney was in the *Book of Lists* as one of two people in history to be All-American in lacrosse and football.* Regardless of the truth or falsity of this rumor, it was believable. He was a person who practiced and preached honor, social responsibility, and general consideration. While walking across campus, he could often be seen picking up a random piece of trash that someone had carelessly dropped. On one of the few occasions when I saw him really angry and saddened, a few students had been caught cheating on a quiz. As he lectured the class, he was shaking. It was clear to me that an honor violation of this type hurt him to his heart, given his tremendous faith in and commitment to the student body at the school.

It was through the leadership of Mr. Finney that Gilman was transformed from what was traditionally a white, Protestant school, to one with a much more diverse student body. He personally pushed for need-based financial aid to help students who were economically disadvantaged.

My experience at Gilman, however, was not merely shaped by Mr. Finney's leadership and the school's struggle to deal with its increasing diversity. There were many dedicated teachers who made the educational experience at once challenging and memorable. One of these teachers was Nick Schloeder. I only took one subject with Mr. Schloeder, United States History Since 1945. It was, however, one of the most memorable of my courses at the school. Mr. Schloeder was an imposing man. He was the kind of man who would have commanded respect merely by his physical presence, but whose intellect alone merited it. His command of the subject matter was clear, whether he was discussing the Vietnam War or sharing an interesting and educational "war story" relating to his personal experiences campaigning for Senator Sarbanes. His ability to "personalize" a political or historical issue made learning history fun and relevant.

Athletics was also an important part of my Gilman experience. I learned a

---

*True. Graduating from Gilman in 1947, Reddy Finney went to Princeton, where he majored in religion. He stuck with his Gilman athletic formula of football, wrestling, lacrosse, becoming the only athlete—with the exception of the professional running back Jim Brown—to become an All-American in two sports in one academic year, football and lacrosse.

tremendous amount about hard work, perseverance, discipline, sportsmanship, teamwork, and leadership, through my participation in athletics, in particular, track and field. I began running competitively in the Middle School in Sixth Grade. Paul Killibrew, the Middle School head, was our coach at that time. We were exposed to almost all of the events in track and field. One day we would run a mile for time. The next day we would attempt to pole vault. The next day we would sprint 100 yards. The end of the season culminated in the Middle School Decathlon. This multi-day event provided each of us with an opportunity to take our awkward little bodies through all of the events which we had practiced so diligently throughout the short season.

Track and field was awesome. I enjoyed the competition and I enjoyed winning. Indeed, I enjoyed it so much that I managed to convince Mr. Killibrew and the Upper School Coach Jack Thompson to allow me to compete on the junior varsity team when I was still an Eighth Grader. As the "baby" on the Upper School team, I did not win often, but I was able to be competitive. The older boys were very supportive, and I learned a tremendous amount from them. Robbie Harrell, Tim Robinson, Chuck Wilder, Doug Riley, Ben McCoy, and other varsity team athletes took me under their wing, harassing me at times, encouraging me at others. It is in part due to their encouragement that I would continue to participate in track and field into my college years and beyond.

The one individual at Gilman who, without question, had the most significant impact on my track and field career was Joseph Duncan. Both on and off the track, Joe Duncan is an impressive person. As an adviser, he provided great personal insights into a broad range of issues and life in general. As a coach, he was a sage who helped me overcome numerous physical injuries and develop the training and knowledge which I would need to excel in the sport. He helped me develop self-confidence. Indeed, I can recall numerous times when I was unsure of my ability to out-run a particular opponent. I would share these uncertainties with Mr. Duncan. At the end of those conversations, I often felt a bit silly. Mr. Duncan's confidence in my ability made me realize that if I ran as hard as I was capable of running, I could win.

Eventually, I internalized this confidence. What I learned from Joe Duncan helped me in later years win several state and collegiate track and field titles in the 800 meters. More importantly, Mr. Duncan was a role model. Not only as a coach, but as a teacher. He has taught Spanish and French to hundreds of Gilman students for almost 20 years. While I did not have the benefit of taking his language class, I have received rave reviews from those who have. This does not surprise me in the least. In many ways, Joseph Duncan, the scholar-athlete, epitomized many of the characteristics which Gilman seeks to inspire in all of its students: academic excellence, social responsibility, honor, integrity, and leadership.

What will the future hold for Gilman School? I hope that Gilman will continue to pursue its mission of preparing young men to be socially responsible leaders and that Gilman will strive to maintain its diversity, even as others begin to lose sight of its importance. I look forward to watching, and participating where possible, as Gilman strides forward into the 21st Century.

Keefe B. Clemons was a 12-year-man at Gilman. His mentor through those years was Joe Duncan, head of the foreign language department and track and field coach. In the Upper School, Clemons was a prefect, a member of the Black Awareness Club, the Traveling Men, the School Band (saxophone) and the Dramatic Club. He ran varsity track and field as well as cross country, winning the Alfred H. Weems, Jr. Track and Field Award at graduation. In addition, he was the recipient of the Fenimore Award.

Clemons attended Princeton, where he majored in International Affairs and Public Policy while maintaining a scholarly interest in urban affairs. Clemons was a five-time Heptagonal Track and Field Champion (800 meters) and an Intercollegiate 4A Track and Field Champion (800 meters). He was team captain in 1989.

Studying philosophy, politics, and economics at Oxford University as a Sachs Scholarship Recipient, Clemons received his master's degree in 1991. In 1994, he graduated from Harvard Law School.

Keefe Clemons is currently an attorney for Hogan & Hartson, L.L.P., specializing in business litigation and education law. In 1995, he began a term of service on the executive committee of the Gilman Alumni Association.

Vociferous Incantations, Sarcastic Barrages, and Death-defying Duelists

ANDREW D. MARTIRE '89

T he psyche—the mind, body, and spirit—of the Gilman student develops through his emulation of Gilman teachers and coaches, and if he enjoys athletics, through the sports into which he pours his passion. In my case, there were three mentor/models, and two sports.

By the late 1980s, Redmond C.S. Finney had been headmaster for 20 years. All students of that era cite him as a major influence in their Gilman experience. The revered Mr. Finney was everywhere, leading a religion class, picking up trash on all corners of the campus, and cheering wildly at sporting events. Students sitting next to Mr. Finney at a game should have been issued protective gear to guard against the headmaster's flailings and vociferous incantations. At football pep rallies, Ted McKeldin '86 was able to perform a striking Mr. Finney imitation, right down to the trademark grey suit and "geezy peezy" mannerisms. Ted's dramatics never failed to leave the student body, as well as Mr. Finney, rolling with laughter. In chapel, mere singing was not adequate for Mr. Finney. He demanded that we deliver the hymns with intense, passionate fervor. If Mr. Finney judged our first verse efforts insufficient, he would briefly halt the music and in his low voice, demand, "Come on, fellas, that's just not loud enough. I know you can do better." Mr. John Merrill, cut off in mid-note, would resume his expert piano playing as the auditorium shook with 400 suddenly energized, booming voices, each student trying to be louder than the next. No one wanted to disappoint Mr. Finney in the classroom, on the athletic field, or in chapel. He holds a special place in my heart and in those of the thousands who graduated during his tenure as headmaster.

Mr. Anton Vishio, Sr. has been a Gilman institution since the late 1960s. As the guru of the Classics department, he has guided countless students through the complexities of Latin and Greek. His devotion to community service as faculty director of the Fellowship of Christian Athletes (FCA) has been remarkable. If a student or member of the community needs help in any respect, Mr. Vishio delivers. As a shrewd Gilmanite, I did not subject myself to the rigors of Latin, but I did have the good fortune to have Mr. Vishio as an adviser for four years. At adviser-advisee meetings, his barrage of humorous sarcasm spared no student, seniors included. When Mr. Vishio distributed report cards, we advisees laughed with glee as he systematically poked fun at each student, regardless of his academic performance. I laughed heartily until it was my turn to be scrutinized, and then I braced for the attack.

Mr. Vishio offered me a plethora (good SAT word, Mr. V.!) of wise academic and athletic advice, but his best recommendation dealt with my social life. In a conference with my parents, he informed them, "My daughter Eva is the perfect girl for Andy." The matchmaker did not know then how correct he was: Eva and I were married in April, 1995. Mr. Vishio, now my father-in-law, still often greets me by asking, "How is my advisee doing?" Readers will be pleased to know that Mr. Vishio acts in the same joke-a-minute mode at home as at school. Family dinners at the Vishios' have provided some of the funniest, happiest moments of my life.

Dr. Mercer Neale, currently headmaster at Boys' Latin School, held a multitude of positions in his long term of excellent service at Gilman. While serving on the Student Council, I had close contact with Dr. Neale, then Head of the Upper School. There was no problem too small or large that he could not attack and solve effectively. Moreover, I had the pleasure of having Dr. Neale as my U.S. history teacher during my junior year. He had a special talent enabling him to draw students into the material so they felt as if they were actually at the event he was describing. Whether it was reenacting the Aaron Burr/Alexander Hamilton duel or exaggerating his slight southern accent into a full drawl to simulate the emotion of Robert E. Lee or J.E.B. Stuart, Dr. Neale transported the class to past eras with unparalleled skill. During my Cooper Fellowship year, one of my assignments was to teach a section of Eleventh Grade U.S. history. Dr. Neale took me under his wing, provided me with voluminous amounts of material, and met with me on demand. His help and advice ensured that I would succeed.

Many a Gilman graduate's longest-lasting memories reflect back to athletic contests. Certain games and plays are embedded in my memory and are as vivid now as when they occurred almost a decade ago. One of these moments involves Matt Eastwick '88, one of Gilman's greatest basketball players. When Matt graduated, he was the school's all-time leading scorer and rebounder. He started for four years at Princeton and captained the team as a senior. In Matt's senior year (my junior year) at Gilman, the "Spiderman" led us to a 22–7 record. While his varied offensive repertoire included outside jump shots, his thunderous dunks were definitely the fan favorites. In a fast-break situation during a game at Carver, Matt dribbled the ball over half court, drove hard toward the basket, and delivered a monster two-handed dunk over a hapless defender. I erupted from my seat, screaming and exchanging high fives with my equally excited teammates. We then looked to the Carver bench, expecting to see long faces. To our shock, they were whooping, hollering, and giving high fives as well! In another game that season, Matt scored over 30 points to carry us to a 56–52 victory over McDonogh in the roaring, ear-splitting "Deafdome." The Finney Athletic Center is a beautiful facility for basketball, but it will never rock like the Old Gym in the "Deafdome Era."

Although the football team, my senior year, produced one of the poorest records in recent years, some good memories from that season do exist. In the second-to-last game of the year, we played at Loyola on a field that had been pushed past saturation by days of rain. It was quickly evident that the contest would be a mud bowl, which was a dream to me and my fellow hogs along the offensive line. The team later discovered that Coach Sherm Bristow's extra-stern game face was a result of an inflamed appendix waiting to burst. At one point in the close game, Jimmy Schmidt '89 was set to return a punt. Jimmy had good hands, but the fact that my 40-yard dash time as a lineman was the same as his time as a receiver/defensive back indicates what kind of speed he possessed. We expected Jim to field the punt, lumber a few steps in the slop, and fall down. In a play that unfolded in super-slow motion, he caught the kick, evaded tackler after tackler, weaved his way down our sideline, and somehow ended up in the end zone 60 to 70 yards later. Jim's touchdown return was one of the most unbelievable, improbable plays I have ever seen. A classic picture taken after the game shows about 10 of us, covered head to toe with mud, jersey numbers indistinguishable, grinning ear to ear, reveling in our 23–20 victory over the Dons.

While I was away at college, my family kept me abreast of developments at "The Tech."* Moreover, summer workouts in preparation for the football season brought me to campus frequently. Now, as a teacher and coach, my affiliation with the school has entered a new phase, and I have the opportunity to try to help young men as Gilman teachers and coaches assisted me just a few short years ago. I welcome and love the challenges that each school day presents. The breakthrough for a Fifth Grader in fractions, the excitement and anxiety of a class play, the laughter at a faculty meeting, the one-point victory over an arch rival, and the heart-breaking last-second defeat all create a unique environment for students and teachers alike.

From the day I entered the Seventh Grade in the fall of 1983, Gilman School has played an integral role in my life. Although my relationship with the school has changed as I have progressed from student to alumnus to faculty member, my positive feelings remain unchanged. In my six years as a student, Gilman instilled in me a strong sense of values while providing a topnotch education. The friendships and experiences I acquired in those years will last a lifetime.

---

*This nickname, and term of affection, evolved from "Gillie Tech" in the early 1980s into "The Tech."

History teacher Mercer Neale, adviser Anton Vishio, and English teacher John Schmick were all important influences on Andrew Martire during his six years as a student at Gilman, along with Francis "Biff" Poggi, who coached Martire in football.

Class and student-body president, Martire was also vice-president of the Fellowship of Christian Athletes and executive editor of the Gilman *News* during his senior year. His academic interests were in history and English, while football and basketball filled his afternoons. Martire was a Sunpapers All-Metro varsity football player in 1988 and captain of the varsity basketball team 1988–89. Upon graduation, he was awarded the William A. Fisher Medallion.

Attending Princeton University, Martire majored in political science. He played varsity football and was a member of the 1992 Ivy League Championship Team.

In 1993, Martire began teaching as a Cooper Fellow at Gilman. He now teaches in the Lower School, Homeroom 5A, along the same hallway with the homerooms of John Xanders '77 and William Merrick '51. Fall and winter afternoons find Martire with either a football or basketball in his hands: he is head coach of the fresh-soph football and basketball squads. In the summers, he teaches U.S. history, high-school level, in the Gilman Summer School.

Andrew Martire is married to Eva Vishio Martire. His half-brother, Hal Turner, and his mother, Ivana Turner, both came to Gilman in the fall of 1995, Hal as a Third Grader, Ivana Turner as the college counselor.

Three Titans

A . J . D O W N S

As one who never heard of Gilman until he happened to drop by one day, then decided to teach there for a year while he decided what he wanted to be when he grew up—and woke up 40 years later to find that he was about to retire as senior master—this writer has had many opportunities to go elsewhere, and dealt with hundreds of incredulous questions like this one: "Do you mean to tell me that this is the only job you ever had?"

It was—and I used to ask myself, from time to time, why I never seriously considered trying anything else. It took me until the last five years or so of my time at Gilman to see that the answer was so obvious that I had not even bothered to put it into words: If you have a chance to work for Callard, Baldwin, and Finney, why on this patient earth would you imagine doing anything else?

They were titans, each in his own way, each so profoundly influential that I simply cannot imagine what I would be like as a person without their pervasive impact on values and personality. I like to think of them as Washington, Adams, and Jefferson—with the same defining impact on the school's history as the others had on the country, the same skyline-dominating loom as their namesake White Mountains.

There were giants in those days; their shadows stretch as far into the future as we can see . . .

HENRY CALLARD
Headmaster, 1943–1963

There was not a lot of money lying around in the '50s for professional development, so the faculty didn't spend much time at conferences and workshops. But we got around, one way and another, and fell into the usual bull sessions with our peers at other schools.

Topic Number One in those sessions was always the same: life at Ivy Prep or

Midwest Country Day, especially as that life was interfered with or made altogether intolerable by the current head (who was usually rumored to be on his way out, or up, or down).

The Gilman members of such groups (as I remember from personal experience, and as I have heard from dozens of others) fell silent as such orgies of complaint and insurrection waxed, increasingly uncomfortable at the realization that, sooner or later, we would have to respond to the inevitable question: "Well, Downs (or Porter, or Gamper, or Barker), tell us about that incompetent Callard at Gilman."

And we would do the best we could, mumbling something about how the kids loved him and . . . well, we thought he was just about the finest man we had ever known, and we couldn't imagine working for anyone else. And one of the gripers would comment derisively that it must be wonderful to work for a saint.

And of course the griper was right. He *was* a saint; and, since saints are no more common in headmaster's offices than they are anywhere else, we had no success at all in trying to tell other people what it was like to work for one. More than that: had we ever dared to hint, anywhere in the said saint's actual vicinity, that we had any such idea about him, he would have been embarrassed, mortified, possibly even angry (though none of us could remember a single occasion when he had ever shown anger at any of us, whatever the provocation).

How do you know a saint when you see one? How did we *know* Henry Callard was one? He was not imposing physically; few saints are, or were. He was not a powerful speaker; the voice was rather high and thin. He would not have been rated above average as an administrator, a manager. He lost things. He was all but incapable of rebuking anyone. He was a great teacher, but he was quick to admit that he had no idea how to help other teachers do better . . .

But when you were in the same room with him, the world looked better. As we recollect him—those who were teachers and students when he walked the earth with us—we remember plodding down the long hall toward "A" study hall, convinced that we had just taught the most inane lesson in the history of education; or dragging back from the gym with the burden of the lost J.V. championship heavy on our shoulders; or on the way to the exam we knew we could not pass; and there he was, with a word or a touch or a smile, and—I have to use this word—we were healed.

The word *charisma* is so over-used it is all but worthless, but if it ever applied to anyone, it applied to Henry Callard. And here is what it meant: You simply could not do less than your best, teacher or student, for him. It was not necessarily easy to be in Henry Callard's Gilman, but it was inspiring; better, use the older form: *inspiriting*. No one, least of all he himself, had the slightest idea how he did it, but he simply *gave* you his spirit, in-spirited you.

A visitor from Britain, confused about where the school office was, asked directions, one day, of a white-haired fellow raking leaves in front of the main building; he was genuinely shocked to find that it was the headmaster. There were certain things, he felt, that headmasters simply did not do. This headmaster, we sometimes thought, was happiest doing the simplest, lowliest tasks. If he had a real soul-mate, it was probably John Krizek, one-time junk dealer, then Gilman's building and grounds superintendent, and one of the two or three certifiable geniuses the school has sheltered. The two of them heard about a barracks the Army was offering free to anyone who would cart it off. They rented a truck, took the building apart, brought it back, and gleefully set it up again. Kids used it for 20 years (It was called The Craft Shop), but none of them enjoyed it as much as those two handymen enjoyed assembling it.

In a time when politicians can't wait to blame somebody, anybody, for anything that goes wrong, it is fascinating to remember Henry Callard. If it happened at Gilman, he was responsible; he would have it no other way. If some callow rookie forgot his study hall duty, it was the headmaster who took it. I went by one day, saw him up there on the dais in "A" and offered to take over. Oh no, he said, it's quiet in here, no phone, and I can get a lot done. (The kids, squirming and spitballing for anybody else, were silent as tombs; they might not want to do their own work, but they would not dream of interfering with his.)

About once a month, he would ease up long enough to sit down with some of us after lunch in the dining room (now the library) and chat. He was an enthusiastic mimic and would "do" some parent or other headmaster, then laugh until tears rolled down his cheeks. "Honest to truth," he would gasp, "honest to truth."

I wrote a little farce of a play about Gilman, including a bit part for Callard playing Callard. He was terrible; he got laughing so hard waiting offstage for his cue that he couldn't say his lines.

In May each year, he would take his teachers aside, one by one, and tell us how much he valued us, depended on us. On one such occasion, he told me how much he regretted that he could offer me only $200 more for the next year. And, knowing that it would not be easy (for we lived on the margin in those days), I found myself saying that we could manage without a raise if we had to—and meant it, and knew my wife would back me (for they loved him as much as we). And went out, my offer of course refused, and full of joy at being on the same planet with such a man. And ran into a colleague, told him the story. He said, "I know. I did the same thing."

I do not expect anyone who did not know him to believe all this; those who know need not be told. But it is good to remember.

LUDLOW BALDWIN
Headmaster, 1963–1968

Imagine Gilman as a Herculaneum, preserved for centuries until some archaeologist, newly arrived from the Saturn station, starts poring over the perfectly preserved records. And Ludlow Baldwin becomes, inevitably, the transitional figure, the caretaker, the regent between two giants (rather like Adams between Washington and Jefferson). Inevitable—and altogether wrong.

For Ludlow Baldwin's impact on the school is in some ways the most dramatic of all. It is also the most difficult to put into words, for he was the quintessential *manager*—and the ultimate achievement of the skilled manager lies in his ability so to "manage" things behind the scenes that his organization, "his people," think that they have pulled all these remarkable things off by themselves.

Now *dramatic* is not a word that managers particularly like; they prefer words like *efficient, civil, smooth, decent*. That last came closest to being Baldwin's motto. "Why can't people," he used to say in despair and frustration at particularly vexing moments, "be just—*decent*?"

So here was this profoundly decent man, presiding over what were probably the most turbulent, the most dramatic five years of the school's history. Consider this partial outline of what went on in that brief span: The road from Gilman to the Ivy colleges, only recently a broad boulevard, was in the process of becoming a goat trail, and Gilman-Princeton alums with sons in the senior class had to be told, as gently as possible, about back-up colleges and selectivity ratings. The drug culture reached full flower, penetrating even into the hallowed halls, and the polarized rage between those who wanted to try to understand—and those who wanted daily strip-searches—called for the most delicate mediation. Viet Nam began tearing the country apart; among other things, it brought about the student deferment (college or "Nam"), which escalated the already agonizing process of college application to almost unbearable levels. The smoldering war between the generations burst into flame; teachers and administrators sometimes felt like U.N. observers caught in a no-man's land between the students and parents, mistrusted by both. Finally, in this town, once described to me in my early months here as Richmond North, the first blacks entered, and graduated from, Gilman. I have studied the record, and I cannot find another half-decade like it.

These were cultural and educational hurricanes, howling across our placid acres, and there were those among us who feared disaster. It is worth noting that, in November and December of 1944, Lt. Commander L. H. Baldwin stood watches on the bridge of the light carrier *Independence* during a typhoon which sent three U.S. destroyers to the bottom—the same typhoon which inspired *The Caine Mutiny*. When pressed in later years, he would pull out an old photograph of that bridge and that officer—against a horizon so steeply canted that viewers safely grounded on Maryland earth felt queasy. Twenty years later, the character tested and annealed in those stirring times lived on in the cheerful fortitude of the skipper of the U.S.S. *Gilman*. Some of us may have thought the ship was sinking; he had seen much worse, and knew better.

What seems almost incredible, in retrospect, is that the school never ran more smoothly than in the heavy weather of the mid-sixties. The skipper's Navy seasoning clearly had much to do with that, but so did managerial skills so innate that he was hardly aware of them. He would never talk about it, but if you got him on the witness stand without a choice, he would say something like this: Look, you keep your ears open; get out of the office and listen to what students and teachers are saying. Keep lines of communication open, and keep a written record of meetings (copies to participants). Let people know, in writing and in public, when they have done well; rebuke and criticize in private. If there is trouble, head right at it, for if you try to dodge it, it will hit you in the back. Care for your people, every one of them. Remember, if you can't have fun at a job like this, don't do it.

You could find all that in the class notes of every freshman at Wharton; what the freshmen probably don't know is how hard it is to get those little maxims out of the notebook and into action. Something else textbooks have trouble with: you can be the greatest manager in the world, technically, and if you have not *rectitude*—you are like the sounding brass, the tinkling cymbal.

Baldwin's greatest gift, when all is said and done, was a granite rectitude—a sure sense of what was right—and the equally sure sense that if he could only stand firm, the much-maligned "establishment" (of which he was himself a charter member) would come around. This is what Baldwin did in his short five years: In a time that Max Lerner characterized as the Era of Polarized Rages, Ludlow Baldwin saw clearly what was the right thing to do; he undertook to help the school to do it—and he managed the whole thing so brilliantly, so delicately, that we remember his time as one when things went particularly smoothly.

They used to call Joe Dimaggio the ballplayer's ballplayer, meaning that he was so skilled he made the impossible look easy. (I have heard fools in Yankee Stadium boo him for missing a catch no other center fielder would even have attempted.) . . . But the players knew.

Ludlow Baldwin was a headmaster's headmaster; only another pro could truly appreciate him. Still, we who worked for him had a pretty good idea, at that.

REDMOND FINNEY
Headmaster, 1968–1992

We remember not so much words or ideas, policies or programs, ceremonies or speeches, though there were floods of words, ideas and policies in bewildering profusion, hundreds of speeches and ceremonies. Reddy Finney lives most vividly in images of action, little freeze-frame pictures . . .

Somebody warned me when I first knew him, for example, not to sit next to him at athletic contests. I should have listened; he nearly detached my arm at an exciting moment in a basketball game. As a coach, he couldn't sit at all; he would crouch at the sideline all afternoon long, methodically pulling up little tufts of grass. It was a curiously precise, almost delicate activity, but it gave the most remarkable sense of barely controlled frenzy—as if the helpless grass was about to be vaporized.

He was frighteningly—and unconsciously—strong. He brought a female faculty candidate to my office one day, needing someone to talk to her while he ran some errand. As he left, he rested a great paw on her shoulder—his usual friendly gesture. I happened to be watching her face; her eyes all but jumped out of their sockets. She told me later that she thought he had snapped her collarbone.

He would occasionally explode into bursts of exuberant animal energy. Delighted by something or other one day, he picked me up bodily (this was in the middle of the Common Room) and held me over his head. He broke up a double play, once, in a faculty softball game, and he, Jack Garver, Dimitri Manuelides, and a 15-foot strip of sod wound up just short of Northern Parkway.

As an athlete, he was a daunting, intimidating blend of power and intensity. I watched him as an undergraduate only once; it was riveting. Somebody discovered, soon after I arrived in Baltimore, that I had no idea what a lacrosse stick was. So they took me to a game between the Princetons and the Blue Jays, and I have never since shaken the notion that it is a remarkably simple game. As far as I could see, you simply gave the ball to this large chap with oak trees for legs, and he would pound along knocking down Blue Jays until he got to a net thing, and that was that.

The walk . . . The head waggle . . . Jeezey Peezey. No year was complete without the designated student "Finney." (The faculty never knew how the mantle was passed; did they have a tournament, or did each graduating "Finney" anoint his successor? We did know that the ones who didn't get to be Finney had to "do" us—and that was tough, for we gave them far less to work with; we just weren't as colorful.) Each of us has his favorite "Finney"; my choice comes down to a dead heat between Bobby Thomas and Teddy McKeldin III.

I doubt that any of us has experienced a more vivid personality, and this makes it difficult to pin him down, analyze, assess his contributions. He just *was*—a kind of elemental force, like a giant meteorite, say, or an earthquake, which makes a colossal, incalculable impact and leaves us trying to figure out how it happened and what it all meant.

Some few generalizations we can be sure of. First is that he was the most approachable, the most instantly likeable adult I ever saw around a school, or anywhere else. Given the Finney Legend—and he was legendary, from the very beginning—you would expect the kids to be in awe of him. Not really; they just liked him; he was their friend. And he liked them. Like a successful politician, he drew strength from human contact; the bigger the crowd, the more it sustained him. And like only the greatest of politicians, he could be in a crowd of hundreds—and be in intimate *personal* contact with each individual. They talk about Bill Clinton working a crowd; Finney makes him look like an amateur. And there was nothing "ulterior" about it; Finney didn't work crowds of students, alumni, parents—to get something out of them, to persuade or convince, to buy a vote. It was much deeper than that; he needed them. In the deepest sense, he loved them. I am perfectly certain, incidentally, that had he chosen to run, he could have won any office the state had to offer.

Another matter we can be certain of: as sure as Alexander modeled himself on Achilles—or for that matter Caesar on Alexander—-so Reddy Finney on Henry Callard. Now that is not in itself unusual in schools like Gilman—and Reddy is far from the only Gilman student to try to replicate HHC. For that matter, Henry Callard was the glass of fashion and the mold of form for a generation of teachers as well as students.

But it went deeper with Finney. It seems to me that over the years Reddy actually began to *look* like HHC. Take the head waggle, for instance; it is, surely, an extension, an elaboration, of the "Callard Tilt"—head bent rather sharply to starboard, right hand flat against cheek and chin as if nursing a toothache. The Tilt meant that he was troubled but engaged, pondering action; so did the Finney Waggle. And campus-grooming! More than once I have felt a tug of nostalgia as I watched Reddy zigzag from one piece of trash to another on his way from his house to school. If I were shooting a movie, I would fade him right into HHC.

Those are externals. As I review my words on Callard, I find I can in almost every case replace one name with the other: the ability to heal with a word or touch, the joy in simple tasks, the automatic acceptance of responsibility, the inculcation of fierce faculty and student loyalty—in short, the aura of saintliness—it is all there.

So far, I cannot imagine dissent: Finney as the most purely *likeable* person any of us ever knew; Finney as Callard. It is good to remember him in these ways. My own view of his most potent legacy, however, will perhaps seem strange, even to him. I close with this perhaps off-beat view of his most important impact because I think it may have implications for the future of the school.

Begin with what I will call a Jungian view of single-sex education. Jung believes that healthy maturation involves, for boys, coming to terms with an inner "femininity"—sensitivity, compassion, nurturing; and for girls, learning to accept and honor in themselves the so-called "masculine" qualities of competitiveness, assertiveness, self-confidence.

Take that theory a step further and apply it to single-sex schools. It is easy to see that a good girls' school—perhaps without consciously intending it—strengthens, validates, nurtures the "masculine" qualities in its students. More than that; recent cultural changes, in the world of work as well as in schools, make it ever easier for growing girls to feel comfortable with what Jung calls the "animus," the inner man.

It is very different for a boys' school. Even if teachers and administrators are aware of Jungian thought and accept the rapidly growing trend in modern life to value men as much for sensitivity, compassion, intuition—the "feminine" virtues—as for the "traditional" male ones, boys' schools tend to become pretty "macho" places, where stoic endurance is king, where sensitivity is all too easily perceived as weakness, and the slightest display of concern or affection—on the part of one's peers or teachers—leads to knowing looks and whispers of "Fag." It is instructive to note that the code of a boys' school places the most severe sanctions upon one student touching another—except in mock fighting, horseplay, and when celebrating athletic triumphs—occasions, presumably, where no hint of weakness or homosexuality is possible.

What has Reddy Finney to do with all this? Why, literally everything. Could a school have had a finer model of caring, compassion and sensitivity? Could the most cynical of students or teachers have imagined for a single moment that this great bear of a man could conceivably be weak or sentimental, "womanish"? Of course not. But they could not imagine, either, a Reddy Finney who did not care, who did not love them, every one, and who was not afraid to show it. Did he care a rap for the code of touching? Not when a frightened little fellow needed above all else a friendly arm about the shoulder. So real men don't cry? Reddy Finney's students saw him do it, in public, and honored him for it. Much, much more important, to be in the same school with Reddy Finney meant to grow up knowing that it is OK to care and to show it, that there is no strength like the strength of gentleness.

Jung would say that Redmond Finney helped us all to come to terms with our anima. What that means is that Gilman is above all a kinder, gentler place, and that its graduates, while imperfect like the rest of us, are more "whole"—because of him. And what it implies for Gilman's future is that nothing is more important in a boys' school than gentleness and kindness; that we may not always be so lucky as to have right in front of us so marvelous, so natural an exemplar of those qualities.

As Tennyson says, "You are a part of all that you have met," and Finney's psychological integrity, along with Baldwin's rectitude and Callard's saintliness, are woven inextricably into the fabric of the school and into the character of each of us who had the blessing of knowing them.

And that, all that, is why I never thought of leaving Gilman.

A. J. Downs worked at Gilman in a vast variety of roles, but most of all as an English teacher, 1950–89. When asked, in 1989, by a Gilman *News* reporter, about his 39 years at Gilman, Downs replied, "I always felt like Peter Pan. It was always a continuing source of astonishment that I was paid for doing something that is so much fun."

A Phi Beta Kappa graduate of Oberlin College who earned his Master's degree from Johns Hopkins University, Downs came to Gilman as an English teacher. From 1955 to 1975, the World War II Marine Corps veteran served as head of the Dramatics Department; from 1963 to 1980, as head college counselor; from 1973 to 1984, as head of the English department; and from 1985 to 1989, as dean of faculty. He also found time to host his own radio show.

Born and raised the son of missionaries in Japan, Downs conducted his life at Gilman with missionary zeal. He created the Upper School's reading skills courses, founded the Senior Encounter Program, and pushed hard for diversification. For 39 years, A. J. Downs was a maverick at Gilman. Briar pipe in the corner of his mouth, reading glasses perched at the end of his nose, a crisp bow tie set against a starched white shirt, Downs spurred a tradition-loving Gilman into more modern educational concepts. A major proponent of coeducation, and one of the engines behind the move to coordinate with Bryn Mawr and Roland Park Country Schools, Downs' only regret while at Gilman was that Gilman did not coordinate with the two girls' schools earlier. He told reporter Michael Blumenfield '89, of the Gilman *News*, "Believing in diversity, how is it that we exclude half of the human race?"

In 1954–55, Downs was an exchange teacher at Tonbridge School in England. In 1969–70, he spent a sabbatical year visiting colleges throughout the country, researching material for his book, *A Long Way from Home*, published in 1970.

Downs has continued to teach, lecture, and write since leaving Gilman. And Gilman continues to call on his wide range of talents. In 1995, between the college drama and literature classes he was teaching, Downs found himself back in the recording studio, narrating the video for The Centennial Campaign: Foundation for a New Century.

1990s

1990

The Redmond C. S. Finney Athletic Center is completed.

The Upper School Building undergoes extensive refurbishing and is named Carey Hall in memory of the school's founder, Anne Galbraith Carey.

The Lower School multi-purpose room is dedicated as the Helen K. Stevens Room.

Tennis virtuoso Reed Cordish '92 begins undefeated streak through sophomore, junior, and senior years as Gilman's number one player. Coached by Jim Busick, Cordish wins MSA singles championship three years in a row.

1991

Ice hockey returns as a varsity sport. Coach Bob Bulkeley leads an inexperienced team through a tough season. Sophomore captain Jason Griswold provides inspiration with rugged forward play. Forwards Dave Iglehart and Tim Elliot lead the team in scoring; Chris Utermohle starts every game in the goal.

1992

Senior wrestler John Kim completes storybook season, compiling a 36–0 record, including a National Prep Championship, Gilman's first since Ted Brown '84 and Dan Miller '84.

Headmaster Redmond C. S. Finney '47 retires. Longtime Gilman teachers John Bartkowski, Fred Brune '41, Graeme Menzies '47, Bill Miller, Charles Pletcher, and Reginald Tickner retire.

President of the Board George Hess '55 leads effort to form The Redmond C. S. Finney Award, to be given to that Upper School student who has been most noteworthy for striving to eliminate racism, prejudice, and intolerance. Approved in a Board meeting, the new award is announced on Founders' Day. The first recipient is David Shapiro in 1993.

Students stroll out of the completely rebuilt Middle School, John M. T. Finney Hall, to play soccer in the fall of 1995. Middle School students and teachers working and studying in this modern building become the envy of Upper and Lower Schoolers, especially in the warm spring months when the central air-conditioning keeps passions cooled. Behind the large window is The Walter Lord Library, the light and airy centerpiece of the building.

Past Board Chairman George Thomsen '48 heads committee to select next headmaster.

Archibald R. Montgomery IV '71 is named the eleventh headmaster of Gilman School.

1993
John M. T. Finney Hall, the Middle School, is completely rebuilt on the original foundation. Second floor doubles the space available. Well-lighted science laboratories, music and art rooms, departmental offices and faculty meeting places, along with the spacious Walter Lord Library, make this a state-of-the-art educational facility.

The Reginald Tickner Writing Center, financed by a $60,000 gift from the Class of 1993 parents and students, is launched under the direction of Writing Center Director Julie Checkoway. The Center helps students with the process of writing through a system of student consultants and college interns working one-on-one with students. Each year a visiting writer-in-residence adds to the inspirational quality of the program.

The A. J. Downs Writers at Work Series is launched through a gift from the Class of 1963. In its first year, the series sponsors eight events. Visiting writers include best-selling novelist Tom Clancy, who dines with 20 Gilman students in the Writing Center and then gives a controversial address to students and parents in the Alumni Auditorium, and Lucille Clifton, former Poet Laureate of Maryland, who

Upper School students operate the student-run radio in 1995 on a shoe-string budget out of a cleared-out shower stall where former boarders once lathered up on Carey's Hall third story.

reads to students and faculty from Bryn Mawr, Gilman, and Roland Park.

1994
An all-fiber-optic local area network (LAN) with an automated catalog and circulation system, numerous data bases, and access to the Internet, is installed in the three libraries of the school under the direction of Jo Ann Davison. Students have entrée to the world's information sources through the Gilman Library Network from any Gilman library terminal, and eventually from modems at home, 24 hours a day.

Jay Homa '96 and Sean Kiernan '96, with help from alumnus Scott Deutschman '89, are instrumental in the founding of campus radio station WGLM.

Under the coaching of John Tucker, the varsity lacrosse team wins its first championship since 1981. The 10–7 victory over St. Mary's gives Gilman its 11th championship. The following spring, 1995, Gilman wins another championship with a victory over Boys' Latin. Midfielders James McIntyre and Kirk Caldroney dominate the face-offs. Attackmen Lorne Smith, Chase Martin, and Lawson Devries put the ball in the goal. Defensemen Packer Rodgers, Chris Tully, and Dave Biddison stymie the BL attack, as does goalkeeper Corey Popham.

With a crowd of thousands gathered on the Gilman campus, the Gilman football team, coached by Sherm Bristow '67, defeats a vaunted McDonogh team in a come-from-behind victory to become MIAA co-champions.

1995
In the fall, the varsity soccer team, coached by history teacher Ned Harris, finishes the year as co-champion.

In September, the first Special Olympics Day is held at Gilman. Handicapped students are invited to spend the day competing in sports activities and games. Classics Department Chair Anton Vishio heads the program.

The Centennial Campaign: Foundation for the Future, the largest campaign in the school's history, is launched under the Board Chairmanship of James S. Riepe. $15 million is sought to expand and upgrade facilities, to increase endowment to provide educational programs for teachers, to sustain the financial aid program, and to develop key programs in technology and the arts. Campaign Chairman Charles C. Fenwick, Jr. '66 vigorously leads the effort, working alongside Stephen T. Scott '64, head of the Financial Development Committee, and William L. Paternotte '63, head of the Leadership Gifts Division.

Annual Giving breaks the $1 million barrier.

Justin Klein '92 sinks one for the alma mater.

New brick-red track, with rubberized surface, is completed. Gone is the old asphalt and cinder track. An entirely new drainage system for the track area and inner field is installed.

After a hiatus of 15 years, an Ancient History course is reinstated as part of the Eighth Grade curriculum. The primary architect of the restored course is Middle School teacher Brandon Neblett '89, assisted by Ned Clapp '59 and S. B. Grimes '59, and with encouragement from Headmaster Arch Montgomery '71. Ancient History, once taught by faculty greats Herbert Pickett, Ludlow Baldwin and Meredith Reese, is now taught with cross-curricular cooperation among the history, language arts, and Latin faculties.

Chris Legg '67 steps down after 13 years as Gilman's head wrestling coach. His teams won the Gilman Duals in 1985 and 1987, the MSA dual meet championship in 1990, and the MSA dual meet co-championship in 1984. Legg continues to teach in the Middle School.

Spencer Finney '95 and Chris Oh '95 lead the varsity golf team to the championship.

During the 1995–96 academic year, Gilman athletes accumulate five championships:

The varsity cross country team, coached by Jack Thompson, finishes in a three-way tie for the MIAA championship. David Chalmers '97 wins all but two of the dual meets Gilman enters.

During the spring of 1996, the baseball team, coached by Marty Meloy, blows away most of its opponents, finishing as MIAA "A" conference champion for the first time. Seniors Jason Mersey, Russell Wren, Jay Homa, and Yani Rosenberg are key players. Head Coach Marty Meloy is picked by The *Sun* as coach of the year and catcher Jason Mersey as player of the year.

The track team, coached by Johnnie Foreman, sprints to another championship year and reaches a milestone by going undefeated in the dual meet season. Alan Hsu '96 anchors the winning 4 X 200 meter relay team. Donald Bocoat '97 wins the triple jump. Patrick Runge '96 sets new high jump record of six feet four inches.

Varsity golfer P. J. Singh '96 wins MIAA individual title under the coaching of art teacher Harvey Peterson. Peterson retires from Gilman after two decades of teaching and accumulating a 163-57-10 record in coaching the golf team 19 out of its 23 years.

1996

After 34 years of working at Gilman, music teacher John Merrill plans a quiet leave-taking. For months ahead of time, past Traveling Men and Glee Club members design a different plot; they secretly gather on Family Day for a surprise performance, eventually serenading Mr. Merrill before a packed audience in the Alumni Auditorium. Mr. Merrill is taken by surprise! Ringleaders in this effort are alumni Ned Worthington '78 and David Whitman '68, and students Gaurab Bansal '96 and George Brown '96.

By June, over $8 million has been raised for The Centennial Campaign. As part of the campaign, all of the Upper School arts programs are brought together in one creative arts center on the third floor of Carey Hall, featuring increased studio space, a well-ventilated darkroom, and computer art facilities. The old "A" Study Hall (the southern wing of Carey Hall, which has been the art room for over a decade) is refurbished and converted into a meeting hall and exhibition center named Centennial Hall.

Student enrollment stands at 946.

The graduating class consists of 107 boys.

1997

The School celebrates its 100th anniversary. *Gilman Voices, 1897–1997*, edited by Patrick Smithwick '69, is published.

A series of Centennial events and celebrations bring alumni back to Gilman from all parts of the globe.

Left, Rafael Lee '92 practices on the clarinet. Gilman's music program continued to expand and flourish in the '90s.

Right, Bill Merrick '51 has been a Lower School teacher since 1958. Whether pulling out his guitar, gathering his Fourth Grade around him, and belting out one of his repertoire of mnemonic songs, or throwing a touchdown pass to a Fifth Grader, Merrick is known for giving the individual student his absolute, empathetic, and focused attention.

Below, Julie Checkoway taught creative writing 1989–95 and was the first director of The Tickner Writing Center. As a published author, Ms. Checkoway brought a modern process-oriented methodology, and at times a controversial feminist point of view, to what in earlier decades had been a tweedy, let-the-red-ink-flow, male-dominated, pipe-smoking Upper School English department.

An inspiration for many students, Johnnie Foreman is renowned for his expertise in and passion for coaching varsity track and football. A Middle School science teacher and director of athletics for the Middle and Lower Schools, Foreman started Gilman's highly successful mentoring program in 1994.

388

389

Andrew Dausch '90 follows blocker Eric David '90 to score ample yardage in Gilman's 35–0 victory over McDonogh.

Right, Varsity tennis star Reed Cordish '92 went undefeated for the seasons of 1990, '91, and '92. His steadiness at the baseline along with his mental toughness made Cordish unbeatable.

Opposite, Lower School teacher Andy Martire '89 leads students to the Finney Athletic Center and the all-school Thanksgiving Day 1995 convocation. Martire teaches Fifth Grade. How many Gilman students could possibly imagine having Classics Department Chair Anton Vishio, Sr. as an adviser and then later as a father-in-law? Read all about it in Martire's "Vociferous Incantations, Sarcastic Barrages, and Death-defying Duelists."

Latin day is capped off by the notorious spring chariot race in which all chariots are home-made.

Below, Martin Rochlin '92 exhibits unlimited school spirit and musical talent by beating on a trash can during a football game.

Opposite, iconoclast, individualist, motivator, raconteur, historian, athlete, political analyst—Nick Schloeder has taught and coached at Gilman under four headmasters. Here he proselytizes to classmates Stewart Becker, Marcus Simms, Michael Kleinman, and J. Spencer Finney, Jr. '95, and they remain uncharacteristically still and quiet: it is 9 a.m. the morning after their senior prom.

A top athete in his student days at Gilman, Sherm Bristow '67 joined the faculty in 1971. Whether in English class or on the varsity football field Bristow has an inspirational quality that he is able to relate to youths. As assistant headmaster, athletic director, head football coach, dean of students, or English teacher, Bristow has been an unforgettable mentor to many a Gilman Upper Schooler.

The Gilman soccer team came into its own in the 1990s, winning its first "A" Conference MIAA Championship (co-champs) in 1995 under the coaching of history teacher Ned Harris. Photographer Steve McDaniel '65 captured this goal-scoring shot of an earlier team.

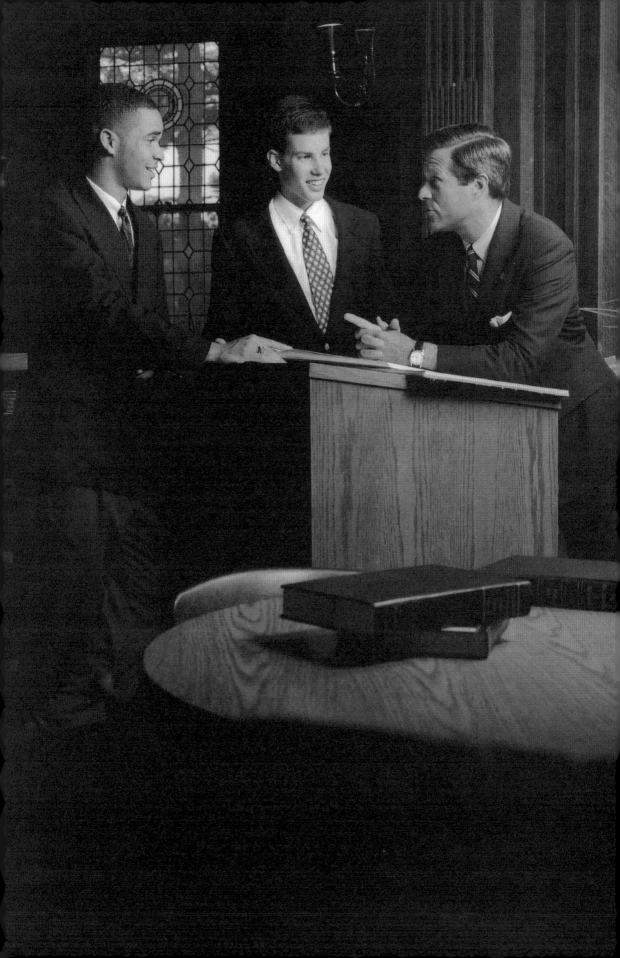

Three Gilman headmasters, hale and hearty, get together at the Alumni Banquet of 1992. Here former Headmaster Redmond C. S. Finney '47 (left) and former Headmaster Ludlow Baldwin '22 (right) give Headmaster Archibald R. Montgomery IV '71 their full support. Later in the evening, Headmaster Montgomery gave his "inauguration address" to the alumni and Reddy Finney received the May Holmes Award.

Left, class presidents "Chaz" Howard '96 and Ted Lord '95 discuss the senior leadership program with Headmaster Arch Montgomery in the Edward R. Fenimore, Jr. Library. For a portrait of headmaster as head mentor, read Howard's "Brand New Shoes."

A Wonderful Present

JOSHUA CIVIN '92

"**G**ilman"—the first time I heard the word, I cried. My parents sat my brother and me down at the polished breakfast table. The strawberry-patterned wallpaper, glued on upside-down by an absent-minded paperhanger, still hung on the kitchen walls. Marc had just turned a rebellious six, and I was a shy, klutzy eight.

"We have a wonderful present for you," Mom and Dad chimed, beaming as if a trip to Disney World loomed in the not-so-distant future. "We've decided to send you to *Gilman*, a private school!"

But what about our friends and the Mt. Washington Elementary School famil-iar—stairwells, science projects, and the walk home up that monstrous hill? Marc and I took one look at each other and burst into tears. Private School—the un-known, even if it bore the name "Gilman"—was too overwhelming for breakfast table discussion.

"You wouldn't *Belize* what I Guat in *Guatemala*, a Honda from *Honduras*, with an *El Salvador*, I got it in *Nicaragua*, and it *Cost-a Rica*, so I did a wheely in my auto-mobily on the *Panama* Canal, Wow!" Mr. Merrick's 4A class chanted the Central America song while he harmonized on his ancient guitar, strumming the same four chords that accompanied all our nifty mnemonic devices. Without a doubt, Fourth Grade was the most challenging year at Gilman—explorer tests, grammar quizzes, punctuation rules. Ask any Mr. Merrick veteran, especially one of the new kids that year, and he will agree. Nights found Mom quizzing me at the breakfast table. "*Obstreperous*," she dictated, "making a great disturbance, clamorous . . ." In the strawberry-papered kitchen, vocab list stress replaced tears, and the overwhelming unknown grew overwhelmingly familiar.

Beware Mr. Merrick's poof gun—one misstep and Poof! Mr. Merrick shoots you; the next morning, poof, you would wake up a day older. Lower School in-grained a firm handshake, eye-contact, and fear of the red leather couch and Lower School Principal Mr. Snyder's wrath beyond. I was never banished to the couch (I am not sure whether to be proud of this accomplishment), but I dreaded forgetting to draw lines with a ruler in the midst of a multiplication problem. When we were constructing our wooden lamps in industrial arts, I cringed every time Mr. Hilliard barked over the sound of the churning machines, "THE SHOP IS NOT A PLAY-GROUND."

But even the playground proved not a playground. It was a jungle where four-square and dodge ball determined social stature. Oddly, victory did not rest on athletic prowess alone. Far more important was securing an invitation on Friday when school spilled out at noon to the house of the coolest Fourth Grader—though, who exactly deserved that title was perpetually and viciously in dispute.

Spontaneously combust—somehow we did not, for if the shop was not a play-ground, it was not always a shop either. Mr. Hilliard doubled as our designated math wizard. He delighted in whizzing us through long division and fractions so fast that Fridays could be reserved for reading. Calming a bunch of Fourth Graders, antsy in blue sweaters and father-knotted ties, his grandfatherly intonations swelled the room. He regaled us with tales of his own childhood spliced into weekly installations of *Rascal* and *Where the Red Fern Grows*. A wonderful haven of slow minutes were stolen from the bustling Gilman halls: the wooden lamp maker and demanding math wizard turned storyteller.

And even the crew-cut, ramrod Mr. Merrick—bard of memorization—sought his own refuge now and then. One day I entered the classroom, back early from athletics. A pair of legs stretched out from under the sink in the corner of the room. Mr. Merrick naps! The obstreperous Fourth Grader in me wanted to swipe the fabled poof gun while the giant slumbered. No more explorer tests, grammar quizzes, or punctuation rules! I was tempted. But the Gilman boy in me reasoned that I had no beanstalk to use to escape the red leather couch and Mr. Snyder's wrath beyond. Feeling intensely guilty, I tiptoed out and swung the door gently closed: the snoring secret—together with Mr. Hilliard's Friday stories—stored for later.

"Late night, Civin?" Mr. Schmick asked. Leaning over my Chapel seat, he nudged me and rolled his eyes. My own snoring secret had been discovered. Nap-time, I thought, should have been a required Gilman activity, regardless of age. In Upper School, the hectic factor had only increased—dashing off to Jewish Students Association meetings or Mr. Bartkowski's chemistry lab, water polo practice or intramural ultimate frisbee, down to the mechanical drawing depths or up to the land of *Cynosure*. That polished breakfast table at home hardly saw any family discussions; if we were not rushing to the next writing assignment, my brother and I were falling into our plates, exhausted from a grueling swim practice.

In Chapel, yet another esteemed Hopkins doctor presented yet another slide show on yet another savory topic such as warts or organ transplants. You could almost excuse the many slumping heads. They did not have, however, convenient sinks to hide their naps induced by "mooching"—another Mr. Merrick vocabulary word—too many Macke French fries during recess.

But Chapel time could also stir the skeptical student body from its contented slumber. Chapel, despite the plush red chairs, served to ignite the controversy and drama of my Upper School experience—as much controversy and drama, that is, as could exist at this 5407 Roland Avenue establishment.

The fall of my junior year a series of Senior speeches set us abuzz. A swastika defaced a locker door, racial slurs were scrawled over library books, and more subtly, lunch tables continued to be populated by exclusive ethnic cliques. Discussions grew passionate. Back from a summer trip to Auschwitz and Israel, my own perceptions as a Gilman outsider had magnified. I was ever-vigilant against racism, real or perceived. And in this instance, it seemed that despite Gilman Experience classes in the Lower School and Talk Seminars in the Middle School, despite nearly 30 years since the first people of color entered Gilman, many issues of diversity remained for Gilman to resolve.

Bring in the artillery: to combat these issues, poof guns were hardly strong enough. But strangely, no official administration response to the events was forthcoming. So we students did what we were best at doing: we mounted a crusade. It took the form of *Open Forums*. Student Council President Peter Daneker and Student Activist Union leader A. J. Julius may have fueled the meetings with very different agendas; but however chaotic, it was democracy of a sort. Teachers banned, we had Chapel time to ourselves.

Heated accusations flew across the aisles. Before we knew it, our rump parliament was voting motions up and down, questioning Gilman admissions policies, advocating non-Western history requirements, restricting potentially un-inclusive hymns from chapel. From the podium, I read my own proposal in a shaky voice. Creating an Upper School Talk program, I argued, would institutionalize the very dialogue these forums promoted. My motion failed. The student leadership staked the future on a student committee directed to respond to discrimination whenever it arose. But as to this committee's membership—a Committee of Six . . . Seven . . . then Eight—consensus began to break down.

Include the leaders of the various minority awareness groups—Asian Awareness Club, Black Awareness Club, Jewish Students Association, Middle East Forum. "But who would speak for the majority?" conservatives cried. The moderates opted for the Student Council President—elected by a majority of the senior class. The radicals hoped to preserve the Student Activist Union seat.

Fine, many said, add both. But a coterie of reluctant revolutionaries demurred. "Make the presentation of the Committee proportional to the population of the student population," they argued.

Student Activist Union leader A. J. Julius shot back, "Maybe we need to found a WASP Awareness Club!"

Pandemonium broke loose. Before Student Council President Daneker understood what had happened, a roaring jeer voted the Student Activist Union representative off the committee. The bell rang before blows ensued.

Before long, passions fizzled, skepticism returned, and the slumbering heads sunk again in their plush red chairs. What became of the committee of much-disputed membership? For its failure, I often fault my own senior class, and myself most of all—as a leader, senior year, of one of those much-disputed awareness groups. After a fruitful Human Relations day which climaxed in a smorgasbord of ethnic food-tasting, coordination among the groups sank under college admissions anxiety.

On no one did the persistent racism weigh more heavily than the legendary champion of Gilman integration, Mr. Finney himself—whose loping gait had assumed a divine presence. Gilman had bravely hurdled the challenges of physical integration—admissions numbers attested to that. Yet, beyond the classroom, socially integrating this diverse student body proved more difficult. In the face of swastikas, slurs, and those nettlesome four-square and dodge ball cliques, even Mr. Finney seemed overwhelmed.

The week after the Open Forums, Mr. Finney finally addressed the student body in a strained voice. In courageous words, he emphasized that Gilman would not tolerate racism in any form. And in just as strong words, he denounced those who looked for "simple solutions"—those who were too quick to criticize before assembling all the facts. Across the aisles, my brother and I flashed each other looks of confusion. Mr. Finney admitted that mistakes had been made. The administration had been slow to react. Yet simultaneously, he appeared to challenge those who insisted on bringing these incidents to the fore. In the bustling of Gilman halls, humble—not ostentatious—reason was preferred over obstreperous revolution.

In the words of Henry James, "To criticize is to appreciate"—and we certainly did a lot of criticizing during our days at Gilman. Crusades had a habit of popping up, briefly intense—slowly dying. Upper School ingrained a firm handshake, eye-contact, and fear of making waves. For instance, to minimize student parking in reserved spaces on campus, the administration issued stickers to identify every car. Fines were threatened, but no students were seriously consulted regarding the policy. Ever-earnest, Jon Goldman organized a protest day. Fliers urged students to wear parking stickers on their ties; but hedging bets, as all Gilmanites learned to do, the fine print at the bottom reminded reluctant revolutionaries that the school provided two stickers per student. One was still left for the car if the protest failed.

Crusades against sending troops to the Persian Gulf, against authoritarian swimming and lacrosse coaches, against losing the senior room, against yearbook censorship: impassioned students, constantly grumbling, yearned to rouse the school from its lethargy. But no one ever thought to challenge at the core, those nettlesome four-square and dodge ball cliques. "Boys will be boys." One administrator belted out his "COMPASSION" theme while turning a blind eye to the din of the playground taunts. And most Gilmanites slumbered on in Chapel or jeered during the Open Forums. Playground bullying graduated to drinking sprees. Condemning swastika and slur scrawling, one Human Relations Day a year, a politically correct multi-cultural assessment—all of this only chipped away at the pressurized and institutionalized cauldron from which such social behavior rose. Mr. Hilliard's rules to keep the playground out of the shop were much easier to understand than the playground jungle itself.

"To criticize is to appreciate"—despite all our criticizing, no one, student or faculty, seemed to do a whole lot of appreciating. Life was too competitive to leave time for appreciation. And that hectic life we led—the crusaders and the slumberers alike—we thought a charmed one. The night the myth shattered, our class was brought together for one brief moment—crusaders and slumberers shedding the skeptical, viciously cool façades. That night, the night before Achievements, no story's swelling intonations could calm our disbelief. Within hours of the crash, a phone chain flowed from student to student, and the news devastated. Alex Semel was the boy whose "wacky sense of humor and the carefree manner in which he lived his life" Ben Jones later memorialized. Alex Semel was the boy who slammed into a tree—a peaceful tree in an open field. Reluctant pilgrims, my classmates and I stopped by that tree in the open field after the funeral; the image was indelible . . . and inexplicable.

I could not bring myself to go up and look in the open casket; I could not bring myself to cry at that peaceful tree. For me, the crying came later—the beginning of senior year. After his wife died, the storyteller Mr. Hilliard grew ill. "You should see him today if at all," his friend Mrs. Brune explained. So my brother Marc and I pilgrimaged to his red brick house on campus. We approached the side of his bed. He looked so fragile. We said, "Thank you." His breathing slowed. I think he heard us— I hope he did. But the moment probably meant more for Marc and me—frighteningly unfamiliar, like the first time we heard the word *Gilman* at the breakfast table nine years before.

Distilling sufficient distance from my Gilman experience is still difficult—only a couple of years gone, my Gilman persona fits like a familiar glove when I visit the old haunts. My friends and I congregate during vacations with the same Bryn Mawr and Roland Park women. We cannot quite prevent ourselves from slipping into the old rivalries, relationships, and gossip. Yet, of all of this, not the Open Forums, not the vocab lists, not the Central America song, not even that first time I heard the word *Gilman*—of all this, what will endure from my Gilman experience will be those blue-sweatered Fridays when Mr. Hilliard wove his tales. Mr. Hilliard's Fridays boiled Gilman down to its essence, shorn of playground taunts, skepticism, and pressurized crusades.

Inquisitive: another Mr. Merrick vocabulary word. When Mr. Hilliard, the shop teacher and math wizard, shed his gruffness, his stories conjured up our inquisitive natures. Mr. Hilliard often did not finish his tales—he left us to discover the book and devour its conclusion, or even better, to imagine our own ending.

What I found towards the end of our many crusades at times proved surprising, unfamiliar, and even frightening. Mr. Merrick napped under the sink in the corner of the classroom; the locker door revealed a swastika; the legendary Mr. Finney wrestled with the same issues we debated; our crusades proved hypocritically overblown. And finally, my Gilman could not escape crashing mortality. But if we could pursue these inquisitive crusades with integrity—this time a Mr. Finney word—the gift presented to Marc and me at the breakfast table years ago was well worth the traumas that have sprung up along the path . . . and those that lurk beyond.

Entering Gilman in the Fourth Grade, Joshua Civin soon established himself as one of the top grade-earners in his class and as a student who was strongly involved in community affairs. Civin was first in his class all four years in the Upper School, and was the valedictorian (The William S. Thomas Scholarship Prize) at graduation. He also was given the Daniel Baker, Jr. Memorial Award for character, the Herbert E. Pickett Prize for General Proficiency in History, and prizes in reading, French, and debating. Civin was a National Merit Scholar, and a Hardie Anglo-American Exchange Scholar, spending a year at St. Edward's School in Oxford, England.*

Civin was a four-year man on the varsity water polo team. He began an avid interest in volunteer work and community affairs at Gilman, volunteering at Bea Gaddy's Soup Kitchen and serving as discussion group chairman of the Lancers' Boys Club.

Upon entering Yale University, Civin threw himself into community organizing. In October of 1994, he was sworn in by the New Haven mayor as the new alderman for the First Ward. Soon he became co-chair of the First Ward Democratic Committee. Over the summer of 1993, he worked in Washington, D. C. as a policy and development assistant at the national headquarters for Public Allies, a program that involves local people in the resolution of neighborhood problems. Soon afterward, he began a Baltimore chapter of the program. He has also worked as a lobbyist and legislative researcher for Young People for National Service.

In 1996, Civin was named one of 20 members of USA *Today's* 1996 All-USA College Academic First Team. The honor recognizes the scholastic and leadership achievements of select college and university students in activities on and off the campus. Yale awarded Civin the Alphens Henry Snow Prize, for the senior adjudged to have done the most for Yale and inspired in his classmates a love of learning. The dean of Yale's Calhoun College noted about the young history major, "He's a tremendous researcher. Some of the professors he's had in the history department say he's the best student they've had in the past 20 years."

In December of 1996, Civin was one of 32 Americans selected to be a Rhodes Scholar.

*The Harry Hardie Anglo-American Prize

In 1969, Thomas G. Hardie II, Class of 1939, established the Harry Hardie Anglo-American reciprocal student exchange program with St. Edward's School in Oxford England. Each year, a junior from Gilman spends the end of the spring semester at St. Edward's and a few weeks of summer in England. A junior from St. Edward's visits Gilman during the last six weeks of the academic year and then lives with the family of a Gilman student for several weeks. The purpose of the grant is to strengthen Anglo-American cultural bonds.

1969 John N. Renneburg	1980 Peter W. Cho	1989 David L. Berger
1971 David D. Cross	1981 Alexander C. Gavis	1990 Kyle J. Ackerman
1973 Henry Lee Stockbridge	1982 David J. Brecher	1991 Joshua I. Civin
1974 Joseph Harrison Young	1983 Dennis C. McCoy, Jr.	1992 Steven D. Ness
1975 John T. Behm	1984 Rishika Fernandopulle	1993 John Bond
1976 Daniel R. Scherlis	1985 Gregory P. Lee	1994 Jonathan H. Park
1977 Hal. I. Gann	1986 Andrew S. Barker	1995 Thomas S. Knowles
1978 Andrew B. Jones	1987 George M. Anderson IV	1996 Vincent J. Tuohey
1979 John P. Sarbanes	1988 Michael E. Blumenfeld	1997 Nikolaus S. Steinberg

Adventures as
Reddy's Secretary

BARBARA HAWKS

One morning I called Gilman and told Mr. Finney I was having a hard time getting to work. The snow was piled high and I had three little kids with me. He said not to worry about a thing, to make some sandwiches and get some books and things together, and he'd be over to pick us up. The kids could have fun in the office.

He pulled up in front of the house, and of course, being the gentleman he is, he didn't just sit in the car and honk the horn. He got out, in just his thin suit on this windy, freezing day, and with no boots on, and he walked up through the snow to the door and knocked. I opened it, and saw over his shoulder that his car was drifting down the road. "Reddy, your car is going down the hill!"

Slipping and sliding, he ran after the car, as if he were going to tackle it, or grab it by the reins and pull it up—and I was so worried he'd get hurt—but luckily he didn't catch it until it had run into a snow bank at the bottom of the hill.

From then on, when Mr. Finney offered me a ride, or to pick me up, I would just very politely say, "No thanks, I'll just take myself."

And then, oh, there was one spring I was trying to sell my house, and I was having a very hard time. Finally, we decided it needed to be painted, and that's about as far as we'd gotten. The next thing I knew, Reddy had recruited a whole group of Upper Schoolers, and there they and Reddy were, all over at my house for the entire weekend.

Reddy was telling them how they had to do the best of jobs, and to be careful and to not make any mess at all—this was a very important project on which they were embarking—when, as he was talking and walking around the house, he stepped in a roller dish full of paint. The dish got stuck on his foot, and he hopped along, landed on the brick sidewalk, and there was this huge footprint right on the sidewalk just a day or two before this prospective buyer was supposed to be stopping by!

"Oh Barbara, I'm so sorry. I'm so stupid. . . ." He tried to clean it up and of course that just made it worse, and by this time none of the students could hold it. They were just rolling on the grass; we were all about to split we were laughing so hard, and Mr. Finney was laughing just as hard right along with us.

 Barbara Hawks has been working at Gilman since 1977. The administrative assistant to the headmaster contributes as much to the homey, family-oriented, country-school feel of Gilman as anyone on the campus.

Upper Schoolers crowded into her office during Headmaster Reddy Finney's years at the helm, and they crowd into her office which now adjoins Headmaster Arch Montgomery's. Mrs. Hawks will be talking to trustees one minute about an upcoming meeting with the Executive Committee, and the next she is counseling a senior on being turned down by his favorite college, or stood up early decision by his number-one prom choice. The following should not leak out to future Upper Schoolers, but the fact is she is also a soft touch for a loan for lunch. (Some students, for fear of ravenous classmates, hide their sandwich bags in Mrs. Hawks' file cabinets.)

Barbara Hawks is a wealth, an encyclopedia, of behind-the-scenes information on Gilman School. And she is the epitome of one of founder Anne Carey's key principles: Above all concerns, in one's daily work, the Gilman student comes first. Students immediately sense this and Barbara Hawks has become an adviser and sometime-mother to many a Gilman Upper Schooler.

Past Headmaster Reddy Finney, by 1996, had still not weaned himself of Mrs. Hawks' assistance. He can occasionally be seen, dressed in L. L. Bean boots, khakis, and work shirt, rushing into her office with a crumpled manila envelope filled with sheets of unlined paper containing swirls and circles and arrows and scrawled sentences, which only Barbara Hawks can interpret and type up into a presentable manuscript for publication or a speech.

A Delayed Withdrawal

MICHAEL MCWILLIAMS '93

Bio. 52: Cellular and Developmental Biology: one professor, two hundred and sixty-five students. Gastrulation II headed the handout, a topic which must be of considerable significance, for on this particular Wednesday morning the lecture hall resembled general admission at Camden Yards when the Yankees are in town. Yet even in Bio. 52, a major requirement overcrowded in typical state university fashion, a student can still count on an empty seat in the front row.

The front row is a peculiar place; the front row sees and hears things the second and third rows do not. I learned many important things in the front row that day. I learned about blastocysts, blastopores, and blastulas. I learned about endoderm, ectoderm, and mesoderm. I learned that my professor shaves between his eyebrows. I learned that the second and third rows get stressed out easily, take tons of notes, and whisper a lot. I learned that the front row, contrary to popular belief, is pretty laid back—due to unlimited leg room I would imagine. And I learned that I miss the front row—the circulating chalk dust, the eye contact from the professor, and the feeling of participation as opposed to observation.

As we worked through classical amphibian, insect, and mammalian examples, Gastrulation II lost me to daydreaming. Regaining my concentration, I raised my hand and blurted out, "Are we still talking about frogs here?" The entire lecture hall fell silent, then erupted in laughter. The professor did not answer my question; he just smiled and continued.

It was a legitimate question, I thought, certainly worthy of a response at the very least. It seems the warm embrace of the front row had caused me to forget, however, that one is not supposed to blurt out questions when Bio. 52 is in progress. It was by instinct that I did it. More precisely, it was by Gilman instinct. For we were never expected to actually wait for the teacher to call on us at Gilman. To raise one's hand was simply a courtesy, a formality in the art of questioning, a signal to teachers to let them know who was interrupting them. My teachers in high school would never miss a beat in quickly responding and getting on with the discussion—for that is what I always felt a class at Gilman was, a discussion.

Only two years into college, any attempt to fully capture and encapsulate my experience at Gilman would surely result in failure. Yet, I am ready to acknowledge that whatever it is that Gilman did to me, for me, is with me, and often, quite unexpectedly and sometimes embarrassingly, creeps out in my actions. And I am also able to reflect and recognize the fact that I miss the front row. I miss the camaraderie, the interaction, interest, and care on a personal level. It was not unusual, for example, in "Rev" Afful's religion class for his marriage or his virtuous sex life to become the topic of discussion. It was not unusual for Mr. Vishio's class to turn into a joke session, despite that he never seemed to learn any new ones. And it was not unusual for Mr. Swanson's Eighth and Ninth Grade science classes to quickly shift to a series of Swanson Sagas—like the time he was nearly castrated by a ten-foot spring when a butter-fingered freshman let go in a demonstration of transverse and longitudinal waves.

The Gilman faculty gave me a license to express myself, an arena in which I could think aloud with no reservations. And I have come to realize only through Bio. 52-esque frustrations that I owe a tremendous THANK YOU to the teachers and staff at Gilman; for teachers who really like their students, who go out of their way to help them, whose concern for and interest in their students is genuine and is expressed.

Perhaps the greatest thing about Gilman is this spirit of the teachers—something most students take for granted. In Middle School, the Latin teachers organized an annual chariot race for us (I believe our team came in second, just after the Kickus Buttus). When we studied birds in biology class, Mr. Siwinski brought in his red-tailed hawk; we watched it fly and fed it raw meat. Rev (Afful) took anyone who scored a 100 on his religion tests to Dunkin' Donuts, Steak 'n Egg, or IHOP for breakfast; he honestly believed his crossword puzzles (with word banks!) would be too much for us. During eighth period, Rev could often be found in the senior room, chatting it up with us on some ethical question, usually focusing on what he would not do for a million dollars.

In the hall, one might be met by Mr. Holly with a helpful hint on fielding a punt or judging a fly ball, or by Mr. Finney with a handshake, a pat on the back, and some words of wisdom and encouragement, or by Mr. Tucker, stopping just to see how life was treating you. Monday mornings there would be little presents for the football players—offensive and defensive statistics compiled by Coaches Bristow and Schloeder and, if you were lucky, an in-action photograph or two from Coach Meloy. Coach Meloy's generosity was endless and his magical Oldsmobile trunk bottomless, often emitting selected paraphernalia in line with a student or player's favorite team or future school—hats, shoes, shirts, and sweats, always colorful and always the right size. Coach Poggi, too, was known to write individual post-season notes. My senior year, he wrote me one in which he elevated my status to "honorary lineman" for my blocking as a wingback—this from a man who categorizes football players into two groups: "pantywaists" and "pantywaists who are okay because they are linemen." I am thinking about getting the note framed.

Yet, of the teachers I encountered in my six years at Gilman, no one person had a greater impact on me than did Mr. John E. Schmick. My senior year at Gilman was his last as dean of students; no dean will ever compare.

Mr. Schmick could be scary. His *See me fast!* notes inspired fear. On his office door, written in big bold letters, were the song lyrics, "I Fought The Law and the Law Won." And on his wall was a chilling picture of a smirking Mr. Schmick, his head enlarged and suspended in mid air, peering into the senior room like an Orwellian Big Brother. However, I never thought he enjoyed being scary. Rather, he enjoyed teaching his Shakespeare and his lyric poetry with wide eyes and dramatic gestures. He enjoyed laughing; his solution to a canceled chapel speaker was to roll a Laurel-and-Hardy film on the big screen. He enjoyed helping students in any way possible. He was an encyclopedia of handy tips. Only he could tell us where we could get the prizes for the Gilman Circus. It was a novelty shop in Essex carrying everything from spider rings to piñatas. I do not remember the name of the store. And Mr. Schmick, if I remember correctly, referred to it with his own pet name—Jerry's or something. Upon entering, he immediately guided us to the back of the store, the budget corner. There he directed our attention to the most popular of the traditional Circus widgets and whatchamacallits (see Mr. Schmick for the actual names), and with a pointed finger and a very businesslike expression on his face began ticking the purchases off—two gross of the spiders, five of the Rainbow Bright rings, three gross of the horse erasers . . . I suggested a couple gross of superballs, but Mr. Schmick was hesitant, warning that Lower Schoolers like to throw things in the gym. We compromised on one gross, and sure enough, come Circus time, the balls they were a-flying.

Most of all, however, I believe he enjoyed instilling a sense of honor in each and every student he encountered. I do not think Mr. Schmick set out to consciously do this; nor do I think he would ever accept any credit for having such a profound impact on the growth of so many young men.

Honor and Integrity. Two words that are thrown around a lot at Gilman but are completely worthless without men like Mr. Schmick to embody and live their meaning. To sit on the Honor committee with Mr. Schmick was one of the most valuable learning experiences of my life. It is something every Gilman student should be able to do. For his sensitivity, empathy, and fairness is unleveled and inspiring when expressed. I am still completely dumbfounded by the duration of the Schmick era. Dean of students could not have been an easy position for him. Even in his last year as dean, the pain and concern he experienced when someone "fought the law" never failed to surface in the troubled wrinkles of his forehead and in his slightly faltering voice.

Indeed, Mr. John Schmick made it clear that only the worst suited for the position, only the poorest stoic, can be the best dean of students and the greatest of teachers. To him and to the countless selfless others who made my experience at Gilman something to write about, I am indebted.

Happy Birthday, Gilman.

One would never discern from the low-key manner in which John Michael McWilliams, Jr. conducted his Upper School student days that in his senior year his classmates would elect him "Most likely to succeed," the faculty would award him Gilman's highest honor, The William A. Fisher Medallion, and he would win awards for being co-valedictorian as well as leading scholar of the senior class.

McWilliams also found success on the fields of Gilman, playing varsity baseball and football, with Marty Meloy (baseball) and Sherm Bristow (football) being among his favorite coaches. In 1992, he was a winner of the National Football Foundation and Hall of Fame Scholar-Athlete Award.

John Schmick (adviser and English teacher), Jamie Spragins (English), and Stephen Siwinski (biology) were his favorite Upper School teachers. In his senior year, McWilliams was both student body and senior class president. He was also co-president of the Earth Awareness Club and a member of Students Aiding Friends.

A Morehead Award recipient, McWilliams is attending the University of North Carolina at Chapel Hill, where he is majoring in biology and creative writing with strong scholarly interests in French and race relations. In 1995–96, McWilliams was co-chair of Students for the Advancement of Race Relations and on the advisory board of the Campus Diversity Training Project. He worked in the Campus Y Big Buddy Program 1994–97, mentoring economically disadvantaged and learning-disabled youth. In 1994, McWilliams worked as a juvenile probation counselor intern in Seattle, Washington, assisting, supervising and making court appearances with youths. He continues to put a premium on social work, serving over the 1995–96 academic year as a representative for the Coalition for Economic Justice and the Human Relations Coalition.

Across the Street

BRENT MCCALLISTER, RPCS '94

It was Senior Year, 8:15 a.m., first day back, and I had just made the 315-yard pilgrimage across Roland Avenue, which, with socializing considered, is perfectly timed to occupy the 11 minutes and 59 seconds provided in "passing time." I strolled past the construction of the new Middle School, into the Common Room, through the sea of short-sleeved button-downs over crumpled and heavily stained ties, and the deep voices that bounced off the walls, only to find myself in United States History Since 1945. A Gilman classic, U.S. Since 45 is taught by none other than "Coach Schloeder."

I should have realized the treat I was in for when in the first five minutes of class, roll was called, I was suddenly "Coach McCallister," and Mr. Schloeder told us the story of how he once hung a student out the window who chose misbehavior as a form of amusement—a fellow I quickly assessed as a masochist of some sort. Then we spent the duration of the class discussing the course curriculum—usually a painful experience but which in Coach Schloeder's case was greatly enhanced by his stories, which we were told to judge as "total truths, half truths, or simply apocryphal." I left class that day, and almost every day thereafter, amused, enlightened, and very interested.

I think that is the strongest specific memory I have of Gilman. I always think about it when new friends at college ask me if I minded attending an all-girls school. The whole concept seems somewhat archaic here, amidst the world of college: the entirely coed four-year experience that exists in a bubble, completely separate from most confirmed realities. I always define my appreciation of the experience with the cliché, "But I had the best of both worlds . . . ," and follow it with a description of the coordinated class structure between Gilman, Roland Park, and Bryn Mawr. I explain how I did attend an all-girls school, but that most of my classes were filled with the presence of "The Gilman Boys," who always seemed to be late to RPCS history classes with Mrs. Goldgeier, but never in trouble.

In retrospect, I realize how lucky I am to have had the experience at Gilman. I do not think my education would have been anywhere near complete had I not heard the story of how Mr. Schloeder was essentially asked to be Kennedy's chief of staff, but was forced to turn the offer down, or had I not been called "Coach McCallister" in almost every one of my Gilman classes.

My high-school experience would certainly have been lacking had I not had Mr. Julius in another Gilman history class. I marveled at his short sleeves in the middle of January, the watch he always placed upon his desk which sounded off the passing minutes, and his bright eyes and red beard which added the final touch to making this man the epitome of the wise professor.

And what would Upper School have been without the closing movement of my Gilman/RPCS education, which was conducted with perfection and ease by none other than "Doc Merrill," an incredible teacher who was able to take a classroom of boys—highly charged and often obnoxious I would guess—and turn them to see the beauty and importance of music. Gilman friends would often describe to me what a great experience 10th Grade music appreciation was, despite its being a requirement. I was lucky enough to have Mr. Merrill for AP music history my senior year, and I looked forward to both the class and the teacher every 6th period.

In my two-year, part-time experience at Gilman, I came to realize how much Gilman has to offer those who walk its halls—from the charisma of both its students and faculty, to the honor and tradition which, though tired from years of wear, still grace the halls with the occasional "Yes Sir." I think it was not so much what I learned in the Gilman classrooms that was unique, as with whom I learned it. So many of Gilman's teachers and students have such dynamic personalities that I found I not only learned from Mr. Spragins' passion for Russian literature and a certain Gilman Conservative Republican Student's adamant-verging-on-obnoxious defense of Nixon, but I sought to equal their passions for both the sake of learning and the desire to remind Gilman what having females in class is all about. Only the occasional hints of chauvinism, mostly lurking in the pages of astrophysics and advanced physical mechanics texts, dimmed the gusto of the coeducational environment, but it was nothing that a few human-relations gender days or mini-week events couldn't keep in line.

So after about six classes at Gilman, eight hundred soccer, baseball, football, and lacrosse games, countless friends, and even more memorable experiences, I have to say that for me, Gilman definitely played a role in that whole experience of "The Upper School Years." As the changes of the past hundred years are considered, as well as those which are to come, the essence of Gilman—its faculty, its students, and its history—will continue to mold and change those who seek to learn.

Brent McCallister attended Roland Park Country School from Seventh to Twelth Grades, becoming president of the Student Government Association as a senior. She was a four-year varsity player in both hockey and lacrosse. During her junior and senior years, she took classes at Gilman, her favorite subjects being the history and literature of South Africa, and the history and literature of Imperial Russia.

Graduating from RPCS in 1994, Ms. McCallister entered Princeton, where she is concentrating on history and continuing to play lacrosse. She hopes to some day work with the government, helping to formulate public policy, especially in regard to educational reforms.

The Priority of Excellence

MARK V. LORD '93

The eyes followed me wherever I went in my years at Gilman. They were the eyes of men I will never meet. Dressed in fine suits, painted in stately, patriarchal poses, and hanging from the walls of the Common Room, most of them are long since dead. I may never know them, but I know without question or doubt what they believed. They believed in the power of education, the maintenance of tradition, and the spirit of children. They believed in Gilman. Those eyes watched as thousands of students shuffled by over the years, serving as both a silent audience and jury.

As I look back on my life at Gilman, emotions surface which are uncharacteristic for me. I remember times when I felt as though I could have walked away from the institution and never returned. I watched, as changeless to a fault and falling back easily on the concepts of tradition, Gilman did little to stop friends from leaving for other schools—other schools which fit to the student and not ones which asked the student to conform to it. Often frustrated, I continued my search for self-definition throughout my time at Gilman, eventually realizing that Gilman was a larger part of me than I had ever known.

With each day away from Gilman, I reach a higher understanding of the magnitude with which my time there affected my life. Beyond a superior text education, I gained an irreplaceable understanding of respect and friendship, and a perception of what is important in life.

The greatness in Gilman lies not in what is taught in classrooms, but in what is learned outside of them. I cannot remember any specific facts about my physics class, but I do remember meeting my teacher, Mr. Shields, every day during his lunch hour, trying to pin down the concepts which had eluded me during class. He was the most meticulous person I believe I will ever meet. Life to him was a science, with every moment predetermined and calculated. Lunch was as unchanging as the periodic table. Skim milk, and some leftover dinner in Tupperware, a napkin in his lap, and perfect posture. I know this because it was not unusual for him to sacrifice his lunch hour, seemingly every day, to help me survive his class. It was not unusual for him to graciously meet with me more than twice a day, so that I would have a complete understanding of his physics.

Mr. Wolf taught us, in his own way, how to earn respect. It could be debated whether or not Mr. Wolf—the polar opposite of Mr. Shields—knew the English word "organization." His classes and teaching methods may have been unorthodox, but his relationships with students rendered a teacher-student trust and friendship which was invaluable. Sitting at his desk among tests and papers (some probably dating back to the mid-1960s) he was never alone, usually chatting with a group of students about pizza deliveries or mathematical probabilities. More students turned to him with their problems and questions than he would ever admit.

Ms. Checkoway struggled with the rigid structure of Gilman for the benefit of her students. A woman in a traditionally male institution, she fought hard for the respect which she gained. She introduced me to the power of writing and literature. When I picture her, it is from the chair next to her desk. She is sitting amongst stacks of papers, binders, and books which cast long shadows in the afternoon, while methodically explaining her unreadable purple markings on my papers. Ms. Checkoway pushed me to pursue education outside of the classroom. Because of her encouragement I began tutoring at Roland Park Public, and I found a love for fiction and writing. I can directly attribute my being a writing major at Johns Hopkins to her influence.

I not only remember Francis "Biff" Poggi as my football coach; I primarily recall the summer weeks I spent in South Carolina with other students at his camp for underprivileged children. I envision Biff standing in a fallow field in rural Beaufort, South Carolina, his PING golf hat tilted to thwart the sun, the children flocked around him asking strings of incessant questions. I see him standing among the children in his white Gilman coaching-staff shirt. Every pair of young eyes are fixed upward at him, and there is a smile on every face.

The quality of the Gilman experience is found not only in the nature of its selfless faculty, but also in friendships formed over the years. Collectively, the class of 1993 was distinctive in its diversity as well as in its cohesiveness. At graduation, I looked at my classmates and the way Gilman had influenced us. I took a moment to examine the friends who surrounded me—the friends who had sat beside me in classes, competed on the athletic fields, and shared each other's successes and failures. We now stood together, having completed a journey. Our paths may not have been the same, but everyone arrived at the same destination, prepared for the next journey.

For me, the importance of Gilman tradition had been felt every time I pulled on a Gilman uniform. I became a participant in history, in the continuance of time-honored rivalries every time I collided with a McDonogh Eagle or a Poly Engineer. Teammates and I listened to the words of Coach Bristow with the knowledge that he had been a part of Greyhound teams of the past.

With my Gilman background, I feel confident in my ability to meet the adversities which life presents. I always knew Gilman was a privilege which I was very fortunate to have experienced. Its name alone has provided opportunities which might have otherwise been unreachable. Gilman prepared me fully for university life and gave me the tools for success in the future.

The shared experience of my classmates has now led us down diverging paths. We are becoming writers, lawyers, and doctors, each one of us uniquely expanding upon the foundations Gilman has provided. The layers of experience may thicken, but our Gilman adventure always remains near the surface. I may walk down the nostalgic halls in the future, among the paintings and trophies, and feel a comfortable sense of changelessness, knowing I had been there before and that those principles which have remained unalterable at Gilman are crucial to the very essence of the institution: integrity, humility, and excellence.

Mark Lord attended Gilman 1988–93, his favorite intellectual activities being the reading and writing of fiction, and his favorite teacher being Julie Checkoway. He was a two-year varsity man in both football and lacrosse. Known for being an extremely hard hitter on the football field, Lord had to spend many an hour in the weight-lifting room packing muscle onto a slight body frame.

Lord entered Johns Hopkins University, where he is enrolled in the Writing Seminars program. He has continued his football career—as well as the weight-lifting program—at Johns Hopkins despite accruing injuries playing against men 50 to 100 pounds heavier, which resulted in four major surgeries. Mark Lord's brother Ted graduated from Gilman in 1995, and his father, Charles V. Lord, was a member of the class of 1960.

December

MICHAEL B. KLEINMAN '95

I have only seen David Payne run on two occasions in my life. The first time was on the football field, and the second was when he ran into the senior room to spread the word that Student "X" (who will remain nameless for legal reasons) was being led out of the building in handcuffs. It is important, though, to keep in mind that Payne was an offensive tackle in football, not a position noted for producing speed-demons.* So, by the time Payne reached the Senior Room with his information, running in during lunch and screaming the news that Student "X" was being led out in handcuffs—which resulted in a mass flight of 30 seniors out of the room, leaving our lunches sitting half-eaten on the tables and the ping pong paddles dropped to the floor—the arrested had already left the building. For this simple reason, I missed witnessing the single most interesting development to occur during my 12 years at Gilman.

To be honest, the whole drug bust did not really affect my life that much. Nor did it really, in a concrete manner, affect most of my classmates. Do not get me wrong, there were quite a few who had to trek into Mr. Montgomery's office and admit to using the evil weed, and there were quite a few who had to spend some sleepless nights wondering if they were going to get probation or more drastic punishment. Yet, a vast majority of my classmates were not put into this predicament. This is not to say that a majority of the class of 1995 did not or has never used drugs. (I have no idea what percentage of my class has used drugs.) This only means that if other students did use drugs, then their dealers were more intelligent than Student "X"—not a hard trick to pull off.

But the purpose of this essay is not to analyze the extent or the severity of the drug problem at Gilman in the mid-'90s. Drugs were used neither more nor less at Gilman than at other private schools. Yet, after the arrest had been made, the press

*Payne, one of Gilman's outstanding football players of the 1990s, attends Notre Dame, where he continues to prove his skills, toughness, and work ethic on the gridiron.

acted like a dog which has found a new bone on which to chew. The story made the front page of The *Sun*, *Baltimore Magazine* published a long article about the incident, etc. Besides the details of the arrest, there was an editorial slant to most of these news articles—a smug comment along the lines that the elite private school of Gilman was no more protected from the drug culture than public schools. Friends of mine from other schools, both public and private, tended to gloat a little over Gilman's misfortune. It was almost as if people were saying, "See, you aren't as special as you thought you were!"* This type of smug, gloating response caught me a little off guard, but I did not have much time to think about it. Along with most members of my class, I had something more immediate to deal with that December: whether or not we got into college early.

Symptoms of college fever had begun to be evident in the spring of my junior year when people began going on their first college visits and had their first meetings with the college guidance counselors—Messrs. Christ, Rogers, and Woodward. By the time senior year began, as early as September, college was one of the most talked about topics: Where are you thinking about applying? Do you think you can get in?, etc.

I was not immune from all this. My classmates and I went through the process of visiting schools, filling out applications, answering essay questions such as "If you were a dog, what type of dog would you be?"—as if I had ever given this question any thought, or even cared what type of dog I would be. A collie? Or maybe the admissions person preferred golden retrievers? It was an infuriating process. I had never before done anything like applying to college, nor did I have any idea what colleges were looking for. Should I answer the essay questions by writing what I really felt, or should I write what I thought college admissions people were looking for? How could I hope to remember how many hours of community service I did in Ninth Grade, and who would know if I exaggerated things a little? Besides these concerns, the problem with filling out college applications is that you have to enter the same boring information on each application. The sheer tedium of it all, combined with the fact that this boring information might very well determine where you spent the next four years, made it a torturous task. Regardless, as the months marched on, the applications were completed. November and the application deadline came and went, and I became more nervous. I had applied to college early, meaning I would be accepted, rejected, or wait-listed at my first choice college, Yale, as early as December.

As December arrived, the college counselors became all but useless. The only thing I wanted to know was whether or not they had heard anything; or, barring

---

*On Friday, December 16, one 16-year-old Gilman student was arrested in Carey Hall by Baltimore City Police for possession of marijuana with intent to distribute. He and three others were expelled from Gilman, while two others were suspended. The student, a minor, was found to have in his school locker: a small film cannister containing marijuana, a small pouch containing the drug, two smoking devices, an electronic pager, and $632 in cash, according to a police report.

that, I wanted to know what they thought my chances of getting accepted were. I was desperate for any type of information I could get my hands on, and so was the rest of my class. Yet, the college counselors were not talking; if they had information, *they were keeping it to themselves.* I pictured myself marching right into Mr. Christ's office and shaking him until he told me what I wanted to hear. I did not give in to this temptation, nor, I think, did any of my classmates.

The worst, though, was Mr. Bulkeley, Gilman's resident hockey coach, counselor, and English teacher. A large middle-aged man with dark hair, glasses, and a perpetually red face. A person you could talk easily to, sitting on the old broken couch in his office. You had to sit slouched down though, to avoid bumping your head on the rows of sagging bookshelves which loomed over the couch. I always thought that if they broke and all those old English textbooks and drug/alcohol education pamphlets came tumbling down on me, it would take hours to dig me out. That is, if they could find me in Mr. Bulkeley's office, his preferred filing system being toss and forget. Most importantly to me, Mr. Bulkeley was Gilman's strongest link to Yale, being an active, superactive, alumnus. I was convinced that he could, if he so wished, get whomever he wanted into Yale.

As December rolled around, he became reticent—refusing to speak with anyone about Yale, or more exactly about whom he thought would or would not get in. Eventually, after he had brushed me off more than once, I stopped asking him for fear that he would, out of annoyance, interfere with the college acceptance gods at Yale and I would not be admitted. This, in hindsight, was clearly not a rational thought, but then again, I was not in a rational state of mind. Then, one cold night, three of my classmates got wait-listed, while I heard nothing. It was the night of the Mountcastle Lecture, and the grim posse approached me as I entered the auditorium that evening, asking if I had heard anything. All I could do was mumble no and quickly walk away—could their bad luck be contagious?

The next day, sitting around the common room, I saw Mr. Bulkeley talking with one of my classmates. I could not contain myself anymore, I HAD TO KNOW. I shuffled over to try to listen to their conversation; maybe they were talking about college. I only heard a few tantalizing sentences from Mr. Bulkeley—". . . and then in the dorms, but do you really want to hear about that now? I mean, what other questions . . ." before he saw me and stopped short.

"What do you want?" he asked of me nicely enough.

"I, I was just curious if, well, if maybe you might know something . . ." I mumbled, getting red in the face.

"What are you saying?" he asked, a smile playing across his lips. I hated him at that moment. I hated him because he knew, and because I did not know, and because he knew why I was so uncomfortable asking him about it.

"Well, well . . . nothing, I guess, I really just wanted to know, nothing, forget . . ." I suddenly realized there was something I feared even more than the nervousness of not knowing whether I was in or not, and that was the possibility that he might actually answer me. I shifted my eyes around the room and then slouched back to the couch where I had been sitting, a "thanks anyway" floating in the air behind me. He watched me sit down, then returned to his previous conversation. That night I told myself not to worry, that of course I would get accepted, after all, I went to Gilman . . .

Over the 12 years of my Gilman education, my class and I had been led to believe that we were the best that Baltimore had to offer. It seemed to be that from the start we were being groomed to join the "establishment"—a web of successful local businessmen, politicians, artists, and community leaders, many of whom were knotted together by their Gilman educations. By dint of our superior education—our sound training in mind, body, and spirit—we were expected to prosper at college and in life beyond. There is nothing wrong with the school expecting its students to succeed. Yet, somewhere along the line, things got a little mixed up: people began seeing success as a right which one was unequivocally granted upon graduation from Gilman. This viewpoint was wrong. Yet, I bought into the myth that because I went to Gilman I had the right to expect nothing but success, especially in the college process. How could they turn me down?—I went to Gilman. On the whole, we as students did not mind this very much. It is a wonderful thing to be told how special you are, and not many people went out of their way to argue that we were not the best.

So, in December of 1994, talk about early acceptance and other college plans dominated the discussions of a large part of the class. Not everyone was wrapped up in this; some people did not apply early, and others simply did not care. Sitting on the ungainly but comfortable couches and the red overstuffed chairs which dot the Common Room like small islands, students would talk about how of course student "A" would get in, after all he was a varsity football player and he would soon be a Fisher Medallion winner and he had already come up with the cure for male pattern baldness, while maybe student "B" would not be so lucky: he only played water polo and his grades were not that good.

This was one of the reasons things got so tense in the Common Room as college decisions began to filter back that December. The credo that Gilman students were the best was about to be put to the test in college admissions offices around the country, and this made me and quite a few of my classmates rather nervous; obviously, colleges did not feel that we as Gilman students had an automatic right to success/admission, not with so many of us getting denied early admission. All of a sudden, many of us found out that we were not special after all, that a Gilman education was not an automatic "get-into-college" card. Among those who did get in there was joy; among those who did not, there were sometimes feelings of bitterness and anger.

Looking back, it is interesting to see how right the media were after all. I did think I was entitled to success simply because I attended Gilman; I just did not admit this to myself at the time. It seems as though many of us thought we were so entitled simply because we attended Gilman, and it took the twin shocks of the drug bust and college acceptances to show us, or at least me at any rate, that we were no more guaranteed success than anyone else.

 A 12-year-man at Gilman, Michael B. Kleinman's main intellectual interest was in history. His advisor and history teacher, Peter Julius, along with history teacher Nick Schloeder and First Grade homeroom teacher Wilma Hilliard, were among his favorite teachers.

In the Upper School, Kleinman headed both the Jewish Students Association and the Peer Counseling Group; he also worked as a Writing Center Counselor. In his junior year, Kleinman was given the Williams College Book Award for his understanding of American history. As a senior, he was awarded the Cleveland Essay Prize, the Herbert E. Pickett Prize for General Proficiency in History, and the Armstrong Prize for Proficiency in Prose.

Kleinman enjoyed football, track, and cross country at the J.V. level, and varsity track, specializing in discus throwing, as a senior. He wrote "December" while working through a heat wave as a summer camp counselor at Gilman before heading off for Yale University. At Yale, Kleinman was secretary of his freshman class and a member of his college council. He writes for the University newspaper and is involved in the campus Democratic party.

Brand New Shoes

CHAZ HOWARD '96

Change is sometimes an unwanted thing. This was most definitely the case for many, if not all Gilman students, upon the arrival of the news that Mr. Finney was to retire in June of 1992. Our disappointment did not necessarily stem from Mr. Finney's departure, however, since we all felt that he had far more than earned his time to rest. Yet, we were sadly aware that we would have to find someone to replace the irreplaceable. And so, towards the beginning of my Eighth Grade year, I, along with the rest of the special "Headmaster Replacement Committee," began my mission impossible to find *some* man or woman who could fill Mr. Finney's humongous shoes.

This committee was made up of students, faculty, alumni, parents, friends, and the Board of Trustees. I am now well aware that my little Middle School opinion did not count for very much, yet there was no way that you could have told me that back then. I felt that finding a new headmaster was as much my responsibility as anyone's. It was with this attitude that I would interview all of the prospective replacements.

Well, we all know how the story ends, or perhaps begins, as the committee elected Mr. Montgomery as the next Headmaster of Gilman School. I can clearly remember what I was thinking as I listened to this man I would ultimately grow very close to, yet at the time felt extremely distant from . . . "What a preppy! He looks like he's straight out of Prep-ultimate Academy. He acts just like a politician. Look at how he shakes hands and smiles and kisses babies! (I may have gone a bit overboard with that one.) What a pretty boy! His hair doesn't move. His clothes are perfectly ironed. He is always . . ."

I went on like this in my head for the length of the interview while the other students in the room asked him an assortment of questions. I remember picturing this man as our headmaster, as I did with all of the candidates. I saw him in his perfectly pressed pin-striped suit, with his unmoving hair, addressing a student body dressed in perfectly pressed pin-striped suits, all with the same closely-cropped haircuts. As scary as that image was to me, I knew that in that imaginary speech to the replicated student body, Mr. Montgomery was, with his strong and caring voice, delivering a meaningful message. For through talking to him, I was introduced to one of the most knowledgeable and honorable men I would ever meet.

Over the years, I grew closer to Mr. Montgomery on a teacher/student level. As a freshman, I had him as a teacher for Ninth Grade religion. One day, we had an in-class assignment to write an essay on Martin Luther King, Jr.'s "A Letter from the Birmingham Jail." In my opinion, my essay was the best piece of writing I had penned that year. However, Mr. Montgomery did not feel the same way. When I eyed that 72 on my desk the next day, I wanted to . . . inflict pain upon him. But then I read the comments. He explained to me how I had pretty much skipped the main points of the letter. But rather than just pointing out my mistakes, he praised the good points of my paper, and that meant a lot to me.

It would not be until the end of my junior year and the beginning of my senior year that I could say I truly knew the man. It was during this time that our relationship evolved from teacher/student, to sometimes big brother/little brother, sometimes father/son, yet most often friend and friend. Being the president of the school is not an easy job at Gilman, as I found out my senior year. With the aid and advice of Mr. Montgomery, this experience became one that helped shape my life.

Over the summer of 1995, the cafeteria food prices were raised significantly, and the student body did not like this very much. So towards the end of the year, the student council held an open forum during assembly. After opinions were sent flying to the senior representatives who were leading the forum, it was decided that the Upper School would boycott the cafeteria. Maybe I should mention that there were no teachers present.

The boycott worked and the food service people suffered a great loss in money and a great waste in food. The student body got what it asked for, and prices were generously lowered. A victory for the students! Or so I thought.

I met with Mr. Montgomery and spoke about what had happened. I was expecting to get a handshake and congratulations for how the students banded together and flexed their muscle in order to make a change. In this meeting, my eyes were opened to the other side. I hadn't even thought how much money it had cost the cafeteria in our few days of boycotting. I hadn't realized that the job security of some of the workers there—who had shown my friends and me nothing but love for 12 years—was shaken. I'm glad that these facts were brought to my attention, but by then it was too late.

What an easy man he is to talk to. There are so many teachers in school that are intimidating. He never seemed that way to me. Not to say that he is a "wuss" either! A fond memory of Mr. Montgomery's courage (or maybe insanity) revolves around the time he decided to wrestle an old friend of mine, Scott So. We used to call Scott "B-train" . . . and all it took was one hit from Scotty for you to understand this nickname. He was big. Anyway, in the middle of the gym hallway, Mr. Montgomery challenges B-train to wrestle him. Scott releases a howl of glee. I'm thinking, "Poor old headmaster. He's been working too hard. Too many meetings with those trustees have affected his brain. He doesn't know what he's getting himself into. . . . hey, hey, hey."

The next thing I know, Scott is up in the air, at least two feet off the hard gym floor.

Scott releases another howl, only this time it is out of fear. Within seconds, the screaming and laughter (from the onlookers) stops, Mr. Montgomery declares his victory and marches down to wrestling practice.

It was little things like that which brought him closer to many students. It was his "talking trash" to Brandon "Bird" Croxton about basketball and his challenging of Terrance Whitehead in different track events that brought him close to them. Maybe it was his encouragement on the sidelines as the football team battled McDonogh on those rainy Saturday afternoons. Or maybe it was his genuine compassion that he shared with my friends and me after an ignorant guy at a lacrosse game made some racist remarks.

If you don't believe me, watch him for a day. He'll still come to work in his preppy suit, but that's O.K. Watch him pick up trash as he walks across the campus. Watch him teach those crazy freshmen in his religion class. Watch him make a Lower Schooler's day simply by calling out the boy's name and saying good morning. Watch him at football practice giving confidence to our young athletes. Then watch him go home to his loving family. Watch him with his wife and two boys. Watch this man in action, and maybe you'll begin to understand.

Everyone wondered how Mr. Montgomery was going to fill Mr. Finney's shoes. Well, to them I say, he can't. Because he's got on a whole 'nother pair of his own.

 Charles "Chaz" Howard came to Gilman in September of 1983 and graduated June 17, 1996. Late afternoons in his Lower School years were spent collecting and trading comic books and baseball cards with his classmates. By Middle School, he was becoming a leader of his class and taking an interest in political science as well as religious topics. His favorite teachers were Johnny Foreman and Jerry Thornbery. Foreman taught him Middle School science and later coached him in track; Thornbery taught him Black History and American Government.

In Howard's senior year, he was co-captain of the track team, which won the MIAA championship for the second consecutive year. On Founders Day, Howard was awarded the school's highest honor, the Fisher Medallion.

As president of the school in his senior year, Howard was known for keeping his cool in the most heated of meetings. Some of this "cool presence" was also exemplified in his many appearances with John Merrill's Traveling Men throughout his Upper School years. Howard was also a member of the Black Awareness Group and the Gilman Mentoring Program.

Following in the footsteps of mentor Arch Montgomery, Chaz Howard is attending the University of Pennsylvania, where he is filling his own shoes.

Appendix

A.

FROM THE FIRST PROSPECTUS
OF THE COUNTRY SCHOOL FOR BOYS
(1897)

BOARD OF TRUSTEES

WILLIAM A. FISHER, PRESIDENT
ALLAN MCLANE, TREASURER
WILLIAM H. BUCKLER, SECRETARY

HERBERT B. ADAMS
CHARLES J. BONAPARTE
WILLIAM CABELL BRUCE

FRANCIS K. CAREY
CHARLES D. FISHER
JOHN W. GARRETT
WILLIAM OSLER
HARRY FIELDING REID
WILLIAM S. THAYER

FOUNDERS

EDWIN F. ABELL
WILLIAM H. BALDWIN
NICHOLAS P. BOND
JOHN W.S. BRADY
LOUISE ESTE FISHER BRUCE
WILLIAM CABELL BRUCE
WILLIAM H. BUCKLER
ANNE GALBRAITH CAREY
FRANCIS K. CAREY
CHARLES D. FISHER
D. K. ESTE FISHER
WILLIAM A. FISHER
GEORGE W. GAIL
JOHN W. GARRETT
FRANK GOSNELL
H. IRVINE KEYSER
R. BRENT KEYSER

LOUIS MCLANE
CHARLES F. MAYER
DANIEL MILLER
BENJAMIN F. NEWCOMER
ISAAC F. NICHOLSON
ALBERT G. OBER
GUSTAVUS OBER
HENRY A. PARR
HARRY FIELDING REID
FRANCIS WHITE

FREDERICK WINSOR, A. B. (HARVARD),
  HEAD MASTER

HENRY H. BALLARD, PH.D. (JOHNS
  HOPKINS), ASSISTANT MASTER
JOHN H. CHASE, A. B. (HARVARD),
  ASSISTANT MASTER

B.

GILMAN HEADMASTERS

FREDERICK WINSOR, 1897–1900

ROLAND J. MULFORD, 1900–1903

SAMUEL W. KINNEY, 1903–1909

EDWIN B. KING, 1909–1912

FRANK W. PINE, 1912–1919

L. WARDLAW MILES, 1919–1926

E. BOYD MORROW, 1926–1943

HENRY H. CALLARD, 1943–1963

LUDLOW H. BALDWIN, 1963–1968

REDMOND C. S. FINNEY, 1968–1992

ARCHIBALD R. MONTGOMERY IV, 1992–Present

C.

BOARD OF TRUSTEES

PRESIDENTS

WILLIAM A. FISHER, 1897–1900

FRANCIS M. JENCKS, 1900–1907

JOSEPH S. AMES, 1907–1912

JOHN M.T. FINNEY, 1912–1942

CHARLES S. GARLAND, 1943–1949(Feb.)

EDWARD K. DUNN SR., 1949(Feb.)–1956

RICHARD W. EMORY, 1956–1965

I. RIDGEWAY TRIMBLE, 1965–1969

OWEN DALY II, 1969–1975

WILLIAM J. MCCARTHY, 1975–1980

J. RICHARD THOMAS, 1980–1985

GEORGE E. THOMSEN, 1985–1990

GEORGE B. HESS, JR., 1990–1994

JAMES S. RIEPE, 1994–

TRUSTEES

ADAMS, HERBERT B., 1897–1900

ALEXANDER, JR., CHARLES B. '26, 1931–33

ALLAN, DAVID W. '64, 1987–93

AMES, JOSEPH S., 1900–04, 1907–37

ARMIGER, JR., JOHN W. '62, 1977–81

AUSTIN, MICHAEL J. '76, 1990–

AYERS, RICHARD A., 1984–85

BAETJER, HARRY N., 1928–38

BAETJER, JR., H. NORMAN '35, 1958–75

BANK, RAYMOND L. '71, 1987–

BAKER, JR., RUSSELL T. '60, 1972–82

BAKER, WILLIAM R. '65, 1984–86

BALDWIN, H. FURLONG '50, 1967–71

BALDWIN, LUDLOW H. '22, 1928–33

BARRETT, ALLEN M. '40, 1951–69

BARRETT, JR., ALLEN M. '67, 1978–81

BARTLETT, DIRCK K. '82, 1996–

BEIRNE, FRANCIS F. '08, 1935–50

BIRCKHEAD, HUGH, 1916–19

BLACK, GARY '35, 1947–60

BLUE, HENRY M. '74, 1996–

BOLTON, PERRY J. '49, 1974–78, 1979–83

BONAPARTE, CHARLES J., 1897–98

BOURNE, JR., KENNETH A. '60, 1976–79, 1989–92

BOUTON, EDWARD H., 1911–12

BOWE, RICHARD E., 1970–78

BOWIE, C. KEATING '32, 1966–70

BOYD, ROBERT F. '62, 1988–91

BOYNTON, JR. GEORGE E. '56, 1972–75

Bradley, J. Brooks '69, 1992–
Bremermann, Jr., H.J., 1972–73
Brewster, Daniel B. '14, 1933–35
Brewster, Gerry L. '75, 1990–93
Broadus, Jr., Thomas H., 1982–90
Brooks, Andrew M. '74, 1989–92
Brown, Jr., Edward W. '57, 1983–87
Bruce, James '10, 1920–28
Bruce, William C., 1897–99
Brune, Herbert M., 1907–48
Buckler, William H., 1897–1906
Burnett, Calvin W., 1983–91
Campbell, R. McLean '42, 1962–66, 1969–78
Campbell, William B. '52, 1988–96
Caplan, Hilary D., 1994–95
Caplan, Mark M. '76, 1994–
Carey, Andrew G. '17, 1927–28, 1938–47
Carey, Francis J. '06, 1916–30
Carey, Francis K., 1897–1944
Carey, Jr., G. Cheston '47, 1975–83
Carey III, James '12, 1924–25, 1928–48
Carey, William P. '48, 1981–89, 1990–
  Lifetime
Chriss, Timothy D.A. '68, 1988–92
Clapp, Ann K., 1985–89
Classen, John N. '34, 1957–61
Claster, John H. '63, 1973–76
Cochran II, Alexander S. '31, 1947–59
Coe, Jr., Ward B. '32, 1964–67
Colston, Frances F., 1981–87
Cooper, J. Crossan, 1913–37
Cooper, Jr., J. Crossan '19, 1935–67
Cooper, Joseph W.J. '21, 1926–29
Daly II, Owen '43, 1952–85, Lifetime
Dates, Victor H., 1975–82
DeGroff, Jr., Ralph L. '54, 1990–
deMuth, David L. '80, 1994–
Dohme, Alfred R.L., 1928–51
Dorsey III, William R. '52, 1973–75
Dunn, Edward K. '18, 1925–79
Dunn, Jr., Edward K. '53, 1969–73
Egerton, J. McKenny '23, 1930–33
Emmons, Charles C. '23, 1951–55
Emory, Richard W. '31, 1946–65,
  Lifetime

Farber, Jr., Dawson L. '35, 1964–81,
  Lifetime
Fenwick, Jr., Charles C. '66, 1985–
Finney, D.C. Wharton '43, 1962–65
Finney, George G. '17, 1933–68
Finney, John M.T., 1906–42
Fisher, Charles D., 1897–98
Fisher, D.K. Este, 1903–47
Fisher, Judge William A., 1897–1900
Fisher, Jr., William A. '31 1928–44
Fisher III, William A. '68, 1990–
Ford, Jr., Harry M., 1980–81
Foster, Arthur D. '22, 1928–29
Fowlkes, Hobart V. '59, 1977–82
French, Jr., George R. '71, 1985–88
Frick, James Swan, 1918–25
Gaines, Jr., W. Lee '69, 1976–80
Galleher, Jr., Earl P. '44, 1971–75,
  1977–85
Garland, Charles S., 1940–61
Garrett, Harrison '29, 1947–50
Garrett, John W., 1897–1901, 1903–06
Garrett, Johnson '31, 1939–42
Gephart, George W., 1971–72
Gibbs, W.T. Dixon '23, 1955–59
Glover, Charles, 1909–13
Godine, Douglas M. '53, 1973–76
Goldsborough II, Brice W. '23, 1926–30
Gordon, Douglas H., 1909–18
Gordon, Jr., Douglas H. '21, 1928–48
Gorman, Douglas, 1928–44
Gorman, Edmund N. '32, 1956–59
Graham, William A. '25, 1950–54
Griswold, B. Howell, 1920–25
Griswold III, Benjamin H. '29, 1947–62
Griswold, Jack S. '60, 1989–94
Grose, Robert W. '59, 1976–79, 1980–88
Hammar, Arthur M., 1911–17
Hardesty, James D. '63, 1985–95
Harris, H. Patterson '04, 1912–16
Harris, W. Hall, 1900–06
Harris, Jr., W. Hall, 1905–11
Harvey, A. McGehee, 1963–75
Harvey, Jr., Curran W. '47, 1971–79
Harvey, John L. '69, 1984–88
Hess, Jr., George B. '55, 1974–Lifetime

REID, HARRY F., 1897–1909
RIENHOFF, WILLIAM F., 1935–57
RIEPE, JAMES S., 1989–
RIGGS, FRANCIS G. '57, 1967–70
RIGGS, JR., LAWRASON '53, 1974–77
ROGERS, BRIAN C., 1995–
ROSENBERG, JR., HENRY A., 1979–87
ROYAL III, WALTER '73, 1992–
RUSSELL II, ROBERT B. '51, 1970–77
RUSSELL III, T. EDGIE '60, 1988–92
RYLAND, WILLIAM H. '53, 1970–73
SAWHILL, JOHN C. '54, 1980–83
SCARLETT, RAYMOND G. '18, 1924–26
SCARLETT, WILLIAM G., 1918–33
SCARLETT, JR., W. GEORGE '23, 1941–43,
    1947–52
SCHMICK, JR., WILLIAM F., 1951–64
SCHMIDT, CARL W., 1986–87
SCHWEIZER, SR., THOMAS, 1960–80
SCHWEIZER, JR., THOMAS '62, 1976–78,
    1979–90
SCOTT, STEPHEN T. '64, 1985–
SHAPIRO, RONALD M., 1977–95
SHATTUCK III, MAYO A., 1992–
SHOEMAKER, JR., DUDLEY '31, 1948–52
SIMMS, LOUISE W., 1973–81
SIMMS, STUART O. '68, 1989–93
SINCLAIR, JAMES L., 1972–81
SLACK, W. CAMERON '46, 1963–66
SLAGLE, JACOB W. '23, 1941–48
SNEAD, JAMES A. '68, 1990–
SNEAD, JR., JOHN E. '61, 1980–83
SPRAGINS, BETSEY R., 1970–84
STAMAS, GEORGE P. '69, 1996–
STANLEY, JR., J. SNOWDEN '60, 1987–91
STEWART, JR., GEORGE A. '39, 1972–76
STEWART, LATIMER S. '25, 1933–46
STIFLER III, WILLIAM C. '59, 1991–95
STINSON, JR., EDWARD '18, 1943–50
STONESIFER, ANN CARTER, 1970–80
SWANN, SHERLOCK '18, 1928–35
SWINDELL, JR., ROBERT H. '51, 1971–74
SYMINGTON, THOMAS H., 1908–13
TESTA, ADENA, 1991–

THAYER, WILLIAM S., 1897–1933
THOMAS, HENRY B. '76, 1995–
THOMAS, SR., J. RICHARD '43, 1978–85,
    Lifetime
THOMAS, JR., J. RICHARD '72, 1988–
THOMAS, SR., ROBERT M. '38, 1953–67
THOMSEN, GEORGE E. '48, 1983–91,
    1992–Lifetime
TILGHMAN, JR., RICHARD C. '65, 1979–91
TRIMBLE, I. RIDGEWAY '18, 1936–71
TRIMBLE, JR., WILLIAM C. '53, 1980–82
TRIPTOW, DONNA, 1996–
TUCKER, EDWARD N., 1989–92
TURNBULL, JR., DOUGLAS C., 1948–57
TURNER, CHARLES T. '36, 1953–56
TURNER, JR., JAMES F. '26, 1950–53
UHLIG II, J. RICHARD '59, 1983–89
VAN DEN BERG, MILTON H., 1970–79
VOHRER, SUSAN S., 1995–
WALKER, M. COOPER '33, 1954–70
WAGANDT, MARY JO, 1995–
WAGNER, JR., FREDERICK W. '27, 1953–55
WAXTER, JR., THOMAS J.S. '52, 1966–69
WEAVER III, ALVA P. '49, 1974–77
WEST III, JOHN H. '61, 1981–84
WHEELWRIGHT, JERE H., 1912–20
WILLIAMS, JR., CHARLES T. '24, 1954–58
WILLIAMS, HUNTINGDON '10, 1936–54
WILLIAMS, MCRAE '54, 1989–93
WILLIAMS, PALMER F.C. '19, 1937–63
WILLARD, JR., DANIEL, 1938–40
WILLIS, RALPH N. '49, 1964–68, 1975–82
WINSTEAD, ELIZABETH M., 1981–82
WINSTEAD III, WILLIAM H., 1983–91
WITTICH, MARGOT O., 1985–86
WOOD, W. BARRY, 1957–65
WOOD, H. GRAHAM '28, 1952–54
WOODS, JR., ALAN C. '36, 1962–66
WOODWARD, THEODORE E., 1976–80,
    Lifetime
WORTHINGTON, HENRY M. '48, 1977–84
YOUNG, HUGH H., 1913–19
ZINK, PHILIP R. '65, 1981–1994

D.

PRESIDENTS OF ALUMNI ASSOCIATION
(Sinces its formation in 1906)

1906–1909 IREDELL W. INGLEHART '04	1955–1956 M. COOPER WALKER '33
1909–1910 F. LAWRENCE GOODWIN '03	1956–1957 ROBERT M. THOMAS '38
1910–1911 H. FINDLAY FRENCH '03	1957–1958 EDMUND N. GORMAN '32
1911–1912 J. MARSHALL H. BRUCE '04	1958–1959 THOMAS R. HUGHES IV '24
1912–1913 J. MARSHALL H. BRUCE '04	1959–1960 ARTHUR W. MACHEN, JR. '38
1913–1914 H. PATTERSON HARRIS '04	1960–1961 JOHN M. NELSON III '36
1914–1915 BEVERLY OBER '07	1961–1962 WILLIAM J. MCCARTHY '49
1915–1916 FRANCIS J. CAREY '06	1962–1963 ALLEN M. BARRETT '40
1916–1920 E. RIDGELY SIMPSON '08	1963–1964 D.C. WHARTON FINNEY '43
1920–1923 D. K. ESTE FISHER, JR. '09	1964–1965 W. CAMERON SLACK '46
1923–1925 JAMES CAREY III '12	1965–1966 WARD B. COE, JR. '32
1925–1926 EDWARD K. DUNN '18	1966–1967 T. COURTENAY JENKINS, JR. '44
1926–1927 EDWARD K. DUNN '18	1967–1968 THOMAS J.S. WAXTER, JR. '52
1927–1928 ANDREW G. CAREY '17	1968–1969 FRANCIS G. RIGGS '57
1928–1929 BRICE W. GOLDSBOROUGH '23	1969–1970 WALTER D. PINKARD '37
1929–1930 BRICE W. GOLDSBOROUGH '23	1970–1971 THOMAS P. PERKINS III '53
1930–1931 DOUGLAS H. GORDON '21	1971–1972 ROBERT B. RUSSELL II '51
1931–1932 LUDLOW H. BALDWIN '22	1972–1973 HARRIS JONES, JR. '54
1932–1933 LUDLOW H. BALDWIN '22	1973–1974 GEORGE E. BOYNTON '56
1933–1934 GEORGE G. FINNEY '17	1974–1975 JOHN H. CLASTER '63
1934–1935 GEORGE G. FINNEY '17	1975–1976 ALVA P. WEAVER III '49
1935–1936 GEORGE G. FINNEY '17	1976–1977 THOMAS SCHWEIZER, JR. '62
1936–1937 I. RIDGEWAY TRIMBLE '18	1977–1978 KENNETH A. BOURNE, JR. '60
1937–1938 I. RIDGEWAY TRIMBLE '18	1978–1979 HENRY M. WORTHINGTON '48
1938–1939 PALMER F.C. WILLIAMS '19	1979–1980 ALLEN M. BARRETT, JR. '67
1939–1940 PALMER F.C. WILLIAMS '19	1980–1981 HOBART V. FOWLKES '59
1940–1941 W. THOMAS KEMP, JR. '22	1981–1982 JOHN E. SNEAD, JR. '61
1941–1942 W. THOMAS KEMP, JR. '22	1982–1983 JOHN H. WEST III '61
1942–1943 JACOB W. SLAGLE '23	1983–1984 DEELEY K. NICE, JR. '58
1943–1944 JACOB W. SLAGLE '23	1984–1985 WILLIAM R. BAKER '65
1944–1945 JACOB W. SLAGLE '23	1985–1986 JAMES D. HARDESTY '64
1945–1946 JACOB W. SLAGLE '23	1986–1987 GEORGE R. FRENCH, JR. '71
1946–1947 EDWARD STINSON, JR. 18	1987–1988 J. RICHARD UHLIG II '59
1947–1948 EDWARD STINSON, JR. '18	1988–1989 STANARD T. KLINEFELTER '65
1948–1949 NELSON T. OFFUTT '30	1989–1990 ROBERT F. BOYD '65
1949–1950 DUDLEY SHOEMAKER, JR. '31	1990–1991 ANDREW M. BROOKS '74
1950–1951 JAMES F. TURNER, JR. '26	1991–1992 GERRY L. BREWSTER '75
1951–1952 NICHOLAS G. PENNIMAN III '27	1992–1993 L. BRYAN KOERBER '79
1952–1953 H. GRAHAM WOOD '28	1993–1994 THEODORE R. MCKELDIN, JR. '55
1953–1954 FREDERICK W. WAGNER, JR. '27	1994–1995 L. BRUCE MATTHAI '75
1954–1955 OWEN DALY II '43	1995–1996 DAVID L. DEMUTH '80

E.

THE WILLIAM A. FISHER MEDALLION

The William A. Fisher Medallion was established in 1903 by Mrs. William Cabell Bruce in honor of her father, Judge William A. Fisher, the first president of the Board of Trustees. It is given only to a member of the Fifth or Sixth Form who has been in the school for three consecutive years and is in complete and regular standing in his form. The medallion is given among boys of high standing in scholarship to that boy who has rendered the highest service that can be rendered the school by leadership based on the influence of character. This is the tangible evidence of the highest honor the school can bestow. The name of the winner is inscribed on a tablet in the Common Room.

WINNERS

1903 LEWIS KINNEY ROBINSON
1904 HENRY PATTERSON HARRIS
1905 DOUGLAS OBER
1906 HUGH KERR GILMOUR
1907 BEVERLY OBER
1908 FRANCIS FOULKE BIERNE
1909 *no award*
1910 JAMES BRUCE
1911 *no award*
1912 D. OLIPHANT HAYNES
1913 CHARLES H. LATROBE
1914 *no award*
1915 DAVID K. E. BRUCE
1916 CHARLES W. MITCHELL, JR.
1917 *no award*
1918 I. RIDGEWAY TRIMBLE
1919 DAVID C. TRIMBLE
1920 ALBERT J. BYINGTON, JR.
1921 FREDERICK ANDREW GIBBS
1922 *no award*
1923 J. MCKENNY W. EGERTON
1924 DONALD P. MCPHERSON, JR.
1925 *no award*
1926 JOHN WHITRIDGE, JR.
1927 HENRY GERHARD HILKEN, II
1928 *no award*
1929 JAMES STANLEY PURNELL
1930 MARION GORDON KNOX
1931 PETER P. BLANCHARD, JR.
1932 WILLIAM CUSHING WHITRIDGE
1933 WALTER MCN. WOODWARD
1934 MORRIS SOPER EMORY

1935 WILLIAM R. MUELLER*
1936 WILLIAM T. DIXON, JR.
1937 BENTON NEAL HARRIS, JR.
1938 ROBERT MASON THOMAS*
1939 TYLER CAMPBELL
1940 JOHN L. CLEMMITT
1941 JOHN CAMPBELL KINDER
1942 RICHARD K. MARSHALL
1943 D.C. WHARTON FINNEY
1944 T. COURTENAY JENKINS, JR.
1945 DAVID BRATT BAKER, JR.
1946 ROBERT MCCLEAN III
1947 REDMOND CONYNGHAM STEWART
      FINNEY
1948 WALDO NEWCOMER
1949 WILLIAM JORDAN MC CARTHY
1950 CHARLES COADY BROWN
1951 ROBERT BROMWELL RUSSELL
1952 JOHN ANDREW GETTIER
1953 JAMES BUTTERWORTH RANDOL
      CARROLL, JR.
1954 ROGER HOWELL, JR.
1955 RICHARD RIDER JACKSON, JR.
1956 GEORGE EDWARD BOYNTON
1957 B. FRANK DEFORD III
1958 LEE RANDOL BARKER
1959 EDWARD ROBINSON FENIMORE, JR.
1960 PETER HUTCHINS WOOD
1961 ROBERT WILLIAMS MOSS
1962 WILLIAM CHATARD WHITMAN
1963 TERENCE HOLLIDAY ELLEN
1964 JAMES WILLIAM ISAACS

1965	Geoffrey LeBoutillier	1981	Robert Hood Moore
1966	Peter Stokes Farber	1982	Stuart Marquand Saunders
1967	Robert Neal Cavenaugh	1983	Gino Marcello Freeman
1968	Edward Smith Harwood	1984	Dennis Charles McCoy, Jr.
1969	Pearson Sunderland III	1985	Rushika Jerome Fernandopulle
1970	William Henry Mueller II*	1986	Bradley Emerson Wheeler
1971	David Jeffrey Rice	1987	Andrew MacGregor Cameron
1972	Christopher Lloyd Taylor	1988	Matthew Clarence Dates
1973	William Sherman Reese	1989	Andrew Dominic Martire
1974	Thomas Gary Hardie III	1990	Andrew Booke Cohen
1975	William Whittingham Harwood	1991	Peter Benjamin Daneker
1976	Robert Mason Thomas, Jr.*	1992	Geoffrey Stuart Berry
1977	Stuart Franklin Gray	1993	John Michael McWilliams
1978	Kraig Jarrett Holt	1994	John Claster Rosenberg
1979	Samuel Thomas Hillers	1995	Charles E. Lord
1980	Stephon Anthony Jackson	1996	Charles L. Howard

*The Muellers and the Thomases are the only father/son winners in the history of Gilman School.

F.

THE WILLIAM S. THOMAS SCHOLARSHIP PRIZES
VALEDICTORIANS

1941 WILLIAM J. HUDSON, JR.
1942 RICHARD K. MARSHALL
1943 WILLIAM ANDERSON GRACIE, JR.
1944 DANIEL WILLARD III
1945 GEORGE HEBERTON EVANS III
1946 JAMES CAREY IV
1947 JAMES GORTER
1948 WALDO NEWCOMER
1949 JOHN NEWELL WELCH
1950 THOMAS HOOKER POWELL
1951 WILLIAM MARCELLUS BURGAN II
1952 DAVID PAINTER MOHR
1953 JAMES BUTTERWORTH RANDOL
    CARROLL, JR.
1954 ROGER HOWELL, JR.
1955 ROBERT GARRETT II
1956 AMBLER HOLMES MOSS, JR.
1957 MILLARD SHERWOOD FIREBAUGH
1958 RICHARD EDWIN KUTZLEB
1959 GEORGE ALLEN COLLIER
1960 CARL STEPHEN PLANT
1961 ROBERT BRUCE MCKIBBEN
1962 WALTER GEORGE LOHR, JR.
1963 JOHN O DELL DUNNING
1964 JAMES IRA CAMPBELL, JR.
1965 ISAAC RIDGEWAY TRIMBLE, JR.
1966 ROBERT ENNIS FARBER, JR.
1967 BRUCE TERRY TAYLOR
1968 JOHN ROCHESTER SPRAGINS

1969 ARTHUR LOUIS RUDO
1970 EDMUND CHARLES SUTTON
1971 JOHN MATTHIAS KOPPER, JR.
1972 STEUART HILL THOMSEN
1973 ANDREW DAVID BERSHAD
1974 THOMAS ALFRED WILLIAM MILLER
1975 GIOVANNI PASQUALE PREZIOSO
1976 WILLIAM HENRY MATTHAI, JR.
1977 JOHN MARSHALL THOMSEN
1978 MARC RICHARD PAUL
1979 JAMES MARC GOLDGEIER
1980 DAVID PAUL OURSLER
1981 PETER WONJIN CHO
1982 MICHAEL LIEBSON
1983 MICHAEL DAVID DANEKER
1984 JAMES ANDREW MAFFEZZOLI
1985 BENJAMIN ROBERT MILLER
1986 EDGAR ROBERT KENT III
1987 ANDREW SNOWDEN BARKER
1988 RAYMOND RAYMOON CHANG
1989 FREDERICK BURTON KANN
1990 RICHARD Y.C. CHANG
1991 RYAN SANG OOK KIM
1992 JOSHUA IAN CIVIN
1993 MICHAEL ELLIOTT GINSBERG
    JOHN MICHAEL MCWILLIAMS
1994 NEIL ANDREW BRENCH
1995 KARTHIK BALAKRISHNAN
1996 JOSEPH JONGCHAN LEE

G.

THE WILLIAM CABELL BRUCE, JR. AWARD

Given to the Gilman Country School in memory of William Cabell Bruce, Jr.
who died while one its pupils after five years of active and honorable participation
in its athletic sports and exercises.

Born: October 26,1896—Died: June 27, 1910

RECIPIENTS

1911 HAROLD WHARTON SMITH
1912 JAMES CAREY III
1913 CHARLES HAZELHURST LATROBE
1914 WILLIAM KENNEDY BOONE, JR.
1915 JANON FISHER, JR.
1916 WILLIAM KENNEDY BOONE, JR.
1917 GEORGE GROSS FINNEY
1918 RAYMOND GORDON SCARLETT
1919 HOWARD KRAMER GRAY
1920 CLARENCE WATSON WHEELWRIGHT
1921 JAMES BARNETT HODGES
1922 JACOB W. SLAGLE
1923 JACOB W. SLAGLE
1924 LATIMER SMALL STEWART
1925 STUART SYMINGTON JANNEY, JR.
      LATIMER SMALL STEWART
1926 WILLIAM DORMAN GILL SCARLETT
1927 RICHARD ARDEN LOWNDES
1928 JAMES STANLEY PURNELL
1929 JAMES STANLEY PURNELL
1930 TEVIS RIDGELY BAKER
1931 WILLIAM PEPPER CONSTABLE, JR.
1932 WILLIAM PEPPER CONSTABLE, JR.
1933 WALTER MCNEILL WOODWARD
1934 MORRIS SOPER EMORY
1935 MAURICE RAYMOND ROBERTS, JR.
1936 ROBERT AUSTIN JOSEPH BORDLEY
1937 JOSEPH SARSFIELD SWEENEY
1938 RAYMOND N. BROWN, JR.
1939 GEORGE A. STEWART, JR.
1940 GEORGE B. FRANKE
1941 GEORGE B. FRANKE
1942 GEORGE B. FRANKE
      FREDERICK W. ALLNER, JR.
1943 OWEN DALY II
1944 EVERETT E. JACKSON IV
1945 WILLIAMS P. FULTON

1946 RICHARD B.C. TUCKER
1947 JAMES P. GORTER
1948 RALPH N. WILLIS
1949 RALPH N. WILLIS
1950 H. FURLONG BALDWIN
1951 ROBERT B. RUSSELL II
1952 GEORGE M. CALLARD
      PAYSON D. JOHNSON
1953 ANTHONY MORRIS CAREY III
1954 CLIFTON T. HARDING, JR.
1955 GEORGE E. BOYNTON
1956 GEORGE E. BOYNTON
1957 FRANCIS G. RIGGS
1958 ALAN D. YARBRO
1959 TIMOTHY C. CALLARD
1960 RUSSELL T. BAKER, JR.
      PETER H. WOOD
1961 HENRY H. HOPKINS
1962 JOHN S. NIXDORFF
      CHARLES HARVEY STANLEY
1963 JOHN H. CLASTER
1964 THOMAS S. BECK
      JAMES W. ISAACS
1965 HARRY C. PRIMROSE IV
1966 MICHAEL J. BOLAND
1967 SHERMAN A. BRISTOW
1968 DENNIS P. MALONE
1969 W. LEE GAINES, JR.
1970 FRANCIS W. SMITH
1971 FRANK W. DAVIS III
1972 PETER L.C. GEORGE
1973 GREGORY B.M. DAVIS
1974 DAVID A. EMALA
1975 ROBERT L. EHRLICH, JR.
1976 MICHAEL J. AUSTIN
      THEODORE T. SOTIR
1977 TIMOTHY HOLLEY, JR.

1978 Kraig J. Holt
1979 James H. Wilkerson III
1980 David L. deMuth
1981 Carlton F. Etchison, Jr.
1982 Michael A. Sarbanes
1983 E. Jerome Hughes
1984 Edward W. Brown III
1985 David M. Rody
1986 Andrew K. Dunkerton
1987 Peter O. Kwiterovich III

1988 Leon Newsome III
1989 Thomas N. Biddison III
1990 Andrew W. Dausch
1991 Jamal K. Cox
        James R. Edwards
1992 Victor Roderick Carter-Bey
1993 David B. Shapiro
1994 James R. Biddison
1995 Corey B. Popham
1996 Thomas Russell Wren

H.
ALUMNI WHO LOST THEIR LIVES IN WAR

World War I

George W. Ewing IV '11
Robert Ober '09
Lucian Platt '09
George Buchanan Redwood '06

World War II

Charles B. Alexander, Jr. '26
Edwin G. Baetjer II '39
Richard K. M. Baughman '43
Hugh Birckhead, Jr. '31
Allen Tupper Brown '36
Tyler Campbell '39
Gearge Hyde Clarke, Jr. '40
Robert F. M. Culver '37
Jesse Andrew Davis, Jr. '35
Auville Eager '37
Arthur Davis Fulton, Jr. '40
John Hamish Gardner III '37
John Work Garrett II '42
Arthur Pue Gorman II '34
William Estes Greble '35
William Hugh Harris, Jr. '37
Johns Hopkins Janney '32
Richard Mott Janney '34
Robert S. Janney '33
Charles Markland Kelly, Jr. '36
McHenry Keyser '44

Charles Phelps King '34
Howard Louis Lambert, Jr. '38
Thomas A. Lanahan '43
David Lapsley '40
Willis Clyde Locker, Jr. '40
Howard May, Jr. '34
Samuel Stockton Miles '32
Marcellus Wiley Nolley '32
George Sterling Patterson '12
Alexander Randall, Jr. '42
John Gregg Thomas, Jr. '39
Ralph L. Thomas, Jr. '43
MacMurtry Walsh '41
Richard W. Warfield '26
John Thomas Wieland '35
George Carl Westerlind '39
Robert B. Womble, Jr. '27

John H. Ballantine, Jr.
   (Faculty Member)

Korean War

Clarence W. Wheelwright, Jr. '49
Theodore Gould III '47

Vietnam

Walter Douglas Williams '52

I.

FACULTY

ABBOTT, FRANCIS H., 1910–14

ABRAMS, DONALD L., 1972–

ACHILLES, H. LAWRENCE, 1922–24

ACKLEY, WILLIAM E., 1948–56

ADAMS, DOROTHY S., 1917–18

ADAMS, SCHUYLER, 1916–17

AFFUL, EBENEZER H., 1987–

ALDEN, STANLEY, 1919–21

ALLAN, DAVID W. '64, 1968–79, 1994–

ALPERT, LILLIAN J., 1977–

ALTMAN, JONATHAN, 1975–76

ANDERSON, EDGAR E., 1942–44

ANDREWS, FRANK W., JR., 1956–75

ANIBAL, CLAUDE E., 1913–17

ANNAN, MRS. RICHARD C., 1939–42

APPLETON, HENRY S., 1910–11

ARAUZO, A. GONZALES, 1961–62

ARMIGER, JOHN W. '62, 1968–72, 1973–75

ARMSTRONG, ALEXANDER '33, 1951–79

ATKINS, RONALD P., 1980–87

AZRAEL, MARY I., 1995–1996

BAIRD, JOHN D., 1987–89

BAKER, WILLIAM R. '65, 1972–76

BALDWIN, LUDLOW H. '22, 1946–68

BALDWIN, SUZANNE P., 1930–31

BALLANTINE, JOHN H., JR., 1939–41

BALLARD, HENRY H., 1897–1903

BANGE, RONALD W., 1971–

BANK, ROBERT B., 1970–71

BARCLAY, ELINORE G., 1969–73

BARD, MRS. J. THOBURN, 1942–46

BARKER, ROY C., 1946–82

BARNES, GARFIELD, 1905–07

BARR, MRS. F. MORGAN, 1952–56

BARRETT, MARGARET R., 1922–26

BARTKOWSKI, JOHN F., 1963–92

BARTLETT, JOSIAH, 1913–39

BAXTER, ARTHUR H., 1898–1900

BEELER, BRUCE H., 1962–67

BEHRENDT, LEO, 1918–19

BELDEN, GEORGE C., 1921–42

BELL, BEATRICE M., 1926–29

BELL, LOIS J., 1943–51

BENDANN, DAVID P., JR. '63, 1971–84

BENEDICT, G. GRENVILLE, 1923–26

BENNETT, GEORGE E, 1928–29

BERGMAN, HELENE, 1969–70

BERTRAND, MIREILLE F., 1963–64

BICHAKJIAN, BERNARD H., 1961–68

BISHOP, A. HAMILTON, III, 1950–60

BISHOP, ALEXANDER H., IV, 1981–86

BLACKWELL, IRVING H., 1903–05

BLOOR, ROBERT I., JR., 1966–69

BLUMBERG, IRENE, 1985–86

BOISOT, MARGOT, 1942–46

BOOCOCK, DANA, 1983–86

BORDLEY, DONALD R., 1969–71

BOURNE, DEBBIE, 1970–75

BOWEN, LOUISE H., 1933–34

BOWEN, MRS. GEORGE A., 1977–79

BOWMAN, ELINOR, 1965–71

BOYD, EDGAR M.B., 1967–72–78–83

BOYNTON, JOHN W., JR. '50, 1957–59

BOYNTON, MRS. GEORGE E., 1961–63

BRAYTON, THOMAS M., 1966–68

BRISTOW, SHERMAN A. '67, 1971–

BROOKS, IAN, 1988–94

BROTCHIE, ELLA M., 1912–14

BROWN, DAVID P., 1978–81

BROWN, EDWARD W., 1923–40

BROWN, EDWARD W., JR. '57, 1961–62,
   1964–80

BRUNE, FREDERICK W., JR. '41, 1965–92

BRUNE, JEAN W., 1968–92

BUCK, PHILIP L., 1971–73

BULKELEY, ROBERT D., 1973–

BURGER, ELIZABETH K., 1920–22

BURGER, JOHN F., JR., 1972–73

BURGUNDER, LILLIAN H., 1974–

BUSICK, JAMES G., JR., 1981–

CABRERIZO, JOAQUIN R., 1967–68

CALAHAN, W. SCOTT, 1943–47

CALLAHAN, JOSEPH F., 1946–55

CALLARD, ELIZABETH H., 1921–22

CALLARD, HENRY H., 1922–24; 1925–27,
   1943–63

CALLARD, TIMOTHY C. '59, 1978–81

CAMPBELL, WILLIAM B. '52, 1961–74, 1984–85

CAREY, MARGARET C., 1944–46

CARR, THOMAS A., 1969–96

CARRAL, FRANCISCO DE P., 1919–21

CARROLL, JOSEPH P., 1962–65, 1969–71

CARRUTHERS, THOMAS N., 1921–22

CARTER, FRANCIS E., JR., 1938–42, 1945–55

CASEY, BETH D., 1980–94

CASLOW, BONNIE B., 1982–

CEYTTE, ANTONIA, 1911–14

CHAE, DAVID, 1985–96

CHAE, HELEN H., 1993–94

CHALMERS, ALLAN K., 1918–19

CHAMBERLAYNE, CHURCHILL G., 1907–11

CHANDLEE, GEORGE M., JR. '32, 1936–40, 1946–78

CHANDLEE, MARY, 1957–59

CHASE, JOHN H., 1897–1899

CHECKOWAY, JULIE A., 1989–95

CHEW, SAMUEL C., 1909–10

CHISHOLM, DANIEL, 1982–83

CHRIST, JEFFREY E., 1977–

CHRISTIAN, DANIEL E., 1980–

CHRISTIAN, EDMONIA M., 1919–23

CHRISTIE, JAMES W., III, 1968–69

CHRISTMAN, MARY BETH, 1995–

CLAPP, EDWARD L. '59, 1969–

CLAPP, MRS. ROGER, 1946–51

CLARK, JOHN R., 1981–85

CLARKE, F. RYLAND, 1964–67

CLARKE, STANLEY, 1921–22

COLLEYE, EDOUARD J., 1918–21

COLLINS, JOHN F., 1911–12

COLTON, HUBERT P., 1910–12

CONLON, CHRISTOPHER S., 1994–

COOK, MRS. ALBERT S., JR., 1946–48

COOK, WILLIAM R., 1962–67

COOPER, EDWARD S. '67, 1975–76

COUTURE, JOHN A., 1996–

COX, NANCY L., 1994–

CRANE, MRS. WILLIAM B., 1939–69

CRAWFORD, WILLIAM C., JR., 1956–61

CRONQUIST, BERNICE A., 1935–37

CUÁN–PÉREZ, ENRIQUE, 1967–69

CULBERTSON, GORDON L., 1986–

CULBERTSON, RONALD L., 1973–

CURRY, ALBERT B., JR., 1913–14

DANIELS, R. BRUCE, 1962–89

DAVID, TOBY J. M., 1985–

DAVIES, THURSTON J., 1916–17, 1919–22

DAVISON, JO ANN G., 1961–67, 1969–

DAWSON, GEORGE A., 1911–12

DAY, ROBERT A., 1963–65

DE JANOSI, CARLETTE E., 1941–42

DE JONG, JANNICK, 1982–83

DEGRAY, JUDY, 1975–77

DELCHER, THOMAS G., 1975–80

DEMEULE, ROBERT J., 1973–

DEMUTH, ETHEL E., 1944–46

DERASSE, FRANCOIS P., 1976–79

DEUVAERT, ARMAND A., 1968–70

DICKERSON, GREGORY W., 1964–66

DICKEY, SUSAN E., 1978–

DICOLA, LUCILLE, 1977–80

DILL, ERNEST A., 1972–76

DODD, JASPER H., 1903–06, 1909–24

DOHERTY, DAVID S., 1996–

DOUGHTY, ANNE P., 1970–71–

DOWNS, A.J., 1950–89

DOWNS, RAY F., 1958–59

DRESSER, J. HERBERT '58, 1965–72

DRESSER, JAMES L., 1926–70

DUGAN, DR. J. SANFORD '56, 1972–74

DUKE, JEFFREY W., 1976–80

DUNCAN, JIM, 1918–20

DUNCAN, JOSEPH N., 1978–

DUNNING, WHITNEY C., 1932–33

DUVAL, EDMUND P.R., 1904–05

EDELINE, CLAUDE, 1964–73

EDSON, GILBERT G., 1947–62

ELLIOTT,, LILLIAN M., 1926–41

ENGLISH, HUGH Y., 1942–44

ENSOR, BROOKS, 1978–90

ERICHSEN, GERTRUD, 1966–69

ESSROG, RABBI SEYMOUR L., 1970–75

ETTER, JOHN L., 1920–21

FARBER, PATTIE, 1976–78

FARIA, DR. NILO S., 1972–85

FAUVER, ALFRED N., 1940–41

FEAGLES, SAMUEL S., 1912–13

FELDMAN, JULIA, 1973–75

FENNEMAN, MRS. LAWRENCE B., 1937–44, 1946–47

FENZEL, LEO, JR., 1979–85

FIELD, EDWIN S., 1910–11

FINNEY, REDMOND C.S. '47, 1954–92

FIROR, DR. WARFIELD M., 1952–71

FISCHER, SHAWN M., 1990–

FITZELL, LOUISE, 1957–77

FITZPATRICK, ROBERT J., 1968–72

FLORIE, PHILLIP, JR., 1978–79

FONTAINE, E. CLARKE, 1911–12

FOREMAN, JOHNNIE L., JR., 1984–

FORMWALT, WILLIAM S., 1936–41

FOX, ARTHUR E., 1914–17

FREY, MRS. FRANK G., 1914–15

FRIDELL, WINN C., 1979–83

FRISCH, JOANNE C., 1980–94

FROELICHER, CHARLES M., 1911–17

FROELICHER, HANS, JR., 1912–15

FROELICHER, MRS. HANS, III, 1957–59

GABBEY, NEIL W., 1996–

GABY, ALAN R. '68, 1972–73

GAINES, MAGGI, 1977–80

GALLEHER, HENRY '81, 1991–92

GAMPER, CHARLES R., 1946–84

GAMPER, THOMAS O., 1991–

GARNER, G. DICKSON, 1918–19

GARRETT, JAMES R. '61, 1975–

GARVER, R. JACK, 1951–66

GASPAROTTI, MARJORIE, 1967–69

GERARDI, WILLIAM J., 1947–53

GIBSON, ROBERT F., JR., 1931–33

GILBERT, RICK P., 1974–77

GOLDBERG, HARRY R., 1979–83

GOODWIN, CHARLES, 1947–57

GORDON, MALCOLM K., 1917–18

GORSKI, S. THOMAS, 1994–

GOSSARD, HARRY C., 1913–14

GRAFFIN, ALLEN L., 1925–26

GRASSI, TEMPLE '65, 1970–75

GREENBERG, JOANNE C., 1973–75

GREENE, WILLIAM A., JR., 1968–

GREENOUGH, THOMAS O., 1937–39

GRICE, MARK R., 1980–81

GRIEPENKERL, MRS. EDWARD C., 1951–53

GRIMES, SAMUEL B., III '59, 1963–

GRISWOLD, ROBERTSON, JR. '38, 1942–43

GROBLER, C. VAN EYK, 1958–59

GUNNING, BERTHE, 1937–41

GUPTA, ANJALI, 1986–88

GWYNNE, SAMUEL C., III, 1974–76

HALVERSON, JAMES T., 1965–68

HANGEN, PAUL S., 1953–55

HARBOLD, MARK B., 1983–85, 1993–

HARDON, FREDERICK C., 1918–23

HARLAN, EDWIN H., 1909–10

HARRIS, EDWARD D., III, 1994–

HARRIS, LEWIS C., JR., 1946–49

HART, ARCHIBALD, M. '22, 1926–28, 1932–38

HARWOOD, RICHARD R., III '65, 1971–78

HASAN, SYED S., 1974–75

HAUPT, WALTER C., 1908–09

HAUSMANN, ADOLAY G., 1923–58

HAUSMANN, MRS. ADOLAY G., 1946–48

HAWKINS, AUBREY L., 1917–19

HAZARD, ROWLAND, 1926–28

HEATH, MELVILLE, 1985–91

HEARN, LEE, 1988–89

HENDERSON, BRUCE M., 1996–

HERING, HAROLD B., 1917–21

HERRMANN, R. LEITH '64, 1969–83, 1995–

HESS, MICHAEL G. '81, 1986–95

HEUISLER, ELIZABETH E., 1995–

HEWETT, JOHN B., 1957–66

HIDALGO, FERNANDO, 1985–92

HIGGINS, PAUL deR., 1926–28

HILLIARD, CLAUDE H., 1958–91

HILLIARD, WILMA M., 1969–89

HOBAN, BERNARD A., 1917–26

HODERNY, ROBERT, 1972–74

HOFFMAN, DONALD, 1925–52

HOFFMAN, MARC, 1993–95

HOFMEISTER, DORIS, 1975–76

HOLBEN, KENNETH P., 1928–47

HOLLEY, TIMOTHY '77, 1984–94

HOLMES, LEE G. '19, 1923–25

HOOPER, DAVID, 1981–82

HOPKINS, THOMAS M., 1961–62

HORNE, JOAN S., 1967–70

HORST, THOMAS '85, 1989–94

HOUGH, MAUD A., 1920–24
HOWARD, ARTHUR J., JR., 1989–
HOWARD, HOMER H., 1921–29
HOWARD, JOHN B. '81, 1985–86
HOWELL, A. ALEXANDER, 1902–03
HUGHSON, MARJORIE, 1941–42
HUKE, MARIE S., 1971–72
HULLEBERG, PAUL, 1986–89
HULSTEYN, JOAN C., 1914–15
HUTCHINSON, LORRAINE M., 1985–
HUTTON, SAMUEL J., 1921–22, 1925–26
IGLEHART, DAVID C., 1969–70
IGLEHART, VIRGINIA H., 1986–
JACOBS, KENNETH W., III, 1981–87
JACOBSON, JOSEPHINE, 1956–62
JAMES, ALAN, 1982–83
JANIAN, LANA L., 1994–
JANVIER, MEREDITH M., 1921–55
JEFFRIES, LYMAN B., JR., 1969–70
JEWETT, IAN W., 1970–79
JOHN, MORGAN S., 1967–69
JOHNSON, CAMILLA, 1973–74
JOHNSON, WEBSTER, 1984–88
JONES, W. RAMSEY, JR., 1939–42; 1946–50, 1952–56
JORDAN, ANNE D., 1980–
JORDAN, ANTHONY W., 1992–
JULIUS, PETER, 1983–
KAUFFMAN, CHARTHELEDA C., 1991–
KEENUM, ROBERT W., 1992–94
KEITH, MARIAN S., 1987–
KELLY, HARMAN O., JR., 1976–78
KERNS, SHIRLEY K., 1898–1899
KERR, ALBERT L., II, 1939–40, 1946–50
KERR, DR. DONALD C., 1968–70
KILLEBREW, PAUL K., 1971–86
KING, EDWIN B., 1909–12
KINNEY, SAMUEL W., 1901–09
KINSOLVING, HERBERT L., 1934–36
KISTNER, LEONARD, 1968–69
KLUG, BONITA L., 1986–
KNIGHT, MICHAEL, 1996–
KNIPP, CARTER, 1984–86
KNIPP, HOWARD F., III, 1978–84
KNIPP, JACKIE A., 1975–
KOEHLER, PATRICIA A., 1972–77

KOZUMBO, WALTER J., 1967–76
KRAMER, NICOLE D., 1990–
KRONGARD, ALVIN, 1969–70
KUMAR, K. SHANTHI, 1976–
KWITEROVICH, PETER O., III '87, 1991–
LADD, EDWARD M., III, 1968–69
LAMB, ARTHUR L., 1899–1933
LAMONT, MARGARET, 1924–26
LANDI, CHRISTINA, 1980–85
LANG, MRS. CHARLES E., 1962–67
LANKFORD, PRISCILLA, 1925–26
LAPOINTE, FATHER LAURENCE A.M., 1966–70, 1973–77
LAPOINTE, JOHN G., 1970–71
LARSON, VANNER T., 1931–33
LAWRENCE, M. GLADYS, 1914–19
LAY, RICHARD B., 1973–77
LAYMAN, JOHN W., 1995–
LEGG, CHRISTOPHER B. '67, 1982–
LEIGHTON, CHRISTOPHER M., 1978–87
LEIGHTON, ELIZABETH, 1978–82
LEMP, KARL C., 1961–64
LEPSON, SUZANNE M., 1989–
LEVIN, ALICE S., 1974–94
LEVIN, KAREN, 1984–92
LEVINE, RABBI ARNOLD, 1975–76
LEVINSON, JOSHUA H. '89, 1995–
LEWIS, DOUGLAS E., 1981–95
LEWIS, EDWIN A.S. '57, 1980–
LEWIS, JAMES W., 1942–45
LINK, STUART M., 1918–29
LIPSCOMB, HERBERT C., 1907–09
LIPSCOMB, THOMAS L., 1912–63
LOCKWOOD, LAWRENCE J., 1963–64
LOOKER, EARL E., 1941–42
LORD, LLEWELLYN W., JR. '43, 1957–67
LORDEN, JOEL E., 1953–61
LORY, GEORGE O., 1916–18
LOTTES, ADELE P., 1973–76
LOUGH, FLORENCE, 1988–90
LOVELACE, CLARENCE S. '40, 1946–48
MACCUBBIN, H. HOBART, 1927–28
MACCOLL, WICKES B., 1984–94
MAGRUDER, WARREN A.E. '46, 1956–71
MALTAS, CHRISTY, 1965–67
MANUELIDES, DIMITRI S., 1956–66

Ottavio Rasetti, Laurea, 1953–60
Parsons, Gay, 1963–65
Paturzo, Louis, 1971–72
Peard, Trevor B. '66, 1980–85
Pearre, Edward D. '76, 1982–88
Peitsch, Julie M., 1994–95
Perkins, William H., 1994–
Persons, Oren H., 1917–18
Peterson, Harvey R., 1977–96
Peyser, Seymour, 1936–37
Pheil, William W., 1963–75
Phillips, Rev. Wendell H., 1969–72
Philpot, Hamlet S., 1903–14
Pickett, Herbert E., 1913–17, 1919–40
Piersol, C. Laurence, 1979–80
Pika, Joseph A., III, 1970–73
Pine, Frank W., 1912–19
Pine, Frank W. '59, 1966–67
Pine, James C. '21, 1929–70
Pitts, Mrs. Thomas D., 1937–48
Pitts, Mrs. Tilghman G., Jr., 1938–39
Pletcher, Charles H., 1972–92
Polasko, John A., 1992–
Pollack, Mrs. Abou D., 1958–68
Porter, William H., Jr., 1947–80
Portnoy, David '79, 1991–94
Post, J. E. Howard, 1900–12
Powell, Bryan D., 1990–
Previdi, Patricia A., 1990–
Pride, Nathaniel H., 1910–12
Privette, Josef, 1925–41, 1946–47
Pryor, John J., 1929–31
Puente, Julius I., 1920–21
Purdue, Margaret J., 1918–20
Pusey, S. Catherine, 1934–37
Quist, Pamela L., 1994–95
Ramsdell, James W., 1995–
Raynor, Charles H., 1965–66
Reahl, David '82, 1986–88
Redwood, John, Jr. '17, 1917–18
Reese, P. Meredith, 1950–79
Reid, Thomas R., III, 1966–67
Reiff, Almer A., Jr., 1930–32
Ribas, Jose M., 1960–61
Rich, Ernest A., 1901–02
Rich, William W. '71, 1975–77

Richardson, Mary R., 1934–42
Ridgely, Julian W., 1905–07
Riepe, J. Creighton '68, 1988–
Riina, John C. '75, 1980–83
Riley, James E., 1966–72
Rinke, Karl–Heinz, 1963–64
Robinson, Alexander C., 1923–26
Robinson, John M., 1946–50
Robinson, Lewis K., 1906–07
Robinson, Marla, 1986–89
Rody, David '85, 1989–91
Rogers, A. Woodward, 1912–16
Rogers, Amy R., 1980–86
Rogers, Burke R., 1987–
Rogers, Diane D., 1988–
Rogers, Donald F., Jr., 1980–
Rosenberg, Candace C., 1971–74
Ross, Craig, 1991–92
Rothermel, Peter F., 1949–51
Roulston, Robert B., 1905–08
Roux, Marthe, 1936–37
Roy, Joaquin, 1967–68
Ruff, Martha, 1985–91
Rusk, William S., 1918–19
Russell, Edward T., 1915–17, 1918–63
Russell, Robert B., IV '81, 1988–90
Ruth, Page, 1943–45
Ruth, Suzanne, 1946–48
Ruth, Thomas D., 1909–10
Ryan, Harry G., 1921–23
Ryan, John R. T., II, 1921–23
Salisbury, David S., 1996–
Sandberg, Margaret C., 1990–94
Sanger, Craig W., 1977–78
Sarbanes, Christine D., 1978–
Savage, Toy D., III, 1975–77
Schloeder, Nicholas C. '85, 1994–
Schloeder, Nicholas M., 1958–
Schmick, John E. '67, 1974–
Schwanke, Frederick W., 1979–
Scroggs, William E., 1969–72
Sengstacke, Charles, 1967–69
Shaw, Harry N., 1907–09
Shaw, Lewis M., 1996–
Shawen, Deborah A., 1977–
Shee, Caroline, 1996–

SHERBOURNE, WILLIAM F., 1912–14
SHIELDS, THOMAS H., 1988–
SHOEMAKER, MARY, 1976–78
SIMMONS, CYRIL H., 1929–31
SIMON, EVELINA C., 1908–10
SIMON, RABBI HOWARD A., 1969–70
SINGHO, KRISHNA P., 1978–80
SIWINSKI, STEPHEN A., 1976–
SLOANE, ROBERT A., 1967–69
SMALL, KEITH, 1976–77
SMITH, BURGESS K., 1967–68
SMITH, CHARLES P., 1945–46
SMITH, ELIZABETH P., 1945–48
SMITH, GARE A. '75, 1979–80
SMITH, MARTIN J., 1970–82
SMITH, ROBERT D., 1972–
SMITHWICK, A. PATRICK '69, 1996–
SNYDER, RICHARD, 1976–88
SOMERVILLE, JEANNE, 1973–74
SOTIR, ALEXANDER, 1971–80
SPEARS, PHILIP E., 1996–
SPEER, WILLIAM, 1941–43
SPENCER, KEVIN M., 1980–81
SPENCER, WILLIS, 1947–70
SPRAGINS, JAMES S.B. '73, 1987–
SPRECHER, HARRY L., 1969–71
STANTON, JOHN S., 1922–23
STARRATT, ALFRED B., 1962–70
STEINER, ROMAN, 1898–1905, 1907–11
STENDEL, HERALD L., 1924–29
STEPHENS, HORACE D., 1960–63
STEVENS, HELEN K., 1935–84
STIEFF, CLAIRE, 1985–88
STILLWELL, CHARLES M., 1994–
STRASBURGER, FRANK C., 1969–71
STRAW, EDITH M., 1929–30, 1931–32
STRAWHORN, JOHN C., 1964–65
STROMBERG, LISA, 1987–90
SWANSON, CRAIG R., 1976–
SWARTLEY, SYLVIA M., 1937–46
SWENEY, JUDITH C., 1975–77
SWETT, MALCOLM, 1938–42
TAGGART, CHARLOTTE C., 1972–
TAGGART, CLIFFORD E., JR., 1970–93
TAGGART, JEFFREY C. '85, 1992–96
TAPPAN, WILLIAM, 1917–19

TASSONI, LORETTA, 1992–
THAYER, DAVID D., 1971–73
THAYER, JAMES A., 1924–27
THOMAS, J. OWEN, 1926–28
THOMAS, ROBERT M. '76, 1981–82
THOMPSON, DONNELL, JR., '91, 1996–
THOMPSON, EDWARD E. '45, 1955–89
THOMPSON, JOHN R., 1967–
THOMPSON, VIRGINIA L., 1992–95
THOMSEN, FERRIS, 1937–47
THOMSEN, LAURENCE W. '85, 1992–96
THOMSEN, LORNE S., 1990–95
THORNBERY, JERRY, 1979–
TICKNER, REGINALD S., 1951–92
TIPPER, MARGARET O., 1993–
TOMPKINS, RAYMOND S., III '69, 1975–79
TOWNSEND, ALFRED J., 1919–63
TRAPP, LINDA S., 1991–
TRUSTY, EDWARD M., JR. '91, 1996–
TUCKER, JOHN R., JR., 1989–
TURNER, IVANA O., 1995–
TUTTLE, ANNIE–LAURIE, 1982–91
TYLOR, MRS. HARRY L., 1945–46
UDOFF, RABBI ALAN, 1970–71
UPHOUSE, NORMAN H., 1937–38
VACCARO, DONNA, 1995–
VAN HORN, MRS. FULLER L., 1951–57
VAN VLACK, ANNE S., 1923–32
VANNIER, LILIANE, 1970–72
VEAZEY, GEORGE R., 1914–15
VENABLE, EDWARD C., 1912–13
VERNER, ELLIOTT K., 1959–67
VERRIL, RAY M., 1919–21
VISHIO, ALEXANDER F., 1994–95
VISHIO, ANTON J., SR., 1965–
WAELCHLI, FR. MARTI, 1916–18
WAPLES, DOUGLAS, 1914–16
WARREN, PAUL A., 1919–21
WATERS, THEODORE '84, 1988–91
WATKINS, ROBERT S., 1919–20
WEAVER, FREDERICK D., 1917–25
WEBB, DONALD F., JR., 1973–80
WEBSTER, JAMES '86, 1990–91
WEILER, PATRICIA, 1979–80
WELLER, DEAN C., 1972–
WETMORE, SEAN P., 1992–93

WHALING, TERRY K., 1973–76

WHEDBEE, THOMAS C. '69, 1983–88

WHEELER, CARLETON A., 1899–1902

WHITE, WILLIAM C., 1899–1900

WHITEFORD, CAMERON, 1917–18

WHITEFORD, WILLIAM C., 1994–

WHITEHURST, WILLIAM R., 1983–85

WHITELEY, JACQUELINE, 1983–84

WHITELY, DANIEL E., 1940–42

WHITMAN, HAROLD F., 1950–58

WIGHT, CLARK E. '87, 1992–

WILDER, RANI M., 1990–

WILHELM, BRUCE P., 1994–

WILLIAMS, FREDERICK R., 1941–42, 1946–85

WILLIAMS, LUCY R., 1989–93

WILLIAMS, RALPH C., 1913–15

WILLIAMS, RUTH W., 1972–79, 1995–

WILSON, DAVID H., 1952–69

WILSON, KATHERINE B., 1911–13

WILSON, MRS. DAVID H., 1952–69

WILTSHIRE, TURNER H., 1911–13

WINSOR, FREDERICK, 1897–1900

WIRTZ, BART, 1914–15

WOLF, JEROME R., 1972–

WOLF, PEGGY K., 1979–

WOOD, ARTHUR E., 1906–07

WOOD, LINDA, 1993–94

WOOD, PETER A., 1993–

WOOD, ROBERT C., 1972–76

WOODRUFF, CYNTHIA, 1992–

WOODWARD, W. M. CARY '53, 1966–

WOODWORTH, ELLERY B., 1956–62

WOOLAVER, FRANCES C., 1912–22

WRENN, HAROLD H., 1948–62

WYATT, EUGENE, 1916–17

WYCKOFF, WILLIAM O., 1914–17

XANDERS, ELLEN H., 1987–94

XANDERS, JOHN S. '77, 1982–

YOST, JOHN S. L., 1914–16

YOUNG, MIRIAM, 1969–73

YOUNG, PHILIP C., 1940–41

ZAMBRANO, MARCELO, 1964–67

Index

Designed by Gerard A. Valerio,
Bookmark Studio, Annapolis, Maryland

Copyediting by Carol Denny

Composed in Adobe Minion by
A.W. Bennett, Inc., Hartland, Vermont

Printed on Mohawk Vellum by
Collins Lithographing & Printing,
Baltimore, Maryland